INSIGHT GUIDE

CUBA

APA PUBLICATIONS
Part of the Langenscheidt Publishing Group

About This Book

Editorial
Project Editor
Danny Aeberhard
Managing Editor
Emily Hatchwell
Editorial Director
Brian Bell

Distribution
UK & Ireland
GeoCenter International Ltd
The Viables Centre
Harrow Way
Basingstoke
Hants RG22 4BJ
Fax: (44) 1256-817988

United States
Langenscheidt Publishers, Inc.
46–35 54th Road
Maspeth, NY 11378
Fax: (718) 784-0640

Worldwide
APA Publications GmbH & Co. Verlag KG (Singapore branch)
38 Joo Koon Road
Singapore 628990
Tel: (65) 865-1600
Fax: (65) 861-6438

Printing
Insight Print Services (Pte) Ltd
38 Joo Koon Road
Singapore 628990
Tel: (65) 865-1600
Fax: (65) 861-6438

First Edition 1995
Third Edition 1999

CONTACTING THE EDITORS
Although every effort is made to provide accurate information in this publication, we live in a fast-changing world and would appreciate it if readers would call our attention to any errors or outdated information that may occur by writing to us at:
Insight Guides, P.O. Box 7910, London SE1 8ZB, England.
Fax: (44 171) 620-1074.
e-mail: insight@apaguide.demon.co.uk

Putting together a rigorously independent guidebook to Cuba is no easy task. With its roller-coaster ride through the 20th century, this island in the Caribbean is a difficult place to view dispassionately. There is a definite urgency about Cuba, and the country engages the mind, not just the senses.

How to use this book
Insight Guide Cuba is carefully structured both to convey an understanding of the island and to guide you through its attractions:

◆ The first section, with a yellow colour bar, concentrates on the region's rich **history** and **culture** in **features** written by experts.
◆ The main **Places** section, with a blue bar, provides a run-down of all the places worth seeing. Places of major interest are cross-referenced by numbers or letters to specially commissioned colour maps. Icons at the top of right-hand pages show where to find the relevant maps.
◆ The listings in the **Travel Tips** section give easy-to-find information on such things as transport, hotels and restaurants. You

Antonio Maceo monument, Santiago

can locate information quickly by using the index printed on the back cover flap, which can also serve as a bookmark.

◆ The book is illustrated with **photographs** selected to convey both the beauty of the island and the character of the people.

The contributors

This new edition was edited with great enthusiasm by Cubaphile **Danny Aeberhard**, who built on the work of previous editors **Tony Perrottet** and **Joann Biondi**. **Gillian Walker**, a correspondent based in Havana, updated the book and helped to broaden its scope, writing new chapters for *Havana* and *Dreaming of Miami*.

Tony Perrottet contributed the chapters on Cuba's early history, *José Marti*, the *Hemingway Trail*, the *Tropicana* and *Pinar del Río*. while Joann Biondi wrote the sections on the *The Revolution*, *Che Guevara*, *Fidel Castro*, *Socialism or Death*, *Tourism*, *Cars*, *Guantánamo* and *Santiago*. **Jane McManus** wrote about the *Sierra Maestra*, *Rural Heartland*, *Guajiros*, the *Southern Islands* and also compiled the original Travel Tips.

Adding a personal note about his friendship with Fidel Castro was Colombian author **Gabriel García Márquez**, who has known the Cuban leader since the 1960s; this chapter, the copywright of Gianni Mina and Ocean Press, is reprinted by permission of the Talman Company.

Other contributors were: **Liz Balmaseda**; **José Antonio Evora**, **Sergio Giral**; **Larry Luxner** (*Varadero, Trinidad and Cienfuegos*); **David Lloyd Marcus** (*East of Santiago*); Naomi Peck (*Afro-Cuban Religions feature*); **James Rodewald**; **Alfonso Silva**; **Ned Sublette**; and **Marjory Zimmerman** (*Around Havana*).

The main photographers to contribute to the book, bringing Cuba to life, were **Eduardo Gil**, **Glyn Genin** and **Fred Mawer**.

Thanks go to **Stewart Wild** for proofreading and indexing the book, to **Alison Copland** for putting Travel Tips in order, and to **Siân Lezard** for her invaluable help in the closing stages.

Map Legend

International Boundary

Province Boundary

National Park/Reserve

Ferry Route

Airport: International/ Regional

Bus Station

Parking

Tourist Information

Post Office

Church/Ruins

Monastery

Mosque

Synagogue

Castle/Ruins

Archaeological Site

Cave

Statue/Monument

Place of Interest

The main places of interest in the Places section are coordinated by number with a full-colour map (e.g. ❶), and a symbol at the top of every right-hand page tells you where to find the map.

CONTENTS

Maps

A map of Cuba is on the inside front cover.

A map of Havana is on the inside back cover.

Introduction

History

Features

Public transportation in Cuba moves at a gentle pace

Insight on ...

Information panels

Travel Tips

◆ **Full Travel Tips index is on page 321**

Places

MARTÍ

TV

MARIETTA 91
DON'T WORRY BE HAPPY

THE ISOLATED ISLAND

It's impossible to arrive in Cuba without any preconceptions. But the country's idiosyncracies soon challenge them

It is difficult to be unemotional about Cuba. The island thrills the senses, befuddles the mind, and tugs at the heart. It is a magical place, full of romantic images: beautiful women who are proud of their ample hips; conga drums pounding late into the night; spicy roast pork and sweet dark rum; baseball, ballet, and dazzling nightclubs; quick conversations spiked with sexual innuendo and wicked humor; people who are warm and expressive and affectionate; the specialist art of the hand-rolled cigar.

However, there are also somber images of Cuba: frustrated youths who dream of futures elsewhere; a communist system that has failed its citizens; political repression and a stubborn, old dictator; anti-American slogans and statues of Lenin; crumbling buildings, empty stores, and over-crowded buses. It is an island frozen in time.

There is a popular joke circulating around Cuba these days. An adult asks a child: "What do you want to be when you grow up?" The child answers: "A tourist." That is because most tourists who visit Cuba today are shielded from the harsh realities of life on the island. For them, Cuba is a taste of the good life, a tropical retreat and an exotic escape. Even so, the average tourist will not leave Cuba unaffected. Slowly but surely this Caribbean island gets under your sunburned skin and touches your soul. Emotions start flowing, and opinions form quickly.

Welcome to Cuba, and decide for yourself. ❑

PRECEDING PAGES: independence hero José Martí shepherds a new generation; carnival in Santiago de Cuba; girls on the Malecón, Havana's seafront promenade; a Cuban family at home.
LEFT: cartoon images supplant revolutionary icons.

Decisive Dates

Pre-Columbian Period: 3500 BC–AD 1492

c. 3500 BC–AD 1200 Arrival of first native American inhabitants, the Guanahatabey – a simple hunter-gatherer culture – in the far west. Later, the Siboney people appear with a similar, but more diverse, culture.

c. AD 1100 The Arawak Taínos settle, living a semi-agricultural lifestyle. Followed by gradual displacement of the Siboney, who become subservient to Taínos.

c. 1450 Warlike Caribs arrive in Cuba, threatening Taíno dominance.

c. 1490 Native population estimated at over 100,000.

c. 1560 Fewer than 3000 indigenous Cubans remain.

1607 Havana becomes official capital.

1662 British pirate Henry Morgan sacks Santiago.

1717 Tobacco trade declared a Crown monopoly. Resistance from tobacco growers crushed.

The British Occupation: 1762–3

1762 Havana falls to a massive British invasion force. The port is opened up to international trade, breaking earlier monopoly of Spanish crown. The British encourage slave trade, opening possibilities of expansion of the plantation system.

1763 Havana returned to Spanish rule as Britain swaps Havana for Florida (Treaty of Paris).

Spanish Settlement: 1492–1762

1492 Christopher Columbus sights Cuba.

1508 Sebastián de Ocampo circumnavigates Cuba, establishing that it is indeed an island.

1509 Diego de Velázquez's first expedition.

1511–15 Velázquez returns to found Baracoa, on the east coast, followed by six other initial settlements (*villas*) around Cuba.

1512 Cacique Hatuey, the great Indian chief, is burnt at the stake. Indigenous resistance crumbles.

1515 Santiago de Cuba becomes capital.

1519 Havana is moved from a site on the south coast to its present position on the north coast.

1523 African slaves brought to work in mines.

1537 First slave revolt.

1555 French pirate Jacques de Sores sacks Havana.

Sugar Boom and Slavery: c. 1774–1840

c. 1790s Sugar replaces tobacco as Cuba's most valuable export.

1795 French Haitians flee slave revolution and settle in Oriente (Cuba's eastern province).

Early 1800s Prices of sugar and land soar. Beginnings of independence movements in Cuba. Simón Bolívar leads anti-colonial revolts across Latin America.

1825 Cuba and Puerto Rico are Spain's only remaining Latin colonies.

1837 Latin America's first railroad in operation between Bejucal and Havana.

1871 José Martí exiled to Spain.

Two Wars of Independence: 1868–98

1868 Carlos Manuel de Céspedes liberates his slaves

near Manzanillo in Oriente and issues call to arms against Spanish overlords.
1869 Rebels issue Constitution of Guáimaro.
1873 Céspedes replaced as rebel President.
1878 Peace treaty signed. Rebel factions split.
1879–1880 The "Little War" breaks out.
1886 Spain abolishes all kinds of slavery.
1892 José Martí founds the Cuban Revolutionary Party from exile in the US.
1895 Martí killed at Dos Ríos. Antonio Maceo killed in Western Cuba. Máximo Gómez assumes command.
1898 US battleship *Maine* sunk in Havana's harbor after explosion. US enters conflict. Spain signs peace treaty ceding control of Cuba to US.

CORRUPTION AND COUPS: 1898–1959
1901 Platt Amendment adopted in Cuban Constitution. Guantánamo naval base ceded to US, and US right to intervene in Cuban affairs accepted. Provokes widespread Cuban unrest and anger.
1902 Tomás Estrada Palma inaugurated as President.
1906–9 Marines invade to protect US interests.
1924–33 Presidency of General Machado, which is characterized by venality and violence. General strike in 1933 forces him to flee.
1934 Fulgencio Batista stages coup. Puppet president installed under army control. Abrogation of Platt Amendment, but Guantánamo left in US control.
1940–4 First Batista Presidency after national vote.
1952 Batista seizes power and cancels elections.
1953 Attack on Moncada Garrison in Santiago.
1956 Fidel Castro's guerrilla force sails from Mexico in the *Granma*. Hideout established in Sierra Maestra.
1957 Failed student attack on Batista's palace.
1958 Guevara opens second front in Sierra del Escambray. Santa Clara falls to rebel troops. Batista flees.

THE REVOLUTIONARY YEARS: 1959–89
1959 Victorious Castro enters Havana. First land reform introduced, and literacy and public health campaigns launched.
1960 Nationalization of major companies.
1961 US-backed invasion results in Bay of Pigs fiasco. Castro declares socialist nature of Revolution.
1962 Cuban Missile Crisis brings world to brink of nuclear war. Cuba brought further into Soviet orbit. US economic blockade begins in earnest.
1964 Castro pays first visit to Soviet Union.
1965 Guevara resigns posts and leaves for Africa.

PRECEDING PAGES: English pirates plunder Cuban coast.
LEFT: the British assault on Havana, 1762.
RIGHT: Fidel Castro argues his case.

1967 Guevara killed in Bolivia.
1968 Small businesses nationalized.
1970 Failure of 10 million-ton sugar harvest target.
1975 Cuban involvement in Angola begins.
1976 Right-wing exile terrorist group bombs plane over Barbados, killing all 73 Cuban athletes on board.
1980 Mariel boatlift: 120,000 leave Cuba for Miami.
1988 Cuban troops withdrawn from Angola.
1989 Execution of General Ochoa for alleged drug smuggling and corruption.

THE SPECIAL PERIOD AND RECOVERY: POST-1990
1991 Russian economic aid axed completely. Chronic food and fuel shortages begin. Industry crippled.

1992 Torricelli Law passed in US, strengthening the embargo and seeking to sponsor dissent in Cuba.
1993 Dollar is legalized, and limited forms of private enterprise allowed. Economic privations continue.
1994 Crisis of the *balseros* (boat people): 35,000 Cubans try to flee to Miami. US tightens immigration controls and limits numbers of asylum-seekers.
1995 Castro seeks direct foreign investment.
1996 Draconian Helms-Burton legislation passed by US Congress tightening embargo's stranglehold.
1997 Return of Che Guevara's remains from Bolivia to Cuba, followed by procession to Santa Clara, where they are laid to rest in new mausoleum.
1998 Papal visit to Cuba. Thousands attend masses across country. Pope attacks the regime's human rights record but also criticizes the embargo. ❑

CONQUISTADORES AND PIRATES

Not much is known about Pre-Columbian Cuba, but its early colonial history was a turbulent one as the new colony experienced its birth pains

The first European to glimpse the coast of Cuba was Christopher Columbus, who on his first voyage in 1492 pronounced it the most beautiful land on earth. Of course, Cuba had already been inhabited for several thousand years by peoples that Columbus wrongly assumed were Indians, and this misnomer has stuck ever since. The oldest groups were the Guanahatabey and the Siboney (originally from Central and South America), whose cultures were characterized by the use of shell implements, and whose people lived in caves or basic settlements mainly in the west of the island. The dominant contemporary group was the loosely-organized, agricultural Taíno Arawak tribe, but their position was threatened by the recently-arrived, warlike Caribs, who were reputedly cannibalistic.

Although they all had complex societies, languages and organized religions based on a cosmic hierarchy of gods, animals and men, the Caribbean "Indians" did not impress Columbus. "They very willingly traded everything they had," he noted in his logbook, "but they seemed to me a people short of everything." His sailors brought back to Europe tobacco, syphilis and news of a world ripe for conquest.

Spanish conquest

The Spanish soldiers and missionaries who arrived in Columbus's footsteps soon discovered gold in the Cuban mountains, and decided that the native population should be enslaved to dig it up. There was some doomed resistance.

Fleeing the Spaniards from modern-day Haiti, the great indigenous warrior Hatuey landed in eastern Cuba with the conquistador Diego Velázquez in hot pursuit. Despite a long game of hide-and-seek in the caves and mountains of the east, Hatuey and his followers were captured and put to the stake in 1512. Offered baptism at his execution, the chieftain asked if there were any Christians in heaven; when told that there were, he preferred to burn as a pagan.

Between 1512 and 1514, Velázquez founded the seven *villas* of Cuba – Baracoa, Santiago, Bayamo, Camagüey, Trinidad, Sancti Spíritus, and Havana – and set about rounding up the rest of the indigenous population for forced

LEFT: in memory of Hatuey, indigenous resistance leader and bane of the Spanish conquistadors. **RIGHT:** Christopher Columbus.

COLUMBUS: THE FIRST LANDING

Exactly where Columbus first weighed anchor is a matter of debate. The generally accepted spot is Bahía Bariay, near Gibara on the northeast coast, and a monument was erected in 1992 to celebrate the quincentenary of the event. But Baracoa, in the far east, disputes this claim. Baracoans have their own plaque pronouncing itself to be the site of Columbus's landing, and they claim that the flat-topped mountain referred to by him in his logbook was, in fact, their *El Yunque* mountain – and not the more probable *Silla de Gibara.* They even have a wooden cross which they claim Columbus left behind on the newly-discovered land.

labor. Many indigenous families committed suicide by hanging or drinking poison rather than be subjected to such an existence. The Spanish put this down to inherent laziness. Others were hunted down like dogs, slowly being forced into the western part of the island, where peninsulas and bays still bear the names given them by the Guanahatabey.

European diseases against which the indigenous peoples had no resistance, such as smallpox, tuberculosis and even the common cold, quickly wiped out the rest. The decline was catastrophic – by the end of the 1500s, the native populations existed only as a faint bloodline amongst the poorer elements of society (Indian features can occasionally be spotted among inhabitants of the remote northeast, near Baracoa); in a few words that have survived in Cuban Spanish (such as *guajiro*, or farmer); and in the shape of the *bohíos* – thatch-roofed huts that still dot the western countryside.

Only a few brave Spaniards dared to speak out against what they were seeing. The most famous champion of the native peoples was Bartolomé de las Casas, so-called "Protector of the Indians". As one of the first settlers in Cuba in 1513, he had exploited indigenous slaves in the mines and on his estate, but turned against this system when a Dominican priest refused him absolution. On becoming a Dominican friar he passionately campaigned for the just treatment of native peoples at the court of the Emperor Charles V. His writings laid the foundations for the "Black Legend," on whose record Spain's colonial history has often since been judged, yet he ultimately failed in his goal of abolishing the harsh *encomienda* system, which granted Spanish conquistadors land and the right to use the inhabitants of that land as forced labor.

Fortress Cuba

Although gold made many of the first Spanish settlers astonishingly rich, the supply quickly petered out. The conquistadores found other, more tantalizing rewards: Hernán Cortés set off from Cuba to conquer Aztec Mexico, and soon afterward Francisco Pizarro had toppled Inca Peru. Plundered gold began flooding into the Spanish coffers and the mines of Potosí, in modern-day Bolivia, began streaming silver. Cuba was reduced to the status of supply post for the more lucrative plundering of South and Central America. While the ports of Panama overflowed with riches and formerly penniless soldiers shod their horses with silver, the seven settlements of the island remained little more than wretched provincial villages.

Cuba's strategic position, however, saved it from oblivion. Treasure from the New World still had to be brought safely back to Spain via the Caribbean Sea, which was becoming infested with foreign pirates. A system of fortresses was established so that treasure could be convoyed in short hops from port to port. Havana was moved from the south to its current spot on the north coast, and acquired massive new walls and fortifications which took nearly fifty years to build. It became the key point in Spain's whole transport system: fleets from Cartagena in Colombia, San Juan in Puerto Rico and Panama City converged here for resupplying, while Latin America's first shipyard turned out merchant and warships. At the other end of the island, Santiago de Cuba was fortified as a secondary port.

WHY "CUBA"?

The name derives from a native term for the island, *Cubanacán*, and not the Spanish for barrel (*cuba*), after the barrel-shaped hills seen by the first sailors.

First signs of wealth

These military accoutrements didn't make life in the towns any less squalid. In fact, the constant parade of seamen and desperate adventurers did the reverse, turning Havana and Santiago into a warren of taverns, brothels and muddy, narrow streets. Even so, some of the wealth rubbed off; merchants could make modest fortunes loading up the galleons with provisions for the long journey to Spain. While the average Spanish sailor was stuck with a scurvy diet of ship's biscuits, the officers could choose from a relatively gourmet menu that included live chickens, turkeys and piglets kept below decks for special meals, and jugs of Spanish wine. Wealthy passengers could bring along dried fruits, brandy, olives, and sweet almond cakes.

With the proceeds of these sales, Cuba attracted a rudimentary high society and a smattering of the magnificent stone buildings that still survive in Old Havana today. Like colonials everywhere, Spaniards trapped in this remote backwater tried desperately to hang on to their heritage: *caballeros* would wear finery and frills despite the tropical heat, keep up with the latest in arts and writing in their homeland, and put on lavish dinner dances in the midst of plagues of malaria and yellow fever.

As one traveler to Cuba remarked: "The

LEFT: Havana, a key link in Spain's colonial defenses.
ABOVE LEFT: Henry Morgan and his fellow pirates sack Puerto Príncipe (Camagüey).
ABOVE RIGHT: the English pirate Henry Morgan.

palaces of the nobles in Havana, the residence of the governor, the convents, the cathedral, are a reproduction of Burgos or Valladolid, as if by some Aladdin's lamp a Castilian city had been taken up and set down again unaltered on the shore of the Caribbean Sea. And they carried with them their laws, their habits, their institutions and their creed, their religious orders, their bishops and their Inquisition."

The Inquisition descended most famously on Remedios in 1682, when the parish priest declared that the tiny village had been invaded by 800,000 devils (making more than 1,000 devils per inhabitant). After burning the odd unfortunate possessed victim, 40 soldiers torched the settlement, ordering the villagers to relocate onto relatively useless land. It was Cuba's first real estate scam: the property was actually owned by the parish priest who had discovered the devils, and who hoped to rent it out at a tidy profit. But the villagers defied pressure and decided to rebuild their town.

Pirates on the rampage

Despite Spain's best efforts, the uninhabited swamps of Florida and the island maze of the Bahamas became havens for freebooters and buccaneers of every nationality, ready to pounce on shipping passing along Cuba's coast. The more brazen found the keys and islands off Cuba's south coast to be perfect bases. The most famous names in piracy all touched on the island's coast, and many became embroiled in the shifting patterns of war between Spain and more recent interlopers in the Caribbean, the English, French, and Dutch.

England's Francis Drake started the habit of calling in at Cabo de San Antonio, Cuba's westernmost point, for fresh water and turtle eggs on the way to and from raids on Cartagena and Panama. It was here that the dreaded buccaneer Bartholomew Portugués, whose small ship had just captured a vast, 20-gun man-o'-war, was surprised by the Spanish. Although he was flung in irons, the pirate knifed his jailers in Mexico and escaped, to be picked up by a band of passing cut-throats who helped him recapture the man-o'-war. They sailed it as far as the Isle of Youth on Cuba's south coast, where Bartholomew Portugués's luck finally turned: a hurricane smashed the ship to pieces.

The most ruthless and successful buccaneer of all was Henry Morgan. Son of a well-to-do Welsh farmer, he was hired by the British government in 1668 to seek intelligence on Spanish activities in Cuba. Morgan took this as licence to sail his 750 men the 50 miles (80 km) inland to Puerto Príncipe (modern Camagüey) and attack it. The Spanish governor got wind of his plan and had a force drawn up to meet Morgan, but "the pirates were very dextrous." The Spaniards were defeated and the town surrendered. Morgan locked the inhabitants in the churches, and set about sacking the town.

According to chronicles, Morgan's men "fell to banqueting among themselves and making great cheer after their customary way, without remembering the poor prisoners, whom they permitted to starve in the churches. In the meanwhile they did not cease to torment them daily after an inhuman manner, thereby to make them confess where they had hid their goods, moneys and other things, though little or nothing was left them. They punished also the women and little children." Morgan went on to sack Panama City, and he later retired to London, where he was feted by high society and even appointed Governor of Jamaica.

Yet crueller than Morgan was the Frenchman L'Ollonois, who came to the Caribbean as an indentured manservant, joined a buccaneer crew and soon won a reputation as a psychopath for his torture of prisoners. This didn't stop the French governor of Tortugas signing L'Ollonois on for raids against the Spanish. On one occasion he attacked the village of De Los Cayos on the southwest coast of Cuba, capturing a frigate from Havana and beheading its surviving crew. Eventually L'Ollonois met his end at the hands of Nicaraguan Indians, who slowly dissected him while still alive.

In 1715, the biggest Spanish treasure fleet ever gathered started off from Havana loaded with nearly 7 million pieces of eight, and thousands of bars of silver. This time, it was nature rather than piracy that was the danger. Although the fleet waited until after the hurricane season and left on a perfect clear morning, it ran straight into a storm in the Gulf of Florida. Nearly 1,000 of the 2,500 passengers lost their lives, and wreckage littered the coast of Florida, to be picked off by passing buccaneers.

LEFT: slaves from Africa working the sugar fields.
ABOVE: domestic scene on a 19th-century porcelain amphora in the Museo Romántico, Trinidad.

The tyranny of "white gold"

Dramatic as these events were, Cuba's real future was being shaped in its first sugar fields. When Columbus first landed in the Americas, sugar was one of the most valuable commodities in Europe, imported for a fortune from the Orient and weighed out by the tablespoon. He realized the Caribbean's potential, and on his second voyage he brought the first sugar cane roots from the Canary Islands and planted them in the modern-day Dominican Republic. Within a century, sugar cane plantations had spread across the Caribbean islands and right to the coast of Brazil.

Cuba too started off as a comparatively minor sugar producer, but gradually more and more lush forests of mahogany and *ceiba* were uprooted to make way for sugar cane plantations, while boat-loads of black slaves were transported from Africa to work them. With the indigenous population wiped out, the Spanish needed an alternative source of labor and black Africans were deemed more robust and resilient.

A Foreigner's View

The great German naturalist Alexander von Humboldt, visiting Cuba at the turn of the 19th century, had the opportunity to witness at first hand life on the island's sugar plantations. He was appalled by the attitude of Cuban slave owners: "I have heard discussed with the greatest coolness whether it was better for the proprietor not to overwork his slaves, and consequently have to replace them with less frequency, or whether he should get all he could out of them in a few years, and thus have to purchase newly imported Africans." The slave trade was booming, and Spain wasn't to grant emancipation for slaves for another 85 years.

Even Fray Bartolomé de las Casas (*see page 22*) had spoken out in favor of the African slave trade, as a way of protecting his beloved "Indians" from rapacious exploitation by colonizers.

With the slaves came African gods, myths and rituals, which the Christian priests could not eradicate despite their zealous efforts. Life on the plantations was brutal. There were uprisings throughout the colonial period, the first one taking place as early as 1537, when slaves rose up and joined in an assault by French pirates on the city of Havana. Some slaves, termed *cimarrones*, chose to escape, fleeing to the mountains where they sometimes developed small communities (*palenques*), but they always lived under the fear of recapture by slave-hunters and their savage dogs. Others, in desperation, even chose mass suicides – many slaves believed that after death they would be resurrected in Africa.

Magical, medicinal powers were attributed to women slaves. "There was one type of sickness the whites picked up, a sickness of the veins and male organs," one former slave recorded. "It could only be got rid of with black women: if the man who had it slept with a Negress, he was cured immediately."

The Last Supper

Just how bizarre Cuban rural society had become by the end of the 18th century can be seen by the events near Santa María del Rosario, a village southeast of Havana (and captured in the classic Cuban film *The Last Supper*). The Count of Bayona, in a fit of religious fervor, randomly invited a dozen of his slaves to a feast on Holy Thursday. Acting out the role of Jesus Christ, he washed the feet of each slave personally. Unfortunately, when the overseer refused to give the slaves a rest day on Easter Sunday, as had been promised by the Count, they rose up in rebellion, burning the plantation to the ground. The Count arrived with armed horsemen to repress the uprising.

Horrified at their perceived ingratitude, he ordered the 12 slaves to be hunted down and executed. Their heads were placed on pikes in the cane fields as a warning to their fellows that, whatever the Bible might say, all men were not created equal in Cuba. ❑

LEFT: the colonial aristocracy set about recreating Spain in the tropics.
RIGHT: an idealized depiction of slave life.

M Pujadas, lit

The Struggle against Colonialism

Cuba was one step behind the liberal changes that spread through other colonies in the 19th century, but Spain's "Ever Faithful Isle" did eventually lose faith

In the early 1800s, every Spanish possession in the New World rose up against colonial rule – except Cuba and Puerto Rico. In Havana, barely a voice was raised in support of the romantic liberation movements being led by heroes such as Simón Bolívar and José de San Martín, much to the embarrassment of modern Cuban historians. On the contrary, Cuba became Spain's military springboard for the many attempts to reconquer her tattered empire, which dragged on for decades and left much of South and Central America in ruins. But by 1825, the Spanish gave up on the New World and retreated to the two loyal Caribbean possessions – the most valued of which remained Cuba, referred to in Madrid as "the Ever Faithful Isle."

Predictions of ruin

Cuban Creoles, masters of a slave society, were in fact desperate to avoid independence. They had been kept in a state of constant terror since the bloody slave rebellion in neighboring Haiti in the 1790s: French refugees had landed on the beaches around Santiago, starving, desperate and telling wild tales of race slaughter, laced with lurid images of voodoo and throbbing African drums. Napoleon's army of 20,000 men was defeated on the shores of the new black republic, and white Cubans were worried that their island might follow suit. "There is no country on earth where a revolutionary movement is more dangerous than Cuba," declared one planter, predicting "the complete ruin of the Cuban race."

Even so, greed was stronger than fear. The expansion of the slave population during the later 18th and early 19th centuries was unparalleled, for two main reasons. Firstly, in 1762, the British had captured the heavily fortified city of Havana, as a consequence of a wider European war against France and her ally, Spain. Although Spain regained possession of her beloved colonial city by handing Florida over to the British Crown, there was one vitally important lasting legacy of the occupation: the British had allowed Havana to trade freely with other nations, thus breaking the jealously-guarded monopoly that Spain had enjoyed since the 16th century. Once broken, this monopoly could not realistically be reimposed by the returning Spanish. Freed from this economic straightjacket, the Cuban economy boomed,

The British in Havana

The British took Havana in August 1762, after storming the main forts guarding the harbor. They then trained the very guns that were meant to protect the city against its own walls, forcing its capitulation in just two weeks. The Governor of Havana was sent back to Spain in disgrace, whereas the heroic resistance of the captain commanding El Morro fort, Don Luis de Velasco, earned him a posthumous ennoblement from his king.

The British divided up the tremendous spoils of the city's public moneys and warehouses, and then endured sickness and disease, until Havana was returned to Spain a mere seven months later.

and there were real incentives to increase production of its chief commodity, sugar.

Secondly, the Haitian rebellion destroyed the sugar plantations there, pushing sugar prices sky-high, and many of the refugees who resettled in Cuba brought with them expertise and improved techniques of production. Cuba soon became the world's biggest producer of "white gold." It was a new era of fabulous wealth and sudden fortunes.

Nothing could stop sugar cane consuming the countryside – citrus fields were replanted, the last forests uprooted, even tobacco fields ploughed over (growth of the crop being restricted to the narrower fields of Pinar del Río province). A steadily increasing supply of slaves was needed for the plantations, especially as workers survived for an average of only seven years. The number of slaves in Cuba leapt from 40,000 in 1774 to 470,000 in 1840, when they made up half the population.

Blacks were bought and sold in newspaper classifieds, next to advertisements for horses and ploughs. In a rare gesture of leniency, some planters allowed their blacks to dance at night to drums, praying that they were not communicating news of rebellion.

A new "sugarocracy" arose in Cuba: the sugar center of Trinidad sprouted resplendent palaces with names like Hope, Gamble and Confidence. Their owners could afford to take shopping trips to Europe, bringing back Persian carpets, Italian paintings and French chandeliers. Sumptuous new mansions transformed Havana from a "large village," in foreigners' eyes, to Spain's "jewel of the Caribbean," a city of iron lace, gracious curlicues and stained glass. The streets were paved with granite imported from New England, and trade boomed with the United States – the beginning of a relationship that would dominate much of Cuba's modern history.

Meanwhile, in 1837, Latin America's first railroad was built from the Güines sugar fields to Havana, using black slaves, Chinese coolies and a bevy of indentured Irishmen. Conditions were so miserable that 13 workers died for every kilometre of track laid.

However, the euphoria couldn't last: in 1857, the bottom fell out of the sugar market, and Cuba went into an economic spiral. The names of mansions in Trinidad went from "Good Results" to "Wit's End", "Woe" and "Disenchantment".

The independence push

By 1868, many Cubans were at last ready to end Spanish colonial rule. In that year, a small plantation owner, Carlos Manuel de Céspedes, freed his own slaves near Manzanillo in the southeast, and declared Cuba independent, sparking off the Ten Years War with Spain. Free and runaway slaves swelled the Liberation Army's ranks: known as *Mambises* – a word

that meant "rebel" in the African Congo – they often fought with machetes for lack of guns and went barefoot and near-naked for lack of uniforms. Antonio Maceo, the "Bronze Titan," was one black soldier who rose from the ranks to become major-general and one of the most popular leaders in the struggle. Like a character in a García Márquez novel, he is said to have fought in 900 battles and been wounded 27 times, survived innumerable assassination attempts, and lost his father and fourteen brothers in the war. Many pro-Spanish whites were afraid that he would try to become president and gathered under the slogan: "Cuba, better Spanish than African!"

LEFT: the bucolic idyll.
RIGHT: Cuban *Mambí* independence fighters charge into the fray as they take on the Spanish.

Adventurers came from around the world to join the struggle against Spain. One was former American Union Army officer Henry Reeve, who signed up only to be captured and shot by a Spanish firing squad. Left for dead, he survived and became a leading general and anti-slavery voice – remembered as *El Inglesito*, the "little Englishman." But the war ground on for a decade, took 200,000 lives and ended in stalemate. It also left a crippled economy, and, with land prices at a level lower than they had been in years, US companies began to invest heavily in Cuban land, developing a significant financial interest in the country's future.

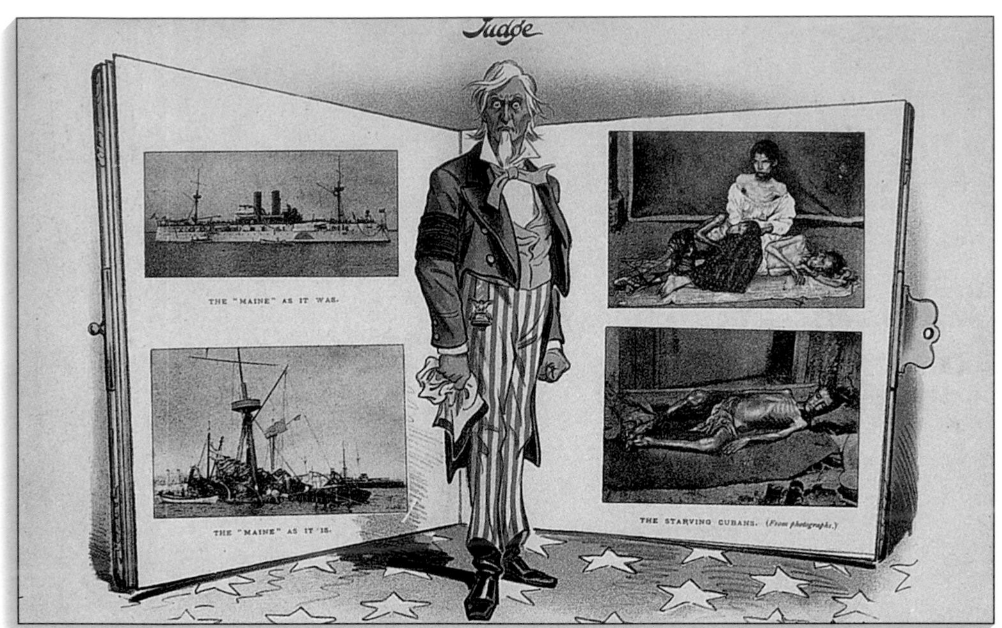

The fighting starts again

In 1895, the carnage began again with the Second War of Independence, this time led by the great Cuban theorist José Martí (*see page 33*). Martí had infused the independence movement with earlier, nascent ideas of social justice: the goal was not just a free Cuba, but a Cuba without its vast inequalities of wealth and racial divisions. Unfortunately, he was shot dead in his first battle in 1895. The seemingly indestructible Antonio Maceo was still around to keep the flame of revolution burning, until he too was killed in a skirmish with Spanish troops in the province of Pinar del Río, later that same year. The tragedy left the Cuban cause in the hands of another stalwart veteran of the earlier war, General Máximo Gómez, who had been persuaded by Martí to return from exile to help lead the struggle.

Also in 1895, the young English officer Winston Churchill decided to take his winter leave in Cuba as war correspondent for the London *Daily Graphic*. The jaunt was "awfully jolly," young Winston found, especially as he was able to celebrate his 21st birthday in a proper war zone. Traveling with a Spanish column, Churchill had his first experience of being fired upon while eating a chicken drumstick one morning; but the guerrillas melted into the countryside and he spent most of his visit, like the Spanish army, "wandering round and round in this endless humid jungle." The future British leader had begun his trip sympathizing with the rebels, but began to feel sorry for the Spanish losing their "Pearl of the Antilles": "They felt about Cuba just as we felt about Ireland," the arch-colonialist later wrote.

Unable to engage the elusive rebels directly, Spanish forces started a scorched-earth policy in the Cuban countryside, executing *guajiros*, burning farms and putting the survivors into labour camps. The strategy failed; by 1898, the Spaniards were exhausted and at the point of withdrawing entirely. But another colonial power had been watching the conflict with increasing interest: the United States.

"Remember the Maine!"

As long as a century before, North American thinkers had decided that Cuba was crucial to their country's strategic interests. Throughout the 1800s, there were calls for outright annexation, and several filibustering expeditions set out from Florida to the Cuban shores, hoping to provoke a popular revolt that would cause Cuba to fall "like a ripening plum into the lap of the Union" (in the happy phrase of John Quincy Adams). Four American presidents even offered to buy Cuba from the Spanish during the first half of the 19th century, seeing the island as part of the natural orbit of their increasingly powerful and expansionist country. With over US$100 million invested in Cuba by 1898, many in Washington were worried that radicals would take over an independent Cuba.

> **NOT FOR SALE**
>
> When in 1848 President Polk offered $100 million to buy Cuba, Spain's foreign minister commented that Spain "would rather see it sunk into the ocean."

American emotions had already been whipped up by the yellow press. Newspaper barons William Randolph Hearst (Orson Welles's model for *Citizen Kane*) and Joseph Pulitzer (who would give his name to America's greatest journalism prize) competed to offer the most lurid and heart-rending tales of the Spanish troops' cruelty: images of Cuban streets awash with blood, bayoneted babies and deflowered virgins became daily fare for millions from Kansas to New York.

The pretext for intervention came on February 15, when the *USS Maine* – a battleship sent to protect American interests – mysteriously blew up in Havana harbour, killing 260 people. Hearst and Pulitzer blamed a Spanish mine (it was Hearst who coined the immortal slogan, "Remember the Maine, to hell with Spain!"), and whereas some Cubans today subscribe to the belief that it might have been a deliberate explosion caused by the US itself to precipitate their involvement in the war, the evidence points to an accidental munitions explosion in the hold. Within a month, President McKinley had declared war; three months after that, the US navy had blockaded the Spanish navy in the harbor of Santiago de Cuba, at the eastern end of the island. A huge American expeditionary force landed north of the city. It was led by an obese veteran of the Indian wars, General William Shafter, and accompanied by a boat-load of eager, if diarrhoea-ridden, journalists.

Although the US Congress passed an amendment stating that they were not claiming sovereignty in Cuba, nationalists quickly had cause to doubt the benefits of

American assistance. Shafter and his men took one look at the ragged Cuban army and refused to allow them into battle – publicly blaming their lack of shoes and poor weapons, in private appalled that so many of them were black and mulatto (the reporter Stephen Crane called them "real tropic savages").

Shafter suggested that the Cubans keep up the rear, digging trenches and latrines. Unsurprisingly, the commanding general, Calixto García, refused to cooperate.

The Spanish army had very little fight left in it, but a showdown of sorts came at the Battle of San Juan Hill, on the outskirts of Santiago. The American Rough Riders were led in a

LEFT: a US postcard whips up interventionist feeling. **RIGHT:** the monument commemorating the sinking of the *USS Maine* on the Malecón in Havana.

famous charge by Teddy Roosevelt, a short-sighted weakling as a child who had taken up *machista* pursuits from tiger-hunting to soldiering in compensation. The Spanish were defeated, although the Americans took heavy casualties. Roosevelt's first missive to the US president was sheepish, but the national press hailed it as an extraordinary military achievement. Roosevelt rode the wave of popularity on to the governorship of New York and, in 1901, the US presidency. Two days after San Juan, the Spanish navy made a quixotic sally from Santiago only to be quickly decimated.

It had been a "splendid little war," as one US official noted, giving the Americans an instant empire (Puerto Rico, Guam and the Philippines were also snapped up). General Shafter arranged a victory march through the streets of Santiago, but the Cuban forces were barred from participating.

The highjacked revolution

The US set up a military government to administer the country. After 30 years of fighting, Cubans had traded one set of colonial masters for another. But not all Americans were caught up in the jingoism of the moment: the vitriolic Mark Twain wrote that the Stars and Stripes should be replaced with a Skull and Crossbones.

In 1901, US Congress agreed to withdraw its troops in exchange for guarantees that the country would remain an American protectorate. The so-called Platt Amendment – composed in Washington to be included verbatim in the Cuban constitution – allowed the US to intervene in Cuban internal affairs: it forced Cuba to lease a naval base at Guantánamo Bay, and gave the US the right to veto Cuba's trade or loan pacts with third countries. News of the legislation caused rioting around Cuba, but the US military governor made it clear to the constitutional convention in Havana that the *yanquis* would not be leaving on any other terms. Tomás Estrada Palma, Cuba's first president, reluctantly signed.

The independence that wasn't

The Stars and Stripes came down in May, 1902, and Cuba began its stunted, compromised freedom. In the coming years, US Congress sent in the Marines on a regular basis to protect American interests and even reinstated US military rule entirely from 1906 to 1909. None of the social reforms envisaged by José Martí would be enacted, elections were regularly fraudulent, and corruption was rife.

At the same time, American investment in Cuba rocketed. US companies snapped up land at bargain prices, and even set up mini "colonies" for American immigrants in places such as the Isle of Youth.

The final tragedy of Cuba's false freedom was the so-called Black Uprising of 1912. Afro-Cubans – many of whom had fought courageously in the wars of independence – were disgusted to find that the new republic was happy to leave them in effective serfdom. They formed their own political party, only to have it banned. Finally, open rebellion spread throughout the country. General Monteagudo crushed the uprising with the help of US Marines and, more viciously, local Creoles, who took revenge on the blacks for a century and a half of fear. "It is impossible to tell the number of dead," the General soon reported, "because it has degenerated into widespread butchery in the hills." Some 3,000 Afro-Cubans are estimated to have been massacred. The "black fear" had been wiped out with blood, and Cuban racism was more brutally ingrained than ever. ❑

Left: the US version of the Battle of San Juan Hill.

José Martí

Even the tiniest Cuban village has a bust of José Martí in its main square. Indeed, images of this incandescent romantic visionary can be found in cities across Latin America and wherever Cubans have settled: he remains Cuba's only historical figure whose greatness is undisputed, both as a man of action and of letters.

Born in 1853, Martí began his career as an independence fighter at 15, when he helped start an anti-colonial newspaper, *The Free Fatherland*, in Havana and denounced a fellow student for marching in a Spanish procession. He was charged with treason and sentenced to hard labor in a stone quarry. A frail youth, the experience ruined his eyesight, gave him a hernia and permanent scars on his ankles (in later life, he would always wear a ring made from the shackles). After six months, Martí was pardoned but sent into exile in Spain – the beginning of a vertiginous journey that took him to France, England, Mexico, back secretly to Cuba for two months, Guatemala, back again to Cuba, exile again in Spain, escape to France, over to the United States and south to Venezuela.

Martí finally settled in New York City in 1881 with his wife and son. New York was a center for Cuban exiles, and Martí was initially intoxicated with the United States ("One can breathe freely," he wrote. "For here, freedom is the foundation, the shield, the essence of life.") The enthusiasm was short lived, and Martí soon saw the US as the greatest threat to Latin American independence. He viewed as crucial preventing "the annexation of the peoples of our America by the turbulent and brutal North which despises them... I have lived within the monster and I know its entrails – and my sling is the sling of David."

For 15 years in the US, the wire-thin Martí kept up a punishing routine of political organizing, lecturing, purchasing weapons, and writing firebrand speeches, newspaper columns and exquisite, avant-garde poetry (his *Versos Sencillos* were married to the song *Guajira Guantanamera* in the 1960s, in what has become the unofficial Cuban national anthem). He ate little, slept only in snatches, but glowed with nervous energy. Traveling to Florida – always in a heavy black suit and bow-tie, his pointed moustache neatly clipped – Martí visited cigar factories to recruit Cuban exiles to his cause. Cuba would not be truly free, he argued, without economic, racial and sexual equality – thus adding an inspiring social element to the provenly potent rhetoric of nationalism.

Martí, though, was not content to remain an intellectual. In 1892, he founded the Cuban Revolutionary Party. Three years later, plans had been laid to rekindle the independence struggle: a message was sent to the black general Antonio Maceo in Cuba, hidden in a Havana cigar. Martí and Máximo Gómez landed secretly on the southeast coast, in a tiny boat that was nearly dashed to pieces in the middle of a storm. Escaping to the sierra of the Oriente, they were joined by hundreds of supporters, but life as a guerrilla was harsh: Martí's emaciated frame, still covered by a heavy coat, was weighed down by pack and rifle, and he often fell on the mountain trails.

RIGHT: José Martí, focused on a worthy goal.

On May 19, 1895, near Bayamo, Martí went into his first day of battle with a picture of his daughter over his heart. He was shot dead almost immediately as he charged toward the enemy, without ever having drawn his gun. A martyr to the cause, he has been worshipped by Cubans ever since. Today, his words have been appropriated by both sides of the political divide: Castro views Martí as the home-grown ideologue of the Revolution, while right-wing Miami Cubans named their anti-Castro broadcast stations Radio Martí and TV Martí. ❑

THE AGE OF DECADENCE

Sex, sin and sordidness: Havana had it all in the decades preceding the Revolution. Behind the hedonistic scenes, the Mafia mingled with the Cuban élite

Basil Woon, author of the classic 1928 travel guide *When It's Cocktail Time in Cuba*, chirped "*Have one in Havana* seems to have become the winter slogan of the wealthy." At the height of the US Prohibition, "personal liberty" had become the euphemistic lure for thousands of American tourists taking the short boat ride to Cuba from Florida. Like a P. G. Wodehouse character, Woon sums up the reasons for visiting Cuba:

1. You may drink as much as you want to.
2. You may buy as many drinks for your friends as you want to.
3. You may chance your luck at the lottery.
4. You may lose as much money as you desire at the casino.
5. You need not carry your marriage certificate with you.
6. You may stare at the pretty señoritas, because staring in Cuba is considered a compliment – not a crime.

Carnal Disneyland

From these innocent beginnings, Cuba in general and Havana in particular were well on the way to becoming international symbols of decadent pleasure. The flow of Americans visiting for sun and sex that began in the Prohibition years would turn into a flood after World War II. In Havana, refined nightclubs raged all night and the casinos were the rival of Las Vegas: long-legged mulattas pranced the stage of the Tropicana for audiences drunk on daiquiris, while the more adventurous headed for live sex acts in seedier surrounds (a regular showtime favorite was Superman, who measured his spectacular erection by lining 12 silver dollars up side by side).

Havana quickly became the prostitution capital of the Western hemisphere. Businessmen could choose their mulatta for the weekend from photographs at the airport; the notorious Casa Marina specialized in 13-year-old girls and boys from the provinces (with only a minor surcharge for virgins). In its prurient, watered-down way, Hollywood helped export Cuba's image as the world's sex capital: in *Guys and Dolls*, Sky Masterson would bring his virgin Salvation Army love down to Havana to be seduced. In real life, stars like Errol Flynn and Gary Cooper came down every winter in their luxury yachts. George Raft, who specialized as a film-star gangster, was full time host of the Red Room at the Hotel Capri.

LEFT: grand hotels like the Sevilla-Biltmore (now the Sevilla) sprang up in Havana in the 1940s and '50s.
RIGHT: casinos were the playground of the rich.

And the whole, rum soaked party went on to the fabulous rhythms of mamba, rumba and *son*. Cuba's 12-piece bands, musicians all decked out in white tuxedos, were in demand from Manhattan to the Left Bank, though the big money in Havana went to American jazz bands and front-liners like Nat King Cole and Maurice Chevalier. Nevertheless, the city became invaded with penniless hopefuls from the provinces. And all this was going on against a sordid background of Cuban domestic politics: the spiralling decadence of Havana was aided and abetted by a series of increasingly corrupt, brutal and authoritarian regimes.

The Batista Era

The Great Depression sparked off a string of riots against President Gerardo Machado, who had been elected more or less fairly in the mid-1920s but found himself making so much money that he refused to leave office. Troops were regularly called out to break strikes; demonstrators were gunned down; hired thugs, called *porros*, abducted, tortured and "disappeared" enemies of the regime. The country was virtually on the verge of civil war in 1933 when a general strike was called. Machado hopped on a plane to Miami, supposedly carrying five revolvers and as many bags of gold bullion.

In the ensuing chaos, the figure who took control was a young army sergeant, Fulgencio Batista, who organized a revolt of lower officers. A mulatto of humble social origins, Batista had mostly only been noticed for a winning smile, but in quick succession he took the rank of colonel, then full control of the Army. Before long, Batista emerged as the major player in Cuban politics, managing the government through a string of puppet presidents.

The "Batista era" had begun. In 1934, the US government, perhaps confident that its interests were secure, decided to rescind the Platt Amendment which guaranteed its power of intervention – although the Americans negotiated a 99-year lease on their naval base at Guantánamo. By 1940, Batista had wearied of running Cuba through others and ran for president himself, winning an apparently fair election.

Playing for the Players

The writer Oscar Hijuelos captures the unequal and divisive atmosphere of those heady days when American high-rollers flooded towards the glitzy Havana scene. In *The Mambo Kings Play Songs of Love,* he describes how "A musician's life in Havana was poor, sociable. Pretty-boy singers, trumpet players, and *congueros* gathered everywhere – in the arcades, plazas and bars. Cuban musicians (were paid) shit. Ten dollars a night, with cleaning charges for uniforms, black skins and mulattoes in one door, white musicians in another, no drinks on the house, no overtime, and Christmas bonuses of watered down, resealed bottles of whiskey."

Havana and the Mob

In a city where fabulous sums could be made from booze, drugs, gambling and prostitution, it's not surprising that the American Mob was not far behind.

In December, 1946, the most important Mafia conference since the Depression was held in Havana. Organizing the meeting was the powerful Meyer Lansky. Known as "the Jewish godfather," Lansky was a diminutive, bookish man who was the brains behind America's national crime syndicate, formed by uniting the various warring families in the 1930s. Guest of honor was "Lucky" Luciano, Lansky's more high-profile Sicilian partner, who had recently been deported from the United States for his notorious activities and was now entering Cuba under a false passport. Every Mafia boss from New York, New Jersey, Tampa, Chicago and New Orleans made the pilgrimage to Havana for the event.

The Cuban capital was a logical meeting place. The Mob had gotten a foothold here during the Prohibition years, using Cuba as a base for running rum to the Florida Keys. But a much more lucrative opening had come in 1938, when the Cuban strongman Batista had invited Meyer Lansky to take over operation of two casinos and a racetrack at Havana's Oriental Park, all of which had gained a reputation for being crooked. Lansky brought in his own pit crews to replace the Cubans and soon had the places "reformed." The establishments flourished, and more casinos followed – with regular kickbacks to Batista, brokered by Lansky. What was better, as far as the Mafia was concerned, was that the whole thing was perfectly legal.

Business was slow in 1946, but the Cuban capital was still the most comfortable and safe place to discuss Mob business. Frank Sinatra was even flown down to sing: the New Jersey crooner came in with two of Al Capone's cousins and a gold cigarette case for Luciano. Top of the Havana agenda was what to do with Benny "Bugsy" Siegel, a charming psychopath who had blown a fortune in Mob money on the Flamingo Hotel, the first casino in Las Vegas. (Meyer Lansky had the last word on his long-time partner and bosom buddy: "There's only one thing to do with a thief who steals from his friends. Benny's got to be hit.")

LEFT: Meyer Lansky, the "Jewish Godfather," who ran the Mob's operations in Havana.
ABOVE: American tourists and ersatz souvenirs.

The Las Vegas of the Caribbean

Although Siegel was duly gunned down the next year, his formula of "high-stakes, high-class gambling joints for high-rollers" soon took off in Las Vegas – convincing Meyer Lansky that the slowly degenerating operations in Havana were chickenfeed. The ever-greedy Batista, who had retaken power after a brief hiatus with a bloodless coup in 1952, agreed. Scandals were again rocking the Cuban casinos, with allegations of rigged games: their rooms were full of American-born dice hustlers, who would fleece tourists of their spending money in games like cubola and razzle-dazzle, even as they dined at their restaurant tables. Worse, a friend of Californian Senator Richard Nixon lost a considerable sum in Havana, creating much poor publicity when he refused to pay up.

In 1953, Batista appointed Lansky his personal adviser on gambling reform, to cleanse Havana as he had done in the 1930s. From his base in the Montmartre Club, Lansky proceeded to turn Havana into a tropical Monte Carlo. Games were regularized, and the secret police were employed to arrest and deport card sharps. The irony was not lost on many. When asked why American gangsters were so welcome in Cuba, the US ambassador replied: "It's strange, but it seems to be the only way to get honest casinos."

The second Batista presidency became the climax of Cuba's age of decadence, a time when corruption reached mythic proportions. The revitalized casino industry was part of a massive push to promote tourism: a new airline was started, visas were waived for visiting Americans, and all new hotels and motels were granted tax-free status. Havana's hotel room numbers nearly doubled in six years. Almost any hotel could and did have a gaming room, so educated Cubans gave up their jobs as doctors and teachers for much more lucrative work as croupiers. Oiling the gears was a Byzantine system of bribes – Meyer Lansky is said to have deposited more than US$3 million in Batista's personal bank account in Switzerland, and this was just a tiny fraction of his own share. The Mafia boss and Cuban president continued to get on famously; according to one observer, they were "like brothers."

Meanwhile, Batista's secret police became less secret and more savage in hunting down opposition figures. The corpses of tortured dissidents were strung from the lamp-posts as a warning for anyone speaking against the relentless turning of the roulette wheels and poker machines in Havana.

The lure of the tropic

Cuba's combination of unlimited sensual pleasures, lawlessness and corruption – along with the *frisson* of danger – exerted an almost irresistible fascination for the many writers and artists who passed through Havana.

In 1923, the 19-year-old Anaïs Nin paid a visit to her high-society family, indulging in a rigorous routine of horse-riding, garden parties, and flirtation. Initially attracted to the sensuality of Havana, the future feminist icon was soon repelled by the city's superficiality and "unsubdued coarseness." "Mental idleness, vacuity, are what I read in most passing faces," she wrote in her *Early Diaries*. "Eyes seeming to wander forever, alighting on everything but carrying no thoughts to the mind, eyes devoid of vision, gleaming only when the senses are pleased."

More impressed with Cuba was the Spanish poet Federico García Lorca, who stayed for three months in 1930. "This island is a paradise," he rhapsodized in a letter to his parents. "If I ever get lost, they should look for me either in Andalusia or Cuba." Already a recognized poet, Lorca was befriended by a string of *habanero* bohemians and took full advantage of Cuba's pleasures. The atmosphere of sexual liberation apparently made García Lorca more overt in his own homosexuality: in Cuba, he wrote his play *The Public*, the first Spanish work to center on male lovers.

Two years later, the American poet Hart Crane had much less success with Cuba's fabled freedoms: arriving depressed from a failed trip to Mexico, he solicited the wrong sailors in Havana harbor and was beaten senseless. Leaving Cuba the next night, he jumped off the boat and drowned himself.

Of all the foreign visitors, Ernest Hemingway was the most notorious, visiting throughout the 1930s for marlin fishing and then moving to Cuba permanently. Although he regularly drank himself into a stupor, Papa's streak of Midwestern puritanism was strong enough for him to remain largely innocent of the seamier side of Havana life.

No such qualms restrained the English writer Graham Greene. During a brief visit in 1957, Greene explored romantic, degraded Cuba and immortalized it in his novel *Our Man in Havana*. He found the Cuban capital a place "where every vice was permissible and every trade possible," and lapped up "the brothel life, the roulette in every hotel, the fruit machines spilling out jackpots of silver dollars, the Shanghai Theater where for one dollar twenty-five cents one could see a nude cabaret of extreme obscenity with the bluest of blue films in the intervals."

Greene even became caught up in his own minor intrigue when he flew to Santiago in the hopes of interviewing guerrillas in the Sierra Maestra, carrying a suitcase of clothes for them. On the plane was a *Time* reporter whom Greene decided was a CIA spy. There were surreptitious meetings with revolutionary contacts in Santiago, and Greene became convinced that he was being followed. The interview fell through and Greene left Cuba soon thereafter.

Last days of the frenzy

For many, the disparity between Cuba's fun-loving image and brutal reality was becoming too great. Many Cubans were disgusted with the levels of corruption into which their country had sunk and the spectacle of the opulent, Mafia-run casinos alongside Cubans sleeping on the footpaths and in burned-out cars. Even some foreigners felt moral qualms. As the Cuban-American writer Enrique Fernández-Más put it: "On the road to pleasure, your driver could turn around at a stop light and show you photos of bodies bloodied with bullets and young faces ripped apart by tortures so savage – vividly described by the *revolucionario* driver – that the daiquiris, the sweet roast pork, the yummy yams, the fine Havanas, the hot sex, nothing tasted good any more."

But not everyone noticed the changing of the winds – including Mob boss Meyer Lansky. In 1957, he opened his own hotel, the Riviera, right on the Malecón; it was the largest and most tasteless place in Havana. Ginger Rogers performed in the Copa Room on opening night; Abbott and Costello flew down to entertain soon after. There seemed to be no limits to the money Havana could produce: gamblers' checks were flown to Miami every morning to make sure that they cleared. In April 1958, the Nevada Gaming Board, enraged that Havana's success was hurting Las Vegas, banned holders of Nevada gambling licences from operating in Havana. Several Vegas operators withdrew their money; Meyer Lansky, oblivious to Cuban politics, stayed put. He gambled everything on Havana – and, as he would later have cause to put it, "I crapped out." ❑

LEFT: Graham Greene, fan of Cuban blue movies.
ABOVE: Sloppy Joe's and other Havana bars were amongst the most famous in the world.

26
ALBUM DE
REVOLUC
CUBA
19
19

A
CION
NA

THE REVOLUTION

One of the 20th century's most distinctive political triumphs for the underdog, the 1959 Revolution still effectively serves as the "year zero" for present-day Cuba

As the age of decadence flourished in Havana, the roots of a revolution were beginning to take hold in the countryside. Under Batista's rule, a small elite enjoyed a grand lifestyle, while the majority of the rural population endured appalling poverty. Few had running water, electricity, or access to health care and education. One-fourth of all Cubans could not read or write, and one-fourth of all adult males were unemployed. The country was rife with corruption, oppression, and inequality.

One year after Batista began his second term in office, a brazen young lawyer named Fidel Castro concluded that an armed uprising was the only way to end the dictator's reign. This was not Castro's first grasp at power. A year earlier he had tried to run for a seat in congress but, in a Machiavellian move by Batista, the elections were surreptitiously canceled.

The Moncada attack

Hoping to spark a mass uprising of the Cuban people, on July 26, 1953, Castro and 125 of his fellow anti-Batistas mounted an attack on the army barracks at the Moncada garrison in Santiago. But as the music of carnival blared in the background, the neophyte revolutionaries were brutally defeated. Despite being a total failure, the hapless coup marked the beginning of the Cuban revolution and served as a harbinger of things to come.

Three rebels died in the attack, and 68 more were later killed by the police. Those who escaped, including Castro, took refuge in the nearby Sierra Maestra mountains. But soon after they were rounded up and sent to jail. Fortunately for Castro, the arresting officer was sympathetic to the rebel cause, and took him to a local jail rather than the government prison where he would have surely been killed. That black officer, Sergeant Pedro Sarría Tartabull, was later court martialed and jailed by the Batista regime, but years down the track, he would be rewarded for his good deed: a grateful Castro appointed him as his personal security guard.

History will absolve me

For Batista, having Castro executed in secret would have solved many problems, but

Castro's capture had become public knowledge, so any such subsequent attempt would have also fomented more anti-government sentiment. Instead, he had to put the rebel on trial. Acting as his own lawyer, Castro delivered a five-hour speech that would sink deeply into the minds of the Cuban underclass. He called Batista the worst dictator in Cuban history, and described in detail the sorry living conditions of the majority of the Cuban people.

He also called out for universal education, agrarian reform, and a total restructuring of the government. He then delivered his famous last words: "Condemn me if you will. History will absolve me." He did not, significantly,

PRECEDING PAGES: history for Cuban schoolchildren.
LEFT: Fidel and his brother Raúl (to his right) in 1957.
RIGHT: time runs out for Fulgencio Batista.

mention a single word about the principles of Marxism-Leninism.

Sentenced to 15 years, Castro was jailed on the Isle of Pines (now the Isle of Youth), where political prisoners were granted an array of privileges. While in jail, he read the works of Marx and studied successful peasant uprisings. He also lectured to fellow inmates and plotted the revolution that would bring him to power. After serving less than two years, Castro was no longer considered a threat to the government and he was released on Mother's Day of 1955. Batista would later regret that rash decision.

Soon after his release, Fidel Castro and his comrades went into exile in Mexico. There, he met a young Argentinian called Ernesto "Che" Guevara and together they created the 26th of July Movement (M-26), named for the attack at Moncada in 1953. M-26, which had roots in Cuba's 19th-century struggles, was the philosophical foundation that became synonymous with Castro's revolution. Castro traveled to New York and Miami to raise money for the impending revolt, gathered guns and ammunition, and campaigned for support from abroad.

In November of 1956, Castro, Che, and 80 other revolutionaries left Mexico aboard a leaky, second-hand yacht. The boat, *Granma*, had been named by its first owner in honor of his grandmother. Later, *Granma* would become the unlikely name of Cuba's Communist Party newspaper, as well as the name of a whole province.

After several days floundering in stormy seas, the rebels landed on December 2 in the Gulf of Guacanayabo, about 100 miles (160 km) west of Santiago. The original plan was to arrive in Santiago at the end of November, at the same time as a planned uprising led by M-26 member Frank País. Lacking the help of Castro and his men, this uprising was crushed in just a few hours. And when the seasick revolutionaries finally disembarked from their boat they were met by Batista's troops who captured and killed about three-fourths of the crew.

Among the dozen or so survivors were Castro, his younger brother Raúl, and Che. Joined by a group of peasants and a few fellow revolutionaries, the ragged dozen quickly slipped away into the Sierra Maestra where they founded the Rebel Army. One of those who joined them was a wealthy revolutionary named Vilma Espín, now the head of the Federation of Cuban Women and Raúl Castro's wife.

Guerrillas in the mountains

Entrenched in the mountains, the Rebel Army saw themselves as warriors of the common people, and set out to infiltrate the country with their revolutionary ideas. During the next few years, they set up an informal government, drew up a manifesto, and organized schools and hospitals in the rural areas. They also established their own radio station, Radio Rebelde, and campaigned on the airwaves for a democratic Cuba. Needing the support of the underground movements in Havana, they aligned themselves with the Students' Revolutionary Directorate and the Civic Resistance Movement.

NOTHNG TO DECLARE

Shortly after midnight on New Year's Eve, Batista fled Cuba for the Dominican Republic and then Florida, supposedly with US$300 million packed in his suitcase.

With his name and face now known the world over, public support for Castro in Cuba multiplied. In March 1957, students stormed the Presidential Palace attempting to kill Batista, while another group took over a radio station and falsely announced his death. The following year a general strike was called in support of the Rebel Army, and disgruntled navy officers tried to stage a rebellion in the port of Cienfuegos.

The turning point of the revolution came in July 1958, when a battalion of Batista's forces

In a clever public relations coup, the rebels smuggled Herbert Matthews, a reporter for the *New York Times*, into their mountain camp for a clandestine interview with Castro. Swayed by the boisterous bravado of Castro and his men, Matthews's story praised the Rebel Army, and gave the world a romantic first impression of the dashing young revolutionary. Matthews' story was fabricated, Batista insisted, and Castro was actually dead. Days later, the *Times* responded with a photograph of Matthews and Castro smoking cigars in the mountains.

LEFT: Raúl Castro and Che Guevara in 1958.
RIGHT: Fidel and long-time companion Celia Sánchez.

surrendered to Castro after a 10-day siege. The Rebel Army, which by this time was about 50,000 strong, charged ahead.

Followed by troops, Castro advanced into Santiago, Raúl into northern Oriente and, in the most decisive move of all, Che into Santa Clara. By December 1958, the rebels had shattered Batista's army, which retreated in defeat. A terrified Batista fled the country.

The following morning, people all over the island rejoiced. Ebullient revellers danced in the streets applauding Batista's downfall. In Havana, throngs of Cuban peasants stormed into the fancy casinos which had been off-limits to them for years. Some vandalized the slot

Che Guevara

To this day, decades after his death, Ernesto "Che" Guevara is a glorified Marxist hero and model for Cuba's ideal socialist man. An icon by government decree, he is known throughout the island simply as Che, an affectionate Argentinian expression equivalent to the cockney/Australian "mate" or the antique American "pal" or "buddy."

Each morning, Cuban schoolchildren begin their day by reciting the patriotic slogan: "Pioneers of communism, we shall be like Che." Throughout the country, posters of his handsome face hang on thousands of living-room walls. Government officials try to emulate his ideals, and women swoon for him as if he were a movie star.

Born in Argentina in 1928, Guevara came from a left-leaning, middle-class family. As a child he developed a severe asthma condition that later brought about his decision to become a doctor. He graduated from medical school in 1953, and then took off to travel through Latin America, seeking political adventure.

After witnessing the CIA-inspired overthrow of the socialist Arbénz government in Guatemala in 1954, Guevara moved to Mexico, where he met the then exiled Fidel Castro. Soon after, he joined Castro's 26th of July Movement and was later to command the guerrilla attacks that led to the flight of Batista. He also became Castro's principal ideological counselor and closest friend.

Once the government was established, he supervised agrarian reform, served as the president of the National Bank of Cuba, and negotiated trade agreements with Eastern Bloc countries. In 1960 he wrote a book, *Guerrilla Warfare*, that became a manual for revolutionary strategies in the Third World. In it, he advocated the use of guerrilla tactics to defeat imperialism; moral rather than material incentives for work; and working class solidarity.

During the 1960s, an entire generation of radical youths idolized his purist Marxist beliefs, selfless devotion and relentless work ethic, and his dramatic image blessed protest movements in Paris, London, Washington, Montreal, Tokyo, Bombay and Baghdad.

A member of the macho world of brave guerrilla fighters, Guevara was impetuous, daring and reckless. He was also a brilliant intellectual who spoke French, wrote poetry, and represented Cuba in international chess competitions. Thrilled by the staccato beat of machine guns, he flaunted his Achilles heel: a total disregard for danger. In 1965 he resigned from his posts (some historians say he'd fallen out with Castro over the growing influence of the Soviet Union in Cuban affairs), and, after a brief spell fighting in the Congo, he settled in the highlands of Bolivia where he attempted to foster revolution among the local peasants. The campaign proved a disaster and Guevara was captured and killed by the Bolivian army in 1967.

After his death, Castro declared a three-day period of national mourning, and then spent years creating a Guevara cult that surpassed his own. When the country began to feel the strain of the collapse of the Soviet Union, Castro tried to rekindle some revolutionary passion by implementing a nationwide "Let's Be Like Che" campaign. Then, in 1997, his mortal remains were discovered in Bolivia and returned to Cuba (*see page 234*).

Che Guevara remains Latin America's most celebrated modern revolutionary. Hindsight reveals him as a martyr glorified by circumstance whose dream of spreading socialism around the world never really had a chance, yet he achieved enough in his brief life for French philosopher Jean-Paul Sartre to describe him as "the most complete human being of our age." ❑

LEFT: Che Guevara, after the success of the Revolution.

machines, while others brought their pigs in to have a look.

The victory drive

On January 1, 1959, the handsome 32-year-old Castro took off with his guerrillas for a victory drive from Santiago to Havana. Euphoric crowds cheered as they passed through the countryside. When they arrived in the capital a week later, tens of thousands of supporters welcomed them. As Castro delivered his first victory speech in Havana, a flock of white doves was released in the air; one of the birds landed on his shoulder, which was taken by followers of Santería (*see pages 92–3*) to be an omen that he had been chosen by the gods to deliver them from oppression.

Cubans in New York and Miami celebrated the fall of Batista and made plans to return to the island. The revolution was praised worldwide as a true victory for the Cuban people, and even the US government was initially optimistic about the changes taking place.

Meanwhile, back at the Riviera Hotel, workers walked out of their jobs. Meyer Lansky found himself in the kitchen cooking dinner for befuddled guests as his wife waited tables and mopped the floors. For Lansky, and his cronies, the good life was over. Words from Castro's speech echoed in his head: "We are ready not only to deport the gangsters, but to shoot them." The notorious Lansky eventually moved his gambling business to the nearby Bahamas, and offered a large bounty for Fidel Castro's head.

A new Cuba

In the spring of 1959, Castro declared himself the prime minister of Cuba, and Che Guevara was appointed president of the National Bank. Hundreds of Batista supporters were jailed and executed, and by 1960 sweeping changes were taking place across the country.

The new government passed an agrarian reform act which limited private land ownership; under Batista, a mere 8 percent of all landowners had owned 70 percent of the land. It also confiscated foreign-owned industries in an effort to end US control of the island (Americans owned more than 165 major companies including 90 percent of the public services and 40 percent of the sugar industry). Farms, plantations, oil refineries, and communications systems were nationalized. The government also outlawed racial discrimination, created a low-income housing program, made free healthcare

ABOVE: a victorious Fidel, accompanied by Celia Sánchez, negotiates the surrender of Santiago.

and education available to all, and implemented new policies for farming, sports, music, the arts, and defense.

The redistribution of wealth meant instant rewards for the peasant class, but just as quickly, the middle and upper classes were stripped of the privileges they had once enjoyed. Already having had their homes confiscated, many feared what might come next and fled the country for exile in Miami. Forbidden to take any possessions with them, most left with nothing more than the clothes on their backs. Women sewed their wedding rings into the hems of their dressses to smuggle them out.

Once in Miami they established a vocal anti-Castro community of exiles that freely criticized the new government, and looked forward to the day they could return to their homes.

In 1960, Fidel Castro delivered his first ever speech to the United Nations and was introduced for the first time to Soviet premier Nikita Khrushchev. While in New York, he also consorted with the radical American black power leader Malcolm X.

At about that time, the US government began to see Castro as a threat to its national security, and mysterious things started happening. A French ship delivering Belgian armaments inexplicably exploded in Havana harbor as unidentified low-flying planes flew over the city. The US was the prime suspect.

In response to America's Cold War antics, Castro took an aggressive stance. In January of 1961, he kicked 11 US diplomats out of Cuba. Soon after, the two countries severed diplomatic relations, and the US began an economic embargo of Cuba which brought the import of American goods to a halt. It also further isolated the island by persuading all but two Western-hemisphere nations (Canada and Mexico) to cut trade and diplomatic ties with Cuba.

The Bay of Pigs

In April 1961, a CIA-trained brigade of 1500 mercenaries, mostly Cuban exiles from Miami, landed at Playa Girón in the Bahía de Cochinos (Bay of Pigs), on Cuba's south coast, hoping to instigate a coup against Castro. Although backed by President Kennedy, the invasion was a fiasco. The element of surprise was lost when US bombers had attacked Cuban airfields days beforehand, and the bombing raids failed to destroy the Cuban airforce completely, thus leaving the attackers open to assault from the air. The counter-revolutionaries were no match for Cuba's military, led by Castro himself; and the local populace, who it was hoped would be sympathetic to the exiles' cause, were in fact strongly pro-Castro. Within 72 hours they were defeated. A few were killed and the rest taken as prisoners. For their release, the US traded US$50 million worth of medicines which Cuba was unable to buy because of the embargo.

Castro emerged as the victor, while Kennedy was humiliated. The invasion was seen by the Cubans as a blatant imperialist stunt, and relations between the two countries worsened. It also garnered support for Castro throughout Latin America, and rendered him forever fearful of a US military invasion. The US did little to alleviate those fears, instigating covert activities including plots to assassinate Castro. The Cuban leader estimates that there have been 20 CIA-inspired attempts on his life; one CIA director, William Colby, expressed surprise, saying he was aware of only five.

By the end of 1961, Castro's platform for a freely elected democratic government had

LEFT: Ernest Hemingway congratulates Castro for winning the 1960 marlin fishing competition.
RIGHT: Khrushchev welcomes Fidel to Moscow.

changed. Following the Bay of Pigs invasion he had shocked the world by pronouncing Cuba's revolution to be a "socialist revolution". Some believe that Castro's conversion to Marxism was merely a pragmatic move to gain favor with the Russians, without whom Cuba did not stand a chance of surviving the US embargo.

On the brink of war

In support of the new socialist Cuba, the USSR supplied Castro with economic aid and shipped nuclear missiles to the island for defense. The threat of nuclear weapons just 90 miles (140 km) away was too much for the US government, and in October 1962, the Soviet Union and the US came face to face with the reality of nuclear war over the Cuban Missile Crisis – what Cubans refer to as the Caribbean Crisis.

The US demanded that the Soviets remove the missiles, threatening to bomb Cuba if they refused. The world watched in horror as the possibility of war came closer. The Soviets eventually relented and an uneasy peace was restored.

Despite the fact that an agreement was reached, the US was not happy with the outcome. In 1963, President Kennedy relegated relations with Cuba to fall under the US Trading with the Enemy Act, which tightened the

embargo and disallowed all commercial and personal contact between the two nations. The US became the only country in the world to forbid its citizens to travel to Cuba, and the political impasse became even more intractable.

Castro himself was incensed that he had not been consulted during the talks between the two superpowers, but the reality was that he had thrown in his lot with the Soviets and was powerless to prevent them from dictating terms. He had to content himself with an unwritten assurance that the US would not sponsor a further invasion of Cuba, and with the fact that, for the briefest of periods, he'd managed to turn the tables on his enemy in the insecurity stakes. ❑

LOOKING AFTER NUMBER ONE

With the Cuban crisis at its peak, the White House Press Secretary, Pierre Salinger, was summoned into the office of President Kennedy, who informed him that there was a special task that he needed carrying out. Salinger was told to buy 1000 of the best Cuban cigars, but was given only one day to do it in – no easy task, even in those days of voracious cigar consumption.

"Have you got them?" the President enquired anxiously the next day. "I've done better than that. I've got 1200," answered Salinger. "Good," uttered a relieved Kennedy, opening his drawer and pulling out the Trading with The Enemy Act to sign, prohibiting trade with Cuba.

CINE
CUMPLIRA
VIVA
MUERTE

CENTENARIO DEL 1RO DE MAYO
AMISTAD
PAZ
LA BRIGADA
NO SE PUEDE
PATRIA y CON

PARE

SOCIALISM OR DEATH.

During the 1960s and '70s, Cuba played a role in world affairs out of all proportion to its size. Since then, this has been curtailed by crippling domestic problems

Although resolved diplomatically, the Cuban Missile Crisis provoked even more Cold War hostility from the US, and pushed Castro firmly into the Soviet camp. In addition, it helped to turn the country into an audacious socialist experiment and feisty Third World power.

Cuba's Communist Party was established in 1965, and the following year, despite Soviet disapproval, Castro was determined to export his revolutionary ideals. In 1966 he claimed that the Andes would become the next Sierra Maestra. But the Soviet Union (whose high levels of monetary and military aid allowed it to wield increasing influence) was pressing Castro to pursue a less independent foreign policy. It seems Che Guevara was determined to carry out a policy of directly fomenting revolution, with or without Soviet support, and left Cuba to fight first in Africa and then Bolivia.

With the death of Guevara in Bolivia in 1967, Castro realized he had to take a different path to global influence. In 1968 he personally endorsed the Soviet invasion of Czechoslovakia, and cemented the bond with his powerful ally.

Castro then directed his energy inward. Trying to lessen the country's dependence on the sugar industry, he attempted to diversify the economy through industrialization. But by this time, thousands of educated Cubans had fled and the country lacked skilled labor. The US embargo limiting the import of industrial equipment was also a hindrance, and eventually the industrialization plan failed. So sugar, once again, became the main force of the economy.

Big Brother is watching

In the name of the revolution, the 1960s marked the beginning of decades of political repression. Anyone seen as non-supportive of the government was deemed "socially unacceptable," and thousands of these "dissidents" were jailed.

PRECEDING PAGES: 1970s May Day parade in Havana.
LEFT: communism, Caribbean style.
RIGHT: the sugar harvest, crucial to Cuba's economy.

Government police sealed off the bohemian neighborhoods of Havana and interrogated artists, writers and intellectuals. Non-supportive poets were silenced. Education and cultural policies became more severe, trade unions were disbanded, and the media fell under absolute control of the government. By the late 1960s,

an ideological straitjacket seemed to have smothered the country.

Practising Catholics, Protestants, Jews, and Santeros were persecuted – religious affiliation was deemed anti-revolutionary. Prostitutes were sent to vocational schools for rehabilitation, homosexuals were imprisoned in labor camps, and all remnants of bourgeois society were eliminated.

To help dissuade counter-revolutionary activities, Castro created neighborhood watch groups known as Comités de Defensa de la Revolución – Committees for the Defense of the Revolution or CDRs. Although the CDRs did organize labor and implement health and education programs, they also served as vigilantes for the government and as the Big Brother of the revolution. Members monitored their neighbors and reported all non-conformist behavior to the government. Still in operation today, there are over 100,000 CDRs on the island, comprising (officially) about 75 percent of the total population. Traditionally, for the ordinary Cuban citizen, belonging to a CDR brings a guarantee of social benefits, while not belonging can bring trouble.

Throughout the 1960s, the "better-dead-than-red" communist-obsessed US continued covert activities against Cuba, including more CIA-backed assassination attempts on Castro. In addition, several of Cuba's trade missions in Europe were bombed by anti-Castro terrorists. As a result, the Soviet Union beefed up its military and economic support to Cuba. Eastern Bloc technicians were sent to the island while Cuban students were invited to study in Moscow. Financial aid steadily increased and was measured in billions of dollars. At the time, Cuba was receiving generous shipments of oil priced far below standard OPEC rates, and about one-half of all Soviet aid to the Third World. Its sugar crop was bought at inflated prices. Boosted by Soviet weapons and fighter planes, Cuba's defense system developed into the most powerful military force in Latin America, much larger than those of Brazil or Mexico.

The heady 1970s

For most Cubans, the 1970s are remembered fondly as the heady days of the revolution. With the utmost confidence, Castro became the international spokesman for Third World causes, traveling to South America, China, Vietnam, and Africa. In 1974 the Soviet premier Leonid Brezhnev visited Cuba and publicly endorsed his Caribbean comrade. In front of enraptured crowds, the two predicted that communism would some day triumph throughout the world. The next year, the Organization of American States lifted its sanctions against Cuba and many Latin American nations resumed ties with the country.

Economically Cuba advanced, and the gains of the revolution were indisputable. Unheard of in most Third World countries, Cuba's health care system eliminated infectious diseases, drastically lowered the infant mortality rate, and curtailed population growth. The number of doctors grew from 6,000 to over 25,000. The government also paved roads throughout the countryside, built low-rent apartment buildings, and eradicated illiteracy. Cubans felt proud.

Although Cuba's political system was redesigned to mimic the Soviet model, Castro remained very much his own man. This was especially so when it came to foreign policy, where he saw Cuba as part of the non-aligned movement. Capitalizing on Cuba's Afro-Cuban heritage, Castro also aligned himself with the Black Power movements in Africa. In 1975 he flexed his military muscles by sending 200,000 soldiers to Angola. Cuban troops fought on the side of the Marxist SWAPO government, following South Africa's decision to assist Angolan UNITA rebels, under Jonas Savimbi. This conflict continued a tradition of Cuban assistance with what Castro saw as anti-imperialist movements in Africa, which went back to the days of Che. In 1978 he did the same for Ethiopia.

MANDELA'S VERDICT

Nelson Mandela believes that Cuba's role in Angola was instrumental in breaking apartheid, as defeat in that war helped to weaken the South African regime.

Back on his side of the world, Castro befriended left-leaning leaders in nearby Jamaica and Grenada and, in 1979, hosted the annual conference of the non-aligned nations. That same year Cuba supported the Soviet invasion of Afghanistan, and the socialist revolution in Nicaragua which brought the Sandinistas to power. An elated Castro strutted the world stage like a proud peacock.

In 1976, Cuba finally approved its new constitution which canonized Marxism-Leninism, and Fidel Castro's position as head of state became constitutional. The new constitution redrew provincial boundaries, adding eight more provinces to the original seven inherited from the Spanish. It also created the assemblies of People's Power (Poder Popular), governing bodies of elected officials who delegate power at municipal, provincial and national levels.

LEFT: Cuba's literacy campaign, begun in the 1960s, created the most literate population in Latin America. **RIGHT:** the military out on show for the anniversary of the landing of the *Granma* on December 2, 1996.

Socialismo o Muerte

At the beginning of the 1980s, Cuba was still a Latin American symbol of independence from US imperialism, but the quality of life in the country was beginning to decline. Productivity dropped off, and healthcare, education and social services deteriorated. Castro blamed the country's problems on the "workers who do not work and the students who do not study," and then fired many government economists.

Many of Cuba's economic problems, however, were caused by blatant mismanagement. The government had appointed Communist Party members to professional positions for which they were not qualified, destroyed the plantation system, and refused to develop the tourism industry. And a political system designed for the Soviet Union did not translate well to Cuba.

SUGAR FOR OIL

A sugar-for-oil deal with the USSR meant that Moscow guaranteed a price for its harvest and payment was made in oil at a price well below the going rate.

In 1980 public protests escalated to the point that the government permitted anyone who wanted to leave to do so – including, it is said, many criminals who were freed in order for them to do so. That year, 125,000 Cubans fled to the US in the so-called Mariel boatlift, adding to the several hundred thousand who had left in the early years of the revolution. In 1985, the Cubans in Miami set up Radio Martí, an anti-Castro propaganda station aimed directly at Cuba. The station's reports of how great life was in the US stirred up even more discontent.

By the late 1980s, Cuba was billions of dollars in debt to the Soviets, and the government was forced to cut food rations. Trying to rejuvenate revolutionary spirit, Castro revised his Patria o Muerte! (fatherland or death) slogan used to punctuate his dreadfully long speeches during the 1960s, and Socialismo o Muerte! became the slogan of choice. Appealing to Cuban nationalism, "100% Cubano" became another motivational motto. Both were plastered on billboards throughout the country.

Criticisms and scandals

On the international level, Cuba received harsh criticisms for its human rights violations. A report filed by Amnesty International condemned the country for its abuse of political prisoners, and the beatings, psychological torture and solitary confinement taking place in Cuba's prisons became a thorny issue.

In 1989, more disgrace fell on the country. General Arnaldo Ochoa, a much decorated military figure, and six other military officials, were charged with corruption and drug trafficking. Found guilty of pocketing millions of dollars and allowing Colombian cocaine smugglers to use Cuba as a way-station en route to the US, the officers were put before a firing squad.

The scandal made a mockery of Castro's insistence that Cuba had an impeccable record when it came to involvement with illegal drugs, and cynics saw the public execution as overly dramatic. Some accused Castro of ordering the punishment in order to mask his own involvement with drugs. Others suggested that Ochoa had been conspiring to oust Castro.

The Eastern Bloc crumbles

As the Ochoa scandal shook the country, the communist dominoes in Eastern Europe were beginning to tumble. When Mikhail Gorbachev assumed power in Moscow and put forth his glasnost goals, many predicted that the Soviet money tree would soon be pruned and that the Cuban government would be thrust into chaos. Castro, however, made it clear that he had no interest in multi-party governments or a free-market system. "For us to adopt perestroika would be like living in our home with another man's wife," he said.

Members of Cuba's Communist Party agreed with their leader. For them, glasnost was a dirty word. Untouched by the brewing crisis, Party members were a privileged class in Cuba. With access to food, cars, gas, travel abroad, and imported goods, they bitterly resisted change.

When the USSR finally fell apart in 1991, the impact on Cuba was devastating. On a yearly basis, the country lost US$6 billion in economic aid, $1 billion in military assistance, 10 million tons of oil, and $6 billion worth of imported goods. It also lost its major trading partner, and now had to sell its sugar at fair market value. The scarcity of available oil paralyzed Cuban industry and transportation systems. Adding to the turmoil, Cuba's sugar harvest was the lowest in 30 years.

The Special Period

Beset by economic crisis, but unwilling to adopt glasnost-style reforms, the Cuban government implemented a belt-tightening survival strategy known as the "Special Period in Time of Peace." In order to compensate for the loss of Soviet subsidies, Castro told the Cuban people to work harder and be patient. He then set about stripping them of the basic necessities of daily life, and demanding sacrifices like none they had ever known before.

Energy consumption was drastically reduced, oxen replaced tractors in the fields, and food rations were slashed to a minimum survival level. Government-produced television programs instructed citizens on how to grow their own vegetables, make their own candles and soap, and turn dried banana peels into san-

LEFT: "We have absolutely no fear of you!" cries a Cuban soldier to Uncle Sam, on Havana's Malecón. **ABOVE:** standing in line has become an inescapable feature of Cuban life.

dals. Horse-drawn buggies were put back in service, and cheap, low-grade oil was substituted to fire electric plants, causing a pall of dirty smoke over Havana.

In addition, the government imported a million Chinese bicycles and ordered the people to start pedalling. Encouraging Cubans to adopt cycling, Fidel Castro told the people: "Expanding the use of the bicycle is an indicator of cultural advancement." But for the millions of secretaries, teachers, and factory workers who had to spend hours a day riding to work, it was more like a step back in time.

Still in effect today, the Special Period means that life for the average Cuban citizen is bleak. Apartments are crowded and in need of repairs. Electric wires dangle in the streets, telephones are few and rarely work, elevators are out of order, and clocks no longer tell the time.

LIVING OFF THE *LIBRETA*

A Cuban's typical ration amounts to one piece of bread a day, three eggs a week, and a portion of fish or chicken once a month. A family of four gets one bottle of cooking oil four times a year, and milk is available only for children under eight. Most of these items are often out of stock at the local shop (*bodega*). Rice is full of grit, while meat rations are often minced and consist mainly of soya and gristle. Many Cubans rarely enjoy the taste of beef or pork: a scrawny piece of meat purchased on the black market or at a farmer's market can cost a month's wages. Some people have sold jewelry and family heirlooms to buy food, and a few admit to turning to cats and dogs for survival.

Cubans are hungry, frustrated, and tired of waiting in long lines for pitiful goods. Sugar, coffee, and rum – the backbone of the Cuban economy – are a luxury for most locals. While Cubans have lived with the *libreta* or ration book since the early 1960s, now it entitles its owner to precious little.

Patients must bring their own bed sheets to hospitals, and surgeons are allotted only one bar of soap per month to wash their hands. Herbal remedies have replaced drugs and hemp is used for sutures. In schools, textbooks are shared and workbooks erased and passed on to the next class. Factories sit idle, there are no fertilizers for crops, and harvests rot in the fields for want of distribution. Newspapers and magazines have shut down because there is no paper. Toilet tissue, toothpaste, shampoo and aspirin are luxuries of days gone by.

Capitalist tinkerings

Faced with rousing discontent on the island, Castro has made some compromises that in the past were non-negotiable. In 1991, he eased travel restrictions abroad, released some political prisoners, permitted more free speech than ever before, and granted autonomy to farmers, who were now permitted to sell a proportion of their produce in the open market.

Prices in the so-called "farmers' markets," introduced in 1994, are cripplingly high, but it has led to more food being available for those who can afford it. In 1993 Castro also permitted people to go into business for themselves by offering licences in over 100 categories, including mechanics, fishermen, farmers, taxi drivers, hairdressers and restauranteurs. The government ensures the self-employed have to pay a small fortune for a trading licence and in income tax to prevent them from benefiting too much from their efforts.

Meanwhile, to make up for lost Soviet subsidies and to combat the United States embargo, Cuba has been avidly wooing new investors – notably Canada, Mexico and members of the European Union – in what are commonly known as "joint ventures". These countries are pumping hundreds of millions of dollars into the economy, above all into tourism but also in the fields of nickel mining, oil exploration, the pharmaceutical industry, and even into sugar production.

CAPITAL SHOPPING

Nowadays, a shopping trip to Havana can take in a visit to a glistening Fiat showroom on the seafront and a branch of Benetton in the old city.

Dollars or death

In 1993 Fidel Castro legalized the use of the American dollar, which previously only a few privileged citizens (including high-ranking members of the Communist Party) had had access to. Decriminalizing the dollar has had a devastating effect on a society brought up at least to pay lip service to egalitarianism. The island is now essentially divided into two classes – those with dollars, and those without. Dollars can be acquired through fair means or foul: on the one hand through relatives living abroad or through a thriving business, on the other from black-market dealing or prostitution. Since there is little of worth that pesos can buy, many Cubans also succumb to converting their hard-earned pesos into dollars at exchange bureaux known as *cadecas*. An average wage of around 200 pesos a month and an exchange rate of 20 pesos to the dollar gives an idea of the disproportionately high value of the greenback.

For those with dollars, life has improved beyond recognition. "Dollar shops", in the form of supermarkets, boutiques, and electrical stores, have sprung up on many a street corner, selling everything from Swiss chocolate to French bread and Japanese TVs to American fridges. This new found consumerism has given Havana a misleading sheen of prosperity. Even though it is estimated that as many as 50 percent of Cubans in Havana have access to dollars, elsewhere the percentage is nearer 30 percent. For most ordinary people, life is still punitively tough.

LEFT: among the new breed of street traders, people that refill disposable lighters are particularly common. **ABOVE:** a bottle of milk is a precious commodity.

Black marketeers

With the advent of dollarization, as it is called, Cuba's clandestine economy has boomed. Black marketeers, known locally as *macetas*, are the new wheeler-dealer capitalists of the country. Buying and selling illegally, many make more money in a week than they could in a year on a government salary. Most sell food, clothes, liquor, medicines, cigarettes, and gas;

while others hawk automobile parts, construction supplies, and electronics. Some steal goods from their government jobs and sell them to people on the streets. For many Cubans, the black market is the only market they have.

Universal Disapproval

In 1997, 143 countries in the UN General Assembly voted against the embargo, with just three in favor (US, Uzbekistan and Israel). The figures for the same resolution in 1992 were 59 in favor, 3 against and 71 abstentions.

Embargo embargoed

While he is still full of anti-American rhetoric, Castro has alluded to a reconciliation with the US. Such hopes, however, received a setback in 1996, when two Cessnas which Cuban exiles from Miami had flown provocatively either close to or actually into (as Havana claims) Cuban airspace were shot down.

Bill Clinton couldn't resist pressure from Cuban-Americans to retaliate against the action of "the firing squad in the sky". He canceled direct flights from Florida to Cuba, and in 1995 passed the notorious Helms-Burton Act. Through this law, trade sanctions were enacted against any company worldwide doing business with Cuba or occupying a building on the island which had been confiscated by the Castro regime in the 1960s. There was an understandable howl of international outrage at the introduction of this bill, which tightened the restrictions imposed under the so-called Cuban Democracy Act, more commonly known as the Torricelli Bill, introduced in 1992. As a result, relations between the US and certain nations, including Canada and some members of the European Union, were seriously strained.

For this reason, and because there is a growing feeling in the US that the embargo has patently failed in achieving its long-term objective – of bringing down Fidel Castro – and is denying American companies major opportunities for investment on the island, the US president appears to be indefinitely postponing the act's implementation.

Since the death of cancer in 1997 of Jorge Mas Canosa, the leader of the ultra right-wing Cuban-American National Foundation, who wielded huge influence in Washington, there appears to be a very gentle thawing in US-Cuban relations. Direct flights between Miami and Havana resumed in July 1998, and increasing numbers of US politicians and businessmen are arriving in Cuba – the former trying to seek an end to nearly four decades of cold war, the latter to be in a position to hit the ground running when the embargo is finally lifted.

A hard-won independence

Cuba's communist regime was given a shot in the arm by the much-publicized visit of Pope John Paul II to the island in January 1998. Though the Pope had words of criticism for Castro about Cuba's record on human rights, he was also outspoken in his condemnation of the US embargo, which he called "deplorable." Yet, ironically, it is probably the embargo above all else that has kept Castro in power, enabling him to pass off his government's failures as not of his own making, and uniting his country against a common foe. Thus has Cuba's "Socialismo o Muerte!" survived while other communist countries have fallen apart.

After centuries of dependence on Spain, the US, and the USSR, Cuba is, for the first time, truly independent. And it is just beginning to learn that the price of independence is steep. ❑

Left: Benetton was one of the first foreign retail outlets to set up shop in Cuba in the 1990s.

Right: refugees at the US base of Guantánamo.

FIDEL

FIDEL CASTRO

Adored or despised? A unique statesman or a megalomaniac dictator? Castro has often been accused of being controversial, but never conventional

He has been called charismatic, brilliant, crazy, tyrannical, omnipotent, paranoid, paternalistic, and ruthless. He is loved and hated, revered and feared. A master of manipulation, Fidel Castro is a complex and mysterious man.

With his erect posture, and piercing dark eyes, he is a physically imposing figure: a talented sportsman in his youth, he once had the chance to try professional baseball. Although he has been seen wearing suits on occasion over the last few years, he still wears crisp military khakis as a matter of choice. He gave up cigars in the 1980s in support of a public anti-smoking campaign, but his beard, now completely gray, remains his distinctive mark. So much so, that his opponents, fearful of using his name, refer to him by cryptically stroking their chins.

As commander-in-chief of Cuba for more than three decades, Castro has survived numerous assassination attempts, nine US presidents, and the collapse of his ideological soulmate, the Soviet Union. Except for Jordan's King Hussein, he is the world's longest-ruling political leader.

Formative years

Fidel Alejandro Castro Ruz was born in Birán in Oriente (*see page 276*) in 1926, the fifth of nine children. His father, Angel Castro, was a brash Spanish businessman who carried a whip and a gun at all times. His mother, Lina Ruz González, was a servant in his father's home who bore Fidel out of wedlock. The couple married several years after Angel's first wife died. With a sprawling farm which employed 300 people, the Castros were wealthy, but not of the cultured class.

Prone to temper tantrums, the young Castro was a loud and troublesome child. When sent to a Jesuit boarding school in Santiago de Cuba, he was called a peasant by the other children and teased about his crude manners. Later, he attended Belén College in the capital, before going on to obtain a law degree from the University of Havana.

While at university, Castro frequently instigated student protests, and was considered a menacing thug. He was said to spend his spare time studying Hitler's *Mein Kampf*, and watching films of Mussolini as he mimicked the dictator's oratory style in front of a mirror.

After graduation Castro briefly practised law, but since he refused to accept money from his impoverished clients, he survived on the largesse of his family. In 1948 he traveled to Colombia where he was arrested for inciting anti-imperialist demonstrations. That same year he married Mirta Diáz-Balart, a wealthy philosophy student with family ties to Batista. The newly-wed couple honeymooned in Miami and New York, and received US$1000 from Batista as a wedding gift. In 1949 their son, Fidelito, was born, but five years later they divorced.

LEFT: immortality on a T-shirt.
RIGHT: the young Castro after being released from jail on the Isle of Pines in 1955.

Mirta remarried and moved to Spain, and has never spoken publicly about her ex-husband.

In 1959 Castro swept into the limelight with his Christ-like demeanor and outlaw charisma, and seized control of Cuba. As an international statesman and icon of the radical left, he mesmerized cheering crowds in cities all over the world, from Baghdad to Hanoi and Prague. For years, he was the self-proclaimed leader of the Third World.

A determined grip

Castro has always ruled his island with absolute power. He surrounds himself with an entourage of government yes-men who cater to his enormous ego and bathe him in adulation. His national security apparatus, embedded in every crevice of the island, enables him to maintain total authority over his people. Anyone who opposes him is labeled subversive, and subversives are harassed or imprisoned.

Although there are many malcontents, Castro still has substantial support. As revolutions go, his was by far one of the most legitimate, and because of this he is adored by many. The former underclass are especially grateful for the cradle-to-grave health care, free education, and social security benefits that they now have.

Castro has many names, including simply *El Comandante* or *El Jefe Máximo* ("The Maximum Leader"). He is sometimes referred to affectionately as *El Caballo* ("the horse"), though perhaps *El Mulo* ("the mule") would be more appropriate: Fidel Castro stubbornly resists change. After about four decades of communist experimentation and costly economic plans, his goal of a socialist paradise has eluded him. Yet he clings to revolutionary goals that are now obsolete.

Castro's personal life

If Castro the politician is hard to understand, Castro the man is even more elusive. Although a public figure, he is a master of self-concealment and a very private person. He rarely gets a good night's sleep, for to sleep is to be off-guard. Instead, he takes short naps at his office. He is fluent in English, but refuses to speak it in public. Grilled fish, turtle soup, and spaghetti are his favorite foods. He is a voracious reader and compulsive gardener. He loves to swim, fish, play chess, and drive his jeep through the Cuban countryside.

Like many Cubans, he is superstitious, and considers 26 his lucky number. He was born in 1926; his father owned 26,000 acres (10,500 hectares) of land; at the age of 26 he planned his Moncada attack on July 26; and he favors the 26th of the month for making significant speeches and important decisions. Such is his superstition that he refuses even to entertain the claim that he was in fact born in 1927.

His older brother, Ramón, tells the story of how the two brothers were sent from their remote mountain home to boarding school in Santiago – an arduous trip that took the boys seven days back in the 1930s. When they even-

ASSASSINATION ATTEMPTS

From the very start, when President Eisenhower was still in office, the CIA planned ingenious (if ineffective) ways of assassinating or discrediting Castro. Cuban exiles in Miami and the Mob were the agency's two natural partners in crime. Apart from simply shooting him, schemes included:

- contaminating his cigars with botulism.
- giving him a toxic dose of LSD.
- lacing a chocolate milkshake with cyanide.
- smearing his wet-suit with tuberculosis.
- plastering a chemical substance on his shoes to make his beard fall out (in an attempt to reduce his charisma).

tually arrived in the city, a family friend took them to the school, only to be told that the young Fidel was still too young to enrol. The exasperated man refused to send the child back across the mountains alone, and, snatching the papers, crossed out the date of birth – 1927 – and wrote 1926. "There," he pronounced, "now he's old enough. Enrol him !"

Rumors say that Castro has had hundreds of romantic encounters and has fathered dozens of children. But since his divorce, he has been linked publicly to only one woman, Celia Sánchez. A vivacious upper-class *cubana* and devoted guerrilla companion during the rebel campaign, Sánchez was Castro's friend and the love of his life. A champion of social causes, she was always popular with the Cuban people, and also held substantial power in the government. Furthermore, she was one of the few people who was brave enough to disagree with Castro. Celia's death from cancer in 1980 is said to have hit the Cuban leader hard.

Isolated like his island

Today, Castro stands at a crossroads, a lonely old man who trusts no one. Many of Castro's closest allies have deserted or betrayed him over the years. His children, Alina and Fidelito, both now live abroad, and his daughter virulently attacked him in a book published after she fled to the US in the early 1990s.

Discontent on the island is rife, but Fidel Castro still has a significant following among the Cubans, particularly those who can remember life under Batista. Old age is more likely to topple Castro than popular rebellion. The Cubans have no wish for a violent uprising, and with good reason they ask themselves what the alternative to *El Jefe Máximo* would be. In 1997 Fidel Castro for the first time openly described his brother, Raúl, as his heir designate – even though his younger sibling, a generally unpopular figure, could not hope to fill his brother's shoes. While Castro has hinted that he might step down should the US lift its embargo, he has also said: "I am a revolutionary, and revolutionaries do not retire."

Castro's place in 20th century history is assured – a renegade leader who has never played by orthodox political rules and who, to this day, is as impossible to predict as he ever was. Meanwhile, from Madrid to Miami, Cuban exiles are positioning for his job. Castro, a prisoner of his own ideals, is facing the tides of change, as Cuba – and the world – wait. ❑

LEFT: Fidel at the height of his oratorical powers.
ABOVE: a suited Castro meets the Pope in 1998.

AN ENCOUNTER WITH FIDEL

Gabriel García Márquez, the Nobel Prize-winning Colombian author, recalls his meetings with his friend, the Cuban leader

Speaking of a foreign visitor who had accompanied him around Cuba for a week, Fidel Castro said, "How that man can talk – he talks even more than I do!" It is enough to know Fidel Castro just a little to realize this was an exaggeration, one of his biggest, because it is impossible to find anyone more addicted than he to the habit of conversation. His devotion to the word is almost magical.

Public events used to begin whenever Fidel happened to arrive, which was as unpredictable as the rain. For some years now he has been arriving at the exact minute, and the duration of his speech depends very much on the mood of the audience. But the endless speeches of the early years belong to a past now confused with legend, and Fidel's style itself has become more compact after so many sessions of oratorical pedagogy.

Even the most difficult speeches seem to be casual talks, like those he held with students in the courtyards of the university at the beginning of the Revolution. In fact, especially outside of Havana, it is not unusual for someone to call out to him from the crowd at a public meeting and for a shouted dialogue to begin.

He has a language for every occasion and a different form of persuasion depending on his different interlocutors – be they workers, farmers, students, scientists, politicians, writers, or foreign visitors. He can put himself on the level of each one and has vast and varied information that allows him to move easily in any medium. But his personality is so complex that any one of them can form a different impression of him in the same encounter.

A man focused on victory

One thing is certain. Wherever he may be, however and with whomever, Fidel Castro is there to win. I do not think anyone in this world could be a worse loser. His attitude in the face of defeat, even when it involves the smallest acts of daily life, seems to obey some private logic. He will not admit it, but he does not have a moment of peace until he manages to emerge victorious from any situation.

Listening to Fidel Castro in so many diverse circumstances, I have asked myself many times if his zeal for conversation does not obey an organic need to hold at all costs to the guiding thread of truth amid the hallucinatory mirages of power. I have asked myself this over the course of many dialogues, public and private, but especially as regards the most difficult and fruitless dialogues with those who, in his presence, lose their naturalness and aplomb and speak to him in the theoretical formulas that have nothing to do with reality.

Everything is different, on the other hand, when he talks to the people in the street. The conversation then recovers the expressiveness and crude frankness of real affection. Of his various civilian and military names, only one is left to him then: Fidel. They surround him without risks, they use the familiar "*tu*" form of address with him, they argue with him, they contradict him, they make demands of him –

with a channel of immediate transmission through which the truth flows in torrents. It is then, rather than in privacy, that the rare human being shielded from sight by the brilliance of his own image is discovered. This is the Fidel Castro I believe I know, after uncountable hours of conversations, through which the phantom of politics does not often pass: a man of austere ways and insatiable illusions, with an old-fashioned formal education, of cautious words and simple manners, and incapable of conceiving any idea which is not out of the ordinary.

He dreams that his scientists will find a cure for cancer, and has created a world-power foreign policy on an island 84 times smaller than its principal enemy. Such is the discretion with which he protects his privacy that his personal life has ended up being the most impenetrable enigma of his legend.

He has the nearly mystical conviction that the greatest achievement of the human being is the proper formation of conscience, and that moral incentives, rather than material ones, are capable of changing the world and moving history forward. I think he has been one of the greatest idealists of our time and this, perhaps, may be his greatest virtue, although it has also been his greatest danger.

Many times I have seen him arrive at my house very late at night, still trailing the last scraps of a limitless day. Many times I have asked him how things were going, and more than once he has answered me: "Very well, we have all the reservoirs full."

I have seen him open the refrigerator to eat a piece of cheese, which was perhaps the first thing he had eaten since breakfast; I have seen him telephone a friend in Mexico to ask her for the recipe for a dish he had liked; and I have seen him copy it down leaning against the counter, among the still unwashed pots and pans from dinner. I have heard him, in his few moments of nostalgia, evoke the pastoral dawns of his rural childhood, the sweetheart of his youth who left him; the things he could have done differently.

One night, while he was eating ice cream in slow spoonfuls, I saw him overwhelmed by the weight of the destinies of so many people, so removed from himself, that for an instant he seemed different to the man he had always been. I asked him what he'd most like to do in this world, and he immediately answered: "Hang around on some street corner." ❑

Left: Gabriel García Márquez, friend of Fidel Castro.
Above: Castro, the subject of many revolutionary tomes.
Above Right: still commanding the affection of many.

CUBA'S ARCANE TRANSPORT SYSTEM

At turns fascinating, exotic, frustrating and divisive, the beleaguered transport situation is also a visible microcosm of the country's economic woes

In the late 1980s, oil supplies from the Eastern Bloc that had provided the island with 90 percent of its fuel began to dry up as the cosy Cuban-sugar-for-Soviet-oil deal came to an end. A scarcity of fuel meant that outside the main cities motorized transport virtually vanished, a situation that has changed little today. Roads are all but deserted, oxen till the fields, horse and traps ply the streets of provincial towns.

But, most noticeably, bicycles are everywhere – more than one million were imported from China in the early 1990s. It's as if the clock has been turned back to a pre-industrial age. Cycling has become part of the fabric of everyday life, with special parking lots for bikes and puncture repair shops everywhere. You might even see a wedding parade on bikes.

CUBAN ODDITIES

The island's current tribulations and its decades of isolation from the western world have resulted in other memorable forms of transport. Wonderful old Cadillacs (*see page 293*) get top billing, but also look out for veteran motorcycles with sidecars, rickshaws created from two bicycles welded to armchairs, and on the railways anything from magnificent steam trains to wheel-less buses that can run along the tracks. And if you think horse and traps are charming, how about goat and traps? They take young children on circuits round the main squares of provincial towns at the weekend.

▽ **HORSE AND TRAP**
Coches, or horse and traps, serve as buses and taxis all over the island. An average ride will cost just a few pesos.

▷ **EMPTY TANK**
The chronic fuel shortage in Cuba means that even main highways can be virtually bereft of traffic, including the six-lane highway from Havana to Pinar del Río.

◁ **HAILING A CAB**
In return for a dollar or two, tourists may be offered a lift in just about anything that moves and therefore takes on the status of a "taxi". Riding around in an old car is a must in Cuba, but not ideal for a long journey.

▽ **KIT CARS**
Many Cadillacs may look ready for the scrap heap, but their owners somehow keep them on the road. The cars are often ingeniously customized with spare parts (even from Ladas) acquired illegally on the black market.

◁ **HITCHING A RIDE**
While tourists have the choice to whizz around in air-conditioned coaches and hire cars, for most Cubans getting around is not much fun. Hitching is often the only option.

△ **DOWNHILL SLIDE**
Cuban ingenuity at its best: in the Sierra Maestra, locals descend mountain roads at high speed on home-made skateboards.

△ **GIANT BUSES**
Nicknamed *"camellos"* for their two humps, these buses were introduced into Havana in the Special Period to counter overcrowding

▽ **GROUP OUTING**
Rare is the Cuban who doesn't get around on a bicycle. And even more rare is the bike with just one person on it.

THE STRUGGLE TO GET AROUND

Buses, called *guaguas*, used to be the backbone of Cuba's public transport system, but now there are simply not enough to cope with demand. Cubans often need to book weeks in advance for a seat on a long-distance bus, while city buses are usually full to bursting. It can take many Habaneros several hours to commute into work.

Hitch-hiking (*la botella*) has become a way of life for Cubans of all ages, but this is not any old hitch-hiking. State officials, known as *los amarillos* ("the yellow ones" – after the color of their uniforms), supervise crowds of hitchers at designated places, usually on the edge of towns and cities. State vehicles are obliged to stop, and *los amarillos* will allocate people to each vehicle on a first-come, first-served basis. Pregnant women and children can go to the front of the line.

It was a free service, but passengers must now pay a few pesos for most journeys.

DREAMING OF MIAMI

Miami's Cuban exile community continues to grow, as economic and political refugees leave the island on rafts or with US entry visas

On Havana's Malecón, a small crowd gathered to watch as fishermen battled to rescue the little raft – a black inner tube lined with fishing net – that had drifted in and out of the bay all morning, held by a current that no one could breach. Finally, three men, fishing for snapper in similar crafts, managed to get hold of the raft and bring it to shore. Too late for the two young men inside. One was already dead of dehydration, the other died soon after the rescue.

A weeping sore

In the weeks following the start of the "rafters crisis" during the summer of 1994, people in Havana began to get used to the sight of bodies washing up in the Bay – many of them chewed up by sharks. Although about 40,000 Cubans made it to the United States that year, it is estimated that between five and nine thousand died in the attempt. Regrettably, this exodus was just the most recent in a series of migrations.

A generational change

In 1959–60, hundreds of thousands of the country's elite left, with many more following in 1961 and 1962, after Castro's declaration that the Revolution was "Marxist-Leninist", and the increasingly evident Socialist slant of policies.

Peasants then came from the countryside and took over the mansions vacated by the rich. Their children grew up living very different lives to themselves – based in cities like Havana, and becoming doctors, professors and engineers. Yet Cubans still wished to emigrate to Miami.

In 1980, after a week-long crisis in which over 10,000 Cubans sought asylum in Havana's foreign embassies, Castro announced that any Cuban who wanted to leave could do so. Around 125,000 promptly did, aided by small craft from Miami, in what became known as the Mariel Boatlift. Denounced by the Cuban state media as *escoria* (scum), the refugees turned out to be mostly respectable, hard-working people: doctors, teachers, academics and members of Castro's new middle class. In other words, people who owed their education and status to the Revolution they had rejected.

What had gone wrong? Why, after 20 years of a Revolution marked by great social changes, of a Revolution that was still popular in some sectors and that was marked by a vehement anti-Americanism, did so many Cubans still yearn for a life in the United States?

Opportunity stifled

Most of those leaving now say the Revolution has failed because it denies two basic freedoms. Political freedom, yes; but, most importantly for the young Cubans of today, economic freedom. Young Cubans complain bitterly about the lack of freedom to "get on" in the world. Those who have trained to be doctors or lawyers often still can't get a house – many married couples have to live with their children in a single room at their parents' house. Doctors earn less in a month than a waiter or taxi driver can make in dollar tips in a day.

As one young émigré – an agricultural engineer – said, "In the United States I will have the chance to live my life. I may fail – there's always a risk. But at least I will have had the chance. Here, if you do not conform, if you are not a Revolutionary Man, you have no chance to succeed. None at all."

Worms in the tropics

The Castro regime continues to brand all who leave, or declare their intention of leaving, traitors or "worms" (*gusanos*) – the phrase often used to describe Cubans in Miami. And it is in Miami where most Cuban emigrants historically end up: a tropical city, near enough to Cuba to keep dreams of a glorious return, of revolution or counter-revolution, alive.

Castro visited exiled Cubans there in 1955 when seeking funds for the overthrow of Batista. Cubans fled there in the 1930s during the brutal dictatorship of Machado. José Martí was there in the 19th century, plotting the overthrow of Spanish colonial rule. After more than a hundred years, the city has taken on a strong Cuban flavor – the Spanish language dominates large areas, restaurants and stores sell American-made replicas of Cuban brands, strong, sweet "Cuban" coffee scents the air of Little Havana (not the real thing, of course – Miami politics ensure that no goods from the island ever reach the United States).

A changing outlook

Over the years, however, the type of people arriving on Miami's shores has changed. The early political refugees who vowed never to return until Castro was gone are now vastly outnumbered by newer, economic refugees like the "*Marielistas*", and the rafters. These later refugees, having left Cuba for mainly economic not political reasons, are not troubled by the idea of holidays in Cuba. In fact, the US has been unable to stop them as they travel to Cuba through Mexico and the Bahamas since Clinton banned direct flights to Havana in 1996. They delight in showering their family with gifts, and boasting about the all-too-obvious benefits of the capitalist life – fueling the myth of a city whose streets were paved with gold.

The obsession with Miami reached a peak in the early 1990s, when Cuba faced crippling hardships after the fall of the Soviet Union, and

PRECEDING PAGES: inner tubes, once a means of floating to Miami, now tend to be used mainly for fishing.
LEFT: Los Malones lookout over US Guantánamo base.
ABOVE: makeshift raft making the hazardous journey from Cuba across the Florida Straits.

people were so desperate to leave that they were willing to risk their lives on a fragile raft on the high seas.

Rafting to Uncle Sam

Of course, most were not sailors and had no idea of the difficulties they faced. A distance which seemed pitifully small on a map actually took many days, even weeks, to reach. All too often, empty rafts would wash up on the Florida Keys. It was estimated that only one person in four survived the journey. The horror stories did not deter those determined to leave. Usually sailing with a large painted banner – to catch

the attention of the Brothers to the Rescue, an exile organization that launched planes from Miami to search for rafters.

Between 1989 and 1994, over 10,000 rafters made it to Miami. The Cuban coastguard stopped a further 37,800 people attempting to leave. During the great exodus of August to September 1994, around 2,000 rafters a week were setting sail. Castro's claims that the US precipitated the crisis – by refusing to grant entry visas to people who were later welcomed as heroes after they had risked their lives on rafts – were supported by a large number of Third World nations. The crisis led to a series of talks between the US and Cuba that all but put an end to the raft as a means of emigration when it was agreed that all would-be refugees picked up at sea would be returned home.

An altering perspective?

Thousands of Cubans began to be held in internment camps, most at Guantánamo Bay, which caused Cubans to start thinking differently about Miami. They began to look to emigration to other Latin countries – Costa Rica and Mexico were favorites. Arranged (and paid-for) marriages to tourists also became a popular means of leaving Cuba.

At about the same time, an upturn in the economy (based on policy changes legalising many forms of private business, the increase in tourism, and more foreign investment) meant many Cubans began to see a real future in their homeland. Also Cubans visiting relatives in Miami came back disillusioned – appalled at the rampant consumerism, the widespread waste of resources and the "hardships" of life there – the hours of work one had to put in to maintain the coveted lifestyle; the constant threat of unemployment; the difficulties of those struck down by accident or illness, confronted by large medical bills and tussles with insurance companies.

In Miami too, refugees began to complain that their families on the island were too demanding, seeing them as no more than cash cows to be milked at every opportunity. Most were working class people with mortgages and heavy financial commitments who were finding the extra burden of helping their family in Cuba too much for them.

The cycle begins anew

However, things changed again with the incident of February 1996 when Cuban MiGs shot down two unarmed Brothers to the Rescue planes. The subsequent US Helms-Burton legislation strengthened sanctions against Cuba, and this, combined with new Cuban crackdowns on the self-employed and "new rich", sent the island's economy back into decline.

Once again, Cubans began to dream of escape. The 1995 emigration agreement had made it possible for a minimum of 20,000 Cubans to receive US visas each year, many of them allocated by lottery. In 1996, over 435,000 Cubans entered the lottery – more than double the number who applied for the first draw in

1994. By 1998, so great was the crush to get applications in on time that police had to close off the streets around the US diplomatic mission in Havana (known as the US Interests Section). Demand is far outstripping supply.

Therefore, undaunted by the huge dangers and uncertainties involved, rafters continue to set sail for the bright lights of Miami. Over 1,000 have been returned to Cuba since the 1995 agreement, and Brothers to the Rescue still find the occasional empty raft in the Gulf of Mexico. In 1997, six Cubans were rescued from a desert island 125 miles (200 km) southeast of Miami suffering from hunger and dehydration – all that were left of 14 people who had set sail weeks before.

The Cuban elite, such as sportsmen (*see page 116*), continue to defect too, although their passage is usually considerably less risky.

WILL THEY EVER STOP?

In the summer of 1998, three Cuban-Americans in their 70s were captured in the mountains of Pinar del Río, trying to incite guerrilla war against Castro.

Exile schizophrenia

Whilst those in Cuba dream of a new life in Miami, the old guard there still dreams of returning to Havana. Veterans of Batista's time and the Bay of Pigs still gather in Miami's Little Havana to plot and scheme over cups of coffee at the Cafe Versailles. Old men now, they haven't given up their dreams that Castro will be overthrown and that they will return in triumph to their homeland.

In recent years, Miami-based terrorist organisations such as Alpha 66 and Omega 8 have organised several incursions into Cuba. They are always quickly captured, though often there have been casualties on both sides. In November 1997, a group of Cuban exiles were arrested by US coastguards apparently on their way to assassinate Fidel Castro during a visit to Venezuela. Exile leaders now admit that the bombs which exploded in Havana's hotels during the summer of 1997, killing an Italian tourist, were organized and paid for in Miami.

These desperate acts, though, are the work of the older generation. Those Cuban Americans born in the US, or who have arrived since Mariel, have a different way of taking on the Communist regime – using their prosperity to fund businesses in post-Soviet Cuba. Most of Cuba's *paladares* (family-run restaurants) started up using Miami money, either as a loan or by direct investment, with the investor taking a cut of the profits. Many Cubans who left on rafts have returned as tourists or entrepreneurs, helping friends and family to set up enterprises, and these new businesses have changed the moribund face of Havana.

However, Cubans who have no family in Miami greatly resent this development: they see the families of exile "worms" able to live well whilst they – the ones who remained loyal to Castro – are suffering on a monthly ration that barely lasts two weeks. The new shopping malls and supermarkets, seen particularly in Havana, are based on the spending power of people who receive money from their families abroad. It is estimated that Cuba now gets more money directly from Miami than from the two main industries of sugar and tourism combined.

Ironically, it is Miami money – the financial power of the exile community – that has kept Cuba from total economic collapse. In the words of one exile, "we, the worms, have finally become butterflies." ❑

LEFT: Cold War barriers at Guantánamo Bay.
RIGHT: a memorial to an older generation of exiles in Miami – the fallen of the Bay of Pigs (1962).

TOURISM: SALVATION OR SELL-OUT?

Cuba's relationship with the tourist industry veers between love and hate. For the time being at least, it favors the former, which is good news for visitors

In the posh dining-room of Varadero's Hotel Meliá, the air-conditioning runs full blast and upbeat disco music plays in the background. Sunburned tourists pass by the breakfast buffet, eyeing the heaps of cold meats, imported cheeses, muffins, and pitchers of fresh juice that have just been laid out for them.

A few miles away, in the city of Cárdenas, local Cuban women jockey for the chance to buy a stale loaf of black-market bread. Welcome to tourism in Cuba. This land of socialist ideals and egalitarian values that once said "never again" to tourism, is singing a different tune these days, and it has a capitalist beat.

Back in the decadent 1950s, Cuba was the king of Caribbean tourism. Before the Revolution, no other island in the region could even come close to Cuba's status as a prime tourist destination. Havana, with its sophisticated clubs and casinos, was an exotic getaway that catered to the whims of wealthy Americans, and the island had a worldwide reputation for gambling, drugs, prostitution, pornographic films, and live sex shows.

To speak of Cuban tourism of the 1950s, however, is to speak of imperialist exploitation. Although the industry was lucrative, many of the hotels, clubs and casinos were foreign-controlled, leaving few in Cuba who actually benefited from their profits.

Part of Fidel Castro's struggle against Batista stemmed from his revulsion at the excesses of tourism, and the neo-colonialism he saw it to represent. Castro denounced tourism as a vulgar example of the dichotomy between the haves and the have-nots. After he took power, one of his goals was to change forever the sinful image of the island. Cuba would never again be a playground for the rich and beautiful, he promised. Instead it would rely on sugar and other natural resources to fuel its economy.

"Social tourism"

Once the new government was in place, its policy toward tourism became inhospitable. The casinos and nightclubs closed, and the hotels were put to use as vacation retreats for local workers. In the 1960s and '70s, many of the foreign visitors to Cuba were either journalists or people wanting to express solidarity with the Revolution. Others were Eastern Bloc communists on a government-paid Cuban vacation. The island promoted "social tourism," whereby sympathetic visitors from around the world were invited to visit model communities, hospitals, schools, and other places where the achievements of socialism were put on display. Between 1963 and 1975, the island received only about 3,000 foreign visitors a year.

When the economy began to show signs of strain in the early 1980s, the government reconsidered its policy toward tourism and "health tourism" became the new trend. Foreigners were invited to Cuba to indulge in a little sightseeing, as well as a face-lift, check-up, or coronary bypass. Hospitals were performing first-rate medical procedures at low-rate costs and many foreigners took advantage.

But by the mid-1980s, the government realized that "health tourism" was not going to provide the economic boost the island needed, and it launched an international campaign to promote pleasure tourism. After the collapse of the Soviet Union, this campaign became much more aggressive.

Tourism is gold

"In the past we feared that tourism would defile us," Castro told his compatriots, "but tourism is gold." So began the push to make tourism the new business frontier of the island. Tourism and hospitality management schools sprung up around the island, European and Canadian advertising campaigns were put in place, and plans for new hotels were drawn up. Castro personally visited construction sites. He also offered international investors some very non socialist incentives that would allow them to operate in Cuba for at least 10 years without paying taxes on income.

Progress came quickly. In 1995, as the sugar industry weakened further, tourism became for the first time the biggest source of hard currency, and the government set out to attract 2 million tourists annually by the year 2000 – a tough target as long as the US embargo is maintained. In 1984, fewer than 200,000 foreign tourists visited Cuba; by 1998 there were well over a million – triple the number that came during the booming 1950s. Cuba is currently counting on investors from Spain, Germany, the UK, Canada, Italy, Mexico and Jamaica.

A pact with the devil

Having come full circle, the tourism industry has created embarrassing ideological problems for the Castro government. Much of the population criticizes it because the situation reminds them of when the island had an elite leisured class, and some see the drive to attract visitors as a pact with the devil. At a time when most Cubans must endure shortages of everything from soap to rice, the government is having a hard time justifying expenditure on imported foods, liquors, toiletries, rental cars, chlorine for swimming pools, and construction supplies needed to support tourism.

LEFT: the contrasting faces of Cuba – tourists lap up the golden sands of Varadero, whilst…
RIGHT: locals line up to buy groceries.

Although tourism employs about 75,000 people, this represents only about 2 percent of the overall workforce. Tourism jobs are highly sought after because of their access to dollars and foreign goods, and many teachers, doctors and engineers have left their professions to work in more lucrative jobs as waiters or bellhops – the average hotel chambermaid earns more than a university graduate working for the peso-paying government. Tourism has also bred corruption. In places like Varadero it has been known for hotel managers to sell positions – the going rate being $250–$300 per post.

There is also the question of the kind of

tourists who come to Cuba. The superb colonial architecture, impressive scuba diving, open-sea fishing and fine flora and fauna will attract a certain number of high-spending tourists, but many more will be deterred by the dilapidated infrastructure, and relatively poor service.

Already the downside of ill-controlled tourism is evident. The industry has brought back something from the Batista days that Fidel Castro promised he would banish forever – prostitution. In major tourist areas of the island, scantily-clad Cuban women called *jineteras* – literally meaning "jockeys" – cruise the streets outside hotels looking for business. Some will offer their services for a night on the town and a new dress. Others earn as much as US$200 a night – more than most professional Cubans, and even senior government ministers, can make in a whole year.

Tourism apartheid

The most distasteful aspect of Cuba's tourism industry is the division it has created between the locals and the tourists. Isolated from the public, most modern resorts have a "Club Med" mentality that accentuates the differences between those with hard currencies and those without. In defiance of socialist ideals, this enclave system, often referred to as "tourism apartheid," is as divisive as the former Berlin Wall.

Hotels are like private country clubs that no Cubans can join. Locals are often not allowed in unless they are accompanied by foreigners. At plush restaurants, the wine flows freely and the steaks are tender, but in most Cuban homes, the walls are crumbling and the cupboards are bare. Electricity, scarce anyway due to low fuel supplies, is channeled to the hotels while private homes suffer regular blackouts (*apagones*). Tourists can easily buy gas for their plush rental cars, while locals must ride bicycles or squeeze into over-crowded buses. And beautiful beaches, once the domain of the islanders, are being gobbled up by developers.

Whether tourism will be the salvation that rescues Cuba's economy remains to be seen. While the gains have been substantial, for every dollar Cuba receives from tourism, it spends about 40 cents on imported goods required by the industry. Compared to other Caribbean islands, Cuba still has a small slice of the tourism pie – nearby Puerto Rico, half Cuba's size, earns twice the income Cuba does from tourism.

There is also the matter of social dissent. Cubans, now exposed to foreign values and ideas, are contemplating quick profits from a free market. Fed up with the inequalities in the industry, they are also voicing their resentment – which in the long run may well prove to be much more socially disruptive than the bad shape of the economy. For the Castro government, tourism may turn out to be like chemotherapy treatment for cancer – the cure may cause more harm than good. ❑

To Have or Have Not

Nicolás Guillén wrote *Tengo* ("I Have") in the 1960s to celebrate the Cuban people's renewed access to the island's beaches and hotels. The poem seems rather ironic today, given that tourists have privileged access to these areas once again.

ABOVE: poolside bar in Guardalavaca, Holguín province.

What the Locals Say

It's 3am on a Saturday: the streets of Havana are blacked out to save electricity, but the disco at the Comodoro Hotel is ablaze with neon. Frank, a middle-aged former oilman from Canada, is in heaven – chomping on a Havana cigar, knocking back *Cuba libres* and leering at a Cuban prostitute who looks about 17, as she wraps herself around his leg and begins to gyrate slowly against his thigh. "Jesus," says the Canadian, "it'd sure help if I could speak some Spanish." A couple of drinks later, he decides that conversation is superfluous and leads the girl off to the connecting hotel.

From the viewpoint of the Comodoro bar, it seems the Revolution has been turned on its head. While the dance floor is packed with holidaying Spaniards, Germans and Canadians, almost the only Cubans are the barely pubescent *jineteras*.

In theory, the Comodoro caters only to foreigners. But at the bar are a couple of Cuban university professors in their forties who, surreally, are here because they have won a prize for political correctness. Using Party coupons, they were able to get in, buy a couple of drinks, and hoard two cans of Coca-Cola for their children.

"You must understand that this is only a small slice of Cuba," says Rosa, a botanist. "Of course, it's a shock to see so much wealth, and worse to know that the girls here can make more in one night than I do in an entire year. But it's a historical moment – and necessary for the country. Also, we may have prostitutes, but it's well known that Cuban *putas* are the most beautiful and cleanest *putas* in the world." Pedro, a professor of the history of imperialism, chimes in: "Cubans are highly educated. Everyone understands that tourism is vital for the Revolution." He blanches when offered a beer, however: it turns out to cost US$7, about three weeks' wages at current rates.

Not all Cubans are so philosophical about being excluded, for example, from former holiday spots such as Varadero, which has now turned into a massive beach resort. "Can you understand what it's like to be effectively banned from a beach that you've been visiting with your family for 30 years?" says a retired teacher. "I'm a Cuban, this is my country, but I can no longer afford a hotel room in Varadero, or even a soft drink."

The only entertainment available to most young Cubans is home-made. An evening spent sitting on the Malecón chatting to friends, drinking home-made rum, and perhaps dancing to music blaring from a car radio, is a good night out for some.

Gathering in a ramshackle mansion one night are a dozen writers and artists, looking as though they are straight out of the 1960s. One by one, each one pulls out a poem and orates theatrically by the light of a kerosene lamp. An exuberant musician in his early thirties has brought a guitar and sings his own compositions – satirical, funny songs about food shortages and problems with bureaucracy. The digs at the system are mild, but in one conversation everyone attacks the regime roundly, particularly the all-consuming censorship and politics encouraging dissident artists to emigrate to Mexico or Miami.

The best-known poet at the gathering, a tiny, fragile woman in her mid-forties, was thrown off the official arts magazine in 1970 for running an article that mentioned both exiled writers and homosexuals. Since then, she has been unable to find work or have her poetry published in Cuba, although it is known in Spain and around Latin America. "It's the psychological climate that destroys you in Cuba," she says. "It's like having to live in a prison." An hour later, the fiesta quickly comes to an end when the hostess's brother-in-law comes home. He is distantly related to a member of the secret police. ❑

RIGHT: travel best described as "communal."

THE CUBANS

Multi-racial and multi-cultural, the vivacious Cuban people are universally hospitable, although complete openness is not always possible in public

How do you describe the Cuban character? It is fun-loving and spontaneous, warm and happy. Regardless of their status in society, Cubans tend to be a generous people. This generous nature, closely linked to the gregarious spirit that characterizes the country, is embedded in the Cuban psyche.

For one Cuban to label another stingy is to tag him or her with one of the worst character flaws imaginable. The song written by popular songwriter Juan Formell and sung by his band Los Van Van captures the idea: "My hands are always empty, giving when there's nothing to give. Oh, but what can I do? These are the hands that I have!"

A mestizo people

Barely a trace of the native Indian peoples discovered by Christopher Columbus in 1492 remains today in Cuban culture. For the most part, Cuba's 11 million people are *mestizo* – a mixture of European, African, and indigenous ancestry. Although the government rarely releases such statistics, other sources estimate Cubans to be only about 35 percent "white."

With the onset of slavery in the 16th century, many Spanish colonizers satisfied their sexual appetites with their slaves. The *criollo* children born of these unions suffered as much social prejudice as did the black slaves. Cirilo Villaverde's famous 19th-century novel *Cecilia Valdés o La Loma del Ángel* explores this theme brilliantly.

During the mid-1800s, Chinese immigrants began to form an important segment of the Cuban population. According to historian Juan Pérez de la Riva, about 35,000 Chinese were brought from Canton to the island to work as servants in conditions similar to that endured by African slaves. Eventually, over 100,000 came to Cuba. Though today only vestiges remain, until 30 years ago Havana's Chinese neighborhood was one of the city's most prosperous. However, the so-called *Barrio Chino* in Central Havana has been revived in the last few years, and now has a popular market and foodstalls attracting both local people and tourists (*see page 169*).

PRECEDING PAGES: a *guajiro* farmer in Pinar del Río province; a 1950s "Yank tank" in Havana.
LEFT: watching the world go by in Old Havana.
RIGHT: relaxing in Trinidad.

Equality for all

Though once common, terms such as *El Chino* (the Chinese man), *El Negrito* (the black one), and *La Mulata* (the mulatto one) are rarely used today – even the mention of racial distinctions is a social taboo. Back in the 1950s, skin color was a divisive issue. Blacks had little access to good jobs, and were forbidden from joining elite country clubs or attending private schools.

With its promise of "equality for all," the revolutionary government has relegated racial discrimination to the collective subconscious, and for a while deleted all questions about race from the official census. Today, Cubans of all races and ethnic backgrounds are born in the same hospitals, attend the same schools and are also buried in the same cemeteries.

Some sociologists, however, argue that, although blacks have advanced dramatically since Fidel Castro took power, the country does in fact suffer from institutional racism. There are only a handful of blacks in the upper echelons of the government, and only about a quarter of Cuba's Communist Party are black or mulatto. According to Carlos Moore, a black Cuban exile scholar, the color of power in Cuba has not changed at all.

A DIVIDED NATION

In the main square of Santa Clara the double sidewalks which once provided separate walkways for blacks and whites are still visible.

by limiting access to schools and job opportunities. To attend mass was to "lapse into the past," and the "past" was regarded by Revolutionaries as a plague. Religious observation, however, continued in private, and following the break-up of the Eastern Bloc, has reappeared in public again.

The Papal visit

A landmark event occurred in January 1998, when Pope John Paul II visited the island – the last place in Latin America that he had not toured. The paradox was not lost on

The Catholic Church

The Catholic Church was officially separated from the Cuban government with the birth of the Republic in 1902. Until the Revolution though, the government considered the Catholic Church its natural ideological ally. As in most Latin American cultures, it served as the foundation of an ordered society. But with the pronouncement of the socialist government in 1961, organized religion was condemned to disappear, and Catholic dogma was replaced by that of Marxism-Leninism. The revolutionary government viewed the church as a dangerous rival and a focus for dissent. For many years practising Catholics were punished

observers: that a Pope who had spent much of his papacy fighting communism should meet a Marxist like Fidel, who had completely relegated the role of the Catholic church and institutional religion under his regime.

The Pope was keen to advance the cause of religious freedom and human rights in Cuba; whereas Castro was gambling on benefiting from the international prestige of the event (demonstrating to the world that his regime had nothing to hide), and on exploiting the fact that the Pope has publicly opposed the US embargo, so as to isolate the position of the US government and the Miami exile community.

Vast crowds greeted the Pope at open-air

masses held around the country, and hopes were high that his visit would herald a period of radical reform. Fidel had declared Christmas of 1997 to be a public holiday for the first time as a one-off "goodwill gesture," and several churches were re-opened as places of worship.

The state's position on religion seems to have altered little, once the furore surrounding the visit died down. It still appears to consider religious faith unacceptable: military recruits continue to be questioned as to their religious practices and it is made clear to them that believers will never reach the top ranks of the military establishment.

changed by then, but the authorities will still remember the names of those who had a picture of the Pope on their door."

Their fears seem to have been realized. Since the Papal visit, the Bishop of Santiago, who made an address seen to be critical of the regime, has been sent away to Mexico and church attendance, after an initial boom, has fallen back to "pre-Pope" levels.

The power of Santería

Cuba's principal religion is not Catholicism, however, but rather *Santería* – in which Catholicism and traditional African beliefs,

Catholic observance has not enjoyed the predicted renaissance either, at least in terms of public observance. During the lead-up to the Papal visit, priests constantly commented on the fears of the people – one young priest said that many parishioners were happy to display pictures of Pope John Paul II inside their homes, but only very few dared put the poster on their doors or in windows, saying, "it might be alright to do this today, but what about next month, or next year? Everything may have

LEFT: guitar-player and friends, Playa Girón.
ABOVE: elderly believer in Trinidad, with a Catholic statue rescued from a vandalized church.

brought across the seas by slaves in the colonial times, merge. The mixture of the rites and rituals of these two beliefs is classic religious syncretism. Though it began as a religion of Cuba's blacks, Santería followers now come from all races and walks of life. It is estimated that at least 90 percent of all Cubans have participated in some form of Santería ritual, despite the fact that for years it, too, was discouraged by the State.

The dominant influence behind Santería comes from the Yoruba religion and folklore of West Africa, which has had wider effects on Cuban popular culture: for example, many common Cuban proverbs are literal translations from the Yoruba language. Originally consisting of various tribes near the African equator, the Yoruba shared a linguistic bond. In her study *The Orishas of Cuba*, Natalia Bolívar wrote that two worshippers who lived in the Havana neighborhood of Regla unified all the Yoruba cults under the name of "Regla de Ocha." Then, the story goes, a black Cuban slave who returned to Africa after the abolition of slavery was recognized there as a descendant of the kings (*obbas*), and ordered to return to Cuba to found the sacred order of high priests, called the *babalawos*.

As in Catholicism, Santería priests offer guidance and counsel, but the source of their divine wisdom differs. Instead of consulting one supreme being, *babalawos* use various instruments to interpret the wishes of the *orishas* or gods. These include the *tablero*, a circular board on which certain items are cast, and a *cadeneta*, a special necklace which is swung onto the floor to produce certain signs. Some *babalawos* use coconut shells or cards as their medium. Each sign carries many myths and stories which the priest will interpret for his client. A *babalawo* might advise a patient to sprinkle Catholic holy water around their home in order to chase away evil spirits. If the problem is caused by the spiritual presence of a dead loved one, they might instruct the patient to "steal a Mass." To do this, the patient would attend a Catholic Mass where the souls of the dead are being prayed for, and when the priest mentions the names of the dead who are being honored, they would whisper the name of their loved one. The annoying spirit then floats away and leaves the person in peace. (*See pages 92–3 for more on Afro-Cuban religions.*)

Machismo prevails

Born of two essentially patriarchal cultures, Cubans are largely *machista*, and traditionally homophobic. Only men are permitted to

THE KOSHER BUTCHER

Prior to 1959, there were about 20,000 Jews in Cuba, many of whom fled here during World War II. Today, fewer than 2,000 remain, most having emigrated to the US during the first years of the Revolution. A few years ago Cuba's last permanent rabbi left the island, leaving the responsibility of passing on Jewish traditions to a dwindling group of pious old men. The kosher butcher shop in Old Havana seems to have survived, however, and is one of the few places in the city that regularly has meat. The government has kept its commitment to supply meat to the shop. Occasionally, food products are donated by Jewish communities abroad to help those trying to maintain a strict kosher diet.

become Santería priests, for example, and women walking alone on the street are often bombarded with overt sexual comments from men. These *piropos* (flirtatious remarks) range from a courteous compliment to a blatant invitation for sex. (Many Cuban women, however, are capable of giving as good as they get.)

More than 35 years of official policy designed to achieve the "equality of women" have undoubtedly improved the lot of women in Cuba, but it has by no means dissolved the island's deep-rooted *machismo* spirit. Far from liberating them socially, the government's goal of incorporating women into the work force has actually led to their having two jobs: one at the workplace and the other in the home, doing most of the cooking, shopping, cleaning, and child-minding. As a result, women have tended to shoulder more of the stress of looking after the family and the home in the difficult conditions of the Special Period.

Another negative side-effect of the Revolution has been the increasing divorce rate. According to government statistics, about 5 percent of marriages ended in divorce in 1953. It is now estimated that, among Cubans aged from 25 to 40, a remarkable 60 percent of marriages fail. One reason for this is the lack of independent living space for newly-weds, who are forced to live in cramped apartments with their families. The decline of the influence of the Catholic Church has also been a factor, though another reason for the rise is the fact that the revolutionary government has made it much easier to obtain a divorce: all it takes is a few hours and about half a month's salary.

Left: looking forward to the future…
Above: and looking back on the past.

Homophobia and gay rights

Although official statistics estimate Cuba's homosexual population to be between four and six percent, the real figure is likely to be much higher since many gays maintain public heterosexual relationships in order to avoid harassment. Since the early 1960s, thousands of gays have fled the island, including a large contingent that left during the Mariel boatlift of 1980 (*see page 56*).

It's important to note that the most deprecating name used to refer to homosexual males in Cuba – *maricón* (queer) – is applied only to homosexuals who are "passive." Active homosexuals are generally referred to instead as *bujarrones*, or "butch." According to the *machismo* thinking that so esteems virility, these "active" gays deserve less disrespect since they are "stronger." But because the political system does not consider them capable of performing "virile" tasks, and given that the cult of virility was so fundamental to the Revolution, even so-called "butch" homosexuals have suffered severe discrimination.

After decades of homophobia, most homosexuals now say that their treatment by society has improved. Several groups of gay men and women have begun to form associations and meet formally to discuss gay rights. The formation of such groups even a few years ago would have raised quite a storm. Also, many say that much depends on where they work. Intellectuals and university students were far more tolerant of individual sexual preferences than blue-collar workers or farmers.

The film *Strawberry and Chocolate* brought the gay issue to the forefront in Cuba in the early 1990s. The film, about a gay intellectual who falls in love with a straight Communist Party militant, played to full houses in Havana and won several international awards. Despite the success of the film, gays are still officially banned from the Communist Party.

CONDOMANIA – NO

The use of condoms is still not widespread in Cuba. Among some people a condom is referred to as a *quitasensaciones* – or "killjoy."

SUICIDAL *ROQUEROS*

Aids brought the macabre phenomenon of the suicidal *roqueros*. Like teenagers in other parts of the world, *roqueros* are heavy-metal music lovers who wear black leather and ripped jeans. But in Cuba, they are sometimes fined and imprisoned for their anti-social behavior. While most are straight, they feel a solidarity with gays, as both are persecuted and seen as deviant.

In 1989, a group of them began injecting themselves with HIV-infected blood donated by friends. The total number of self-infected rockers reached 100, virtually all of whom have since died. Opposed to everything the Cuban government stood for, they took Castro's "Socialism or Death" slogan literally.

Aids in Cuba

The appearance of Aids did not help the status of gays in Cuba. When the country's first Aids case appeared in 1985, the government quarantined patients at special sanitariums. The policy was condemned abroad as an abuse of human rights, but helped contain the spread of the disease initially; many Aids-infected gays voluntarily checked themselves into these sanitariums, where they had better access to food and medicines, and could live together openly as gay couples.

The picture has changed substantially over recent years. Rocketing levels of prostitution, coupled with a general hostility to the practice of safe sex and the rampant promiscuity of Cuban society, has caused the number of heterosexual cases of HIV-infection to rise rapidly, and fears have been expressed that Cuba may be about to experience an Aids epidemic.

The sanitarium system too has begun to break down due to lack of funds. The cost of keeping a single patient in a sanatarium is $46,000 a year – just too great to be sustainable. The places are falling apart – broken furniture and equipment is not replaced, there are not enough light bulbs and food quality has deteriorated badly. As a result, new inmates are not accepted until they are actually ill with Aids and many are treated on an out-patient basis. Certainly, HIV-positive people are no longer confined there and the government's original purpose of isolating the infected has failed. ❑

LEFT: a young couple in Sancti Spíritus.
RIGHT: bicycles and baseball, this must be Cuba.

CU

SANTERÍA AND AFRO-CUBAN RELIGIONS

Three main religions developed in Cuba out of the rich heritage of West African slaves. Of these, Santería is the most important

Santería (the "Way of the Saints"), also known as Regla Ocha or Regla Lucumí, stems from the beliefs of the Yoruba people of West Africa – the dominant ethnic group of slaves in Cuba. Forbidden by their Spanish Catholic masters to practise their native religion, believers hid their worship by syncretizing traits and characteristics of individual African *orishas* (gods) with those of particular Catholic saints. For this reason, the religion became known as Santería, and for this reason, too, the term "Santería" is considered to be derogatory by many believers.

In the Regla Ocha, Olofí is the highest god – the source of *ashé* or spiritual energy that makes up the universe and everything in it. He interacts with humankind through his emissaries or lesser gods called *orishas*, who rule over every aspect of life and every force of nature.There are hundreds of gods in the Yoruba pantheon, but around 15 feature regularly: Oshun, the goddess of sweet waters, love and fertility, is represented by Our Lady of Charity – Cuba's patron saint.

NOT JUST A FAITH BUT A WAY OF LIFE

Walk down a street in any Cuban town and you are likely to find someone dressed all in white who has recently been initiated into Santería – an *Iyawó* – and is undergoing a year of communion with their *orishas*. In the religion, communication between *orishas* and humankind is by means of ritual, *ebó* or offerings – including sacrifice and divination. The latter can be performed only by a *babalawo* or priest of Orula – the *orisha* of Knowledge and Wisdom – who will use pieces of coconut or shells. Music, dance and trance possession are also ways through which believers interact with the *orishas*, and are integral to the spiritual experience.

◁ **THE SACRED BATÁ**
The three *batá* drums, tuned to the tones of the Yoruba language, are used to call the *orishas*. Each rhythm acts as a prayer to a particular god.

◁ ***BOVEDA*: SPIRIT ALTAR**
Glasses of water, candles, a rosary and photos of the dead are placed at this altar, to aid communion with the spirits of deceased or *eggun*.

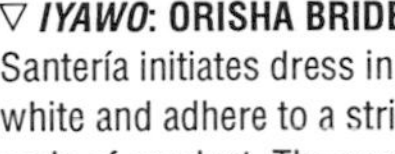

▽ ***IYAWO*: ORISHA BRIDE**
Santería initiates dress in white and adhere to a strict code of conduct. The necklaces worn are sacred; each represents one of the *orishas*.

▷ **ELEGGUA**
Guardian of roads and doors, Eleggúa stands at the crossroads of the human and the divine. Nothing should be done without his permission.

▽ **TRANCE**
During a *bembé* (drumming party) a *santero* or *santera* may be "mounted" by an *orisha* who is able to counsel through its human host.

▷ **CHANGÓ**
Fiery god of lightening, passion, and dance, Changó is represented by Santa Bárbara, a double headed axe and the colors red and white. For many believers, he embodies manhood and virility.

ABAKUA AND PALO MONTE

Abakuá is the name given to the esoteric religion practised by all-male secret societies that still exist in Cuba, especially in places like Guanabacoa near Havana and Matanzas. Visitors, however, are only likely to see it as part of a tourist show, characterized by the hooded figure of the *diablito* (little devil), who dances amongst the *ñáñigo* "initiates", ritually cleansing them. Real initiates join by invitation, and then only after their good character has been verified. The way of the religion is laid down in the sacred book called *Estatuto*.

Another all-male religion is Palo Monte, also known as Regla de Palo (the "Rule of the Stick"). It is similar to Santería, but has its roots in the Congolese Bantu religion. Most importantly, its practitioners, who are called *paleros*, work with the darker forces, and can be consulted by anyone except a *babalawó*.

CUBA'S SIZZLING SOUND

There's nowhere else like it: for "Cuba", read "Rhythm." Here you'll find a depth of musical talent that is, perhaps, unequalled anywhere in the world

Music in Cuba seems to come from the ground, from rooftops, from everywhere. It never stops. According to official statistics, there are 12,000 people classified as professional musicians in Cuba – that is, people who don't have any other job – and that doesn't include the amateur musicians.

By the time of the 1959 Revolution, Cuba had already exerted a great influence on world popular music for decades. After 1959, the presence of Cuban music in other countries declined, above all in the US, the world's principal music merchant and trend-setter. Even so, in Cuba the music continued to evolve.

African roots

At the core of Cuban music is African culture and percussion. Various African religions are widely practised and in the singing and drumming of African religious ritual is a mother lode of rhythmic polyphony that permeates Cuban music. Each African culture had its own musical repertoire, all of which are assiduously conserved in Cuba. Indeed, the musical repertoire of the Yoruba may well be the great musicological treasure of the Western hemisphere – a living African classical music.

Spanish music, itself a mixture of North African, Sub-Saharan, Middle Eastern and European influences, has also played an important role in Cuba's musicological development. So too did French styles, especially in Oriente, where many French colonizers and their slaves settled after the slave rebellion in Haiti at the end of the 18th century. In Cuba, the French trio of piano, violin and flute grew into the ballroom orchestras known as *charangas*. The "contredanse," a French version of the 18th-century English country dance, evolved into the *danzón*, which first appeared on the island in the late 1870s.

PRECEDING PAGES: serenading in Havana.
LEFT: a Santiago bandleader blows his horn.
RIGHT: the incomparable Beny Moré, or the "Barbarian of Rhythm," from the 1950s.

Behind all Cuban popular music is the *clave* (pronounced "cla-veh"), a two-bar pattern with a three-two or two-three beat that alternates with syncopated and unsyncopated measures. It sounds complex, but you don't have to be a musician to feel it: when 17 Cuban musicians are playing, the music has tremendous momentum, and no one can stay still. The beat of the *claves* – two fat wooden sticks about 8 inches (30cm) long – provides the lead for all the members of the band, setting the basic rhythm for them to improvise from.

The Rumba and jazz

Rumba is thought to have emerged in the late 1800s, after the abolition of slavery, probably in the former slave port of Matanzas. The word *rumba* applies to the dance, the music, as well as the party where they both happen.

It appears to be derived from music played on the Congolese drums: in its older form, it was often played on boxes; in its more modern version it is played on *tumbadoras*, the hand drums of Congo origin made world-famous by Cubans as "congas." Three drummers play in a rumba, each with a different sized drum. The three principal varieties of rumba today are: the *guanguancó*, the *columbia*, and the *yambú*.

From the 19th century, there was a busy sea route between the port cities of Havana and New Orleans, Louisiana, and a great deal of musical interchange occurred between the two. Rumba arrived in New Orleans, where it has become a basic part of the musical vocabulary of the city; and jazz came to Havana, almost as quickly as it appeared in New Orleans.

A raw-edged sound that utilizes African call-and-response vocals and cyclical background riffs, *son* became a worldwide hit in 1930 when the record *El Manicero* ("The Peanut Vendor") was produced by Don Azpiazu. The record created an international rumba craze, even though it was a *son* not a *rumba*. Why the confusion first appeared is not certain (possibly it was because rumba was a more exotic-sounding name than *son*), but it has persisted to this day. *Son* can be played by a big band or by a trio, but its classic instrumentation is a sextet consisting of *claves*, bongos, maracas, guitar or the Cuban *tres* (*see page 100*), and double bass.

Modern Cuba is an almost entirely literate society, and this applies to music as well. Many Cuban musicians know both European-style musical theory and Afro-Cuban traditions. This, in effect, gives them two different languages in which they can communicate at will – most commonly heard in Cuban jazz.

Where it all began

The music known as *son* came from Cuba's Oriente province: from the mountains of the Sierra Maestra, and the area around Santiago and Guantánamo, possibly in the late 18th century. In the 1920s, *son* experienced a wave of popularity, which took Havana by storm.

Sometimes a trumpet is added to the ensemble, and you may see many other Afro-Cuban percussion instruments being used, such as the *güiro* (a grooved gourd that is scraped in the manner of a washboard), and the *chekeré* (a typically West African shaker, made of a calabash surrounded by a net of beads).

Mambo

In the 1930s, audiences craved lively types of music, so Cubans added a more rhythmic sec-

LEFT: the original rumba, Cuban style.
RIGHT: a percussionist with his *güiro* (gourd); Cubans learn to perform at an early age.

tion to the *danzón* and it became known as mambo – a word of Congolese origin. Born in Cuba but raised in New York, the mambo subsequently took on a much more brassy sound and became a big hit in North America.

Also at about this time the conga (not to be confused with the drum), a Cuban street dance popular in Santiago, became popular in the States. The characteristic rhythm of the conga is a kind of "*dubba dubba dubba dubba dom... BOM!*" The Santiago tradition, in which competitive neighborhood groups dance congas in the street, dates back to the Lenten carnivals of the 17th century. A conga dance is usually led by a drum-major-like figure playing a *corneta china* (a Chinese cornet – a reed instrument introduced by Chinese laborers), followed by a group of people playing bells and drums.

Trova and boleros

The Cuban *trova* is a Spanish-derived ballad style, generally romantic, sung by troubadours. In many cities, most famously Santiago, the tradition is demonstrated for tourists regularly at the Casa de la Trova, although *trova* is only one of many styles played in these venues. The Cuban *nueva trova* (new trova) comes more recently from artists who were members of a

kind of think-tank experimental group that existed at the Cuban film institute in the 1960s. A bitterly romantic urban folk music, *nueva trova* combines traditional Cuban music, international pop trends, experimental classical music, and socio-political commentary.

Of the *nueva trova* performers, Pablo Milanés and Silvio Rodríguez are two of the most popular. Milanés, known for outspoken political commentary in his music, performs throughout Latin America. Rodríguez, a shy man who creates a theater of intimacy in concert, is also a songwriter of major importance. Compared to these two, the younger generation of *nueva trova* performers tends to be more

The Cha-cha-chá

Enrique Jorrín (1920–07), band leader of the Orquesta América, provided a new dimension to the already brimming cup of Cuban rhythm. He had noticed that the Americans often had great difficulty dancing to the complex rhythms of Cuban music, and so he deliberately invented a style that was easier for the fun-seekers to move in time to.

In 1949, Jorrín set about composing "La Engañadora," in a new rhythm based on the *danzón* of the late 19th century, and it was finally recorded in 1953. This new rhthym, the *cha-cha-chá* (never just the *cha-cha*) quickly caught on, and soon after created the greatest Cuban music and dance craze of the 1950s.

aligned with rock music: Carlos Varela, for example, is a Cuban rock-and-roll proponent and poet with a gift for metaphor.

Salsa

During the early 1970s, the music known as salsa came into being. In Spanish *salsa* means sauce, preferably hot and spicy. In the old days, audiences used to call out to the performers "Give it some sauce," and this is likely to be how the name caught on. Although the base of salsa is the rhythms of Cuban *son*, it actually first appeared in the urban jungle of New York, and whereas *son* has always retained an earthy, acoustic, rural feel, salsa reflects the brash – or smooth, sophisticated – sounds of its city roots.

CUBAN BOLERO

The bolero has a strong hold on the Cuban national consciousness. The slow, sentimental music lets the singer take center-stage, and is a treat when performed live.

Early Cuban performers

As the *danzón* was being redefined into the cha-cha-chá, a blind Cuban musician of Congolese descent named Arsenio Rodríguez was updating the *son*, extending the repetitive, driving instrumental part of the music to create *son montuno*. Rodríguez, one of the greatest Cuban musicians of the century, was red-hot with the dancing public in the 1940s. He was a master of the *tres*, a uniquely Cuban instrument which looks like a small guitar, but is strung with three pairs of strings, each pair tuned to the same note, but at different octaves. The slack-sounding wire strings give an evocative quality to the music of *son* and *son montuno* that immediately marks it out as Cuban. Rodriguez's compositions have been paid extensive and sympathetic homage by modern groups such as the excellent Sierra Maestra.

The group Sonora Matancera occupies another important place in the history of Cuban music. The group formed in Matanzas in the 1920s, moved to Havana and, in the late 1940s, added a fireball of a singer named Celia Cruz, who brought a more African feel to its music. Cruz left Cuba at the time of the Revolution and became an institution in the US, where she is still a leading star, known both for her ferocious singing and her anti-Castro politics.

The biggest singing star of Cuba in the 1950s, however, was Beny Moré. Beny (even today he is referred to by his first name) traveled to Mexico in the late 1930s and performed there throughout the 1940s, singing with bandleaders and appearing in Mexican films. When he returned to Havana in the late

1940s to start his own group, he became the greatest attraction in Cuba, comparable perhaps to Elvis Presley in the US. His horn-driven band was perhaps the crowning glory of Cuban popular music in the 1950s. Moré stayed in Cuba after the Revolution but died in 1963. Nicknamed *El Bárbaro del Ritmo* – the "Barbarian of Rhythm" – Moré lived the life of a true showman, and drank himself to an early grave, aged only 44.

Leading lights of Cuban Jazz

Havana's jazz scene by the 1950s was extremely sophisticated. In 1957 the bassist Israel "Cachao" López produced a legendary recording session, which is available on CD to this day. Cachao revolutionized Cuban music by introducing the concept of the "*descarga*," or jam, into the Cuban jazz vocabulary. This new jamming meant there was no music written down: it was all improvised electrically while on stage. Cachao's records from this time still sound as fresh today as they ever did.

Jazz is still popular in Cuba, but its exponents are often easier to catch on tour abroad. Irakere, a 15-piece group founded in 1970 by Chucho Valdés as Orquesta de la Música Moderna, has fused North American-style jazz with Afro-Cuban percussion. Two of its original members, Paquito D'Rivera and Arturo Sandoval, are now international Latin stars, based overseas. Irakere's music is intense and full of compositional brilliance, and the band is in great demand by jazz clubs overseas.

Groups like AfroCuba, Cuarto Espacio, and Perspectiva are also popular. Old-timers still active in jazz include Frank Emilio Flynn and Tata Guinés. Gonzalo Rubalcaba, Cuba's best-known younger jazz musician, is based in the Dominican Republic, but still performs in Cuba.

LEFT: time for dancing between socialism and death.
ABOVE: young Cubans whirl in a Havana club.

THE OLD BOYS SHINE UP AS NEW

Since the mid-1990s, there has been a great upsurge of worldwide interest in traditional Cuban music. Pride of place amongst the old-timer stars who have recently been "re-discovered" goes to Compay Segundo, one half of the superb duo Los Compadres from the 1950s, who came out of retirement and recorded a Grammy-winning CD in 1998. Now aged in his 90s, he tours the world playing with his own band or as part of the Nueva Trova Santiaguera. So, too, do other greats from the 1950s, such as the pianist, Rubén González, and vocalists, Pío Leyva and Ibrahim Ferrer, who record as part of the Afro-Cuban Allstars. "

Later performers

After the Revolution, the music never stopped in Cuba, not for a moment. But the reorganization of Cuban society was dramatic, and it was not until the end of the 1960s that new musical movements had a chance to be felt. By the late 1970s, an original modern Cuban music was in full flower.

Turn on and Tune in

Channel 6 shows different music programmes at 8.30pm on most nights of the week, ranging from folk music to modern Cuban Rap.

Consistently the most popular group in Cuba for the past 30 years has been Los Van Van, founded in 1969. This 14-member dance band is practically synonymous with modern Cuban music. Led by composer and vocalist Juan Formell, the group invented their own peculiar style, which they call *songo*. Similar to salsa, it mixes trombones and violins with synthesizers, call-and-response vocals, jazzy solos, and shimmering rhythms.

Capturing the modern salsa audience is NG (Nueva Generación) La Banda, one of the most famous salsa bands in the world. Founded in 1989, NG had an instant hit with their first recording, and has had over 25 hits since. This powerful band best defines the first half of the 1990s in Cuban music.

Adalberto Alvarez – a bandleader since the 1970s – has recently shifted toward a more pan-Caribbean beat, but it is still 100 percent Cuban. Founded by manic pianist Juan Carlos Alfonso in 1988, the trombone band known as Dan Den is intensely Cuban and very funny. Particularly popular with teenage audiences in Cuba, its sound is funky and very electronic.

Other popular salsa bands in Havana are Yumuri y sus Hermanos, Issac Delgado, and the wild Charanga Habanera, once banned from performing by the government for its lewd behaviour on stage.

Afro-Cuban Music

In the Afro-Cuban tradition, one of Cuba's most famous singers of African religious music is Lázaro Ros, a native of Havana who estimates he knows 800 songs in African languages. Besides working with his own group, Olorun, Ros has collaborated with Cuban rock groups to make albums that blend Afro-Cuban religious music with modern styles. The key instruments in most Afro-Cuban music are the sacred hour-glass shaped drums called *batás*.

Another type of folk music is the *punta guajira*, which is well represented by Celina González, best known for her anthemic invocation of the Santería God, Changó, in the song *Santa Bárbara*. It's worth trying to catch her live in concert.

Where to catch the sounds

Most of Cuba's tourist hotels and restaurants provide some kind of live music, with the most impressive probably being the Havana Riviera Hotel's Palacio de la Salsa. The more intrepid visitor can seek out the wilder Salón Rosado (also known as the Tropical), a place where Cubans pay pesos to enter. More folkloric events include Rumba Saturdays, held on alternate Saturdays in Havana's Vedado area, and in front of the Teatro Sauto in Matanzas.

At night, Cuban television gives a lot of airtime to home-grown music (including everything from salsa to *campesino* folk songs), and Cuban music videos compete in popularity with those of mainstream stars from Whitney Houston to George Michael. ❑

Left: the larger-than-life exile Cuban singer, Celia Cruz, was one musician who rejected the Revolution.
Right: tourist band in Old Havana sings the classics.

THE ARTS

Elitist and derivative art of colonial times has been replaced by a more creative, inclusive, home-grown tradition, but censorship has inevitably taken its toll

Due to its location and a unique cross-cultural history, Cuba is one of the most privileged islands in the Caribbean as regards its art forms. Forming a geographical, maritime crossroads between Europe and the Americas, it has long been one of the Western hemisphere's most important cultural centers.

Although originally inhabited by different indigenous groups, Cuba is, compared to the rest of the New World, poorly represented in the Pre-Columbian arts. Native Cuban artefacts that have been discovered are fairly crude, especially when compared with the contemporary marvels produced in Peru or Mexico, for example. The first chroniclers were noticeably unimpressed with the material culture of the people they came across on the island.

With the rapid extermination of the indigenous population, whatever else there was of the non-material side of native culture died out too, leaving the Spaniards with a cultural blank slate on which to write their own forms of music, dance, and decorative arts – a situation unlike that of most of their other colonial possessions. The one-sided nature of this cultural imposition was tempered, however, by the Chinese and, above all, Africans, brought to the island as slaves, as well as by the French who escaped from the Haitian revolution in the 1790s. America's intercession in Cuba's war against Spain in 1898 added another cultural outlook – best exemplified in the grandiose Capitol in Havana, a replica of the Capitol in Washington, DC – but this waned when Castro came to power.

The sugar industry and concomitant slave trade brought great wealth to the Spaniards, who then bought gold and silverware, precious stones, and fine furniture from Europe to adorn their *nouveau-riche* Cuban palaces. They also built fortresses and churches, mixing baroque styles with the distinctive *mudéjar* style – a blend of Christian and Arabic traditions that was born from centuries of contact between the Spanish and the Moors, mainly in Andalucía. While Cuba was endowed with fine colonial architecture, the pictorial arts were staid – stiff portraits of wealthy ladies and tepid landscapes decorated aristocratic homes and offices, mimicking the high-society tastes of Europe.

International acclaim

In the early 20th century, Art Nouveau and Art Deco filled cities like Havana with their gracious or outlandish forms – a notable example of which is the Bacardí Building in Old Havana. From 1900 to the late 1950s, Cuba made great advances in the arts. Cuban paintings gained international acclaim and, thanks to the many foreign artists visiting the island, Havana became one of the most celebrated cultural centers in Latin America.

Among Cuba's most prominent artists from this era are Wilfredo Lam, who incorporated the mystical dimensions of his own Afro-Cuban heritage with erotic and magical symbolism,

PRECEDING PAGES: Santería-inspired naive art.
LEFT: catching the Caribbean light, Havana Bay.
RIGHT: *Revolution and Culture* arts magazine.

and was greatly influenced by Picasso's cubist legacy; Carlos Henríquez, who portrayed an epoch of legendary bandits painted with amazing transparency; Romanach, with his peculiar world of old maids and gloomy rooms; Ponce, who painted young maidens and saints with faint monochromes; Mariano, who explored the brilliance of roosters; Amelia Peláez, who evoked the Cuban spirit in her tropical still-lifes; René Portocarrero, who created fantastic versions of Havana and beautiful Creole women; Servando Cabrera, who painted robust country men with rifles and machetes; and Antonia Eiriz, who fascinated the art world

with her Goya-esque monsters and ghostly nightmares. The best place to see these artists' works is in the Museo Nacional de Bellas Artes in Havana.

Art and revolution

When Castro seized control, a new class of artists rose to power. Along with social and economic reforms, Castro brought an aggressive program of cultural reforms that tried to enhance artistic expression. In 1959, one of the first acts of the new government was the creation of the Cuban Film Institute (ICAIC) and the National Cultural Council (CNC). The National School for Art (Cubanacán), also founded in 1959, served as the cradle for new artists in the fields of painting, music, dance and theater, and teachers of art were sent out all over the island.

State sponsorship opened the door to many artists. However, having the state as patron could have its drawbacks, in terms of artistic sacrifices concerning freedom of expression. In 1962 Castro defined his political policy toward artists and intellectuals: "Within the Revolution, everything; outside the Revolution, nothing," and during the mid-1960s the position of the government became more extreme. This forcibly removed all those who had differing opinions about the cultural program, as well as those who were noncommittal. Many liberal artists were condemned to silence, while others were forced to seek asylum. Others were persecuted as "anti-social elitists," or exposed as homosexual. The most unfortunate were despatched to prison or to one of Cuba's new labor camps known as UMAPs – "Military Units for Aid to Production," set up in 1965.

After this, the strength of the arts was greatly diminished. Directors and writers who were not prepared to disappear into oblivion became more cautious as they were forced to fulfil the government's artistic and cultural requirements. Socialist ideology began to dominate. In 1973 another Education and Cultural Congress introduced further reforms designed at increasing censorship. Hundreds of actors, writers and directors were fired, and the totalitarian ring tightened around the art world.

Theater

Following the 1959 Revolution, Cuban theater experienced its best, and its worst, years. At the outset, there was tremendous development in different theatrical currents; everything from Sartre to Ionesco was performed, and an annual International Theater Festival which attracted playwrights and directors from across Latin America was established.

The Teatro Escambray, a mobile drama group which took theater to the peasants, is trumpeted as a great revolutionary achievement, but it did more to spread the message of the Revolution than to entertain the people. While theater remains the least developed of Cuba's art forms, there are a few companies worth looking out for, most notably Teatro Buendía, based in Havana but often away on tour.

Dance

Ballet is held in high esteem in Cuba. The Cuban National Ballet Company, led by Alicia Alonso, has won international acclaim for its repertoire which includes classical and modern ballets, many choreographed by Cuban masters. When not touring abroad, the company performs mainly in Havana's Gran Teatro or Teatro Nacional. The Camagüey Ballet, a newer company founded shortly after the Revolution, once had an impressive reputation, but has lost some of its best dancers to the bright lights of the city.

The Cuban Folkloric Ballet performs ritual dances and chants from the Afro-Cuban cultures, and many amateur dance groups across the country dedicate their efforts to maintaining the heritage of African culture.

Painting

Painting is a field in which Cuban artists have managed to retain a fairly healthy degree of freedom of expression, in spite of the difficulties involved. Surviving the sclerosis of socialist realism, the contemporary generation of Cuban artists has developed diverse styles, many with strongly anti-establishment undertones, through their often abstract art.

Afro-Cuban mythology and folklore are more apparent in Cuban art than ever before, as seen in the works of Manuel Mendive, one of Cuba's most famous contemporary artists. He has cultivated an intricate, primitive style laden with Afro-Cuban symbolism, and his work is appreciated worldwide. Look out, also, for the work of Flora Fong (of Cuban-Chinese descent), who combines Caribbean colors with a light touch that hints at her oriental ancestry.

In recent years there was a movement known as Street Art, whereby young artists displayed their highly expressive work outdoors, away from the official galleries where their paintings could be censored. The streets of Havana became a living exposition where painters not only displayed their canvases, but also turned the streets into studios where they created their work. Because of its dissident style, this rejection of official art was finally suppressed. Some exponents were harassed by the police and most of their work was confiscated. Many young artists left Cuba for other countries, although some established themselves abroad without breaking their ties with the government.

Painters such as Humberto Castro and Moises Finale established themselves in Paris, while Ana Mendieta based herself in Mexico. Many others moved to Miami, where a Cuban artistic network was already in place. Respected artists José Bedia, Luís Marín, José Iraola, Tomás Esson, Nereida García, Frank León, Juan-Si, and the outstanding Tomás Sánchez have all defected, and are now leaders of a new generation of Cuban artists residing in the US.

It has become much easier to buy Cuban art during the Special Period. Old Havana is now chock-a-block with state-run art galleries and artists selling their wares on the street.

Literature

Cuba has produced some outstanding writers, some of whom have won an international reputation in their field. Names like Guillermo Cabrera Infante, Alejo Carpentier, Servero Sarduy, Lézama Lima, Miguel Barnet and, of course, José Martí, share a glorious space in Latin American literature.

Before the Revolution, many Cuban writers had gone abroad, and several returned during a

LEFT: detail from *Always Che* by Raúl Martínez (1970). **ABOVE RIGHT:** the renowned Cuban National Ballet company in performance.

period of literary renaissance in the early 1960s, when they received preferential access to housing and a guaranteed income. Writers like the poet Nicolás Guillén were given official patronage by the revolutionary government, and some were even sent overseas as cultural attachés.

NICOLÁS GUILLÉN

Nicolás Guillén (1902–89) was a lifelong communist and after the Revolution enjoyed the prestige of being Cuba's National Poet.

However, the international literary scandal known as the Padilla Affair changed all that. In 1968, Herberto Padilla won an award for his book *Out of the Game*, a collection of poems which discredited the myths of revolutionary society.

Though the award was given by a prestigious international jury, the book was banned in Cuba, and Padilla was arrested. The affair caused an outcry among intellectuals abroad, including writers like Gabriel García Márquez and Jean-Paul Sartre who had until then been supportive of the Castro's regime. After this, a large number of writers were marginalized from public life and their books taken out of circulation. The era of limited toleration of literary dissent had ended. Many writers left the island, including Guillermo Cabrera Infante, who is still often described as Cuba's greatest living author. Living in London, he remains highly critical of Fidel Castro and his regime.

In 1987, the Cuban leadership re-evaluated the issue of artistic censorship, and in recent years, because of the massive exodus of writers and artists, the government has taken a more lenient attitude towards literary taboos.

In addition to the writers mentioned above, other Cuban writers well worth reading are Miguel Barnet, whose best-known work is *Biografía de un cimarrón*, published in 1967 and translated into English as *The Autobiography of a Runaway Slave*; Lydia Cabrera (famous for her studies into Afro-Cuban religions), Lisandro Otero, Fernando Villaverde, and the late Reynaldo Arenas.

Cinema

Film is the most favored of the arts. Cuban cinema really kicked off with the arrival of Castro and the creation of the Cuban Institute of Cinematography (ICAIC). A militant cinema set about promoting the advantages of the socialist system. Cuban documentaries were shown in even the most remote corners of the island. Inspired by this Cuban movement, other Latin American filmmakers created documentary political films that became a vehicle for left-wing liberation movements around the world.

Following the suggestion of Gabriel García Márquez, Castro founded an international film school in the town of San Antonio de los Baños (*see page 192*) near Havana in 1986. Sponsored by a group of Latin American film-makers and by García Márquez himself, the school caters to students from Asia, Africa and Latin America, and is relatively free from the constraints of having to follow the official party line.

THE LATIN OSCARS

The New Latin American Film Festival, held in Havana every December, attracts film-makers and actors from all over the world. Its Coral prizes are the Latin American equivalent of the Oscars.

The leading light amongst Cuba's post-revolutionary film directors is Tomás Gutiérrez Alea (1928–96). His 1969 movie *Memorias del Subdesarrollo* ("Memories of Underdevelopment") – about a middle-class Cuban who refuses to leave for Miami in the early 1960s but is, at the same time, unable to fit into revolutionary society – is a modern classic. His1966 comedy *La Muerte de un Burócrata* ("Death of a Bureaucrat") is also well worth seeing.

Although Cuba is full of creative energy, most of the country's cultural institutions are feeling the crunch of economic crisis. The film industry has all but shut down, most new movies being made with foreign money, and book publishing has been badly hit. Like most other Cubans, writers, artists, actors, and film-makers are struggling to survive. Indeed, the more tolerant government attitude – which saw the release of films looking honestly at the difficulties of the Special Period – seems to have been somewhat of a false dawn. Films such as the well-received comedy *Guantanamera* and the Oscar-nominated *Fresa y Chocolate* (Gutiérrez Alea's last hit) were harshly criticized by Castro in a speech in 1997, arousing fears in the artistic world of a return to the dark days of total censorship. The head of ICAIC, Alfredo Guevara (a lifelong communist and personal friend of Castro) gave an emotional press conference defending the films. But after a flurry of resignations and a long meeting between Castro and Cuba's leading artists, the official position has prevailed. Guevara has publicly stated that artistic "mistakes" were made, and that the artistic community must be more careful so as not to damage public morale or moral values. Has Cuba seen the last of "open cinema" for the time being? ❑

LEFT: the Museum of Fine Arts, Havana.
ABOVE: *The Evening Meal* and *The Lady of "El Cerro"* by René Portocarrero (1912–85).

EL PUEBLO GOBIERNA
MASIVIDAD
Garantía
DE CA
DEPORTIV

ESTILO
más

SPORT

One irrefutable triumph of the Revolution has been in the domain of athletics. Cuban sportsmen and women regularly dominate world-class opposition

Gregorio Fuentes, Ernest Hemingway's fishing guide and skipper, still lives in Cojímar, a fishing village outside Havana whence the pair would set out on their expeditions. One day, Papá, as Fuentes still refers to Hemingway, turned to him and said he was having trouble coming up with a title for the novel he'd just finished. Fuentes already knew the story line, since one inspiration for the book came from an old fisherman they had spotted on a trip to Paradise Key. Fuentes recalls telling his friend, "You already have the title. Where did this story take place? On the sea. And the fisherman was an old man, no?"

The Old Man and the Sea was published in 1953, forever fixing Cuba and marlin fishing in the world's imagination. Cojímar was the original site of the Ernest Hemingway International Billfish Tournament, which began in 1950, but it now takes place in Tarará, nearby. Although the boats these days are decidedly smaller, the fish are still exceptionally large.

Fidel Castro has participated in the international fishing tournament, though scuba diving and snorkeling are more to his taste. Castro's love of water sports may be responsible for the conversion of the Isle of Youth into an international scuba diving center.

In 1944, Castro was voted athlete of the year at Belén College, a Jesuit preparatory school in Havana, where basketball was his specialty. "If I hadn't been an athlete, I wouldn't have been a guerrilla," Castro has said. He was also once offered a professional contract to pitch for an American team but, by his own admission, he was not major league material. Had Castro's arm been better, perhaps he would never have taken up arms against Batista, Cuba might still be a playground for wealthy Americans, and it is extremely unlikely that there would now be a large sign displayed outside Cerro Pelado, the Cuban national sports training center, proclaiming "*Fidel: Atleta Número Uno.*"

The right of the people

In January 1959, less than a month after taking power, Castro addressed the assembled sports organizations of his country and decried the state of sport in Cuba: "It is a shame that sport has been so undervalued. Less than 10 percent of our youth participate in sports. We must promote them at all costs. We must inundate every corner of the island with sports equipment. We should strive to improve our athletes rapidly."

Today, plastered around sports arenas throughout the island is another Castro quotation: "Sport is the right of the people." With the creation of the National Institute of Sports, Physical Education and Recreation (INDER) in 1961, Cuba was definitely on the way to fulfilling this pledge. Today, nearly half the population of 11 million has participated in organized sports.

The base of Cuba's sporting pyramid is its 80,000 elementary school children. Every year students compete in a variety of athletic competitions in the School Sports Games. Those that excel are invited to be tested for admission to the Schools for Sports Initiation (EIDE), whose students range in age from 11 to 16. EIDE students attend regular classes, but they are also given advanced coaching and face high-level competition. Those who perform best will graduate to one of the Schools of Higher Athletic Performance (ESPA) where students hope to be noticed by a coach from the national ESPA in Havana.

THE SPIRIT OF SPORT

Sport in revolutionary Cuba is seen as an integral part of one's physical and moral education. In the the words of Castro himself, 'Sport is an antidote to vice.'

It took more than a decade for this system to make an impact on the sports world, but when it did, it did so with a bang. Teófilo Stevenson, a heavyweight boxer from eastern Cuba, won a gold medal at the 1972 Olympics in Munich. Stevenson won another gold at the 1976 games in Montreal, where the world was introduced to another great Cuban athlete: Alberto Juantorena won gold medals in the 400 and 800 meter races, the first man ever to win both events in one Olympic Games. Stevenson won a third gold medal in Moscow in 1980, but one fight that the world missed out on was a bout between Stevenson and the other outstanding boxer of his age, Muhammad Ali. The two never met, due to politics and the Cuban's amateur status. Both Stevenson and Juantorena now hold posts in INDER. They are two illustrations of another Cuban sports philosophy: "The greatest incentive that can be given to an athlete," Castro said in 1959, "is security in their retirement and a proper reward for champions."

At the 1992 Olympics in Barcelona, Cuba was the fifth-highest medal winner with 31, surpassing larger countries such as France and Britain. In Atlanta in 1996, they came eighth with 25 medals. "To beat an American is the most important thing," said one Cuban boxer. "Knocking out an American is better than knocking out a better boxer. It's transcendent."

Baseball

Baseball came to Cuba in the late 19th century as the country's allegiance was shifting from Spain to North America. The game was brought by travelers going in both directions, with the first games played in around 1865 between Cuban dock workers and American sailors. Spanish authorities associated the game with the cause of Cuban independence, and revenues

PRECEDING PAGES: winding up for the pitch.
LEFT: waiting for the big marlin to bite.
ABOVE: slugging in the backyard.

from baseball games did indeed find their way into the coffers of Martí's independence movement. As a result, the game was banned in parts of Cuba in 1895. Repeated visits from US marines after independence heightened baseball's popularity, as did the increasing numbers of US players seeking Caribbean warmth and winter paychecks. Though the sport was originally the realm of Cuba's economic elite, it quickly caught on among all classes of society.

Major league riches

Cuba's presence at the Barcelona Olympics provided a rare opportunity to watch some of the best players in the world, but it was also a sad reminder that the world's baseball fans have been deprived of the thrilling play of some of the world's best players. Cuban players, for their part, consistently assert that they play for the love of the game and their country, and are not interested in the millions of dollars they could earn in the major leagues. Defections, however, have become increasingly common, and some of the island's finest players have abandoned Cuba for multi-million dollar contracts in the major leagues in the US. It is going to be hard to prevent defections in the future, too, as few top sportsmen are able to resist the twin lure of instant wealth and the chance to compete against the best the world has to offer.

It is not only Cuba's baseball players, perhaps, who are foregoing major league riches: INDER would reap a tremendous windfall if they allowed their best athletes to sign professional contracts. Based on the old formula by which INDER took half the earnings of coaches and athletes working abroad, it has been estimated that Cuba's current infield players would be worth some $50 million a year in the US major leagues. However, the US would not permit professional players taking back American dollars to Cuba, certainly not during the current climate of the Helms-Burton legislation.

DEFECTIONS AND PROTECTIONISM

When star pitcher Livan Hernandez defected in 1997, the ensuing crackdown on Cuban players was swift. After investigators claimed other players were planning to flee, they were removed from their teams. Livan's brother Orlando, said to be an even better player, was dismissed from his team and given a menial job at Havana's psychiatric hospital. He later escaped to the Bahamas and now plays for the New York Yankees.

The defections led to a major shake-up in Cuba's sports world, with mass sackings and resignations. Some US players must be thanking their lucky stars for the continued embargo. Protectionism on both sides?

Economic difficulties, however, forced Cuba to export some of its athletic talent. Agreements were made with professional Japanese baseball leagues, and over 400 Cuban sports personnel worked in some 40 different countries. This strategy earned Cuba some much-needed hard currency, but it also lost the country at least one medal. At the 1991 Pan-American Games in Havana, Cuba's softball team lost to Argentina, which was coached by a Cuban on loan from INDER. Finally, faced by the high numbers of defecting sportsmen, Cuba ended the practice of allowing them to work abroad in 1998.

The Pan American Games

When Cuba committed to hosting the Pan American Games – the largest sporting event in the Western hemisphere – its economy was still protected by the financial support of the USSR. But by the summer of 1991, the Soviet Union had collapsed, placing further stress on Cuba's economy, which was already in a downward spiral. Many wondered whether it was wise to invest so much money and manpower in the construction of stadiums while there was barely enough food for the Cuban people.

In the midst of all that uncertainty, sports remained a high priority, and the completion of the stadiums became a matter of international prestige. World-class athletes helped construction workers prepare the sites for the games. Cuba won 265 medals – second only to the US total of 352 – but remarkably the gold medal totals were Cuba 140, the United States 130.

By any measure, the 1991 Pan-American Games were a tremendous triumph for Cuba's sporting establishment, as were the Olympics the following year. All the same, given the further deterioration of conditions in Cuba, its results in the 1993 Central America and Caribbean Games in Puerto Rico may be the most amazing of all. Cuban athletes won 227 gold medals, 75 more than the rest of the 31 other competing nations combined.

In the footsteps of the greats

Two of Cuba's outstanding athletes of the 1990s have been the runner, Ana Fidelia Quirot, who triumphed in the 800-meter race at the World Championships in 1997 – having made a remarkable comeback from a severe burns accident – and the phenomenal highjumper, Javier Sotomayor (who now enjoys the additional prestige of being a deputy in Cuba's National Assembly). Sotomayor could rightfully lay claim to the title of greatest highjumper of all time, having frequently broken the world record (pushing the mark up to 2.45 meters), claimed Olympic gold in 1992, and taken World Championship gold in 1995 and 1997. Such domination has ensured that the profile of Cuban sport has remained as high as the bars over which he leaps. ❑

LEFT: two world beaters in track and field: highjumper Javier Sotomayor; and 800m runner Ana Quirot.
RIGHT: working out is now part of the culture.

OPEN TO ALL – BIG AND SMALL

In Havana, top budding gymnasts train at the Provincial School for Gymnastics, housed in an ornate colonial building on the Prado. While they practise their world-class routines, on the other side of the building a group of five-year-olds might be working on cartwheels. Despite the disparity between these extremes of talent and experience, there is an air of accessibility to the elite athletes that meshes nicely with the pleasing irony of this formerly exclusive club being put to popular use. It is hard to imagine a top-level national athlete in any country training alongside kindergartners, but, like so many of Cuba's seeming contradictions, it works.

THE ESSENCE OF CUBAN CUISINE

The delights of a Caribbean cuisine which all too often is difficult to track down in Cuba itself, because of the widespread food shortages

There is a certain music to Cuban cooking: the rhythm of onions dancing on a hot skillet, the sizzle of garlic and peppers that foretells the most classic of Cuban dishes – slowly simmered beans, stews thick with tubers, seared or braised meats, fillings infused with spices.

THE VERSATILE PLANTAIN

Cuban cooking exalts lowly ingredients. Take, for instance, the plantain, *el plátano*. A Cuban cook can give it many different personalities. You can fry it ripe (*maduro*) in slices cut diagonally, or green (*verde*) in paper-thin chips. You can fry thicker wedges of green plantain, squash them, and fry them again for *tostones*. You can boil plantain chunks, ripe or green, mash them with a fork, drizzle with olive oil and sprinkle with crunchy fried pork rinds for *fu fú* – a dish of western African origins but an acquired taste for some visitors. You can fill mashed plantains with *picadillo*, meat hash, and melted white cheese for a *pastel de plátano*. You can do anything but eat them uncooked.

Mostly, Cuban food is simple. It is fare of *el campo* (the countryside), which reflects local harvests and carries earthy suggestions of its Spanish and African roots. It allows, for instance, a dish of Galician inspiration to be served with African accompaniments. The art of Cuban cooking doesn't involve fancy molds or gelées. If some dishes are time-consuming, it's only because of Cuba's obsession with food.

This culinary obsession permeates even the language, the music, the romancing. Entire songs are dedicated to things like the mango or the *palomilla* steak. The rhythm of the *guaguancó* often accompanies mouth-watering lyrics: one of Cuba's first international hits, in the 1930s, was about food: "The Peanut Vendor." Years later, the island's most famous singer, Beny Moré, teased the *marranito*, the little pig, in danger for his life: "We're going to make you *jamón* (ham) and *chicharrón* (pork scratching)" And what does Celia Cruz, exiled Cuban salsa queen, shout in the middle of her songs? *Azúcar!* Sugar!

Like the music, the Cuban language is infused with allusions to food. A good guy is *un pan*, "a piece of bread." A good-looking guy is *pa' comérselo*, "good enough to eat." A good-looking man or woman is *un pollo*, "a chicken." A *pollo* might get this dubious compliment: "If you cook the way you walk, I'd scrape the pot."

The Cuban staples

If Cuban creole (*criollo*) cuisine had a national dish, it would be roast pork (*puerco*) served with black beans (*frijoles*), white rice (*arroz*) and plantains (*plátanos*). Rice and beans are traditionally prepared in two forms: black beans with rice known as *moros y cristianos* (Moors and Christians) or red kidney beans with rice (*congri*). A soupy stew of black beans (*potaje*) is sometimes served alongside plain white rice. Root vegetables are also popular, particularly *yuca* or cassava (a starchy tuber), *malanga*, and *boniato*. *Malanga* is rather challenging to the uninitiated palate, while *boniato*, a kind of sweet potato, is delicious.

The ingredients and spices most used in traditional Cuban cooking are cumin, oregano, parsley, sour oranges and *ajo* – garlic and more garlic. The *sofrito*, a paste of chopped onion, garlic, and green pepper sizzled in good olive oil, is the basis of many dishes. In these days of scarce ingredients, a popular seasoning for vegetables and meat is a tasty mixuture of lime, garlic and oil, called *mojo*. You won't often find meat stews on the menu, but look out for the *ajiaco*, a classic infusion of meat and vegetables.

For the Sweet Tooth

Sugar is the basis for Cuba's fine rum, but also for one of its favorite non-alcoholic drinks, *guarapo*, which is the cloudy, sweet juice of raw, pressed sugar cane.

In the Special Period, the native food of Cuba has seemed close to extinction at times, with hotels often relying on bland international dishes. Cuba has become the land of "*no hay*" – "there isn't any." Cubans have had to learn to cook with what's available. Lean times have forced a new kind of cuisine upon the Cuban people, who have become masters of improvisation, stretching rice with whatever is available, planning vegetarian meals in a culinary culture obsessed with meat. It wouldn't be unusual to find a Cuban bartering a chicken for a bar of soap, or any other items considered luxuries in Cuba. Fortunately for some, the opening of farmers' markets has made a wider choice of ingredients available to those who can afford the high prices. Visitors to Cuba can sample these in the private restaurants or *paladares*, which these days can often serve up a better meal than the state restaurants – and for much less money. (*See Travel Tips for more information on eating in Cuba.*) ❑

PRECEDING PAGES: barbecued chicken in the park.
LEFT: dining out is a luxury most Cubans rarely enjoy …
ABOVE: …unless it's in the fields!

The Doyenne of Cuban Cooking

Traditionally, It has been non-Cuban novelties that have been featured in the few Cuban cookbooks in print. There are few Cuban recipes in the pre-revolutionary classic, "*Cocina Criolla*" (Creole Cuisine), written by the culinary guru Nitza Villapol. She offers recipes for everything from "Yankee Pizza" to Swiss fondue.

More recently, she has offered tips on Cuban TV on how to cope with a ration book and food shortages. She advises people to substitute lemon peel, dried avocado and celery leaves for hard-to-find spices. Her old cookbooks now stand as a testament to a kind of eternal national phenomenon that anything Cuban is considered too down-home, too rustic for fancy dining.

FLORA AND FAUNA

As one might expect from so original an island, Cuba has a varied and beautiful array of wildlife, but many of its endemic species are under threat

Cuba is an intensely green island of the American tropics. At 775 miles long and 100 miles wide (1,250 by 160 km), it is the largest island in the Greater Antilles. Including the Isle of Youth and hundreds of surrounding islands and cays, the country occupies over 44,000 sq. miles (114,000 sq. km). It has a wide range of habitats: from beaches to coastal mangrove swamps; from broad plains to rugged mountains; from cactus semi-desert to remaining indigenous forests of cedar and ebony.

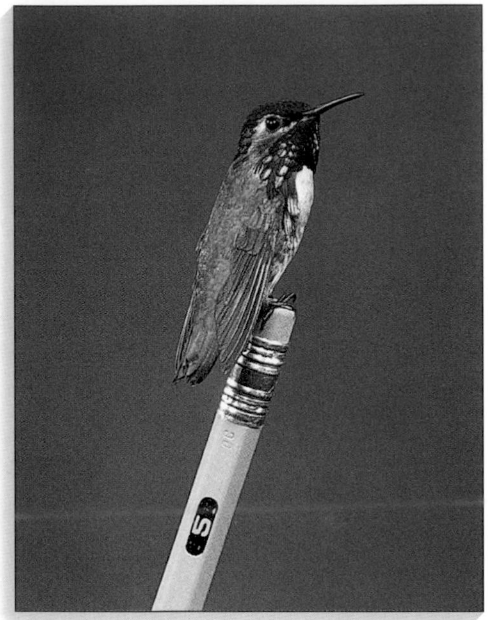

THE ORIGIN OF SPECIES

Like many other large islands in the world, Cuba contains a rich collection of rare birds and animals found nowhere else on earth. As with its unusual plants, Cuba's rare animals are also distantly related to others found elsewhere. Many arrived on huge rafts made of natural debris thousands of years ago. Some were blown here by strong winds. Others walked their way from North and South America along an arch-shaped land mass that millions of years ago formed a bridge between the lands. Once Cuba separated from the continents, most species followed a unique evolutionary path and developed into something very different from the ancestors they left behind.

Graceful and remarkable flora

About half of Cuba's 6,000 species of plants and trees are endemic to the island. Many are directly related to African varieties, apparently having drifted across when the Atlantic Ocean was a narrow, embryonic body of water.

The stately **royal palm** tree, rising to 80 ft (24 meters) high, graces the national emblem and is a prized resource protected by legislation. Its fronds are used for thatching in roofs; its bark for siding; its palm hearts make a delicious salad; its seeds are used for animal feed; and bees gather its palm honey. Another fascinating Cuban palm is the endangered **cork palm**, a stumpy prehistoric plant with scrubby fronds that has somehow survived as a relic from the age of the dinosaurs. It can be found only in a few areas of Pinar del Río Province.

The fragrant white **mariposa**, or butterfly jasmine, is the national flower, even though it is not actually indigenous to the island. During Cuba's wars of independence, women wore it in their hair as a symbol both of their patriotism and purity.

About 350 species of birds can be found in Cuba, more than half of which use the island as a winter resting spot as they make their annual migration from North to South America. There are also 185 species of butterflies, and over 1,000 species of insects.

If you're lucky ...

Few visitors to Cuba will leave the island without seeing the ubiquitous white cattle egrets feeding in the fields or the ugly turkey vultures soaring overhead, but with patience and good fortune, nature lovers might be able to glimpse one or more of Cuba's specialties. The **almiquí**, a cat-sized native mammal that resembles a mole, is a nocturnal insectivore that gives off a strong, foul odor. On the brink of extinction, a few remain in the eastern mountains of the island, but it is only otherwise found in the western part of the Dominican Republic. The **jutía**, an indigenous, edible rodent that can weigh as much as 10 lbs (4 kilos), is also endangered, because of overhunting, but can still be found in forest preserves and on some of the small mangrove keys.

Crocodylus rhombifer, known as the **Cuban crocodile**, lives in the freshwater swamps of the Zapata Peninsula and on the Isle of Youth, but it is threatened by hybridization with the island's other species of crocodile, the more ubiquitous **American crocodile**. A rare iguana, the **Cyclura hubita** – a red-eyed armor-plated reptile – is found only along the shores of Cuba and the Cayman Islands.

Cuba is home to 16 species of hummingbird (*colibrí*). If you don't do any serious bird-watching, you may still be lucky enough to spot one feeding off a flowering bush in a provincial town. But don't expect to see the *zunzuncito* or **bee hummingbird**, which is the smallest bird in existence. With a length of about 2 inches (5 cm) – bill and tail included – and weighing about 2 grams, at least 30 are needed to equal the weight of one chicken egg.

The **Cuban trogon**, or *tocororo*, with its pagoda-shaped tail, was chosen as Cuba's national bird, as its coloring of red, white and blue matches the Cuban flag. It still thrives in the forests, where it perches very still for long intervals. However, it is more often heard than seen, shrieking a piercing "*to-co-roro*" sound.

The **greta cubana,** an exquisite butterfly, is one of only two clear-winged butterfly species in the world. Its translucent wings are edged in black and rimmed with a bright red band. It inhabits the humid forests near Santiago.

Cuba's **land snails** (*polimitas*), over 90 percent of which are indigenous, are often multicolored – white, yellow, orange, striped in green or spotted in black, for example. They are found mostly in Cuba's eastern mountains. Local people in and around Baracoa often try to sell bagfuls of *polimita* shells to tourists.

As elsewhere, though, Cuba's biological heritage is threatened. Tourism development has led to the destruction of ecologically valuable land, and oil shortages have meant the clearing of forests to be used for fuel. Worryingly, about 200 species of Cuba's plants and animals are now on the United Nations official list of endangered and threatened species. ❑

PRECEDING PAGES: Cuban crocodile, Zapata Peninsula.
LEFT: bee hummingbird, the world's smallest bird.
ABOVE: a watchful Cuban chameleon.

P.GUINART

PLACES

A detailed guide to the entire archipelago of Cuba, with principal sites cross-referenced by number to the maps

Most visitors to Cuba arrive at either Havana or Varadero – two places which, while only 85 miles (140 km) apart, mark the opposite extremes of the Cuban experience. Varadero is a holiday resort built purely to extract tourist dollars, with glitzy high-rise hotels, restaurants and nightclubs, and golden beaches that are largely free of locals. Havana, on the other hand, is where five centuries of Cuban history coalesce, a city saturated by romance, nostalgia and intrigue. Although slowly falling to pieces, it should not be missed, for there is nowhere else like it in Latin America.

Whichever city you choose as a jumping-off point, the "real Cuba" lies out in the provinces. A shortage of parts and fuel has greatly reduced public transport services but, with a judicious combination of short domestic flights, organized tours, informal taxi rides, and rental cars, you will be able to penetrate the less-frequently visited hinterland. For those with a sense of adventure, hitching is a viable alternative – it's safe, and is the manner in which most Cubans travel.

More time-pressed visitors can take day trips from Havana into Havana Province, or from Varadero into Matanzas. For a purer taste of rural life, to the west of Havana lies the province of Pinar del Río, the tobacco-growing region that is one of the lushest and most spectacular parts of the main island. A journey to the central south coast should include visits to Playa Girón on the Bay of Pigs, the wildlife-filled Zapata Peninsula, the port of Cienfuegos, and Cuba's colonial jewel, Trinidad. Offshore, Cayo Largo is the favored beach resort, while the Isle of Youth is a major diving center.

The vast sugar cane fields of the rural heartland make up perhaps the slowest and least-visited part of Cuba, and the East – what was formerly Oriente Province – has its own thriving identity and traditions. Separated by distance and official indifference from Havana, the Oriente was where 19th-century independence movements took root. In the 1950s, Santiago saw Castro's attack on the Moncada Barracks, symbolic start of the Revolution, whilst the Sierra Maestra was where the guerrilla campaign was fought. Santiago, Cuba's second city, is often a few steps ahead of Havana in culture and music, and exploring the shattered highways, remote beaches and craggy mountains of the Oriente remains one of Cuba's great adventures. ❑

PRECEDING PAGES the *mogotes* of the Viñales Valley, in Pinar del Río province; Playa Ancón, on the south coast; colonial street scene in Trinidad.
LEFT: *plátanos* for sale, Santiago.

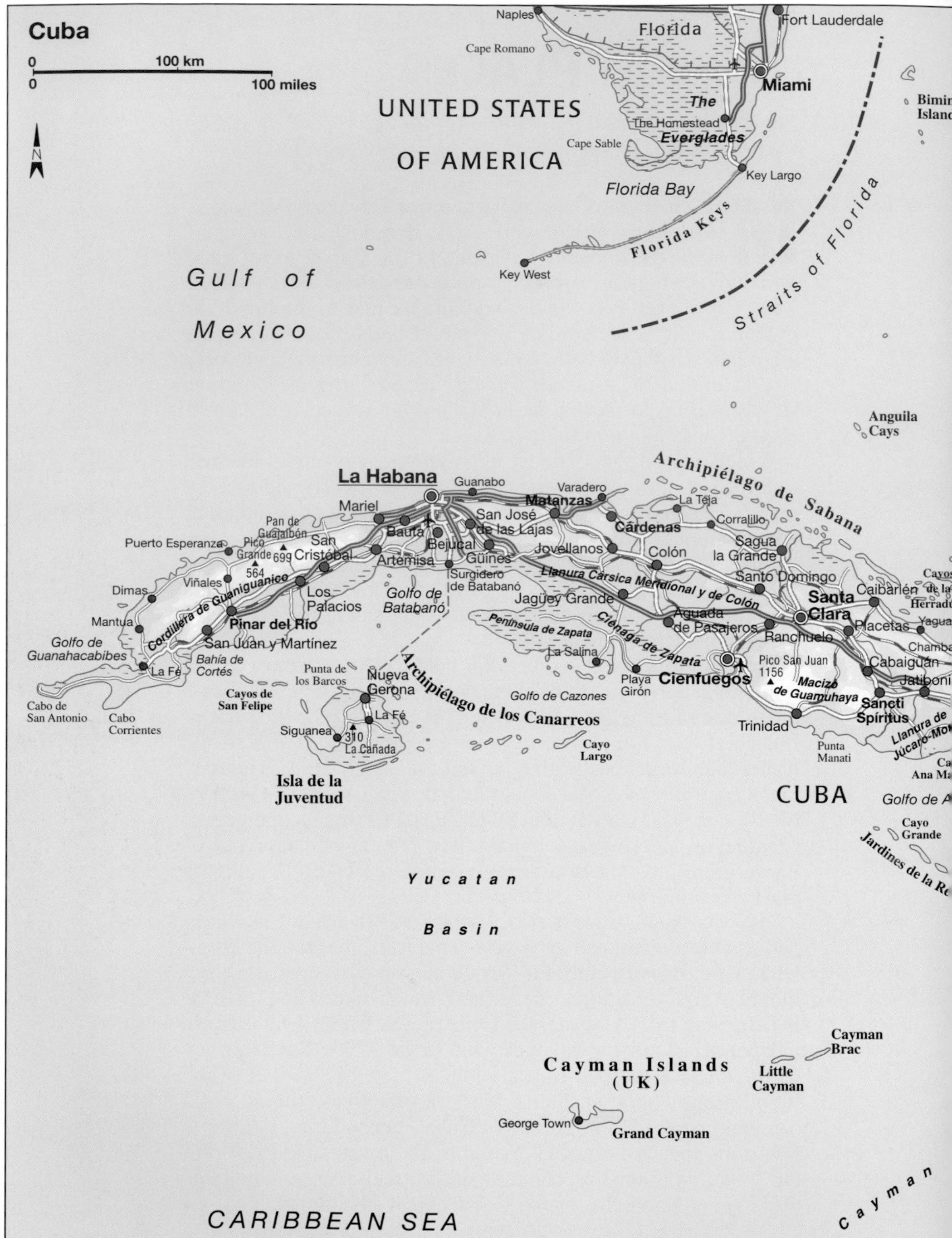
Cuba
0 100 km
0 100 miles
N
UNITED STATES OF AMERICA
Florida
Naples
Fort Lauderdale
Cape Romano
Miami
Bimini Islands
The Everglades
The Homestead
Cape Sable
Key Largo
Florida Bay
Florida Keys
Key West
Straits of Florida
Gulf of Mexico
Anguila Cays
Archipiélago de Sabana
La Habana
Guanabo
Varadero
Matanzas
Mariel
La Teja
Corralillo
Pan de Guajaibón
San José de las Lajas
Cárdenas
Puerto Esperanza
Pico Grande
699
564
San Cristóbal
Bauta
Bejucal
Jovellanos
Sagua la Grande
Artemisa
Güines
Colón
Viñales
Surgidero de Batabanó
Santo Domingo
Caibarién
Dimas
Los Palacios
Golfo de Batabanó
Llanura Cársica Meridional y de Colón
Jagüey Grande
Santa Clara
Cordillera de Guaniguanico
Aguada de Pasajeros
Mantua
Pinar del Río
Península de Zapata
Ciénaga de Zapata
Ranchuelo
Placetas
Golfo de Guanahacabibes
San Juan y Martínez
La Salina
Bahía de Cortés
Punta de los Barcos
Nueva Gerona
Pico San Juan 1156
Cabaiguán
La Fé
Playa Girón
Cienfuegos
Macizo de Guamuhaya
Jatiboni
Cabo de San Antonio
Cabo Corrientes
Cayos de San Felipe
Archipiélago de los Canarreos
Golfo de Cazones
Sancti Spíritus
La Fé
Siguanea
310
La Cañada
Trinidad
Cayo Largo
Punta Manati
Isla de la Juventud
CUBA
Cayo Grande
Jardines de la Re
Yucatan Basin
Cayman Brac
Cayman Islands (UK)
Little Cayman
George Town
Grand Cayman
CARIBBEAN SEA
Cayman

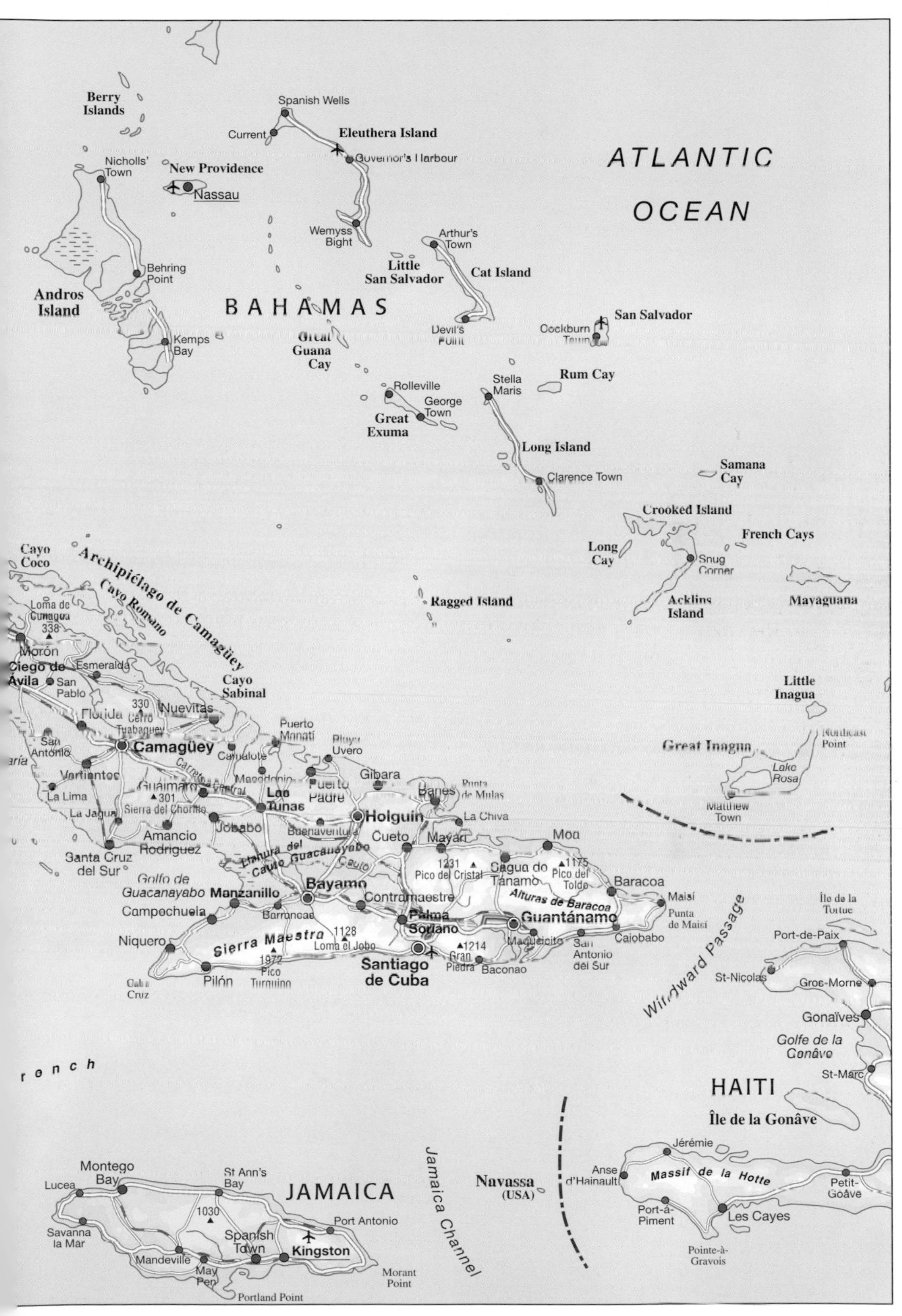

ATLANTIC OCEAN
BAHAMAS
Berry Islands
Spanish Wells
Current
Eleuthera Island
Governor's Harbour
Nicholls' Town
New Providence
Nassau
Wemyss Bight
Arthur's Town
Little San Salvador
Cat Island
Behring Point
Andros Island
Kemps Bay
Great Guana Cay
Devil's Point
Cockburn Town
San Salvador
Rum Cay
Stella Maris
Rolleville
George Town
Great Exuma
Long Island
Clarence Town
Samana Cay
Crooked Island
French Cays
Long Cay
Snug Corner
Ragged Island
Acklins Island
Mayaguana
Cayo Coco
Archipiélago de Camagüey
Cayo Romano
Loma de Cunagua 338
Morón
Ciego de Ávila
Esmeralda
San Pablo
Cayo Sabinal
Florida
330 Cerro Tuabaquey
Nuevitas
Camagüey
San Antonio
Puerto Manatí
Playa Uvero
Camalote
Vertientes
Guáimaro
Carretera Central
Macagonio
Puerto Padre
Gibara
Las Tunas
La Lima
301 Sierra del Chorrillo
La Jagua
Banes
Punta de Mulas
Holguín
La Chiva
Amancio Rodríguez
Jobabo
Buenaventura
Santa Cruz del Sur
Cueto
Mayarí
Moa
Llanura del Cauto
Guacanayabo
Cauto
1231 Pico del Cristal
Sagua de Tánamo
1175 Pico del Toldo
Baracoa
Golfo de Guacanayabo
Manzanillo
Bayamo
Contramaestre
Alturas de Baracoa
Maisí
Punta de Maisí
Campechuela
Barrancas
Palma Soriano
Guantánamo
Niquero
Sierra Maestra
1128 Loma el Jobo
Santiago de Cuba
Maquicito
1214 Gran Piedra
Caiobabo
San Antonio del Sur
1972 Pico Turquino
Pilón
Baconao
Cabo Cruz
Little Inagua
Great Inagua
Northeast Point
Lake Rosa
Matthew Town
Windward Passage
Île de la Tortue
Port-de-Paix
St-Nicolas
Gros-Morne
Gonaïves
Golfe de la Gonâve
St-Marc
HAITI
Île de la Gonâve
Jérémie
Anse d'Hainault
Massif de la Hotte
Petit-Goâve
Port-à-Piment
Les Cayes
Pointe-à-Gravois
Navassa (USA)
Jamaica Channel
JAMAICA
Montego Bay
Lucea
St Ann's Bay
1030
Port Antonio
Savanna la Mar
Spanish Town
Kingston
Mandeville
May Pen
Morant Point
Portland Point
rench

INTRODUCING HAVANA

A city of more than two million inhabitants, Cuba's capital offers far more than just its astonishing colonial core

When seen from a distance, Havana looks spectacular. Waves crash over the city's famous promenade, the **Malecón**, where lovers stroll before pastel-colored buildings. Stone fortresses turn golden in the Caribbean light, recalling the days when Havana was the jewel in the Spanish Crown, its harbor full of galleons loaded with South American silver.

Closer up, the grandeur fades: Havana has been consumed by tropical decay. Most of the city hasn't had a lick of paint since the Revolution triumphed and the revolutionary government turned its energies towards developing the countryside. Although a major UNESCO-funded restoration program is now in full swing within the colonial quarter, **La Habana Vieja** (Old Havana), many of its narrow 17th-century streets are still literally falling to pieces, as is most of **Centro Habana**, the area that borders it to the west.

The next suburb, **Vedado**, was modelled on Miami, and most of its tallest buildings are still the hotels originally financed by the American Mafia in the 1940s and '50s. Here and in the other main western suburb, **Miramar**, the pre-revolutionary mansions of the rich are today occupied either by ordinary Cuban families, whose homes lie rotting splendidly amid lush foliage — or by a growing number of embassy officials, foreign investors, and Cuban bureaucrats.

The above-mentioned areas are all most visitors see of Cuba's capital city, but Havana also has some fascinating outlying districts that ought not be missed.

Havana is an exhilarating place, but it can also be exhausting. There is a neurotic, anxious edge to life here, quite unlike anything you'll find in the rest of Cuba. Foreigners walking the streets attract a constant stream of interlocutors: *jineteros* (hustlers), selling everything from cigars to bootleg rum; school kids after some change (in dollars, please); *jineteras* (prostitutes) after single men; and squadrons of taxi drivers on the lookout for a fare.

Unquestionably, however, these hassles are a small price to pay to see one of the most peculiar and fascinating places on earth, a city of great paradox and great presence. As Cuba's political and economic center, it has become a museum to a broken communist dream. Yet it is much more than just that: it is the focus of Cuba's youth culture; the place where you'll find the most magnificent hotels and the liveliest discotheques, where the Revolution seems to have come full circle and, uncannily, recreated the absurdly decadent world of Graham Greene's *Our Man in Havana*. ❑

PRECEDING PAGES: looking eastward from the Hotel Habana Libre in Vedado.
LEFT: Old Havana.

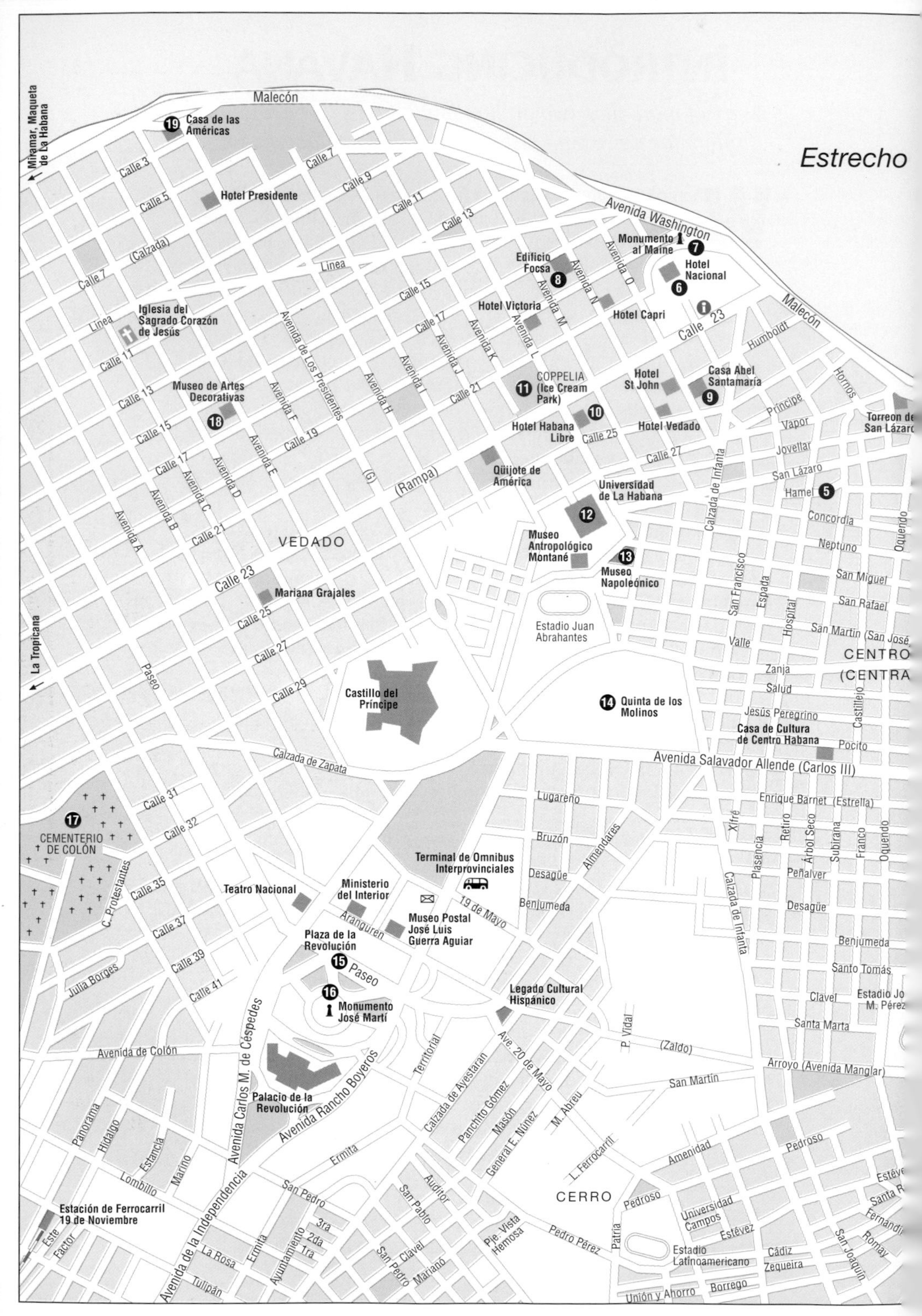

Malecón
Casa de las Américas
Miramar, Maqueta de La Habana
Estrecho
Hotel Presidente
Avenida Washington
Monumento al Maine
Hotel Nacional
Edificio Focsa
Hotel Victoria
Hotel Capri
Iglesia del Sagrado Corazón de Jesús
COPPELIA (Ice Cream Park)
Hotel St John
Casa Abel Santamaría
Museo de Artes Decorativas
Hotel Habana Libre
Hotel Vedado
Torreon de San Lázaro
Quijote de América
Universidad de La Habana
VEDADO
Museo Antropológico Montané
Museo Napoleónico
Mariana Grajales
Estadio Juan Abrahantes
La Tropicana
Castillo del Príncipe
Quinta de los Molinos
CENTRO (CENTRA
Casa de Cultura de Centro Habana
Avenida Salvador Allende (Carlos III)
CEMENTERIO DE COLÓN
Terminal de Omnibus Interprovinciales
Teatro Nacional
Ministerio del Interior
Museo Postal José Luis Guerra Aguiar
Plaza de la Revolución
Monumento José Martí
Legado Cultural Hispánico
Palacio de la Revolución
Avenida Rancho Boyeros
Avenida Carlos M. de Céspedes
Avenida de la Independencia
Avenida de Colón
CERRO
Estación de Ferrocarril 19 de Noviembre
Estadio Latinoamericano
Estadio Jo M. Pérez

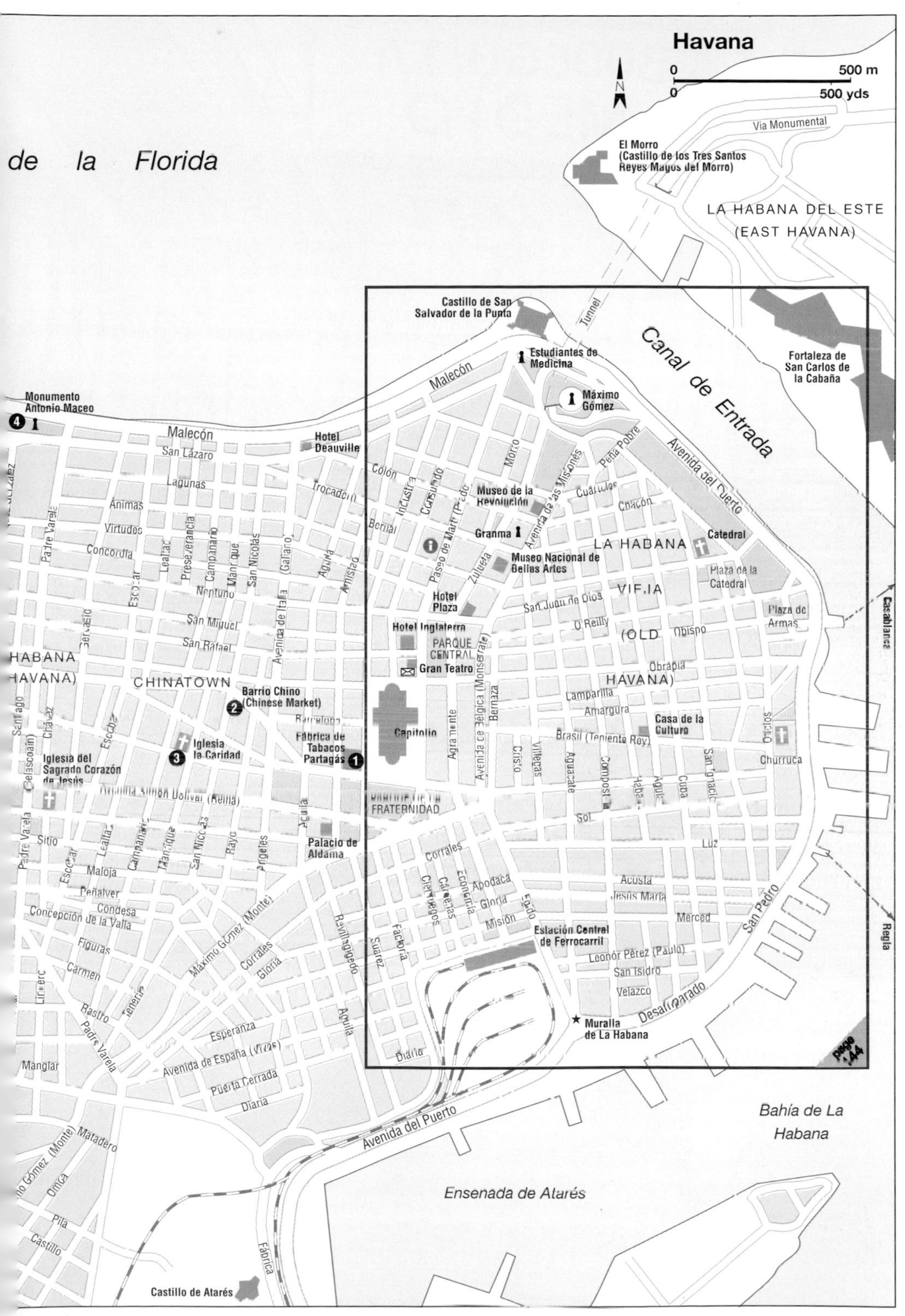
Havana
0 500 m
0 500 yds
de la Florida
Via Monumental
El Morro (Castillo de los Tres Santos Reyes Magos del Morro)
LA HABANA DEL ESTE (EAST HAVANA)
Castillo de San Salvador de la Punta
Tunnel
Canal de Entrada
Fortaleza de San Carlos de la Cabaña
Estudiantes de Medicina
Máximo Gómez
Malecón
Monumento Antonio Maceo
Hotel Deauville
San Lázaro
Lagunas
Trocadero
Colón
Museo de la Revolución
Granma
Catedral
LA HABANA VIEJA (OLD HAVANA)
Museo Nacional de Bellas Artes
Plaza de la Catedral
Plaza de Armas
Hotel Plaza
Hotel Inglaterra
PARQUE CENTRAL
Gran Teatro
Capitolio
CHINATOWN
Barrio Chino (Chinese Market)
Fábrica de Tabacos Partagás
Iglesia la Caridad
Iglesia del Sagrado Corazón de Jesús
FRATERNIDAD
Palacio de Aldama
Casa de la Cultura
Estación Central de Ferrocarril
Muralla de La Habana
Churruca
Casablanca
Regla
Bahía de La Habana
Ensenada de Atarés
Avenida del Puerto
Castillo de Atarés
page 144

LA BODEGUITA
DEL MEDIO

OLD HAVANA

Restored grandeur reveals the might of Spain's most precious colonial city, but Old Havana is more than just a living museum. Life on the streets holds as much interest as the fine architecture

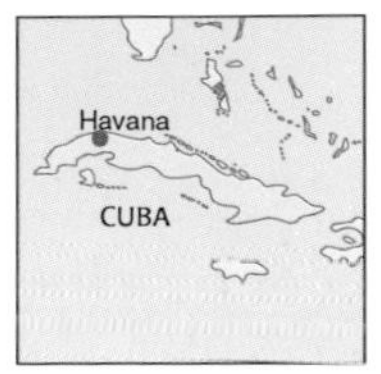

A good place to get an idea of Havana's basic layout is actually from the opposite side of Havana Bay, from the imposing fortress of **El Morro** (*see page185*). The view from the Morro's walls encompasses much of what a visitor will see in the city, making it an excellent place for orientation. Although this is a sprawling city of some 2.1 million inhabitants, most visitors find themselves shuttling along the seafront boulevard, the Malecón, between two main areas: the hotel and restaurant district of Vedado (where the only skyscrapers are clustered) and **La Habana Vieja**, or **Old Havana**, the city's touristic heart. This is likely to be where most visitors to Cuba spend the first day of their trip, and it is a tremendous place to begin any holiday.

Exploring Old Havana

The compact grid of narrow colonial streets, graceful squares and aristocratic mansions that make up Old Havana was, for some 350 years, the entire city. It was only in the 1860s that the massive city walls were knocked down and *habaneros* began distinguishing the district as "old." For many years, the area was allowed to languish – a blessing in disguise, since it meant Havana escaped the Disneyland-style restoration of other Caribbean relics such as San Juan in Puerto Rico. The Castro government put money into developing the impoverished countryside, and left the capital untouched. In spite of the decay everywhere evident after such chronic neglect, the 1959 Revolution ironically actually saved Old Havana. The Batista regime had had the area scheduled for demolition: cars could not easily pass down the Old City's narrow streets, and more land was needed to satisfy the fever for high rise hotels, casinos and night-clubs.

Since the Old City was placed on the UNESCO World Heritage List in 1982, and with the added incentive of turning it into a major tourist attraction, the authorities, have embarked on an ambitious process of restoration. This has rescued sections of the city from decay, but in other areas, buildings continue to collapse after bad weather – more than 600 have been lost in this way over the past 10 years. Still, some 150 of Havana's remaining buildings date back to the 16th and 17th centuries, 200 from the 18th, and 460 from the 19th, making it the most authentic colonial city in the Americas.

Although it is Cuba's most important historical site, Old Havana is also very much alive – in fact, it is one of the most densely populated parts of the island. After the Revolution, people from the countryside came to Havana by the thousand, taking over ancient mansions abandoned by the rich, and dividing them up into *ciudadelas* – little tenement cities where dozens

LEFT: one of Old Havana's most famous landmarks.
BELOW: La Giraldilla, symbol of Havana

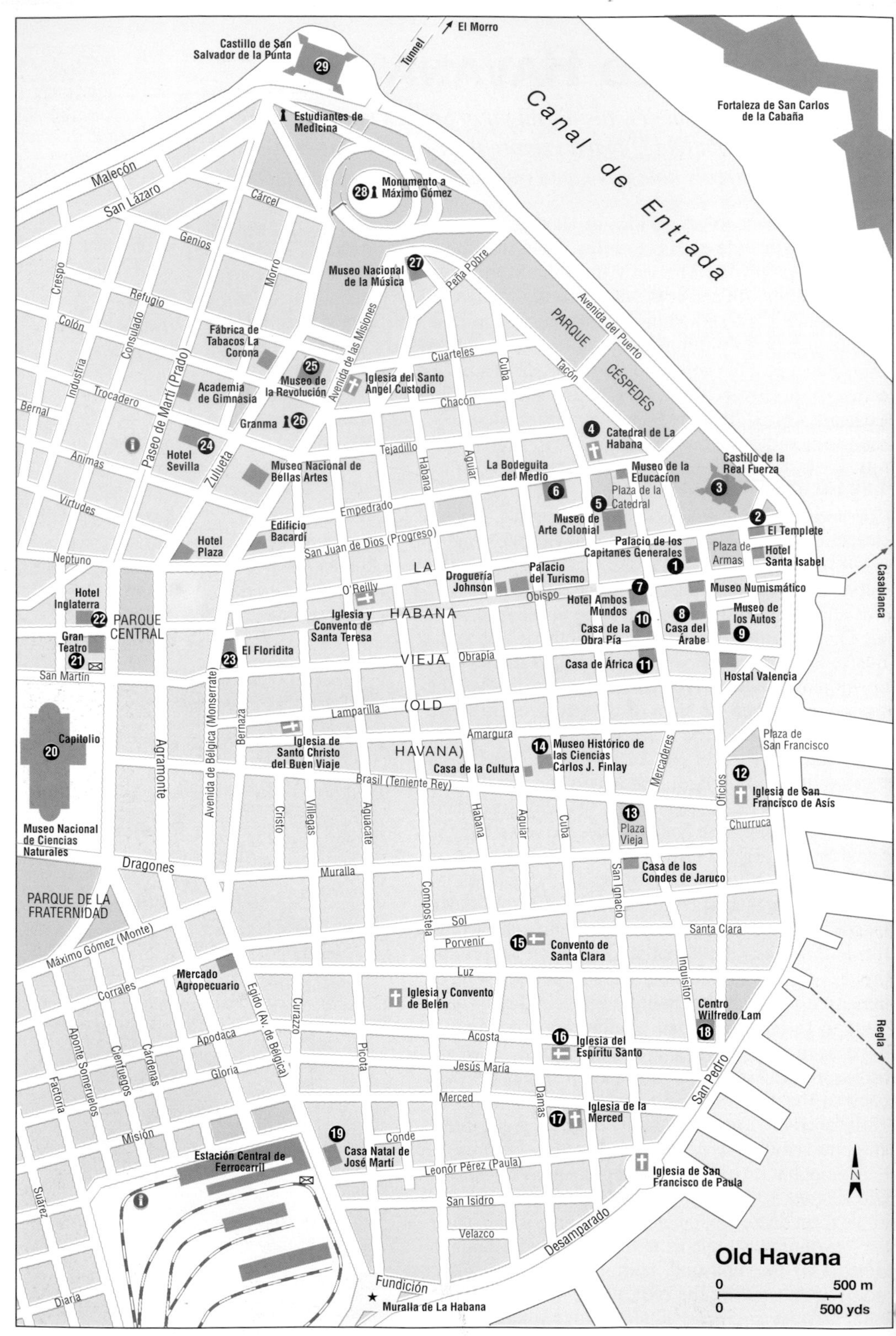

Old Havana
El Morro
Tunnel
Castillo de San Salvador de la Punta
Fortaleza de San Carlos de la Cabaña
Canal de Entrada
Estudiantes de Medicina
Monumento a Máximo Gómez
Museo Nacional de la Música
Fábrica de Tabacos La Corona
Academia de Gimnasia
Museo de la Revolución
Iglesia del Santo Angel Custodio
Granma
Hotel Sevilla
Museo Nacional de Bellas Artes
La Bodeguita del Medio
Catedral de La Habana
Museo de la Educación
Plaza de la Catedral
Castillo de la Real Fuerza
Museo de Arte Colonial
El Templete
Palacio de los Capitanes Generales
Plaza de Armas
Hotel Santa Isabel
Casablanca
Edificio Bacardí
Hotel Plaza
Hotel Inglaterra
Gran Teatro
PARQUE CENTRAL
Droguería Johnson
Palacio del Turismo
Hotel Ambos Mundos
Museo Numismático
Museo de los Autos
Casa de la Obra Pía
Casa del Árabe
Iglesia y Convento de Santa Teresa
El Floridita
LA HABANA VIEJA (OLD HAVANA)
Casa de África
Hostal Valencia
Capitolio
Museo Nacional de Ciencias Naturales
Iglesia de Santo Christo del Buen Viaje
Museo Histórico de las Ciencias Carlos J. Finlay
Casa de la Cultura
Plaza de San Francisco
Iglesia de San Francisco de Asís
Plaza Vieja
Casa de los Condes de Jaruco
PARQUE DE LA FRATERNIDAD
Convento de Santa Clara
Mercado Agropecuario
Iglesia y Convento de Belén
Centro Wilfredo Lam
Iglesia del Espíritu Santo
Regla
Iglesia de la Merced
Casa Natal de José Martí
Estación Central de Ferrocarril
Iglesia de San Francisco de Paula
Muralla de La Habana
PARQUE CÉSPEDES
Malecón
San Lázaro
Cárcel
Genios
Crespo
Refugio
Colón
Consulado
Morro
Industria
Trocadero
Bernal
Paseo de Martí (Prado)
Animas
Virtudes
Zulueta
Neptuno
San Martín
Avenida de las Misiones
Peña Pobre
Avenida del Puerto
Tacón
Cuarteles
Cuba
Chacón
Tejadillo
Habana
Aguiar
Empedrado
San Juan de Dios (Progreso)
O'Reilly
Obispo
Obrapía
Lamparilla
Amargura
Brasil (Teniente Rey)
Mercaderes
Oficios
Churruca
Avenida de Bélgica (Monserrate)
Bernaza
Agramonte
Cristo
Villegas
Aguacate
San Ignacio
Dragones
Muralla
Compostela
Sol
Santa Clara
Porvenir
Máximo Gómez (Monte)
Luz
Inquisidor
Corrales
Egido (Av. de Bélgica)
Curazao
Apodaca
Acosta
Aponte
Someruelos
Cienfuegos
Cárdenas
Gloria
Picota
Jesús María
Factoria
Merced
Damas
San Pedro
Misión
Conde
Leonor Pérez (Paula)
Suárez
San Isidro
Velazco
Desamparado
Fundición
Diaria
0 500 m
0 500 yds
N

of families share one roof. These tenements usually have one family per room, often without running water, and sometimes a couple of pigs are even kept inside, in the bath or a home-made pen. Ground floors have been converted into shops, and in true Caribbean style, socializing is done on the sidewalks, with music blaring from cassette decks and kids playing in the mostly traffic-free streets. One sad consequence of the city's wide-scale restoration program is that it's taking some of the life out of Old Havana, as families are moved out of historic buildings and rehoused, but you'll find the backstreets are still full of vitality.

Speak no evil at the Cafe Mina in Plaza de Armas.

The heart of the Old City

The **Plaza de Armas** is Havana's oldest square, and the best place to begin any walking tour of the city. By day, this beautiful, regal square is home to a second-hand book market and a large bustling artisans' market, which runs off into the surrounding streets. It is touristy, but there are many lovely things to be bought here at bargain prices. Check out the crochet work, Tiffany-style lamps and other objects made from stained glass, painted papier-mâché toys and wonderfully carved wooden statuettes. There is plenty of jewellery – everything from the bead *collares* of the Santería saints, to beautiful pieces featuring small native pearls, coral, shells and hematite – but refrain from buying black coral and tortoiseshell since these are seriously endangered species. Modern artists sell their gaudy works here too. In the evening, the square is lit by antique filigree lamps, and on many nights an orchestra plays in the open air. It is the focus for much of the street life of the newly restored city, and is surrounded by elegant cafes, bars and restaurants, such as the **Cafe Mina**.

In the center of the leafy square is a statue of Carlos Manuel de Céspedes, rebel President and leader of the first War of Independence in the 1860s. The majestic building on the west side of the plaza is the **Palacio de los Capitanes Generales** (Palace of the Captain Generals) ❶, perhaps the finest example of baroque architecture in Havana. Completed in 1780, this was home to the Spanish governor until independence, and of the US military governor for the few years thereafter. Cuban presidents lived here until 1917, when they moved to the Capitolio and this became the mayor's office.

Today it houses the **Museo de la Ciudad** or Museum of the City (open daily 9.30am–6.30pm; entrance fee; camera extra), which has by far the most lavish of Havana's many collections of colonial artefacts. Keep an eye out for the machete of independence fighter General Antonio Maceo, and the dining room with 400 plates hung on the walls. The King of Spain's Hall was kept constantly ready in case His or Her Majesty ever decided to inspect Havana, though no monarch ever did. The courtyard garden is delightful, hung with vines and bougainvillea, with a statue of Christopher Columbus at its center. An excellent value **special museum ticket** is available here, which covers entry into all of Havana's museums.

At the plaza's northeast corner is the open-air Doric temple, **El Templete** ❷, with a large religious paint-

BELOW: El Templete.

Havana Cathedral's door knocker.

ing by the French artist Jean-Baptiste Vermay inside. A column marks the spot where the city was founded in 1519 as "La Villa de San Cristóbal de la Habana", with a Mass being said under the sacred *ceiba* tree. The original tree was knocked down by a hurricane in 1828 and has been replanted several times. The current descendant is still credited with magical powers, partly because *ceibas* are considered sacred in the Yoruba religion (on which Santería is based). During a festival every November 16, *Habaneros* celebrate that first mass: thousands of people fill the square, and wait many hours to fulfil a ritual – circling the tree three times and throwing coins at its roots to bring good luck in the coming year.

Nearby is the beautiful **Hotel Santa Isabel**, which was originally built in the 18th century as the Palacio del Conde de Santovenia; a ruin for many years, it has now been restored to five-star status. Across the street from El Templete is the **Castillo de la Real Fuerza** ❸, the oldest building in Havana. This powerful fortress, complete with drawbridges, iron cannon and murky green moat, was built on the orders of King Philip II after the city was sacked by pirates, and it was completed in 1577.

Topping its tower is the city's symbol, the bronze figure of **La Giraldilla de la Habana** (a replica, in fact – the original is in the Museo de la Ciudad). Called Inez de Bobadilla, she was the wife of conquistador Hernando de Soto, who left Cuba to search Florida for the fountain of youth. Instead, he found only miserable death. La Giraldilla spent every afternoon for four years in the tower, expectantly watching for his return. There is a small museum and gallery in the castle, and on the roof is a pleasant terrace coffee shop with good views of the harbor.

BELOW: hanging out at the Castillo de la Real Fuerza.

"Music turned to stone"

Two blocks north is the **Plaza de la Catedral**, named for the baroque **Catedral de La Habana** ❹ (open Mon–Fri, 9–11am, and 2.30–6pm) which dominates the square and forms part of the most harmonious collection of buildings in the city. Officially termed the Catedral de la Virgen María de la Concepción Inmaculada, the building was finally finished in 1777, after several setbacks. It was begun as a church by the Jesuits in 1748, but was halted when King Carlos III ordered them out of Cuba in 1767, and gained cathedral status only in 1793. There are bells in both of the towers: the shorter tower has a bell from the Cuban city of Matanzas; the taller, a bell from Spain. At midnight on New Year's Eve, the cathedral bells ring and crowds gather to rap at the great timber doors for luck in the New Year. The surprisingly small and rather somber interior holds an altar of Carrara marble inlaid with gold, silver and onyx.

For many years, this cathedral held the supposed ashes of Christopher Columbus, brought from Santo Domingo in 1796. His ashes were taken back to Spain after Cuba won her independence in 1899, though most people now believe the ashes are actually those of Columbus's son Diego. The Pope held his final mass here, in January, 1998, shortly before he flew back to Rome. Then, the square was packed with the faithful (and the merely curious), and the surrounding buildings were decked with flowing silk banners in the Vatican colors of yellow and white. A small shop to the right of the cathedral sells postcards, T-shirts and other memorabilia of the historic papal visit. A morning mass is held every Sunday at 10.30am, and on Tuesdays and Thursdays at 8am.

The delightful Cathedral Square

This beautiful square was once a rather seedy place, known as the Plazuela de la Ciénaga (Little Swamp Square). It was the place where the city's rainwater drained, and was once dominated by the Zanja Real or "royal ditch." The site of a fish market before building began in the 18th century, it was the last square to be built in Old Havana. On the east side of the square is the **Casa de Lombillo**, built in 1741. The former mansion of a Cuban slave trader, it housed Cuba's first post office, and now houses the **Museo de la Educación**, detailing the events of the literacy campaign that followed the Revolution. Beside the Casa de Lombillo is the **Casa del Marqués de Arcos** which was built in 1742 for Cuba's royal treasurer. Today it is an art gallery.

Directly opposite the Cathedral is another beautifully restored colonial building, the **Casa del Conde de Casa Bayona**. Built in 1720 for the then Governor General Chacón, it now houses the **Museo de Arte Colonial** ❺ (open Wed–Mon, 9am–5pm, Sun closing at 1pm; entrance fee), packed with glorious artefacts from four centuries of colonial rule. Most of the rooms, centered on a typical colonial courtyard, are open to the public, including a handful of rooms furnished to give an idea of the lifestyle of a wealthy Havana family in the 19th century. There is a room dedicated to the city's famous *vitrales*, the stained-glass

TIP

You can still see Cuba's first "post box" set into the wall between the Casas Lombillo and Arcos – but don't post your letters in the face's ugly mouth, as it seems to devour them on many occasions without trace.

BELOW: Havana's baroque Cathedral, lording it over Plaza de la Catedral.

Colonial balcony, painted in "Havana blue," in Plaza de la Catedral.

windows and panels that are a Cuban specialty, including the distinctive swing doors known as *mamparas*. Note also the superb wooden *mudéjar* (Moorish-inspired) ceilings upstairs, known as *alfarjes* *(see pages 164–5)*.

In the southwest corner of the square is the **Callejón de Chorro**, a tiny cul-de-sac, where a wonderfully restored Art Nouveau building houses the **Taller Experimental de Gráfica** (Experimental Workshop of Graphic Arts). Here you'll find good quality silk screening and printing for sale, and you can watch the artists at work. This alley is also the home of one of Havana's most popular *paladares* (private restaurants), full of plants, parrots and moodily lit by Tiffany lamps – you will often see a queue outside.

Next around the square is the **Casa de Baños** (Bath House), rebuilt in 1909 over a 19th-century original; the water was fed directly into the baths from the Zanja Real water ditch. A plaque marks the spot. Today, the building houses the Galería Manuel which sells excellent art, clothes and Cuba's famous Tiffany-style lamps. Next door, taking up most of the west of the square, is the **El Patio** restaurant. This beautiful colonial building was formerly the **Casa de los Marqueses de Aguas Claras**, the 16th-century former home of Governor General Gonzalo Pérez de Ángulo. Outside, a talented house salsa band plays sets for those sipping cool *mojitos* on the terrace, and at night the bar puts out tables and chairs in the delightfully floodlit square. Inside, the tremendous courtyard is the setting for the restaurant, which extends from the ground floor (where you can eat surrounded by palms and be serenaded from the grand piano if there's no competition from the salsa band) to the balconies upstairs. The surroundings are grand, but the food is mediocre and over-priced.

BELOW: souvenir stalls await the tourist dollar.

To the east of the Cathedral is **Calle Tacón**, a good place to park, as official "minders" keep parked cars under watch – theft from cars is rife in this part of town. They will expect a dollar for their pains. Likewise, this is a place for the footsore to find a taxi. At Tacón No. 4, a lovely blue and white colonial building with a cool tiled patio is home to the D'Giovani Italian restaurant, with a small pastry shop tucked into the corner. The maze of tenements behind here teems with illegal *paladares* (the ones which don't register with the authorities, so as to avoid taxes) – ask any taxi driver.

Behind the Cathedral

Between Calles Empedrado and Chacón is the **Seminario de San Carlos y San Ambrosio**, a solid building of coral limestone that runs along the harbor front. Built by the Jesuits in 1721, it is still used as a seminary and the doors are rarely opened to the public; when they are, step into the deliciously peaceful green courtyard, perfect for quiet contemplation amidst the noise and heat of the Old Town. Behind this building you may notice a miniature castle that looks disturbingly like the Castillo de la Real Fuerza. Attempting to sightsee here would be a mistake, however, since it is in fact a police station.

Just around the corner, on Calle Cuba No. 64, is the **Palacio de Artesanía**, another delightful colonial building which has an artisans' market on three floors around a plant-filled courtyard. It's an obligatory stop on the coach party trail. Most of the shops are government-run, selling postcards and Che Guevara T-shirts.

Calle Empedrado

Leading off the Plaza de la Catedral, this street's first main site is the justly famous bar and restaurant, **La Bodeguita del Medio** ❻. It started life in 1942

A popular departure point from Old Havana if you are not on foot is the seafront square adjacent to the Plaza de la Catedral. You'll find taxis eager for custom and Cuba's new breed of cycle rickshaws or *bicitaxis*.

BELOW: Hemingway's old watering hole, La Bodeguita del Medio.

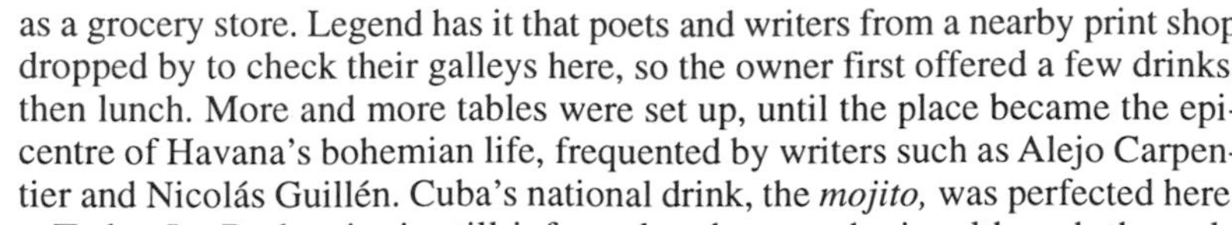

as a grocery store. Legend has it that poets and writers from a nearby print shop dropped by to check their galleys here, so the owner first offered a few drinks, then lunch. More and more tables were set up, until the place became the epicentre of Havana's bohemian life, frequented by writers such as Alejo Carpentier and Nicolás Guillén. Cuba's national drink, the *mojito,* was perfected here.

Today La Bodeguita is still informal and atmospheric, although the only Cuban bohemians here are likely to be working as waiters. Photos and memorabilia from famous diners clutter the walls, which have been tattooed with so many signatures that they are almost black. A sign over the bottles in the front bar was supposedly written and signed by regular customer Ernest Hemingway: *"My Mojito in La Bodeguita, My Daiquirí in El Floridita."* Not perhaps, his most profound statement, but typically pithy, and a whole lot less banal than some other people's contributions to the great graffiti debate that plasters the bar's walls. According to Tom Miller in *Trading with the Enemy*, it was a hoax anyway, made up by Papa's drinking pal Fernando Campoamor to attract customers. If so, it has certainly worked: from morning to closing, the barman can't pour out *mojitos* fast enough. Errol Flynn was once another frequent visitor, but nowadays the mix is mainly tourists and *jineteras*. The food is not great value but if you decide to eat here as well, pork is the specialty, served with *moros y cristianos* (rice and beans), and plantains.

At Empedrado No. 215 is the beautiful **Museo Alejo Carpentier**, dedicated to the famous Cuban writer. The house, also called the Casa del Conde de la Reunión, centers around a lovely courtyard and contains many interesting Carpentier artefacts, including his car, a Volkswagen Beetle. All the artefacts and the house itself, built in 1820, were given to the state on Carpentier's death by his widow, along with the rights to his royalties, to be used for maintaining the museum.

One block south along Calle Cuba is the **Calle O'Reilly**, named after a Spaniard with Irish ancestry, Alejandro O'Reilly, who was the first Spanish Governor after the island was handed back by the British in 1763. A plaque on the corner of Tacón reads "Cuba and Ireland: Two island peoples in the same seas of struggle and hope." This street is still awaiting restoration – it is fairly run down and dirty for the most part, but there's the enjoyable **Cafe O'Reilly** at No. 205, with good, friendly service and some fine little upstairs balconies.

Faded opulence on Calle Obispo

The **Calle Obispo** is one of the best known and most pleasant streets in Old Havana: it was the first street in Old Havana to be pedestrianized and restored. One classic 1920 guidebook to Havana likens Obispo's open-air shops to caves,with windows full of "diamonds and Panama hats, tortoise shells, Canary Island embroidery and perfumery." Cafe windows were stacked with chocolate and almond cakes, wine shops offered Russian liqueurs in miniature glass bears. Things have changed a lot since the 1920s, but though Havana is still far from being a consumer paradise, many interesting shops are beginning to open (all

TIP

To make your own heavenly and refreshing *mojito*, crush fresh mint leaves with sugar and lime juice; add ice and a liberal measure of a white rum such as Havana Club Silver Dry; top up with soda water, and garnish with more fresh mint. Then apply to the Bodeguita for a job.

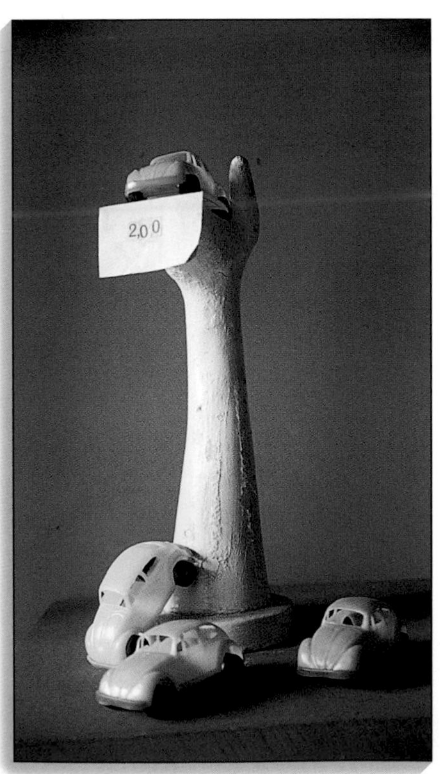

BELOW: only in Cuba: a shop window display in Calle Obispo.

Map on page 144

selling goods for dollars, at prices well out of the reach of all but a handful of Cubans). Obispo has both types of shop: expensive looking dollar ones selling everything from designer clothes to sheets and duvets; and Cuban peso shops with almost nothing for sale.

Art lovers will enjoy a stroll along Obispo, as many artists rent space at the front of private houses. A considerable number have exhibited abroad and have international reputations. Most are worlds away from the often tacky art exhibited in the Plaza de Armas, but they are, of course, much more expensive.

Walking west up Obispo from the classical, columned **Banco Nacional de Cuba** on the corner of Calle Cuba, you find the former **Hotel Florida**, which has been in the process of renovation for some time. For a look into the past, peer into the dark interior of the **Drogería Johnson** (on the corner of Aguiar): its polished mahogany bench and ceramic medicine jars are straight from the 1920s. Its half-empty shelves give it the air of a museum, but it is still a working pharmacy, selling mostly state-produced herbal tinctures.

Visitors who wish to buy Cuban art should note that they need an export permit for any work of art from a state-run shop or gallery. See *Travel Tips* for more details.

A Hemingway haunt

Heading back down Obispo towards the Plaza de Armas, you pass the **Hotel Ambos Mundos** ❼, at No. 153. For $1 you can visit room 511 where Ernest Hemingway wrote *For Whom the Bell Tolls*: the room is tidily kept, with an antique typewriter (not Ernesto's) and several copies of American 1930s magazines (likewise). The hotel has been extensively refurbished and has a wonderful piano bar in the lobby. Opposite the hotel hangs a bell marking the original site of the University of Havana, which was founded here in January 1728. This bell originally tolled to signal the start of classes.

BELOW: the oldest house in Havana, Calle Obispo.

The next cobbled section of Obispo joining up with the Plaza de Armas has many historic buildings, and be sure to look for the holes in the street revealing the old water-course, which used to supply fresh water to the heart of town. The center for the city's restoration works, the Office of the City Historian, is at No. 117–119. This, the oldest surviving house in Havana, dating back to 1570, (and also one of its most photographed) now sells a number of books and souvenirs of Old Havana as well as the Havana Museum Pass (*see page 145*).

Few Habaneros *haven't heard of Eusebio Leal. He is the dynamic City Historian who is energetically spearheading the campaign to restore Havana to its full glory.*

South along Calle Oficios

Turning south out of Plaza de Armas, onto Calle Oficios, you reach almost immediately the **Museo Numismático** (open Tues–Sat 1–8pm, Sun 9am–1pm; entrance fee) – one of Old Havana's least visited museums, dedicated to money. Next door at Oficios No. 12, the **Casa del Arabe** ❽ (open Tues–Sat, 2.30–9.45pm, but closed 6.30–7pm; Sun 9am–1pm). A surprising number of Cubans are of Middle Eastern origin and this beautiful colonial mansion of Moorish appearance celebrates Arab culture. It has a museum, a one-room mosque, and a restaurant where you can eat tabbouleh and houmous.

Across the street is the **Museo de los Autos** ❾ or Car Museum (open daily 9am–6.30pm; entrance fee) – although just about any street in Havana would also have a case for this title. Here reside a fabulous collection of venerable roadsters and limos, including vehicles that the revolutionary youngbloods like Camilo Cienfuegos and Che Guevara would tour around Havana in, on affairs of state. Down the little Calle Justiz alongside is a place for dance enthusiasts: the **Caserón del Tango**, dedicated to the promotion of this Argentinian art form, which is a world apart from some of the more spontaneous, lively Cuban dances.

BELOW: inside the beautiful Casa de la Obra Pía.

On the corner of Oficios and Obrapía is the **Hostal Valencia**, the first colonial home in Old Havana to be converted into a hotel. It has just 11 rooms, grouped around a vine-draped courtyard with a pleasant bar and a restaurant. While a lovely place to stay, the hotel is invaded regularly by tourists during the day.

Obrapía and neighboring streets

Turn right into Obrapía, and you pass the **Casa de Oswaldo Guayasamín**, the city house of one of Latin America's foremost contemporary artists. Though Ecuadorean by nationality, he has always had a close affinity with Cuba and belongs to the same left-leaning artistic community that finds inspiration here, along with Gabriel García Márquez. The house has a shop selling costly lithographs, and possesses a couple of original paintings, including a striking portrait of his friend, Castro, presented to him on the occasion of his 70th birthday – but which *El Jefe Máximo* apparently did not consider particularly flattering.

One block south of Obrapía runs Calle Lamparilla, where Wormold had his vacuum cleaner shop in Greene's classic novel "Our Man In Havana." Sadly, there's nothing to see: No. 37 does not exist.

You then cross over **Calle Mercaderes**, which has several noteworthy buildings one block either side. Towards the Hotel Ambos Mundos is the Cuban-Mexican Society for Cultural Relations, housed in the **Casa de Benito Juárez** (entrance fee), which has a display of artefacts and costumes from different parts of Mexico. Then, at Mercaderes No. 117, you'll find one of the many new and elegant shops springing up in Old Havana – the **Tienda de Los Navegantes**, a shop beautifully fitted out in polished wood which sells maps (including plans of Cuban towns) and navigation charts, both old and new. On the opposite side of the street are the **Casa de Puerto Rico** and the **Casa del Tabaco** (open Tues–Sat 10.30 am–5pm, and 10.30 am–1pm; free), a fascinating little museum of tobacco and smoking well worth a quick visit. Many of the exhibits were donated by the world's most famous ex-smoker, Fidel Castro himself. Notice the cigar box in the shape of the house where Castro was born. You can also buy cigars fresh from a large humidor.

Back on Obrapía at No.158 is the delicious lemon-yellow **Casa de la Obra Pía** ❿ (open Mon–Sat 10.30am–4.30pm; entrance fee), once the home of the Calvo de Puertas family. The *obra pía* ("pious act") commemorates Martín Calvo de la Puerta's action in providing dowries for five orphan girls every year. The imposing doorway leads into a creeper strewn courtyard and one of Old Havana's finest colonial mansions. First built in 1665 and then enlarged in the 1700s, the building's best rooms are upstairs. Highlights include the rare *cenefas* or painted floral borders on the staircase (*see pages 164–5*), and the elegant, open-sided dining room.

Opposite is the **Casa de Africa** ⓫ (open Mon–Sat 10.30am–4.30pm; entrance fee), which has an impressive display of African artefacts, many of them donated by the city's African embassies or donated by Cuban leaders who received them as gifts whilst on trips to African nations. This museum gives ample demonstration of the way the Cuban authorities have allied themselves with that part of the Cuban heritage that had been ignored before the Revolution. The second floor is dedicated to the Afro-Cuban religions of Santería, Abakuá, and Palo Monte (*see pages 92–3*).

BELOW: selling vegetables from a street stall.

Running off the northern end of the Plaza de San Francisco is Calle Baratillo, where there's a sculpture garden in memory of Diana, Princess of Wales, and which is also the place to organize carriage rides around the Old Town.

A waterfront square

Walking in the rest of the Old City can be pleasant in any direction. Returning to the Hostal Valencia and walking south along Oficios brings you to another historic square, the **Plaza de San Fransisco**. At its center is the Fountain of Lions, built in 1836, and on one side the immense **Lonja del Comercio**, recently restored to house the offices of many foreign businesses. However, the main landmark here is the **Iglesia de San Francisco de Asís** ⓬ (entrance fee).

First built in 1608 and rebuilt in 1737, San Francisco's 130-ft (40-meter) campanile is one of the tallest on the continent and was once Havana's best lookout for pirates. The building was taken over by the English from 1762–3, and as it had been used for Protestant worship, Catholic *Habaneros* would never again use it as a place of worship. Since the 1840s, it has been a customs office, a post office and a warehouse. It is now a concert hall with regular performances of classical music, while its cloister houses a museum of Spanish colonial art and artefacts. One of the strangest exhibits inside is the pickled remains of Teodoro, a Franciscan monk, in jars set into the left side of the church.

Around Plaza Vieja

Stretching away from Plaza de San Francisco on all sides are newly restored cobbled roads and freshly painted mansions, many of them now cafes, stores, or art galleries. A short distance southwest is **Plaza Vieja** (Old Plaza) ⓭, built in the 1500s to create a space for bullfights and fiestas, and once one of Old Havana's principal squares. A famous fountain of four dolphins once stood here, but it fell victim to a 1930s "modernization." For decades an underground parking lot ruined any chance the square had of being picturesque, while the sur-

BELOW: the Lonja del Comercio, overlooking Plaza de San Francisco.

rounding buildings crumbled. But the square is now the center of renovation work, and by the time this book is published the traditional cobbles should have been relaid and a new fountain built. Several colonial buildings have already been restored. On the south is the **Casa de los Condes de Jaruco**, now home to the Fondo Cubano de Bienes Culturales (Cuban Fund for Cultural Products). This fine 18th-century colonial house has various galleries of art and glass work, with a pleasant café in the courtyard and rare murals upstairs. Its trio of *mediopuntos* are among the best examples of stained-glass windows in Havana.

On the western side of the square at San Ignacio No. 356 is a building where the native *malanbueta* (a reed-like plant) is woven to make items for the tourist market. Touring these workshops is much more interesting than you'd imagine. Next door more handicrafts (mainly dolls and wooden objects) are gaudily but attractively painted for sale in the tourist markets. Upstairs is an art gallery which often holds art and photographic exhibitions. On the southeastern corner of the plaza is the amazing Art Nouveau **Hotel Palacio Viena**, built in 1906, which has long been a *solar* – a residential hotel where many families live cheek by jowl. On the corner, next door, is the cosy little Bar Plaza Vieja.

Just to the northeast of the plaza is the **Museo Histórico de las Ciencias Carlos J. Finlay** ⓮ (open Mon–Sat 8–11.30am and 1.30–5pm; entrance fee), a museum to the history of science in Cuba named after the Cuban doctor who discovered the vector for Yellow Fever, a massive killer at the time, but something that has now fortunately been stamped out across the land. With its elegant Neoclassical lecture theater (where Einstein once gave a lecture) and 19th-century pharmacy (moved from Plaza Vieja), the museum is well worth a visit.

On the corner of Cuba and Sol is the **Convento de Santa Clara** ⓯ (open Mon–Friday, 9am–4pm; entrance fee), an enormous 18th-century convent, famous as a refuge for dowerless girls. Take a guided tour and you will see the vast tree-filled main courtyard, the Clarisa nuns' cells, and the lovely cloistered courtyard with a café-restaurant. The convent also houses a conservation institute where you can see all the restoration techniques being utilized in the renovation of Old Havana – including carpentry, the restoration of old tiles and the making of new ones. All the works in Old Havana have been undertaken using, wherever possible, the same materials and techniques as the original craftsmen.

Map on page 144

Restoration is giving a new lease of life to the Plaza Vieja.

BELOW: Palacio Viena, on the corner of Plaza Vieja

A duet of churches

South of here is the delightful **Iglesia Parroquial del Espíritu Santo** ⓰, Havana's oldest church. Built in 1638 as a religious retreat for "free Negroes," this fully-renovated gem displays Moorish influence in its façade and the cedar ceiling, and it features catacombs whose roof is supported by tree trunks. The chapel vault has a mural (sadly almost erased by time) of the Dance of Death.

A little further down Cuba you'll reach the lavish **Iglesia de la Merced** ⓱, dating from 1746. This is one of Havana's most famous churches as it's dedicated to Saint Mercedes, who becomes Obatalá in Santería. The day to visit is September 24, when hundreds of worshippers – often wearing white or carrying white flowers (Obatalá's color) – congregate to give tribute. At any time, you will see Santería devotees worshipping here, many of them initiates dressed all in white. Note the flower-sellers all around – flowers are a common gift of thanks for requests granted by the saints. The church itself is dark and ornate with wonderful *trompe l'oeil* frescoes.

A diamond set in the floor of the lobby of the Capitolio marks the theoretical center of Havana, and all distances from the city are measured from here. Don't be fooled – the stone is a fake.

Along the waterside

The atmosphere changes as you hit the busier streets on the fringes of Old Havana. This is not an area that attracts many tourists, but there are a few sights if you have time to spare.

By the harbor, where San Ignacio meets the dock road (here called Almeida de Paula), is a pretty little former church, the **Iglesia de San Francisco de Paula**. Now used as a study center for modern Cuban music, it has an interesting collection of art and photographs of Cuban bands and popular orchestras. North of here along the dockside road is the **Centro Wilfredo Lam** (open Mon–Fri and alternate Sundays, 8.30am–4.30pm; usually free, but there may be a small charge for some exhibitions; tel: 61 3288). This is dedicated to one of Cuba's most famous 20th-century artists, but also shows works by other Cuban and Third World artists in frequent exhibitions.

Back along the waterfront road you come to some interesting remnants of the old city walls, the **Cortina de La Habana**. Slaves worked for 23 years to build these walls, which were 5 ft (1.5 meters) thick and over 30 ft (10 meters) tall. The first walls were begun in 1674, but were altered and expanded up until the late 18th century. They ringed the old city until 1863, when they were torn down to allow the city to expand. Nearby stands a stark, dramatic monument to the Belgian ship **La Coubre**. This ship, carrying armaments for the Cuban army, blew up on 4 March, 1960, killing 72 sailors and dock workers: was it an accident or – as the Castro Government has always maintained – the work of the CIA?

BELOW: inside the Hotel Inglaterra.

Three blocks northwest up Avenida de Bélgica (or Egido) at No. 314 Leonor Pérez (also called Paula), is the house where Cuba's most revered figure was born. The **Casa Natal de José Martí** ⓳ (open Tues–Sat 10am to 6pm, Sundays, 9am–12.45pm; entrance fee), is just a small simple house, painted yellow and blue in typical Havana style. He lived here until he was five years old and the house contains everything pertaining to his life: letters, first editions, even locks of his hair. There is sometimes a queue to get in as the house is a popular place for school visits. Around the corner is the Moorish-Victorian **Estación Central de Ferrocarril** (Central Railway Station) – unmissable with its soaring twin towers.

Capital projects

Avenida de Bélgica follows the line of the old city walls, and you can follow it north (past a small farmers' market) to the enormous, grandiose **Capitolio** ⓴ (open Tues–Sat 10.15am–5.45pm, Sunday 9.15am–12.45pm; entrance fees for museums), which dominates the skyline all around. Built in the 1920s as the new presidential and governmental palace, it copied stone for stone the design of the Capitol in Washington DC, continuing the process of Americanization begun in 1902 when the United States effectively took over from Spain as Cuba's colonial master. Guided tours run through its proud interior into the former presidential offices and halls of Congress. The building now houses the Academy of Sciences, which is closed to visitors, but also several museums open to the public: the **Museo Nacional de Ciencias Naturales** (National Museum of Natural History), with some moth-eaten displays of fauna; the **Museo de Ciencias y Técnicas** (Science and Technology Museum); and the **Planetario** which holds shows every hour after 4pm.

Next door to the Capitolio is the flamboyant **Gran Teatro** ㉑, completed in 1837, and sometimes called El Teatro García Lorca. It contains several auditoriums – the gold auditorium is grand, if surprisingly small inside, with plush red seats and a bewitching painted ceiling – and cultural institutions, including the Centro Gallego for descendants of Galician immigrants, one of several Spanish social clubs in the city. Tours are offered through its many halls: ballet dancers work out in the sunny front rooms, while theater productions are rehearsed in the semi dark. The upstairs dance hall, where 2,000 couples once came for high-society events, is falling to pieces and used by set painters. There are still regular performances by the national ballet and opera companies, with tickets costing between $10 and $30 for foreigners (Cubans pay in pesos).

Washington DC comes to Cuba in the dome of Havana's Capitolio.

Parque Central

The Gran Teatro occupies one corner of the **Parque Central**, which, with its stately royal palms (many bearing tourist graffiti from the 1940s and '50s), always seems to be buzzing with activity from early morning until midnight. In

BELOW: the ornate façade of the Gran Teatro.

the center is a white marble statue of José Martí. The corner of the park nearest the Capitolio is called the Esquina Caliente or "Hot Corner" where men gather and debate, mainly about baseball.

Next door to the Gran Teatro is the splendid, neo-baroque façade of the **Hotel Inglaterra** ㉒, popular (not surprisingly) with travellers from England. The sidewalk outside its doorways, nicknamed "the Louvre Sidewalk," has been one of the busiest spots in Havana for generations. It was once a popular spot for pro-independence conspirators to come and speak, and one such occasion in 1869 prompted Spanish soldiers to open fire. Not all Spaniards were so ruthless: an officer who was protesting the execution of eight Cuban students in 1871 broke his sword against the hotel door, and a plaque commemorates his bold, humanitarian gesture. The Inglaterra was once one of the most opulent hotels in Havana, and the Moorish-influenced dining room off the lobby is still impressive – unlike the food. The small rooftop bar holds a salsa cabaret every night except Tuesday (entrance fee).

The rooftop restaurant of the Hotel Plaza is the best place from which to view the Bacardí Building, and provides a good view over the Parque Central too.

On the east side are the Cuban Supreme Court and a rather seedy shopping mall – thankfully in the process of restoration – and on the northeast corner the **Hotel Plaza**, with its grand columned lobby. The café-bar on the ground floor behind the lobby, with its stained-glass skylights, parrots and plants, is a popular meeting place for foreign businessmen cutting deals. Behind the hotel is the outrageous Art Deco **Edificio Bacardí**, an extravagant confection topped with the statue of a giant bat. This was the headquarters of the Bacardí Rum Company, which was based in Cuba until the family fled the island in the early '60s. The building dates from 1929, and looks like a giant three-dimensional mosaic – a strange mixture of Swedish granite, Cuban limestone, tiles and terracotta.

BELOW: Art Deco in full bloom with the Edificio Bacardí.

Hemingway's bar

Two blocks south of the Edificio Bacardí is **El Floridita** ㉓, made famous as Ernest Hemingway's favorite haunt (it features in his novel *Islands in the Stream*). It was frequented by the Hollywood set who came to Havana in the 1950s – Errol Flynn, Frank Sinatra, Eva Gardner, Gary Cooper and Marlene Dietrich were all regulars. *Esquire* magazine in 1953 ranked it with the 21 Club in New York, the Ritz in Paris and Raffles in Singapore as one of the world's best bars. It is claimed that the daiquiri cocktail was invented here, though some say it was actually concocted by miners in Santiago province. Certainly it was at El Floridita that the drink became famous, and Hemingway even invented his own version, the "*daiquirí special*," which is still served.

Not much else is the same as in Hemingway's day, when it was an informal, old-fashioned place, with ceiling fans and a three-piece band. Like an ordinary *bodega*, it opened out onto the street (which made it convenient for Hemingway to throw people he'd beaten up directly onto the sidewalk). Today it has been renovated and polished up into one of the most expensive restaurants in Cuba, with a bronze bust of Hemingway right near his favourite seat, on the far left of the original wooden bar. It still serves the best daiquiris in town, if overpriced at $6 each, but the bar lacks the atmosphere of the Bodeguita del Medio and the air conditioning battles with your frozen daiquiri in an attempt to freeze you first.

Map on page 144

The Zaragozana, a long-established restaurant next door to El Floridita on Monserrate, serves decent Spanish food.

The faded glory of the Prado

Running north of the Parque Central is the **Prado** (officially known as the **Paseo de Martí**), the historic, popular, promenading avenue lined by trees and lion statues that stretches all the way to the Malecón. Though officially part of

BELOW: shoeshine on the corner of the Parque Central.

Central Havana, it is generally considered to be part of Old Havana, and forms an easy landmark in the transition between touristy Old Town and the real city of working *Habaneros*. This boulevard, with its raised walkway set with colored marble and stone, has seen better days. Construction began in the late 1700s and continued until 1852, and its buildings were once home to Havana's richest, most aristocratic families. The area began to decline in the early 20th century when the mansions of the rich were mostly turned into casinos and nightclubs. The upper levels became notorious brothels, adorned with skimpily-dressed girls who would stand on the balconies to lure in custom.

Non-residents can make use of the Hotel Sevilla's oasis of a swimming pool for a daily charge of $5. Towels are available.

The practice has not entirely died with the Revolution, since nowadays the Prado attracts some of the worst pimps and *jineteras* in Havana, along with the odd bagsnatcher. However, they are outnumbered by ordinary folk going about their daily business or simply going for a stroll. Furthermore, some of the old buildings nearby have been turned into schools, and as they have no playgrounds, you will often see the children in their red and white uniforms having sports lessons or just playing on the Prado's raised walkway.

The Prado's most obvious landmark is the towering **Hotel Sevilla** ㉔ at No. 255, which featured prominently in Graham Greene's *Our Man in Havana*: the secret agent Hawthorne stayed in room 501. Beautifully restored in 1994, the Sevilla has a wonderfully Spanish ambience, with its cool lobby and a delightful blue-tiled patio café complete with fountain. The best view in the area is to be seen from the lavish 9th-floor restaurant: it is closed during the day, but the person on the door should happily let you in for a look.

Slightly further along is the **Academia de Gimnástica**, where Cuba's budding gymnasts and current stars train together. Strictly speaking, the building is not

BELOW: Arabic influence amongst the Prado's neglected mansions.

SEALING DEALS AND TYING KNOTS

The Prado is important territory. The area between Colón and Refugio has become widely known as an unofficial property market. Cubans are not permitted to sell property – only to exchange it. "*Se permuta*" signs pinned to doors and balconies around the city mean the residents want to exchange their house either with another in a different area, or, more commonly, because family pressure means they want two small houses for one large one. These are more difficult to fix since almost everyone has one large house and wants two smaller ones. This means money as well as property usually changes hands, illegally, and so people gather on the Prado to make illicit deals. Sometimes thousands of dollars change hands, in a country where the average wage is $9 per month.

Prado No.306 on the corner of Animas is the **Palacio de Matrimonios** (Palace of Weddings), where on Mondays, Wednesdays, Fridays and Saturdays, you can see wedding parties in hired tuxedos and frothing white dresses make their grand entrances and exits. Take a look inside too at the gilded, chandeliered luxury of this former aristocrats' palace. The non-religious ceremony has a strong socialist feel – the man promises to help his wife with housework and child care (though few Cuban men ever do).

open to the public, but you can sometimes persuade the caretaker to let you have a look at the stunning galleries upstairs.

The national art collection

Between Agramonte (Zulueta) and Avenida de las Misiones are two of Havana's most important museums. Coming first in a grim, modernist building is the **Museo Nacional de Bellas Artes** (National Museum of Fine Arts). The museum, which has suffered for years from architectural decay and lighting problems, is closed for renovation until mid-2000. This museum has Latin America's largest collection of antiquities, and fabulous works by Goya, Rubens, Velásquez, Turner, Gainsborough, and Canaletto. The collection of Cuban artists is the largest in the country, and although many of the earlier 20th-century styles seem derivative from movements in Europe and the US, there is still some fine work. Curiously, the post-revolutionary painting seems more energetic in the 1960s and '70s – inspiration seems to peter out by the 1980s.

The Museum of the Revolution

North of the Bellas Artes is the **Museo de la Revolución** ㉕ (open Tues–Sun, 10am–5pm, Sat until 6pm; entrance fee; extra charge for cameras), housed in deposed dictator Fulgencio Batista's former palace. You come first to a replica of the yacht **Granma** ㉖ – used by Fidel, Che and 80 other guerrillas to cross from Mexico to Cuba in 1956. The boat is painted brilliant white with green trim and set in a huge glass case as one of the Revolution's great icons. Around the *Granma* outside are other curious relics: a tractor converted into a "tank" by revolutionary troops; an old Pontiac with a double floor for smuggling arms

The Museum of Fine Arts possesses one half of Canaletto's View from Chelsea Bridge, *which the National Gallery of London tried (in vain) to buy in 1997. The artist originally divided the work into two since it proved impossible to sell as one piece.*

BELOW: recruits inspect the remains of a spy plane outside the Museo de la Revolución.

Map on page 144

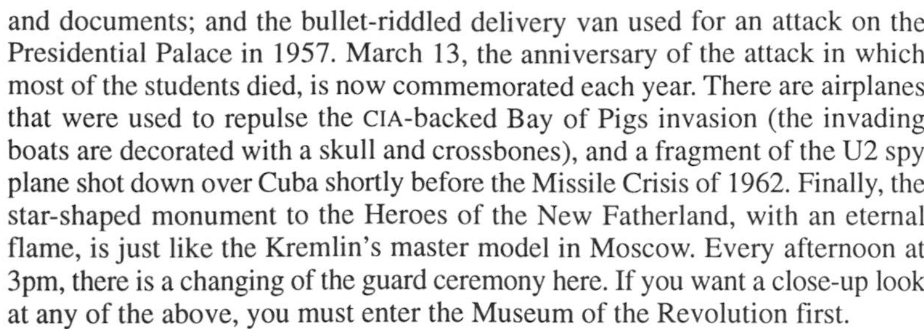

and documents; and the bullet-riddled delivery van used for an attack on the Presidential Palace in 1957. March 13, the anniversary of the attack in which most of the students died, is now commemorated each year. There are airplanes that were used to repulse the CIA-backed Bay of Pigs invasion (the invading boats are decorated with a skull and crossbones), and a fragment of the U2 spy plane shot down over Cuba shortly before the Missile Crisis of 1962. Finally, the star-shaped monument to the Heroes of the New Fatherland, with an eternal flame, is just like the Kremlin's master model in Moscow. Every afternoon at 3pm, there is a changing of the guard ceremony here. If you want a close-up look at any of the above, you must enter the Museum of the Revolution first.

George Bush, one of the US presidents in the Rincón de los Cretinos.

Permanently parked outside the front of the museum is a SAU 100 Stalin Tank, which Fidel Castro used during the battle at the Bay of Pigs. The Presidential Palace was worked in and lived in by all Cuba's presidents from its completion in 1913 until 1957, when Batista built the present Palacio in what is now the Plaza de la Revolución. The delicious white and gold interior was created by Tiffany's of New York.

Although the museum's exhibits are identified only in Spanish, the hallowed halls and the memorabilia laid out with quasi-religious reverence make excellent viewing. There are bloodstained uniforms from the failed attack on the Moncada Barracks, as well as the heavy black coat that Fidel wore during his famous trial (although the photos of a beardless Castro are perhaps more shocking); a guitar that revolutionary prisoners played in prison; and old poker machines from the casinos of the 1950s. Graphic black and white photos show victims tortured by Batista's secret police alongside little-seen images of Fidel and his band in the Sierra Maestra. Giant, complicated three-dimensional maps show the various guerrilla campaigns, while a somewhat disturbing life-sized dummy of Che bounds through a model forest looking serene, gun in hand. There is now a separate Che Guevara museum which tells his own story, complete with exhibits including cuttings from his beard, his Bolivian body bag – an old US mail bag – and his (over-) stuffed horse.

RIGHT: want to make a call?
BELOW: cruising in a timewarp town.

A small gift shop on the way out sells Che T-shirts, and don't miss **El Rincón de los Cretinos** ("Cretins' Corner"), devoted to former US President Ronald Reagan (shown in life-sized caricature with a cowboy hat and six-shooters), George Bush and the deposed Fulgencio Batista.

The end of the road

A stone's throw from the Presidential Palace, on Avenida de las Misiones, is the **Museo Nacional de la Música** ㉗, which has an extensive collection of Cuban instruments and a shop selling cassette recordings and CDs. In front of this museum you will see the mounted **monument of Máximo Gómez** ㉘, one of Cuba's great independence campaigners. Nearby, people queue for the *ciclobus*, which takes cyclists through the tunnel under the bay to Habana del Este. Right on the waterfront is the small fortress of **Castillo de San Salvador de la Punta** ㉙ (due to be transformed into yet another museum) in an area bustling with congregations of hitchers trying to get home. ❑

LOCALES (5c para cada 3 minutos de conversación)
Descuelgue el manófono.
2. Después de escuchar el 'TONO DE DISCAR' inserte la moneda
3. Disque el número deseado.
4. Añada una moneda al recibo del tono de aviso o su
llamada sera desconectada a los 20 segundos.
5. Si su llamada no es completada, cuelgue el
y su moneda sera devuelta.
DEVOLUCION

CUBA'S COLONIAL ARCHITECTURE

Colonial architecture in Havana may not be as decorative as that found in other Spanish colonies such as Peru, but it has a simple, solid elegance

Old Havana is, without doubt, the finest showcase of colonial architecture in Cuba. Its features are seen all over the island, however. Other places particularly worth visiting for their architecture are Camagüey, Gibara, Remedios, Santiago, and Trinidad.

MUDEJAR MAGIC

The strongest influence on Cuban colonial architecture came, of course, from Spain. In particular from Andalusia, where the so-called *mudéjar* style – a fusion of Christian and Muslim traditions that developed in medieval Spain – predominated at the time of the colonization of Cuba. Many of the early buildings in Havana were built by *mudéjar* craftsmen, who came by ship from Seville and Cadíz and adapted the styles they knew to suit the conditions in the Caribbean: primarily the hot climate and the relative paucity of materials. The talent of these craftsmen lay above all in carpentry. Woods such as mahogany and cedar were abundant in Cuba at that time, and were used to construct ceilings, doors, columns and railings, as well as furniture.

BOLD BAROQUE

The Baroque style reached Havana in the late 18th century. This more showy, sophisticated architecture proved to be a perfect medium for expressing the new-found confidence of a nation enjoying its first real economic boom – though the wealth was concentrated in the hands of a few. While undoubtedly grander than anything that had gone before, fusion with the existing *mudéjar* styles kept Cuban Baroque simple.

▷ **CUBAN BAROQUE**
Havana's Palacio de los Capitanes Generales marks the peak of Baroque refinement, but still uses *mudéjar* features, like the courtyard.

△ **GRILLED WINDOWS**
Grilles (*rejas*) across windows are a common feature. Originally made of wood, bars of wrought iron became popular in the 1800s.

△ ***MUDEJAR* CEILINGS**
The Museo de Arte Colonial in Old Havana has some of Cuba's finest *alfarjes* – the wooden ceilings built by Spanish carpenters, who would often adorn them with Islamic, geometric designs.

◁ **THE SQUARE**
This image of Havana's Plaza Vieja shows a typical square in the colonial period. The arcades at ground level enabled people to walk in the shade.

HOW TO BE COOL IN CUBA

The most striking features of Cuban colonial design are solutions to the problem of how to keep cool – namely, by creating the maximum amount of shade and ventilation.

- *Courtyards*: many houses were laid out around a courtyard, with arcades to enable residents to move from room to room in the shade.
- *Doors*: these were very tall and had small windows or *postigos* that could be opened to provide light and ventilation without having to disturb the residents' privacy by opening the whole door.
- *Ceilings*: vaulted ceilings (*alfarjes*) were not easy to build but were high and cooler than flat ceilings.
- *Mamparas*: these swing doors, with decorative glass panels and fancy woodwork (above), were popular in the 1800s and allowed air to circulate between rooms.

◁ **BAROQUE FLOURISH**
The swirls of Havana's Cathedral façade are typical of Cuban Baroque. Since the local limestone was hard to work with, the style was less elaborate than in Europe.

▽ **FLORAL FRESCOES**
Murals, called *cenefas*, often with floral motifs, were used to decorate the lower half of interior walls. Those in the Casa de la Obra Pía (*see page 153*), seen here, are among the few to survive.

◁ **GLASS AS ART**
Colored glass panels (known as *lucetas*, *vitrales* or *medio puntos*) over doors or windows were decorative but also functional since they filtered the harsh sunlight.

CENTRAL HAVANA, VEDADO AND MIRAMAR

The Miami-style hotels of Havana's tourist district contrast with the dilapidation of Central Havana, a place made colorful by its scenes of everyday life and its bustling markets

Bounded by the giant avenues of the Malecón to the north, Prado to the east, and Calzada de Infanta to the west, **Centro Habana** is a bustling, overcrowded district seething with life and noise. The area dates mostly from the 19th century, when Havana, having burst out from its city walls, began to spread across the swampy lands and rocky pastures to its west. The buildings are salt-pitted and tumbledown, and unlike in the historic Old Town, you will not see restoration programs in progress here. One-time graceful mansions and town houses have been divided up between many families and become *ciudadelas* – little tenement "cities."

But look beyond the crumbling façades and you will see that many of these houses are true palaces, even if their glory has faded: pizzerias lit by priceless chandeliers; a narrow passageway lined with lofty marble columns; a pink marble bathroom with gold fittings, but nevertheless waterless and shared by 30 families. The city may slowly be falling into ruin, but the inhabitants certainly don't let that interfere unduly with their lives. Centro Habana is full of life. The street theater of everyday normality (Cuban style) lights up each corner, and for the traveller searching for an experience beyond the world of cafés and museums, this is the place to be.

LEFT: statue of Independence hero, General Máximo Gómez.
BELOW: waiting for customers at the market.

Behind the Capitolio

Tucked just behind the Capitolio at Industria No. 502, on the corner of Dragones, is the **Fábrica de Tabacos Partagás** (Partagás Cigar Factory) ❶. The famously strong Partagás cigars have been rolled here since 1845 (*see pages 206–7*). There are two guided tours a day (Mon–Sat, 10.45am and 1.30pm), but you may have to book in advance – check with reception. The factory has a cigar store, but prices are often higher than in hotel stores. Real cigar smokers should resist the temptation to buy from the hordes of *jineteros* gathered outside. Despite the many stories they tell, all are fakes and definitely not worth the asking price of $20–$50 a box. Immediately behind the factory at Amistad No. 407, the equally famous **H. Upmann** cigar factory also offers guided tours. Some of the best Montecristos are rolled here.

Flanking the southern side of the Capitolio is the **Parque de la Fraternidad**, a busy, pleasant park with the Friendship Tree at its heart. This tree was planted in the soil of 17 nations by the delegates of the 1928 Pan-American conference to cement friendship between the countries of the Americas. Also here is an unofficial car museum – rows of old American cars in varying states of repair whose owners tout for business from passers-by. On the west side is this area's main bus terminal, and you will see long lines for the buses and *camello* road-trains that roar out to all parts of the city. A ride in one of these monsters costs 20 Cuban *centavos*. On the south-west corner of the park is the beautiful 19th-century **Palacio de Aldama**, which houses an institute detailing the serious matter of the history of Communism and Socialism. The building has some unique painted ceilings, now somewhat spoilt by strip-lighting, but it is not open to the public on a routine basis.

Cuatro Caminos is a good place to change money on the black market if you need Cuban pesos, but branches of "Cadeca" usually offer better rates and are generally a safer option.

The Queen's Avenue

The hectic **Avenida de la Reina** (also known as Avenida Simón Bolívar, and which becomes Avenida Salvador Allende as it heads out towards Vedado) effectively forms the southern boundary to Centro Havana as far as most tourists are concerned. Two sites are worth noting from amongst the multitude of shops and apartment blocks along its length. Firstly a magnificent Gothic church, the **Iglesia del Sagrado Corazón de Jesús**, and a little further on, the splendid **Casa de Cultura de Centro Habana**, which is always alive with musicians, dancers and other aspiring artistes, who rent magnificent, decaying rooms for a pittance in order to conduct practice sessions. Running southwest from the end of Reina is Calle Máximo Gómez, better known as **Monte** (meaning "Hill"). This is an area that has been crumbling away for decades but is now in the process of renovation, and only just in time. The imposing 19th-century mansions were once the summer homes of the city's colonial aristocracy, as it was cooler here than in the rest of the city during Havana's sweaty summers.

The street begins south of the Parque de la Fraternidad, at the bustling farmers' market of **Cuatro Caminos** – the largest market in the city, with separate

BELOW: stately cars parked near the Parque de la Fraternidad.

sections for fruit and vegetables, meats, flowers and prepared foods. There is a *guarapera* selling frothing, freshly-pressed sugar cane juice for a peso a glass. This entire area is good for peso street food: peanut *turrón* candy bars (2–3 pesos); reasonably cheesy pizza (5–10 pesos); *refresco* soft drinks; and *granizados* – shaved ices flavored with syrup, costing about 20 *centavos*, for those with stronger stomachs. The area is thick with good *paladar* restaurants too. There is an interesting herbalist opposite the market with strong links to Santería, selling medicinal herbs alongside votive jars, candles and the bead necklaces dedicated to the *orishas* or gods of the religion.

Map on pages 140–41

A handful of stalls on Cuchillo in Barrio Chino sell snacks and delicious fruit batidos *(milkshakes).*

Chinatown

Easily reached by heading west along Dragones from the Partagás cigar factory is the **Barrio Chino** ❷ – Havana's tiny Chinatown, centered around Calle Cuchillo and San Nicolás. The first Chinese arrived in Cuba in the mid-19th century to build the country's railways, but the community lost much of its homogeneity after the Revolution, and has to a large extent been integrated into the wider melange of Cuban society. Still, many people in the area have distinctly Asiatic features and, confusingly, almost everyone is known by the nickname "*Chino*".

This area used to be notorious as the center of Havana's red-light district. Times have changed, and the infamous **Shanghai Theater** – described in *Our Man in Havana*, and which once specialized in live sex acts and pornographic movies – has now re-opened as a nightclub specializing in karaoke. There is a good Asian restaurant, the **See Man**, inside the theater. However, the **Restaurante Pacífico**, at the end of Calle Cuchillo on San Nicolás, is the most

DRUMS, DANCE AND A DREAM

Those who take an interest in Afro-Cuban religions and the powerful, percussion-driven music and dance that accompanies their ceremonies, should check out the Callejón Hamel in the district of Cayo Hueso – a tiny backstreet off San Lázaro and Lucena in northwestern Centro Habana. The area has been dedicated to Palo Monte and Santería, with shrines to the various *orishas* and tiny shops selling art and artefacts.

The walls and houses of the alley have all been plastered with enormous, boldly-colored murals that are the work of a single man: the artist, Salvador. A nattily-dressed man with the air of a showman, he began this project in 1990, fired by his religious heritage, and there is considerable local pride in his achievement, especially considering the scarcity of resources available to him.

Sunday is the day to go, since then an Afro-Cuban band strikes up with *batá* drums and fierce dancing for the mixed crowd of tourists and locals. The atmosphere is good, but you'd be wise to take care of your valuables, or better still, leave them behind in your hotel. You are welcome to take photos, but expect to make a contribution. Likewise, women sit at the gated entrance offering good luck charms and fortune telling for an "offering" (dollars preferred!).

BELOW: Afro-Cuban dancer on Callejón Hamel.

famous Chinese restaurant in Havana. Castro and Hemingway were both regulars once, but these days the food is mediocre and not even distinctively Chinese. Hemingway's son Gregory described a 1950s visit to the Pacífico with a five-piece Chinese orchestra on the second floor, a whorehouse on the third floor and, on the fourth floor, an opium den. On Calle Cuchillo, a small, not especially Chinese market is a hive of activity and does sell a few unusual things – fresh lychees and goose eggs for example – but watch out for pickpockets. There are also a few places specializing in Chinese medicine.

Cubans love their rum, but can rarely afford brand names, so they turn to the homemade stuff. The quality varies: it is always fairly rough, but the worst is known as chispa-tren *("train sparks") and can literally take your breath away.*

An interesting Santería church, the **Iglesia La Caridad** ❸ is to be found at the edge of Chinatown on Manrique and Salud. This glorious frescoed and golden church – its dark interior lighted by candles and full of incense, flowers and choral music – is undergoing restoration, and the entire church is held up by wooden props along one side. Just inside the door is a shrine to the eight saints who are the most powerful *orishas* of Santería.

The famed Malecón: artery of the city

The more common side of Central Havana to visit is to the north. Emerging from the Castillo de la Punta at the top end of the Prado, the 3-mile (5-km) **Malecón** seafront drive is Havana's main artery, running straight through to Vedado. Hitchhikers, young lovers, prostitutes, families on a stroll, wheeler-dealers, elderly couples walking the dog – the cross-section of city life you will see here is complete. By day, children splash in the crashing (and heavily polluted) surf as salsa bands rehearse in the buildings above. At weekends, by night, the Malecón turns into one huge party. Hundreds gather to dance and drink rum. The houses along the front here, having suffered from decades of neglect, are now

BELOW: the Malecón, Havana's famous promenade.

undergoing desperately-needed renovation, with many individual buildings having been sponsored by different Spanish provinces. A Portuguese company also plans to completely rebuild the dangerously pitted seafront walkway.

Alas for the romantics, the plans also include preventing waves crashing over the sea wall. The spectacle of the sea roaring up against the Malecón is a part of the Havana scene, but the "big seas" (in storms, giant breakers reach as high as 30 feet, or 10 meters) do tremendous damage to the roads, paths and buildings. In winter, the road often has to be closed to traffic, and on some occasions the sea wall is severely breached, flooding vast areas of Central Havana. For the time being at least, you can still enjoy the dramatic spectacle from September to April – the biggest and best waves are to be seen in Vedado, by the Hotel Riviera and the statue of Calixto García, where the Malecón meets Presidentes. In contrast, when the tide is low and seas less enraged, you can see the eroded remains of 19th-century stone baths carved from the coral limestone of the shore at the Old Havana end of the Malecón. The area was known as the **Elysian Fields** and was a fashionable place to see and be seen. There were once separate bathing areas for white men and women, and blacks.

The **Hotel Deauville** at Malecón and Avenida de Italia (Galiano) is Centro Habana's only tourist hotel. Halfway along the promenade is the **monument to Antonio Maceo** ❹, a huge bronze statue of the 19th-century revolutionary hero. There is a code to the city's equestrian statues of heroes: when the horse is rearing up, with both hoofs in the air, the subject died in battle; if only one hoof is raised, the man died of wounds sustained in battle; if the horse has all four hoofs firmly on the ground, the hero in question died peacefully in his bed. Maceo's horse is rearing since he died fighting the Spanish in 1896. The large tower block behind the statue was built before the Revolution as a bank, but it is now Cuba's flagship hospital, the **Hermanos Ameijeiras**. A couple of blocks inland is **Callejón Hamel** ❺ (*see page 169*).

Vedado

West of Centro Habana, the Malecón courses through to the green and leafy suburbs of Vedado. The whole district of Vedado was loosely modeled on Havana's alter ego, Miami: the streets are identified by numbers (running east to west) or letters (running north to south); and some Art Deco buildings now vaguely recall the shabbier corners of South Beach in the 1970s before its restoration. With palm trees lining many streets, it is a pleasant place to stroll or stay, even if it has less character than Old Havana.

The suburb is heralded by the twin towers of the **Hotel Nacional** ❻, Havana's most splendid hotel, perched on a rocky outcrop overlooking the Malecón. Modelled in the 1920s on the Breakers Hotel in Palm Beach in Florida, it has serene gardens with good views of the sea and a long, shaded verandah with comfy wicker chairs where you can escape for a while the hubbub of the city. The café bar has walls lined with pictures of the "in crowd" who stayed here in its glory days – the likes of Errol Flynn, Frank Sinatra, Ava Gardner, and Clark Gable. The Malecón rolls on past the **Monumento al Maine** ❼, dedicated to the

Map on pages 140–41

TIP

Surf's up! When the waves are big you can see young boys indulging in the highly dangerous sport of riding the manhole covers as the seas rush in along the drains, forcing the heavy metal covers up into the air.

BELOW: boys playing the national game.

To see Coppelia ice cream park as it was, watch it feature in the Cuban film Fresa y Chocolate *("Strawberry and Chocolate") – a wry, metaphoric reference to the limited choice of flavors actually available in a place (or system) which claims to be offering so much choice.*

memory of the 260 American sailors killed when the ship blew up in Havana in 1898 (*see page 31*). A plaque on the monument declares, "Victims Sacrificed by Imperialist Voracity in its Eagerness to Seize the Island of Cuba." The American eagle that once topped the two graceful columns was felled by an angry mob with a crane, in 1960.

The **US Interests Section** – a faceless mass of concrete and tinted glass – lies a little futher west. Directly facing the building is the most filmed and photographed billboard in Cuba (*see page 73*). Large numbers of over-dressed Cubans hoping to join the "*Señores Imperialistas*" with an entry visa gather in a little park on Calzada and K as they wait to be interviewed by the consulate. There are always throngs of people here: many come from out of town and sleep in their cars for days waiting to be interviewed.

A couple of blocks south, on Calles 13 and L, is a building right out of Gotham City. It was designed by the same architect who built the Empire State Building in New York. The families of many famous revolutionaries live here. Next door by the park is the **Hospital Camilo Cienfuegos** – now a dollar-only hospital specializing in eye diseases. Another Vedado landmark is the blunt, curved **Edificio Focsa** ❽: although it looks like Stalinist architecture, it was actually built in the capitalist 1950s, and the Russians liked it so much that they copied the design for 10 buildings in Moscow. The name is an acronym for a defunct company.

Vedado's hotel zone

Inland from the Nacional are numerous hotels: the elegant **Hotel Victoria**, on 19 and M, has a pleasant coffee bar; the **Hotel Capri,** on 21 between N and O, still retains the sleazy 1950s air it had when George Raft co-owned the hotel (and the basement bar opposite – the **Monseigneur** – was the scene of many Mafia meetings in the days when the mob ruled Havana). Calle O continues across the famous commercial artery of 23rd Street – known as **La Rampa**. Here there are a couple of budget hotels, the **Hotel Vedado** and **Hotel St John**, many of the city's airline offices, a few nightclubs and a whole host of fairly cheap but good snack bars. One block away, on the Calzada de Infanta, is the **Casa Abel Santamaría** ❾, the home of the joint leader of the 26th of July Movement with Fidel Castro in the 1950s, who was brutally tortured to death after the failed Moncada attack of 1953. Castro himself attended many meetings here.

To the west is the rather squat, ugly form of the **Hotel Habana Libre** ❿. For only three months before the Revolution, it was open as the Havana Hilton, but afterward Fidel himself and his embryonic government took over an entire floor for several months. The ground floor cafe was the scene of a famous attempted poisoning of Castro, who used to spend late nights here chatting to kitchen staff (the cyanide capsule intended for his chocolate milkshake broke in the freezer). Although the lobby is rather dismal these days, it parades Havana's most baroque selection of suspicious characters and prostitutes. The view from the 25th-floor bar is one of the best in the

BELOW: the casual look on a Vedado street.

Map on pages 140–41

city, but the hotel knows this and charges non-guests several dollars to visit.

Opposite the Habana Libre is the famous **Coppelia Ice Cream Park** ⓫, built by the revolutionary government to replace the notoriously elitist Vedado ice cream parlors (where poorer and darker-skinned clients need not have bothered queuing up). This famous institution has been closed for "repairs" for some time – but no repairs appear to have yet started: some *Habaneros* say that the closure for building work is just a ruse as the government simply can't afford to import the ingredients for the ice cream any more.

Around the University

The **Universidad de La Habana** ⓬, two blocks southeast of here, is a lovely group of classical buildings in golden stone, placed around a cool and leafy garden: reached by climbing an impressive flight of steps at the head of San Lázaro. Anyone can stroll around the campus, and it is a good place to meet young Cubans, who love to practise their English. In the campus lies the **Museo Antropológico Montané** (open Mon–Fri, 9am–noon and 1–4pm; entrance fee), an excellent collection of Pre-Columbian artefacts including the famous wooden Tobacco Idol, found in Maisí, at the far eastern tip of Cuba.

The fastest-spreading fast food chain in Havana.

Opposite the University is a stark, fascinating **monument** containing the ashes of **Julio Antonio Mella**, a student here who founded the Cuban Communist Party and was assassinated in Mexico in 1929. On January 28 – José Martí's birthday – a tremendous torchlit march starts from the monument. Around the corner, the **Museo Napoleónico** ⓭ (open Mon–Fri 9am–4pm; entrance fee) is housed in a delightful mansion at San Miguel No. 1159. Orestes Ferrara, a 19th-century politician, brought much of this unexpected collection

BELOW: the famous Hotel Nacional.

of Napoleonic memorabilia from his travels in Europe. It includes Napoleon's death mask, his pistols from the Battle of Borodino and a fine library.

Where Calzada de Infanta meets Avenida Salvador Allende (also called Carlos III) you'll find the **Quinta de los Molinos** ⓮, reached via a tree-shaded drive. This was the site of 18th-century snuff mills built alongside the Zanja Real watercourse to Old Havana (*see page 147*), and parts of the original 16th-century aqueduct have been incorporated into the water garden and grotto. The grounds are somewhat neglected but provide a quiet haven; you sometimes find musicians practising beneath the trees. The gardens were a popular place to promenade in colonial days, when the rich had their summer palaces across the road in the Cerro area. Mixing business with pleasure, people could inspect slaves here before they went to market. The lovely house at the center of the gardens was once the colonial Governor's summer palace, and is now a museum to General Máximo Gómez.

Private license plate.

Revolution Square

South of here is the **Plaza de la Revolución** ⓯, the governmental heart and soul of modern Havana – though the word "soul" is hardly applicable to such a barren place. The whole region has been given over to Eastern European-style monolithic architecture, where faceless bureaucrats can labor unseen behind thick concrete walls. Yet the Revolution is not entirely to blame: many of the office buildings were built during the Batista era, when the dictator expressed his own taste for intimidating, colossally uninspired design, as seen in the flat, grey former Justice Ministry, which was finished in 1958. It now houses the Central Committee of the Communist Party, which includes Fidel's office.

BELOW: Che Guevara surveys Revolution Square from the Ministry of the Interior building.

Map on pages 140–41

The plaza is the scene of Cuban political rallies several times a year, and the site of Fidel's most famous eight-hour speeches. On the anniversary of Che's death, schoolchildren come here to lay flowers. At the center is the mighty **Monumento José Martí** ⑯ (open Tues–Sat 10am–6pm and Sun 10am–2pm; entrance fee, with hefty extra charges for cameras and videos), which now houses an informative museum, including the original design plans for the Plaza and Martí monument. Ascend the monument (which costs extra) for an impressive 360° view of the city: Habana Vieja looks a very long way away. Behind the monument is the monolithic **Palacio de la Revolución**, where senior ministers, including Fidel Castro, have their offices. Visitors are not permitted to photograph the Palacio, or even loiter behind the monument.

The **Ministerio del Interior** is Cuba's most sinister and secretive organization (though vast, it has just one number listed in the phone book, which no one ever answers), and yet it is housed in Cuba's most photographed building. The outside wall has a giant **mural of Che Guevara** executed in black metal, and best viewed at night when clever lighting gives the face an eerily three-dimensional look. Inexplicably, the plaza is also the location for the **José Luís Guerra Aguiar Museo Postal** (open Mon–Fri 9am–5pm; entrance fee), which has stamps from every corner of the globe and a philately shop. Also nearby, on Boyeros and Bruzón, is the **Museo de la Historia de Deportes** (Sports Museum) (open Tues–Sun 10am–5pm; entrance fee).

One woman's tombstone in the Colón Cemetery is carved as a domino with two threes on it: a passionate player, she died of a stroke when she failed to draw a double three during a crucial game.

City of the dead

You could take a taxi from outside the main bus terminal (just down the road from the Plaza de la Revolución) to the arched stone entrance to the **Cementerio de Colón** (Columbus Cemetery) ⑰ (open 6am–6pm; entrance fee includes a guided tour). This is one of the largest necropolises in the world. Construction began in the 1860s, when *Habaneros* ran out of church catacombs. A competition for its design was won by a young Spaniard, Calixto de Loira y Cardosa. Although the cemetery's Latin motto reads "Pale Death enters both hovels and the palaces of kings," Calixto used a pattern to ensure that the dead could be separated by social standing. The 15-year work of building the cemetery was, however, too much for the designer and he died at the age of 32, thus becoming one of the first to be buried in his own creation.

Wealthy *Habaneros* competed to create the most impressive family tombs, and the result is a decadent, morbid atmosphere that would have appealed to Edgar Allan Poe: a stone forest of Grecian temples, urns, columns, angels, Madonnas, crucified Christs, and angels of mercy. The mausoleums are an eclectic mix of Gothic and Neoclassical styles, and statues of faithful dogs lie supine at their masters' feet.

Among the more famous sites is the Monument to the Medical Students, eight young men who were executed in 1871 for desecrating the tomb of a Spanish journalist who attacked the independence movement. The image of Justice over the tomb does not wear the traditional blindfold of impartiality, and the scales she holds are tipped to one side. Cubans also make

BELOW: the monolithic Martí Monument.

pilgrimages to the tomb of Amelia Goyre de la Hoz: though buried in 1901 with her child at her feet, when she was exhumed the child was supposedly found in her arms. There are also two pantheons dedicated to the Afro-Cuban secret society of Abakuá (*see pages 92–3*).

Western Vedado

Avenida de Los Presidentes runs northwest from the Plaza de la Revolución, crossing La Rampa, which is here a pleasant avenue, lined with formal gardens and the former homes of the rich, most now government buildings. At Calle 17 No. 502 between D and E is the **Museo de Artes Decorativas** ⓲ (open Tues–Sat 11am–6.30pm and Sun, 9am–1pm; entrance fee). It has a wonderful collection of decorative arts, especially porcelain, which is displayed in a series of furnished rooms ranging from a Rococo salon and Regency dining room to a gorgeous Art Deco bathroom.

Heading back to the Malecón along Presidentes, you pass a gigantic marble tribute to past Cuban presidents. It is a favored hangout for disaffected, long-haired youths, or *frikis,* and is one of the few places in the city where graffiti is tolerated: the monument is covered in it, much being witty and politically pertinent. Next door to the Hotel Presidente, the **Casa de Las Américas** ⓳ cultural center, founded by Che Guevara, has a collection of art and archives and is housed in a landmark Art Deco building with blue glass windows.

Towards Miramar

From here, the Malecón heads west. There is a dusty, open-air artisans' market on the corner of Calle A, and just beyond rises the **Hotel Riviera**, built by Jew-

BELOW LEFT: the tomb of Amelia Goyre de la Hoz in the Columbus Cemetery.
BELOW RIGHT: dressed up in Miramar.

ish mob boss Meyer Lansky as a last attempt to recreate Las Vegas by the Caribbean. He had a suite on the 20th floor, but for tax reasons he was listed as the hotel's kitchen manager. The interior of the Riviera is still pleasantly evocative of the 1950s, and there is a very decent swimming pool, but the hotel has now been both dwarfed and outclassed by the **Hotel Meliá Cohiba** next door.

The Cohiba – which took five years to build using voluntary labor – is one of Cuba's rare five-star hotels. In addition to downtown Havana's only escalators, it has a series of outrageously exclusive stores, a good cigar bar (where you can purchase single classic cigars if you don't want to invest in a box of 25), and the **Disco Aché**: techno music used to be the order of play here, but this has been replaced by live bands playing Cuban tunes.

A couple of blocks west of the Riviera is the expensive, over-rated **Club 1830**, with a Spanish restaurant in the **Torreón de la Chorrera** castle by the sea. Right alongside, the Malecón disappears into the tunnel under the Almendares River, re-emerging as Quinta Avenida in Miramar.

Miramar

There are various ways to cross into Miramar: via the **Túnel de Almendares**, across the road bridge from Calle 23, or by the **bicycle bridge** that carries Calle 11 over the river. This bridge crosses the river at a particularly picturesque spot, where ramshackle wooden houses come down to the river amidst gardens of palms and hibiscus, and a motley collection of wooden fishing boats lie moored to homemade piers or rotting away against the bank; the scene has a peculiarly Asian feel. The bridge is the only bicycle and foot bridge over the Almendares, and it is usually jammed solid with bicyclists, all ringing their bells.

Map on pages 140–41

The Meliá Cohiba outdoes the Riviera in most respects, but the Riviera still has the number one dance venue in town: the Palacio de la Salsa – where most of Cuba's top salsa stars play in front of an exuberant crowd.

BELOW: private enterprise in full flow, selling peanuts and coffee.

La Maison, at Calle 16 701, on the corner of 7 Avenida (tel 33-1543) in Miramar, houses several boutiques selling clothes and accessories, but far more entertaining are the nightly fashion shows.

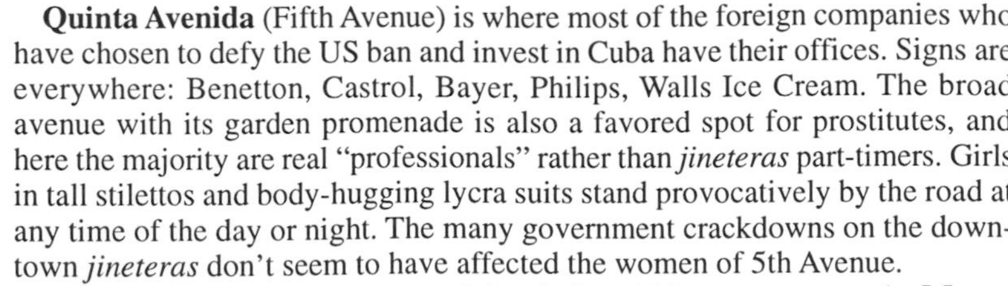

Quinta Avenida (Fifth Avenue) is where most of the foreign companies who have chosen to defy the US ban and invest in Cuba have their offices. Signs are everywhere: Benetton, Castrol, Bayer, Philips, Walls Ice Cream. The broad avenue with its garden promenade is also a favored spot for prostitutes, and here the majority are real "professionals" rather than *jineteras* part-timers. Girls in tall stilettos and body-hugging lycra suits stand provocatively by the road at any time of the day or night. The many government crackdowns on the downtown *jineteras* don't seem to have affected the women of 5th Avenue.

Quinta Avenida is home to one of the city's quirkiest museums – the **Museo del Ministerio del Interior** (MININT), which has displays cataloguing the CIA's many attempts to assassinate Castro; the gadgets on show include a camera disguised as a cigarette lighter and a radio transmitter hidden inside a fake rock. At Quinta No. 6502, between 62 and 66, the giant **Russian Embassy** towers over Miramar. This enormous complex of offices and apartments once housed the various offices of the Soviet Union. Now the independent former Soviet States have moved out and have their own embassies, leaving the greatly-reduced Russian mission somewhat lost and lonely.

Primera Avenida (First Avenue) is where you will find the Teatro Karl Marx, good for concerts and movie premieres. On Primera between 60 and 62 is Havana's Aquarium, which gives dolphin shows. It also has an endangered species breeding program, and treats injured animals before returning them to the wild. Che Guevara's youngest daughter Celia is a vet here. The building work seemingly forever in progress between Quinta and the sea is to be luxury apartments and houses for foreigners, and yet more hotels.

Miramar has one other interesting exhibition – the **Maqueta de La Habana**, located at Calle 28, No. 113 between 1st and 3rd Avenidas (*see map page 186*). This vast scale model of the city (open Tues–Sat, 2pm–6pm; entrance fee) took nine builders 10 years to construct, and is the second largest of its kind after a model of New York. Every street, every house, every vacant lot, every tree is faithfully represented, constructed out of cigar boxes; different colors show which districts date from which period. The model sits inside the so-called **Pabellón** (Pavilion), with an office responsible for overseeing the development of the capital attached.

BELOW: the unmistakable Russian Embassy in Miramar.

Further out

South of Miramar, in the Alturas de Belén district, is the famous **Tropicana** nightclub, while to the west extend endless green suburbs, such as **Cubanacán** and **Siboney**, where many government offices are located. Many party functionaries also live out here, and though the remote location might seem inconvenient, Cubans will tell you that it makes perfect sense to them – it gives them the least chance of being seen.

At the furthest outskirts of the city is the **Marina Hemingway** (*see map page 186*). Today there are accommodations and several expensive restaurants and duty-free stores here, but don't be fooled – apart from the name, there is not the slightest connection to the writer. From the marina, the road carries on west towards the province of Pinar del Río. ❑

A Night at the Tropicana

The roulette tables may be gone, but not a great deal else has changed in the Tropicana nightclub – Havana's most famous cabaret spot since it first opened in 1931, and the only place of its kind that has operated more or less continuously throughout the austere years of the revolution. Kitschy, crass and gleefully sexist, the Tropicana (between Avenida 43 and Línea T in the Marianao district in western Havana) is everything that Cubans love in live entertainment.

Shows start at 9.30 every evening except Monday, weather permitting (billed as an open-air "paradise under the stars," it is forced to cancel shows regularly in the rainy season). Guests arrive from 8.30 for drinks or dinner. The place is lit up like a Christmas tree: blue neon signs announce the entrance, and a huge fountain with statues of frolicking naked women is bathed in blue and red. A small band warms up the crowd at the entrance, to add to the carnival atmosphere.

Whatever you think of the actual show, the Tropicana's setting is breathtaking. Tables fan out like sunbeams around the semi-circular stage, with enough room to seat 1,400 and stand many more; tropical trees enclose the amphitheater in a sheltering cocoon; and amongst the foliage, large neon lights spell out the names of musical demigods like Carmen Miranda and Nat King Cole. On a good night, the warm tropical air is seductive and the stars are visible through the treetops (this being Cuba, there is also the odd cat running around between the audience's legs, bringing the tone back down to earth).

With the triumphant blare of a 20-piece band, the show begins. Women in silver lamé coats and top hats float across the stage on trapezes. Dancing mulattas leap past in a blur of feathers, glitter and long legs. A bizarre pageant may be thrown in. Then, as if to mock the power shortages elsewhere, dancers appear with giant, blazing candelabras sprouting bizarrely from their heads.

It's the sort of extravaganza preserved in the rest of the world only in old black and white movies. In fact, to enjoy the Tropicana, it's best to turn your mental clock back about 40 years. Despite the Revolution's progressive social legislation, Cuban women are still brought up to titillate men with their appearance, and Cubans genuinely love their vast, hectic tit-and-bum shows; lesser versions can be seen around the island – the best being in Santiago de Cuba.

Another reason that Havana's Tropicana has survived is that it earns tourist dollars: the entrance fees ($50 for the best seats) include a thin cocktail, but not the use of a camera. Meanwhile, the Tropicana is a prime haunt for Cuba's most gorgeous and voracious *jineteras* on the hunt for single men, introducing themselves as "dancing students" who just happen to be catching the show.

The first half of the performance, lasting from 9.30 to 11pm, is the most spectacular; the second half, from midnight to 1.30 or so, is a relatively sedate round of singers with a few backup chorus girls. The discotheque attached to the club goes on till dawn. ❑

RIGHT: a candlelit dinner with a difference.

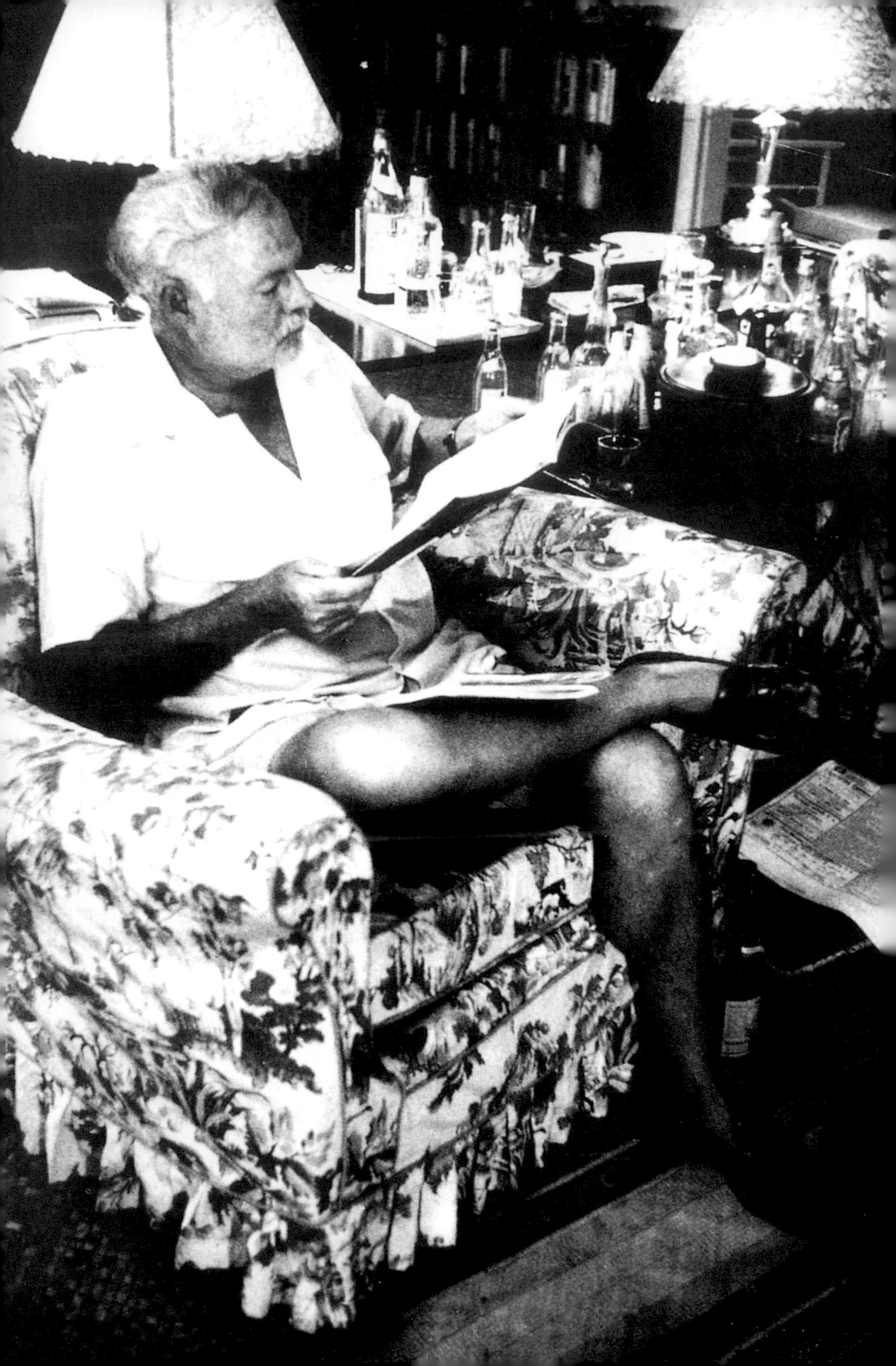

On the Trail of Hemingway

Still loved in his adopted country, Papá Hemingway has left a trail of sites connected with his life, including his beautiful estate residence and the fishing village of Cojímar

Maps:
Area 186
City 144

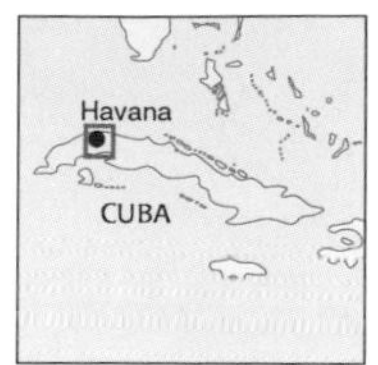

For more than 20 years, the Nobel Prize-winning writer Ernest Hemingway lived in and around Havana, drinking in its bars, fishing off its shores and using Cuba as the background for some of his most famous writing, including *The Old Man and the Sea*. Often called simply Ernesto or *Papá*, he is the Cubans' favorite *yanqui*. Only José Martí receives more literary accolades, and even Fidel has sung his praises: when he went to the Sierra Maestra during the Revolution, Castro took *For Whom the Bell Tolls*, Hemingway's epic of the Spanish Civil War, to learn about guerrilla warfare.

Hemingway's interest in Cuba began in the late 1920s, when he began crossing the Straits of Florida from his home in Key West on marlin fishing trips. The island's laid-back, sensual atmosphere seemed the perfect antidote to the values of his Midwestern Protestant upbringing, and he soon became a regular in the bars of Old Havana. Returning from the Spanish Civil War in 1938, he moved into the Hotel Ambos Mundos on Calle Obispo; from there he could stroll the nine blocks to his favorite bar, El Floridita, cutting a distinctive figure in his cotton shirt, scruffy khaki shorts and moccasins.

The journalist Martha Gellhorn, soon to become Hemingway's third wife, was not content to live in a hotel room. She found a house advertised called Finca Vigía – a former cattle farm on the site of a Spanish fort with magnificent views over Havana. The couple bought it in 1940 for $18,500 cash, and, though Gellhorn later divorced him, Hemingway stayed on there for virtually the rest of his life.

The world's most famous writers and movie stars made the pilgrimage to his tropical refuge, joining the writer on marlin fishing trips in his custom-made luxury yacht, the *Pilar*. Hemingway may not have always been the most gracious host (one biographer describes him as "boastful, lying, obscene, boring, overbearing, ill-tempered, touchy, vindictive and self righteous"), but few could resist an invitation.

During World War II, Hemingway honed his macho persona by converting the *Pilar* into a gunship and searching the Cuban coast for lone German U-boats (luckily for him, he never found one, although he claimed to have spotted one which submerged before he could approach). He left Cuba for a stint as war correspondent in Europe, then returned to settle into a famous and drunken old age. His ponderous figure and bristly white beard became so well-known in Havana that a chorus of "*Papá! Papá!*" greeted him wherever he walked, but strangers approaching him in bars were not always welcome, as the inebriated writer was as likely to punch them as to say hello – though he always apologized afterwards.

In the mid-1950s, Hemingway donated his medal

LEFT: Hemingway in the Finca Vigía. **BELOW:** Hemingway's room in Old Havana's Hotel Ambos Mundos.

A very old man of the sea: Gregorio Fuentes, friend and assistant of Ernest Hemingway, is still living in Cojímar, but go soon if you want to meet him.

for the Nobel Prize for Literature to the Cuban people. It was installed in the Virgin of Charity church at El Cobre, near Santiago, and remained there until 1988, when it was briefly stolen. It was recovered however, and is now kept in a Santiago bank vault. He stayed in Cuba until 1960, when serious illness provoked his return to the US for cancer treatment. This proved unsuccessful and, in 1961, he killed himself with a shotgun in Idaho.

The Old Man and the Revolution

Hemingway's attitude towards the Cuban Revolution is still hotly debated, with both pro- and anti-Castro forces claiming his support. While in Cuba, Hemingway had kept a distance from the activist artistic community in Havana, and although he had been so vocal in his attitude to the Spanish Civil War 20 years before, he remained silent on the situation in his adopted home.

He reserved his verdict for private conversation. Biographers agree that Hemingway was heartily sick of how Batista had been changing Cuba (in 1958, some government soldiers even shot his dog). And the writer's macho instincts were aroused by the drama of the guerrilla war and the characters of Fidel and Che. "This is a good revolution," he wrote to one friend; "an *honest* revolution." When Batista fled, he commented: "*Sic transit hijo de puta*," (there goes the son of a bitch). One of his last comments before he died, however, was that he hoped the US would not push Castro into the communist camp.

Politics didn't get in the way during Castro and Hemingway's only meeting, during the Hemingway Fishing Competition in Havana in 1960. Fidel won an armful of prizes, and Ernesto awarded the trophies. They had a long conversation – about marlin, what else? After Hemingway's death, Castro escorted his widow, Mary Welsh Hemingway, to the former home, which had been confiscated by the government, to retrieve some possessions and papers.

BELOW: memorial bust at Cojímar.

The Hemingway Trail

Today there is a well-worn route for Hemingway fans to visit in and around Havana. The best place to start is in the Old City, where the recently restored **Hotel Ambos Mundos** (*see page 151*) has preserved his room as it was when he wrote *For Whom The Bell Tolls* in the 1930s. **El Floridita** (*see page 159*) bar and restaurant has a Hemingway bust by his favorite chair and serves up the writer's own daiquirí mix. **La Bodeguita del Medio** (*see page 149*) retains more atmosphere than most Hemingway haunts, and is where he would drink his *mojitos* (a drink he helped to popularize), even if the authenticity of the sign bearing his signature behind the bar is in doubt. Avoid the remote **Marina Hemingway** to the west of the city – as there's little to see or do (*see page 178*). The famous annual marlin fishing tournament held in Hemingway's honor actually takes place out of **Tarará** marina to the east of the city, and is held in July, when some of the biggest marlin run.

It is worth hiring a taxi to visit the two other great Hemingway attractions. The first is the **Hemingway Museum** at **Finca Vigía**, 7 miles (10 km) from Havana city center in the suburb of **San Francisco**

de Paula. The house lies at the end of a long, leafy driveway and is surrounded by gardens. The mansion is much as Hemingway left it (his last wife, Mary Welsh, took only some letters and paintings), although as a precaution against theft visitors can only peer in through the windows. Among the relics are 9000 books, Hemingway's original Royal typewriter and innumerable animal heads on every wall, trophies from African hunting safaris.

Also on display is Hemingway's Mannlicher carbine: with it unloaded, he used to show his friends and wives how he one day planned to commit suicide, much to their consternation. He did indeed remain true to the jest. Connected to the main house is a four-story tower, from which the estate gets its name – *vigía* means "look-out". Mary Welsh had intended that Hemingway should write on the top floor, but he never liked the tower and used it instead to store his fishing gear. The pool where Gary Cooper once lolled and Ava Gardner swam naked is still there – as is, nearby, Hemingway's yacht, the *Pilar*.

Maps: Area 186 City 144

"Don't know how a writer could write surrounded by dead animal heads," sniffed Graham Greene, after he had seen the large number of Hemingway's hunting trophies.

The fishing retreat

The most relaxing stop on the Hemingway circuit is to the little fishing village of **Cojímar**, some 6 miles (10 km) east of Havana (*see page 188*). Hemingway kept the *Pilar* moored here, and used it as the setting for *The Old Man and the Sea*. When a film version of the book was made, most of the fishing scenes were shot off Cabo Blanco, Peru, since Cuban marlin rarely make dramatic leaps out of the water when hooked.

The palm-fringed village has kept its laid-back Caribbean flavor. A charming seafront promenade starts at a cube-shaped Spanish fortress, now occupied by the Cuban military. Opposite is Cuba's most affectionate memorial to Hemingway: a bronze bust made from boat propellers donated by local fishermen. At the other end of the promenade, overlooking the sea, is **La Terraza** restaurant, which figures in *The Old Man and the Sea* and was Hemingway's local favorite. Today it has been done up and does well out of its literary connections. You can eat some of Cuba's best seafood here and the views and sea breeze cannot be beaten. Photos of Hemingway fishing cover the wall but, oddly, like the scenes from the film, most were taken in Peru.

Finally, no visit to Cojímar is complete without an encounter with Gregorio Fuentes, Hemingway's fishing guide for nearly 30 years (and a model for Santiago in the novella). Fuentes was also involved in Hemingway's attempts to hunt down German U boats. Having celebrated his 100th birthday, Gregorio's mind is still surprisingly sharp, and he seems unfazed by the parade of tourists who come to take his photo. In fact, as a good revolutionary, he sees talking to tourists as his patriotic duty, to help Cuban tourism bring in foreign exchange.

Fuentes' memories of his long years with Hemingway may be a little faded and formulaic, but the reservoir of affection is limitless. "Of the Americans as a people," he declares to anyone who will listen, "there are good and bad. But I have never met a more intelligent man in the world than Ernest Hemingway, nor one more humane." ❑

Below: Old Man and the Sea sculpture at Marina Hemingway.

LA EMP M MIXta
SALUdA EL 35
ANIVERSARIO de LA
REVOLUCION
VENCEN LOS QUE
LUCHAN Y RESISTEN

AROUND HAVANA

Grand fortresses, suburbs soaked in Afro-Cuban traditions, and a rare head of Lenin are among the attractions here. There's also a notably bizarre religious procession

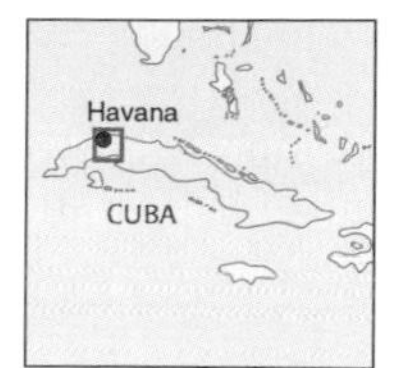

Over the past century, Havana has sprawled away from its well-protected bay and port facilities to incorporate what were once separate towns and villages. As a result, several day trips from the capital's center are actually still within what is officially known as the **City of Havana Province**. Further into the capital's rural hinterland is known as **Havana Province** – often referred to as *Havana Campo* ("rural Havana").

This confusing distinction is worth knowing: city maps stop dead at the borders of the City of Havana Province, and there are no separate road maps of Havana Province. Tourist attractions in both areas are few and far between, but if you're not going anywhere else in particular, it's certainly worth considering an excursion to get an idea of Cuba's provincial life. Even within Havana City, once you get past the endless suburbs of low-rise apartment blocks and factories, there are farming areas and small towns that could be almost anywhere on the island.

LEFT: farmers in Havana Province.
BELOW: El Morro, seen from the Malecón.

The great fortresses across the bay

From Old Havana, a short tunnel dips beneath the bay to the **Castillo de los Tres Santos Reyes Magos del Morro**, which is fortunately known by the simpler title of **El Morro** ❶ (open daily, 9am–8pm; entrance fee). This 16th-century fortress, with 10 ft (3 meter) thick walls, was constructed from blocks taken from Cuba's coastal reef and took more than 40 years to complete. It still dominates the Havana skyline to the east, especially at night when floodlit. The views from here are superb, whether around the bastion's vertiginous ramparts, back towards the city, or out at sea, from where the main **lighthouse** can be seen 50 miles (80 km) away.

The castle was once a vital part of the city's defenses. On the lower level, closer to the harbour, is the **Batería de los Doce Apóstoles** (Battery of the 12 Apostles), with each of its 12 cannons bearing one of their names. In colonial times, these guns would be fired at 9pm (a rite now re-enacted in the neighboring fortress of San Carlos de la Cabaña, *see page 186*) to announce the closing of the city gates and the raising of a great chain, which was hauled up between El Morro and the Castillo de la Punta in Old Havana. The chain closed the bay to pirate ships in the days when Francis Drake sailed these seas. The pirate Henry Morgan was told by former English prisoners in Havana that he would need at least 1800 men to take the city – he didn't try. Bizarrely, there are still several pieces of modern artillery directed out from El Morro towards the Straits of Florida, as a symbolic defiance against a *yanqui*-inspired invasion.

Havana's San Carlos de la Cabaña fortress is the largest of all the Spanish colonial fortifications in the New World.

There are three **museums** at the Morro castle: one dedicated to navigation, one to the history of the castle itself, and one to pirates. There is also one of Havana's most atmospheric restaurants, **Los Doce Apóstoles**, on the seafront.

Nearby, the **Castillo de San Carlos de la Cabaña** ❷ (open daily, 10am–10pm; entrance fee), was built from 1764–74, after the departure of the British invaders. It too has some interesting **museums**. One of these documents the fortress in colonial days, when many independence fighters were shot here. A good number of Batista's followers met the same fate after the victory of the Revolution in 1959, when Che Guevara used the fortress as his headquarters. Another small museum contains some fascinating Che memorabilia.

At 9pm every evening, the atmospheric ceremony of the **firing of the cannon** (called *El Cañonazo*) is conducted in period military dress, to signal the obsolete practice of the raising of the harbor chain. Although nowadays they only fire blanks, the noise is authentic, and the ceremony is fun, especially as locals often outnumber tourists. Much of the fortress, although in the process of being

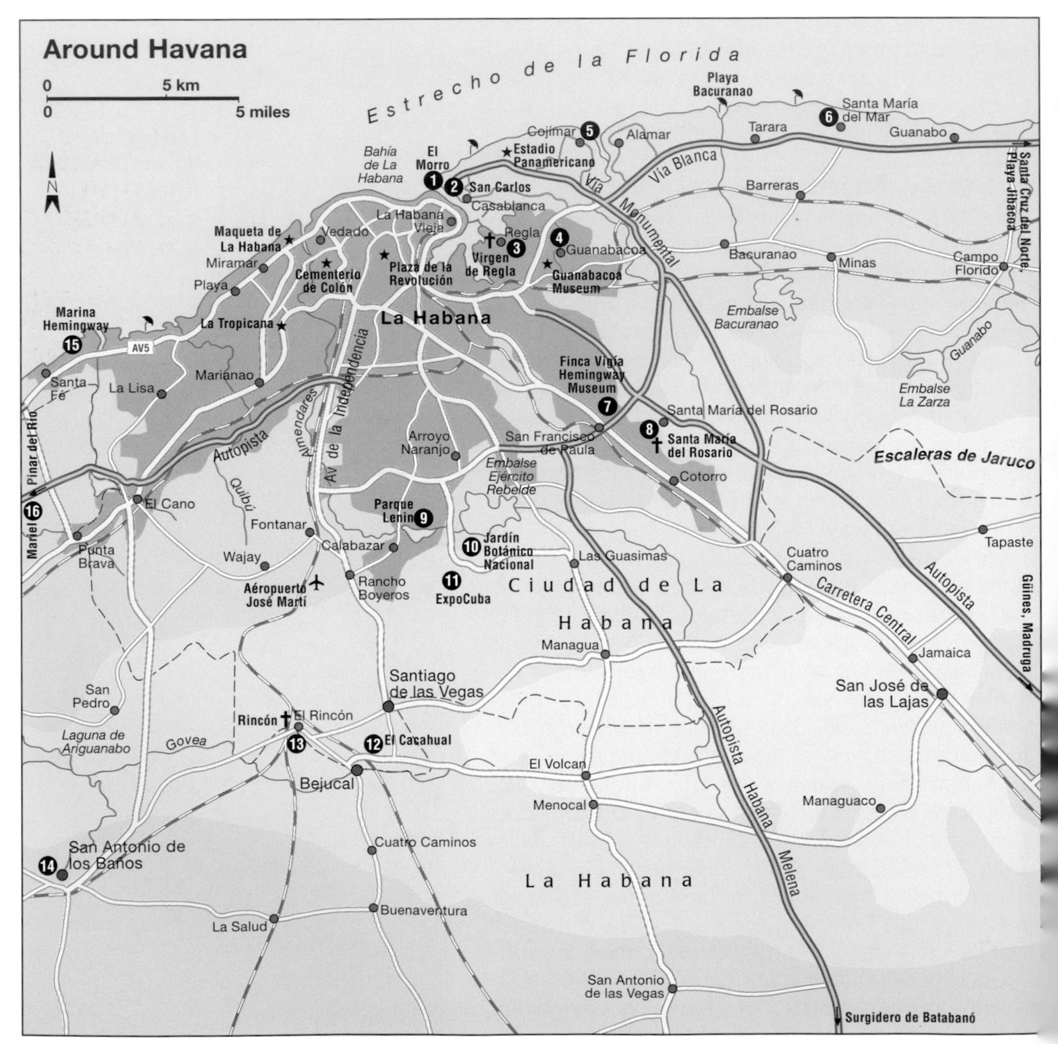

restored, is in a fairly dangerous condition – there are a lot of sheer drops from the high walls, which are neither roped off nor signposted, so take care when exploring. There is one of Havana's most scenic bars, **La Tasca**, and an excellent restaurant, **La Divina Pastora**, at the foot of the fortress on the waterside.

Map on page 186

The eastern suburbs

The most enjoyable way to reach the ramshackle little town of **Casablanca**, to the south of the fortress, is actually by ferry from Old Havana, costing only 10 centavos. You may see passengers dropping paper into the sea – they are ridding themselves of their problems in a Santería ceremony. Ferries for Casablanca leave from the foot of Calle O'Reilly behind the Plaza de Armas, and others leave for Regla and Casablanca from the foot of Calles Luz and Santa Clara.

Casablanca has balconied houses scattered along the shoreline, and exudes a sleepy air. One of its principal buildings is the domed, white national observatory, the **Observatorio Nacional**; and here, too, is the statue which dominates the bay – **El Cristo de Casablanca**. This statue of Christ, carved from Italian marble by Cuban sculptor Jilma Madra, was inaugurated in December 1958, only shortly before the fall of Batista. In the early years of the Revolution the statue was struck by lightning and the head fell off. The Government had the figure repaired – to the consternation of some Communists who felt it a "waste of the people's money" to repair a religious monument.

When Havana residents are suffering from a streak of bad luck, they sometimes say, with a roll of their eyes, "I'm heading for Guanabacoa" – to perform a cleansing ritual.

South of Casablanca, **Regla** ❸ is an old town famous in the past for smugglers, and which once held Havana's bullring. Today the only ring in sight is the ring of heavy industry surrounding it, though the old town is still appealing. The **Museo Municipal de Regla** (open Tues–Sat 9.30am–6pm, Sun 9.30am–1pm; entrance fee) on the pretty Calle Martí, tells the town's history and has a strong Santería bias. Santería is also featured in the **Fiesta de los Orishas** ceremony, held every Tuesday night at 8pm in the Palacio de Turismo, right by the ferry landing. However, this has little to do with the real business of Santería, and is put on only for tourists.

BELOW: an imposing statue of Christ looks across the harbor from Casablanca.

Near the Palacio is the lovely early 19th-century **Iglesia de Nuestra Señora de Regla** (open daily). This church is dedicated to the black **Virgen de Regla**, the patron saint of Cuba's sailors. Her counterpart in Santería is **Yemayá**, goddess of the sea, a woman prone to sudden rages and anger. You will see worshippers making offerings here, many dressed in blue, or wearing blue and crystal beads – the colors of Yemayá. Her day is September 8, when there is a fascinating procession in honor of the Virgin. The church also has an altar to Santa Barbara, twinned in Santería with **Changó**, God of war and machismo. Offerings here are in red, the color of Changó, and his day is the 4th of December. There is another **Santería shrine** – this time to San Lázaro, or Babalú-Ayé – near the Parque on Calles Juan Bosco and San Joaquín in Guanabacoa.

Afro-Cuban center

Santería is strong not only in Regla but also in several of the towns across the bay. **Guanabacoa** ❹ is renowned in Cuba for its connections with Afro-Cuban

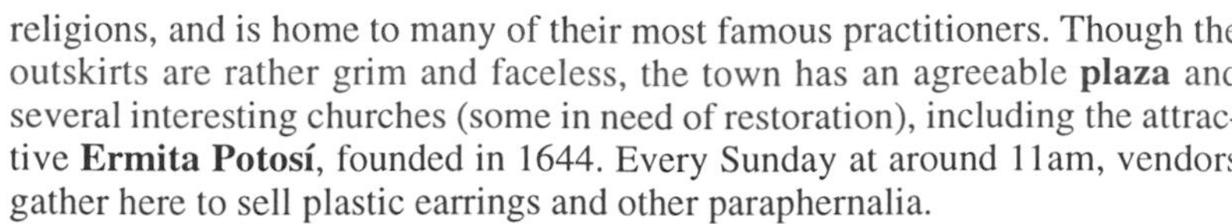

religions, and is home to many of their most famous practitioners. Though the outskirts are rather grim and faceless, the town has an agreeable **plaza** and several interesting churches (some in need of restoration), including the attractive **Ermita Potosí**, founded in 1644. Every Sunday at around 11am, vendors gather here to sell plastic earrings and other paraphernalia.

The **Museo Municipal** (Calle Martí 108; open Wed–Mon & Sun pm) is most famous for its exhibitions on Afro-Cuban cults, but it also has plenty on the town's past – though this will be of limited interest if you speak no Spanish. There is lots about Pepe Antonio, who headed local resistance to the English invasion of 1762. Less heroically, Guanabocoa was a nexus for the slave trade from the time of its foundation in 1607. Wander along **Calle Amargura** ("Bitterness Street"), where slaves were dragged en route to their executions.

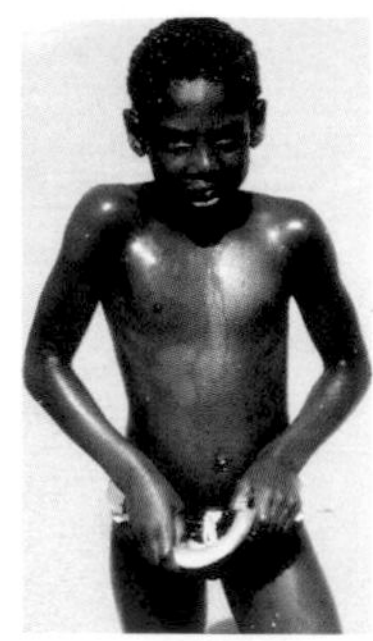

The coast east of Havana has a string of beaches frequented by both Cubans and tourists – at least in summer; don't expect to see many locals on the beach in winter.

As for modern religion, the best known priest in Guanabacoa is Enriquito, whose house is on the official tourist circuit. It contains rooms devoted to the two main Afro-Cuban religions, Santería and Palo Monte, while Enriquito's "family compound" up the street includes animals, an African-looking yard and a fine example of the religious vessel of Palo Monte, known as a *nganga*, which looks rather like a small cauldron. It's a commercial deal: Enriquito charges to be photographed and his grandchildren are not in the least camera-shy either. Another photogenic spot is the **Cementerio**, a true city of the dead with above-ground mausoleums littered with offerings.

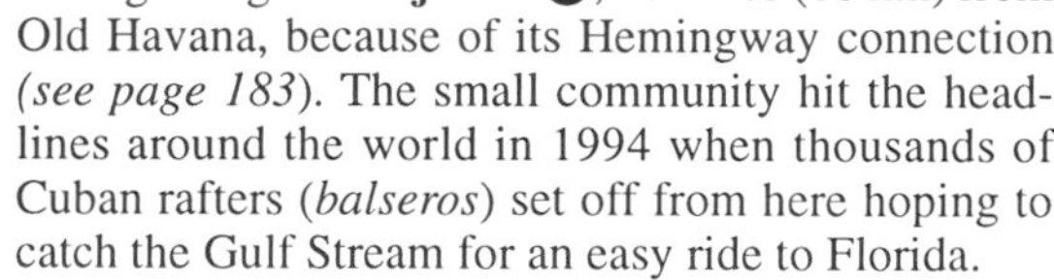

Swimming spots

Scattered along the coastline east of Havana are several sights worth visiting. A popular destination is the fishing village of **Cojímar** ❺, 10 miles (16 km) from Old Havana, because of its Hemingway connection (*see page 183*). The small community hit the headlines around the world in 1994 when thousands of Cuban rafters (*balseros*) set off from here hoping to catch the Gulf Stream for an easy ride to Florida.

BELOW: a Cuban beach bum.

Just off the highway before Cojímar is the **Villa Pan Americana**, a complex of sports facilities, apartments and a hotel built for the 1991 regional games (*see page 117*). The Cuban volunteers who took on the huge task of building the complex now live in the athletes' apartments, though some are still used for athletes competing at the nearby stadium.

Across an inlet to the west of Cojímar lies **Alamar**, a suburb built by volunteers, known as micro-brigades, after the Revolution. Originally planned for 40,000 people, it now has closer to 100,000, mostly in a depressing array of five-story walkup apartment blocks. Supposedly it is the grimness of the place and its distance from Havana which have earned Alamar the nickname of "Siberia" in some circles.

Beyond Alamar stretch a series of beach resorts known collectively the **Playas del Este** (Eastern Beaches). The natural settings are pleasant enough, and there are a couple of resorts catering to tour groups, but many towns and facilities range from drab to dismal. The closest beach is **Playa Bacuranao**: on a small horseshoe-shaped inlet, it is a favorite with families and is packed in July and August. Then comes a 10-mile (16-km) stretch of open sea, sand dunes, coconut palms, and, in some places, a distressing amount of litter. The sand starts at **El Mégano** and continues to **Santa María del Mar** ❻, which has a good beach and is the most pleasant section of this coast, with a number of seafront hotels. Further on, you come to **Guanabo**, an old seaside town with a number of wooden bungalows built in the 1920s and 1930s – looking like Key West conch houses, they are very popular with Cubans. The beach here is usually much livelier than almost anywhere else along this stretch of coast.

Map on page 186

Further east lies **Santa Cruz del Norte**, site of Cuba's largest rum distillery (the home of Havana Club). Just inland from here is the sugar mill **Central Camilo Cienfuegos**, originally founded by the American Hershey Chocolate Company in 1917, during the sugar boom. The adjacent company town itself still retains many of its original American buildings, although largely in sad decline. The Hershey train, as it is called, still runs through the town daily, on its route between Casablanca and Matanzas: to go the whole way is a bumpy, four-hour journey in an old ramshackle train, but it is an unforgettable trip.

Opposing ideological backgrounds, but a happy partnership.

The coast road continues past the attractive **Playa Jibacoa** and then along the **Litoral Norte** (North Coast) beach resort complex, consisting of a series of rustic cottages amongst coastal vegetation. Most geared up to international travelers is **El Abra**, with an Olympic-sized pool and a gorgeous beach nearby. From here, the highway continues into Matanzas Province (*see page 213*).

Southeast of Havana

To the south of Regla is the suburb of **San Francisco de Paula**, with the Hemingway Museum at **Finca Vigía** ❼ (*see page 182*). Heading southeast out

BELOW: Cubans at the beach.

TIP

Parque Lenin has a famous restaurant, Las Ruinas, inside a 1960s building which incorporates the lichen-covered walls of an old plantation home. The simple but elegant interior and good food attract diplomats and other expats, but the menu caters to all budgets.

of the capital along the Autopista Nacional (National Highway) and turning off at El Catao, you come to the town of **Santa María del Rosario** ❽, a lovely place with tall trees, old houses and pleasant inhabitants. The main attraction is the 18th-century **Cathedral** – best visited on a Sunday afternoon (mass is held at 2.30pm), which is the only reliable time of the week when the baroque paintings and statues can be seen. Across the shady plaza is the restored **Casa del Conde de Bayona**, once home of the Count of Bayona, a sugar baron notorious for executing a group of rebellious slaves (*see page 26*). The site where the leaders were executed is marked on the **Loma de la Cruz** (Hill of the Cross), up a steep street from the plaza. The plain wooden cross was erected as a warning to other slaves, and two flanking crosses were erected in 1959 to stand for the thieves crucified in the New Testament.

Continuing onwards, to the east of the highway you'll find the **Escaleras de Jaruco** nature park, which marks the highest point of the area inland from Guanabo (which is not saying much). From here you can head back along the winding country roads to the coast, passing **Campo Florido**, an old rural village in the heart of a cattle-raising area. Alternatively you can carry on further southeast to **Madruga**, a town with strong Afro-Cuban religious connections, where a Santería house is open to tourists.

Lenin lingers on

Directly south of Havana on the airport road (officially called Rancho Boyeros, but Avenida Independencia on most street signs) is **Parque Lenin** ❾, a vast stretch of gently rolling parkland with tall trees and bamboo stands (open Wed–Sun, 9am–10.30pm). After years of stagnation in the Special Period years, the park is gaining a new lease of life. Some rides, shows and the miniature railway have reopened and there are many new cafes serving Cuban people in pesos and foreigners in dollars. Amongst the many general attractions there is a monument and museum to the park's creator, Celia Sánchez and, most famously, a giant, well-tended stone head of Lenin – one of the last such monuments left in the world. There is also an equestrian and health center, **Club Hípico** (open to tourists and Cubans Wed–Sun, 9am–4.30pm), which offers horsey sports as well as saunas and massages for those who are less active.

South of the park is the **Jardín Botánico Nacional** ❿, the largest botanical garden in Latin America. Looking after the vast areas of pasture and woodland is a struggle, and some areas are sorely neglected. The Japanese garden is well maintained, however, and there is a series of attractive greenhouses with tropical, desert and temperate flora, as well as an extensive herb garden, which supplies medicinal plants to many of Havana's *yerberos* (herbalists). The garden has a herbal tea room, a botanical bookstore, a plant shop and Cuba's only vegetarian restaurant (serving such daring things as potato ice cream). A tour, including guide and transport, costs $3.

Across the road lies **ExpoCuba** ⓫, a sprawling area of pavilions celebrating Cuba's achievements in science, health, education and the arts.

BELOW: a rare chance to see a monument to Lenin, in Parque Lenin.

Further South

A well-maintained two-lane road continues onwards towards Cuba's south coast. The town of **Managua** has many traditional wooden houses with high ceilings and plant-filled patios, but the region is full of military installations, so make sure there are no "Zona Militar" signs about before taking photographs. Back in the country, the houses all maintain vegetable gardens and fruit trees. There are rows of *ceiba* (silk cotton) trees, their bark looking like elephant skin.

About 13 miles (20 km) from the coast, the soil becomes red and the terrain flatter. This is the "Banana Republic" of Batabanó. Endless banana groves are guarded by armed farmer militias, some on foot, others on horseback. These work to scare away "banana bandits" who make off with the ripening fruit for sale on the booming black market.

At a well-marked crossroads, turn left for the town of **Batabanó**, or press on straight ahead for **Surgidero de Batabanó** (*see map page 198*) on the south coast. In the 16th century, this was the first site of Havana. Today, it is a rather seedy and depressing place, and most people come here only because it is the departure point for hydrofoils and ferries heading for the Isle of Youth. Just two blocks from the Caribbean is the old **Hotel Dos Hermanos**: lobster and shrimp fishing are important in the area, and the hotel restaurant often features them on the menu. During the Prohibition era in the United States, both hotel and town were stops along the bootleg trail, and veteran staff members can recall tales of visits by Hollywood and gangland celebrities.

Heading back towards Havana, the road passes through **Bejucal**, once the last stop for Cuba's first railroad, completed in 1837. Thanks to enormous sugar wealth, the "iron horse" was pioneered in Cuba before Spain. It was built by

Ceiba *trees are almost never cut down, in keeping with beliefs of Central American and African origin that regard them as sacred.*

BELOW: fishermen near Batabanó.

The El Rincón pilgrimage on the night of 16 December is a startling, and sometimes disturbing, spectacle. Many penitents walk, while others crawl for miles on bleeding knees, or drag themselves by the palms of their hands, with a rock or box of stones chained to an ankle.

enslaved blacks and indentured workers from Ireland and the Canary Islands, all of whom worked 16 hours a day on starvation wages. The town today has an 18th-century **church** and restored colonial residence that has been turned into a restaurant, **El Gallo**. For an alternative cultural experience, catch an outside cinema screening on fine nights. Further north is **El Cacahual** ⓬, where Cuban independence hero Antonio Maceo is buried, and where ceremonies were held welcoming back troops returning from Angola at the end of the 1980s.

The small town of **Santiago de las Vegas** is a sleepy place which wakes up just once a year for the **Procession of the Miracles**. On the eve of December 17, the Day of San Lázaro – patron saint of the sick – people come from all over Cuba to the little church of **San Lázaro** at **El Rincón** ⓭, just south of town, to pray for help or forgiveness. Thousands of people – a mixture of penitents and people who come just to join in – process slowly through the town to the church, where the pilgrimage culminates with a mass held at midnight. The scenes inside the church are often emotional, with people shouting "Viva Lázaro", "Viva Cristo." Spirits run so high that the security forces always turn out in force in case of trouble. The Pope gave his penultimate mass here during his visit to Cuba in January 1998.

Otherwise, Santiago de las Vegas is most famous for its Aids sanitarium, which is the largest of its kind in Cuba. Patients from the institution are often present at the mass in El Rincón church on the Day of San Lázaro.

Points southwest of Havana

To the southwest of Havana, some 22 miles (37 km) along the Autopista del Mediodía, is **San Antonio de los Baños** ⓮. This must be the most filmed small

BELOW: *artesanía* for sale.

town in the Third World: just 5 miles (8 km) away is the **International Film School**, whose students from Latin America, Asia and Africa often use San Antonio and its residents in their graduating projects. Gabriel García Márquez is the founder and benefactor of the school, which he visits frequently to teach classes in screenwriting. Other notables who have worked with the school include Robert Redford and Francis Ford Coppola.

San Antonio is famous too for its annual **international humor festival** (held every April), and as the birthplace of both the composer-singer Silvio Rodríguez and the late Eduardo Abela, whose Batista-era cartoon character, El Bobo ("The Fool"), created biting social criticism. El Bobo is now the town symbol, standing at its entrance.

*The route west of Mariel is delightful – and is recommended as an alternative route to Pinar del Río. But note that stretches are within a miliary zone (*Zona Militar*), so be wary of taking pictures. If you are thinking of hitching, be prepared to wait all day.*

Traveling west

The coastal route west from Havana begins at Miramar's Quinta Avenida, and runs past **Marina Hemingway** ⓯ (*see page 178*) to a few small resorts. Don't expect to find many foreigners at **Santa Fé** or **Playa Baracoa**, both charming, sleepy places with wooden homes along the seafront and small rocky beaches where a few locals let rooms or houses by the sea. A little further west, **El Salado** has another pebbly beach and a pleasant cabin motel.

During the summer of 1994, *balseros* (rafters) embarked on the hazardous crossing towards the US from all along this coast, in a great refugee crisis that strained political relations between the two countries. **Mariel** ⓰ (*see map page 198*) was also the scene of a great exodus in 1980, when over 120,000 Cubans were allowed to leave, picked up in boats from Miami. This port used to be filled with Soviet ships, and now, after a long hiatus, it is beginning to get busy again, especially as there is a new free-trade zone *(Zona Franca)* for foreign investors. A horrendous cement works rains white powder on the town, giving everything the grey, ashy look of recent disaster.

Beyond Mariel, the scene grows more rural. The coast road passes glorious blue seas edged with scrubby beaches, and inland the landscape is agreeably pastoral. This is the beginning of cattle and sugar cane country, and has some of the easiest sugar mills to visit from Havana. Until 1959, the mills were all named after saints, leading one historian to dub them "the heavenly court," but they were subsequently renamed after Cuban and Latin American heroes. It is difficult to visit these mills during the *zafra* or harvest, which runs from December to May or June, but quite possible off-season. Many roads are unmarked, but farm workers will happily give directions.

Before the town of **Artemisa**, a large town south of Mariel, you will find the fascinating but unmarked ruins of **La Bellona** sugar plantation, dating from the 19th century. Walls and columns are spread over a large area, the most identifiable structures being the main house and the slave quarters, which have a tall iron gate and the remains of a watch tower at one end. Artemisa is full of monuments to the 24 revolutionaries from here who fell during the assault on the Moncada barracks in 1953; they are also commemorated in the town's **Mausoleo de los Mártires**. ❑

BELOW: always ready with a smile.

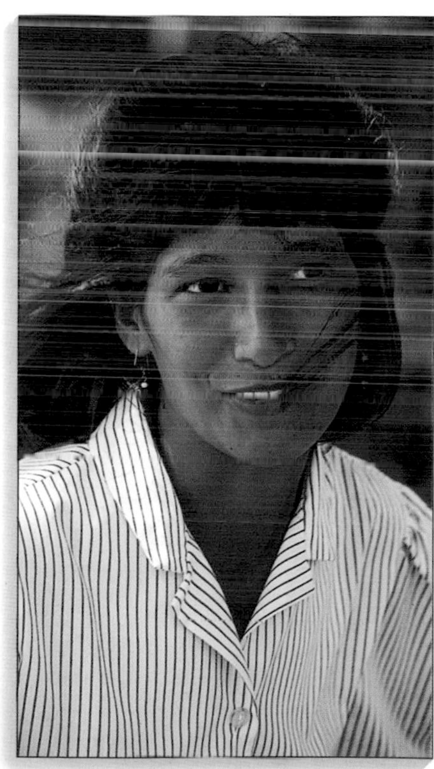

PINAR DEL RÍO

More than just the region where the world's finest tobacco is lovingly cultivated, this rural area offers some superb scenery, diving, cave exploration and a strong liqueur for afters

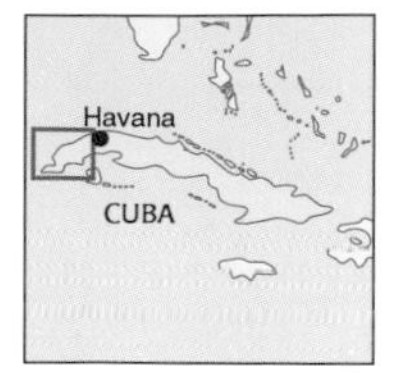

Jutting out like a swollen thumb to the west of Havana, the province of Pinar del Río looks and feels quite different to the rest of Cuba. This is the country's tobacco heartland. Physically, it is dominated by a unique string of rounded limestone mountains called *mogotes*, around Viñales; in their shadows are the lush green *vegas* or fields that produce the world's finest tobacco leaves, the dream of cigar connoisseurs from Paris to New York.

The atmosphere in Pinar is several degrees more gentle and relaxed than the rest of Cuba – a fact that the great Cuban intellectual Fernando Ortíz has argued is a direct legacy of the centuries-old tobacco tradition. While eastern Cuba is devoted to sugar cane – a crop whose harvesting is back-breaking work in the fierce Caribbean sun – the cultivation of tobacco is refined, intimate and even elegant. Pinar's plantations are minuscule compared to the endless cane fields of the east, and only a fraction of the numbers of workers are required. Everything is done by hand, from the picking of the leaf to the rolling of the cigars. In some *vegas*, linen nets protect the plants from the sun; in others, harvesters remove their hats, so as not to bruise the fragile, valuable leaves accidentally.

"Tobacco, despite the phallic shape into which it will be rolled, is Cuba's feminine side," says one Cuban-American writer. "Sugar, in spite of its sweetness, is violent masculinity; it fosters the machismo I abhor." Whatever the emotional benefits of growing tobacco, Pinar del Río has historically been one of the least developed provinces of Cuba. For centuries, the central Government looked first towards the east of the country (after Havana, that is), and even holidaying *Habaneros* instinctively avoided Pinar for the beaches of Varadero and attractions of Santiago.

One of the Revolution's aims was to bring Pinar more up to par with the rest of the country but rural life here is still beguilingly lethargic and, with the current fuel shortages, often reminiscent of the 19th century. Bullock carts are the main form of transport and regularly block traffic on roadways; the use of oxen and mules for transport is not exlusive to this region, but Pinar's reliance on them is greater than elsewhere. Tall, thatched *casas de tabaco*, with their steeply pitched roofs – for drying the leaves – dot the landscape, as do traditional palm-thatched cottages, or *bohíos*. At a time of severe building shortages, the government is building new *bohíos*, using traditional, abundant, natural materials. The villages are small and dreamy, each with its crumbling colonial church, palm-fringed plaza and inevitable bust of José Martí.

Head west, compañero

In its efforts to bring Pinar closer into the national fold, the Castro government pushed through an

PRECEDING PAGES: Viñales Valley from Hotel La Ermita.
LEFT: in the fast lane in Puerto Esperanza.
BELOW: bullock carts are still a vital form of rural transport.

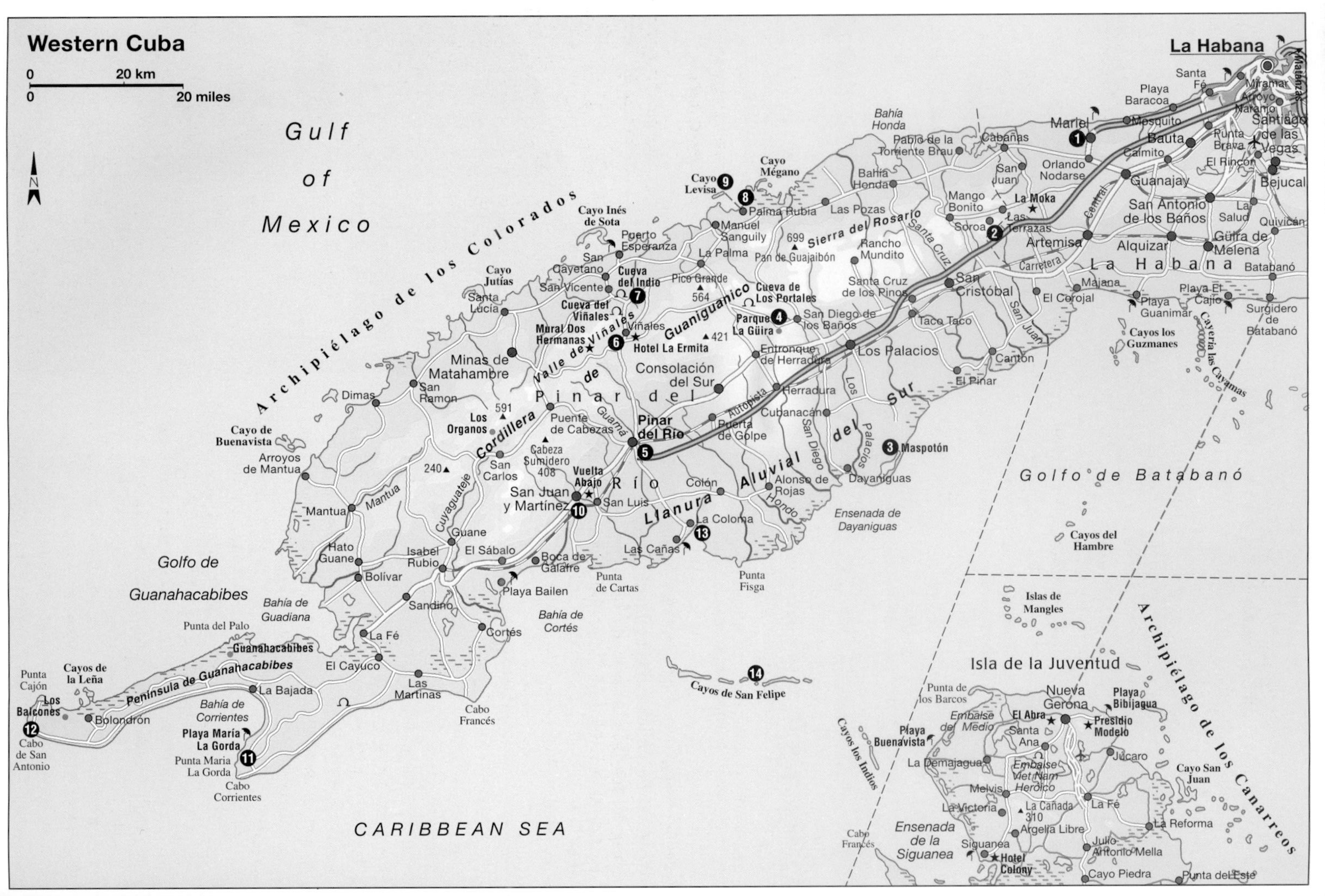
Western Cuba
0 20 km
0 20 miles
N
Gulf of Mexico
CARIBBEAN SEA
Golfo de Batabanó
Golfo de Guanahacabibes
Archipiélago de los Colorados
Archipiélago de los Canarreos
La Habana
Matanzas
Miramar
Arroyo Naranjo
Santiago de las Vegas
Bejucal
Quivicán
Batabanó
Surgidero de Batabanó
Punta Brava
El Rincón
La Salud
Güira de Melena
Santa Fé
Playa Baracoa
Mosquito
Bauta
Caimito
Guanajay
San Antonio de los Baños
Alquízar
La Habana
Playa El Cajío
Playa Guanimar
Cayería las Cayamas
Cayos los Guzmanes
Mariel
Orlando Nodarse
Artemisa
Majana
El Corojal
Carretera Central
La Moka
Las Terrazas
Cabañas
San Juan
Mango Bonito
Soroa
San Cristóbal
Cañón
El Pinar
Santa Cruz
Taco Taco
Bahía Honda
Pablo de la Torriente Brau
Rancho Mundito
Santa Cruz de los Pinos
Los Palacios
Maspotón
Dayaniguas
Ensenada de Dayaniguas
Las Pozas
Sierra del Rosario
699
Pan de Guajaibón
San Diego de los Baños
Cueva de Los Portales
Parque La Güira
Entronque de Herradura
Herradura
Cubanacán
San Diego
Palacios
Alonso de Rojas
Hondo
Cayo Mégano
Palma Rubia
Manuel Sanguily
La Palma
Cayo Levisa
Pico Grande
564
421
Hotel La Ermita
Consolación del Sur
Puerta de Golpe
Autopista
Los
Colón
La Coloma
Punta Fisga
Llanura Aluvial del Sur
Cayos de San Felipe
Puerto Esperanza
Cayo Inés de Sota
Cueva del Indio
Viñales
Valle de Viñales
Guaniguanico
Pinar del Río
San Luis
Las Cañas
Punta de Cartas
San Cayetano
San Vicente
Cueva del Viñales
Mural Dos Hermanas
Puente de Cabezas
Guamá
Cabeza Sumidero
408
Vuelta Abajo
San Juan y Martínez
Boca de Galafre
Bahía de Cortés
Cayo Jutías
Santa Lucía
Minas de Matahambre
591
Los Organos
Cordillera
San Carlos
Playa Bailen
El Sábalo
Cortés
Cabo Francés
Cuyaguateje
240
San Ramon
Guane
Isabel Rubio
Sandino
Las Martinas
Dimas
Mantua
Bolívar
La Fé
El Cayuco
Hato Guane
Cayo de Buenavista
Arroyos de Mantua
Bahía de Guadiana
Guanahacabibes
La Bajada
Punta del Palo
Península de Guanahacabibes
Bahía de Corrientes
Playa María La Gorda
Punta Maria La Gorda
Cabo Corrientes
Bolondrón
Cayos de la Leña
Los Balcones
Punta Cajón
Cabo de San Antonio
Isla de la Juventud
Islas de Mangles
Cayos del Hambre
Playa Bibijagua
Presidio Modelo
Nueva Gerona
El Abra
Santa Ana
Embalse Viet Nam Heroico
Embalse del Medio
Júcaro
Cayo San Juan
La Reforma
La Fé
Julio Antonio Mella
Cayo Piedra
Punta del Este
La Cañada
310
Argelia Libre
Melvis
La Victoria
Siguanea
Hotel Colony
La Demajagua
Punta de los Barcos
Playa Buenavista
Ensenada de la Siguanea
Cayos los Indios
Cabo Francés

impressive six-lane **autopista** (highway) from Havana. Today it is hardly used; except for a few trucks and army vehicles, your hire car or tour bus is likely to be the only moving thing on it. Clustered in the shade under bridges are droves of hitch-hikers on a mission to buy food in the provinces or visit relatives – be generous with your space since many of them may have been waiting for hours.

Following the highway, the provincial capital of Pinar del Río, 110 miles (178 km) from Havana, can be reached in only three hours. Slower, but more appealing, is the old **Carretera Central**, a two-lane road that winds through smaller towns and is thick with cyclists. The third and most picturesque option is the rough-and-ready **Carretera Norte**, which follows the coast. (Note that it is considerably easier to get out of Havana and join any of these three routes by first following the coastal road to **Mariel** ❶.) Drivers should also note that there are no filling stations and few refreshment stops along any of the routes between Havana and Pinar del Río.

If you've decided to hitch-hike yourself, and are having problems getting a lift, do as the locals do: wave a couple of dollars at the passing traffic.

The verdant Sierra

Traveling through the interior, the highways enter the steep hills of the **Sierra del Rosario**. The first detour, just before the provincial boundary, is the eco-resort of **Las Terrazas**. In 1967, the Government built an artists' colony here. More than three decades on, the community looks a little like a faded hotel complex, tumbling down the forested terraces to a long lake. The latter is lit by night and has a small café suspended over the water on a pier. The community is the base for several artists who sell crafts and paintings from their workshops. There is also a **museum** of Pre Columbian artefacts from the region.

On the road passing under the apartment block and through a pair of green gates is the **Eco-Center** where you can hire guides who specialize in the forest's flora and birdlife. Guides cost $3 per person per hour, or $1 per person for groups of over four. There are two excellent *paladares* in the village. The San Juan River Trail ends at the fabulous **Baños de San Juan** where you can bathe in a deep mountain pool fed by a tall waterfall. Foreigners stay at the **Hotel La Moka**, a beautiful modern hotel built in traditional Cuban style, and with live forest trees piercing its split levels and patios. You can hire bicycles from the hotel for $1 per hour.

Across the provincial border, 5 miles (7 km) from the main highway, is **Soroa** ❷ – less a village than a crossroads in the dripping forest (much of the Sierra has been declared a UNESCO Biosphere reserve). Soroa is best known for its **botanical garden** (*orquidería*), maintained behind large gates: in its extensive, pleasant grounds are some 700 types of orchids, more than 200 of them indigenous (open Sat–Thurs, 10am–5pm; guided tours $3). Signposts by the roadway also direct hikers to a *mirador* (lookout) – the walk is 20 minutes – and a **waterfall**, as well as the modern resort complex called **Castillo en las Nubes**, the Castle in the Clouds. This is a good place for a break from the road, with a pleasant dining-room and views across the sierra to the plains from a sunny, silent terrace. Soroa is now very much a part of the tourist trail with its bar and souvenirs, though the **Bar Eden** is a pleasant place

BELOW: cooling off at Soroa.

to sit and watch the river and listen to the cicadas – an incredible rattling sound that rolls through the forest like a Mexican wave. Visitors can stay at the **Villa Soroa** in cabins set in a lush landscape.

Spiced with rum, Guayabita del Pinar firewater comes in sweet and dry forms – but though it is renowned in Cuba, it tends to win few foreign converts.

West of Soroa, the Carretera Central passes the provincial town of **San Cristóbal**, whose red tile roofs and colorful buildings are all falling to pieces. As in all such outposts, motor traffic is non-existent: only the police seem to have fuel. Slightly to the south, on the railway line, is **Los Palacios**, and a rough dirt road that heads to the remote and barely populated southern coastline. In the swampy land here is **Maspotón ❸**, where a Club de Caza (hunting club) operates small bungalows. Pigeon and wild duck are common here in the winter months, and trout fishing is good all year round.

Che's redoubt

Back on the Carretera Central, the route passes the **Presa La Juventud**, Lake of Youth, and a detour north to the village of **San Diego de los Baños**. This pretty little town, by the side of a gorge cut by the fast-flowing Los Palacios River, was once famous for its spa. The spa is still there, mainly used by Cuban convalescents, but it is also available to foreign visitors for massages and treatments with volcanic mud and mineral water . There is a milky radioactive pool which glows in the gloom of the domed bath house, which is said to stimulate the hypothalamus area of the brain and rejuvenate the nervous system. Visitors stay at the delightful **Hotel Mirador** next door. The tropical forests of the **Parque Nacional La Güira ❹** can be reached by road, or by crossing the suspension bridge across the river by the spa. This was part of an aristocratic estate in colonial times and still contains a mansion and sculpted garden. The surrounding forest, dotted with lakes, plays host to a rich birdlife and is home to the native Cuban deer.

BELOW: the local x-rated beverage.

The neighbouring **Cueva de Los Portales** was the cave HQ for the western army under Che Guevara during the 1962 Missile Crisis. The camping complex here, with log cabins amongst the pines joined by rope walkways, was designed by Celia Sánchez. It had been long deserted and was falling down but is in the process of renovation and should re-open in time for the millennium.

Provincial capital

The one exception to the prevailing laid-back atmosphere is the hectic capital city of **Pinar del Río ❺**. A settlement had existed here since the 1570s, but development really began only after 1774 – comparatively late in the Spanish colonial period. Pinar lacks the clear grid pattern that makes other Cuban towns so straightforward to explore. The streets are unusually narrow and confusing, packed with cyclists going in several directions at once. Be warned, too, that for a relatively small place, the town contains an unusual concentration of *jineteros* (street hustlers).

Although it has been a long time since anyone called Pinar attractive, with a little imagination you can tell it once was. In fact, inhabitants will rave about how pleasant life could be before the Special Period began and shops and storefronts began to be shut up.

The main street, José Martí, has no shortage of impressive, decrepit buildings: the **Palacio Guasch**, dating from 1909, stands out for its fairytale Moorish design mixed with various other architectural styles. Today it houses the **Museo de Ciéncias Naturales** or **Natural History Museum** (Martí 202 at Avenida Pinares; open Tues–Sun; entrance fee), which is crammed full of stuffed animals and has a curious collection of concrete dinosaurs in the courtyard behind.

A short walk east is the **Museo Provincial de História** (Martí 58; open Tues–Sat & Sun am; entrance fee), housed in a colonial mansion and with a collection of local memorabilia ranging from 18th-century furniture to the pistols, radios and rifles of local revolutionary heroes. Next door is the **Teatro Milanés**, dating from 1845,which has been fully restored to its former glory. Visitors can see the interior, made entirely from polished wood, for a small entrance fee.

More interesting for visitors are two factories in Pinar. Near the Plaza de la Independencia, at the eastern end of Martí, is the tiny **Fábrica de Tabaco Francisco Donatién** (open Mon– Fri & Sat am; fee for compulsory tours), where the workers are pleased to receive visitors to watch them rolling a variety of cigars, and where there is also a small shop. South on Isabel Rubio is the **Casa Garay** (Isabel Rubio 49; open Mon– Fri; fee for compulsory tours), which produces a liqueur called *Guayabita del Pinar* from the pink-fleshed *guayabita* fruit which grows around Pinar like a weed. Tours of the factory take you past the vats of liqueur and end up in the gift store, where the concoction can be tasted straight.

Marking the route back to the *autopista*, the **Hotel Pinar del Río** is something of a local landmark: squat, ugly and shabby, it is a classic post-revolutionary Cuban hotel. There are a handful of hard currency stores and a couple of dismal bars, while the swimming pool is usually only half-filled with brown water.

Next to the hotel is a curiously Stalinist-style **monument** – an inverted "V" with a star on top and portraits of local revolutionary leaders on each limb. Foreigners can also stay at the **Hotel Globo** on Calles Martí and Isabel Rubio, or the **Hotel Italia** on Medina and Rubio. Just north of town, the road to the Viñales Valley passes the camping resort (*campismo*) of **Aguas Claras**, where comfortable cabins overlooking a swimming pool are surrounded by the lush wooded gardens of a former colonial estate.

Map on page 198

Jurassic Park comes to Pinar at Palacio Guasch.

BELOW: a skilled roller in Pinar's cigar factory.

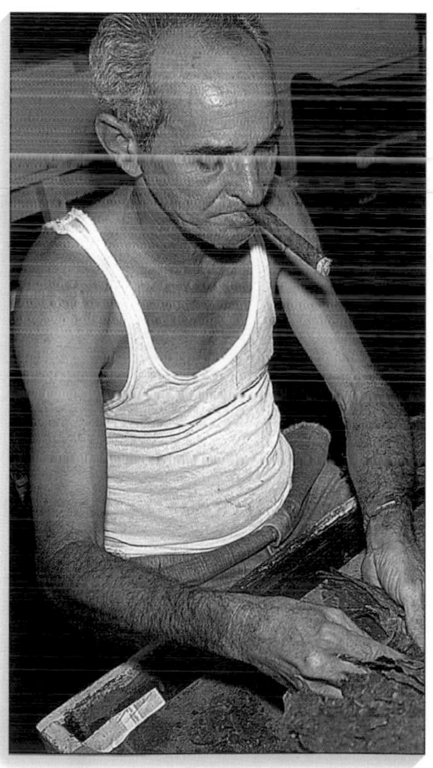

The Viñales Valley

The touristic core of the province lies north of the city of Pinar, in the **Sierra de los Organos**. This is the region dominated by the bizarre mountains that protrude sheer from the fields. Like other peculiar protrusions such as the desert buttes of Arizona and Australia's Ayers Rock, these *mogotes* are fists of hard stone that were left behind when the softer soil around them eroded over millions of years. In the Jurassic period they supported a level ocean floor like a series of blunt pillars; today, covered in luxuriant foliage, they have the air of overgrown ruins.

From Pinar, a narrow, slippery road with splendid views winds 17 miles (27 km) up into the sierra until it reaches **Viñales** ❻. The local authorities, recognising the importance of their little tobacco town as a center for this important tourist region, have worked

There is a delightful state-run restaurant in the very center of Viñales – the Casa de Don Tomás. The blue timber house with an attractive garden was built in 1822 and is the oldest surviving building in town.

hard to make it appealing to visitors, who used simply to drive on through having admired the view. The long rows of houses and their porches have been freshly and colorfully painted, and the shady plaza, with its typical rural colonial church, is looking wonderful after recent renovation work. The townsfolk too have discovered the benefits of tourism: Viñales appears to have more *paladares* and rooms to let than any Cuban small town except Trinidad (even Viñales's mayor lets rooms and serves dinner at his tobacco farm just out of town).

There are two hotels in the area. The **Hotel Los Jazmines** is the most attractive, both in itself and in its position. The views across the valley are exceptional, whether from the rooms in the main hotel, the annexe, or from the terrace, which provides a spectacular spot for the swimming pool. The hotel is the main stopping point for tour buses, so inevitably a string of vendors have set up stalls selling the usual plethora of low-grade tourist items, but luckily the car park is set slightly behind the main hotel buildings.

The **Hotel La Ermita** is closer to Viñales (a 20-minute walk, above the town to the east). It has more distant views of the valley, but almost all of the rooms have balconies facing out to the *mogotes*, as does the swimming pool and the pleasant, open-air restaurant. At dusk the scenery in this area is particularly stunning: the sun turns brilliant orange as it slides behind the mountains whilst a thin mist gathers in the valleys, isolating the distant strings of palm trees in a haunting tropical soup.

Agricultural heartland

It is a short drive down from Viñales into the shaded valleys between the *mogotes*, whose rich soil is perfect for tobacco growing. Along these isolated

BELOW: Hotel Los Jazmines.

Map on page 198

roads, *guajiros* bicycle past wearing straw hats and puffing huge cigars, or, equally as likely, trot past on horseback. In the fields, ploughs are pulled by oxen or *bueyes* instead of tractors, and these are often used for carts as well; one favored form of transport is simply hooking two wooden planks into a "V" behind a couple of brahmin bulls, and allowing them to drag the passengers along as if they were water-skiing.

The must-see attraction – according to the tour guides, that is – is the **Mural de la Prehistoria**, an enormous and garish painting that covers the flank of the Dos Hermanas Mogote, about 2 miles (4km) west of Viñales. The mural was commissioned by Fidel Castro himself in the 1960s to portray the emergence of Socialist Man from the primal wilderness. One of Diego de Rivera's students, Leovigildo González, took on the commission, directing dozens of local painters. It is regularly touched up by the local artists who worked on the original by dangling precariously from the cliff top on rope swings. The mural is brash and certainly not to everyone's taste, but it is certainly out of the ordinary. Like it or hate it, you can't but help appreciate the pleasantness of the location, and there is a good restaurant below the cliff, which serves excellent *criollo* meals.

The controversial Mural of Prehistory certainly never disappoints on size.

Caves and cays

The *mogotes* are riddled with underground rivers and limestone caves. Heading north of Viñales, the road first passes the **Cueva de Viñales**, a cave that has been turned into a discotheque and is strictly for students of Cuban kitsch. A couple of miles further on is the **Cueva del Indio** (Indian Cave) ❼ – so named because the local indigenous Guanahatabey peoples used it as a cemetery and refuge during the Spanish Conquest. For a small entrance fee, visitors pass through the

BELOW: the view across the Viñales Valley from Los Jazmines.

TIP

At the river, stone steps lead down to the black waters. A boatman takes visitors a further five minutes out of the caves, but have cameras ready, as the impressive exit comes upon you very swiftly.

café, bar and souvenir shop into the cave and follow a contorted limestone tunnel down to an underground river. When visited alone, the cave's ambience is eerie – it looks like the underwater escape passages from old horror films. On emerging, refreshments can be had at a small bar, where you can sip coconut and rum drinks from a coconut shell, enjoy the view of the deep blue pool surrounded by cascading jungle plants, and listen to the chattering birdlife.

The road north of Viñales continues through spectacular countryside directly to the coast, ending up at **Puerto Esperanza**, a small and soporific fishing outpost, where benches are laid out beneath palm trees by the mangrove-lined coast. One of the province's few Cupet filling stations lies just to the south at San Cayetano. Some 22 miles (35 km) to the east of Esperanza is **Palma Rubia** ❽ – accessible either by way of the unsurfaced coastal road or the better-maintained route through La Palma further inland – from where the ferry to **Cayo Levisa** ❾ leaves (daily at 11am and 5pm; $10). This small island, some 40 minutes off the coast, has by far the best beaches in Pinar del Río Province, with sparkling white sands. There is a reasonably comfortable resort, where, thanks to the fishing industry, lobster is the lunch specialty. This is a place to chill out and do little, though there is some good diving: the nearby reef has abundant black coral and other rarities. East of Cayo Levisa lies a tiny cay with an outsized name, **Cayo Mégano de Casiguas a Paraíso**, which was a favourite retreat of Ernest Hemingway, and which offers superb scuba diving off the coral reef. All the hotels in Viñales can arrange trips to Cayo Levisa.

The coastal route heading back to Havana via **Las Pozas** (where there is the only *paladar* for miles around: the excellent value **Restaurante El Mambí**) and **Bahía Honda** is often rough, pot-holed and narrow, so should be driven with caution. This is a return to more traditional sugar-growing areas, and in the winter harvesting time the road can be jammed with trucks. The views of the Caribbean are pleasant, but the beaches are not Cuba's finest, especially since much of the coastline is taken up by mangroves rather than sand. The best is probably **Playa Herradura**, some 5 miles (8 km) off the main road, to the north of Cabañas.

BELOW: at the Indian Cave, Viñales.

The end of the road

Heading west from Pinar del Río, the route passes the town of **San Juan y Martínez** ❿. Between here and **San Luis** is the district of **Vuelta Abajo**, where it is generally regarded that the very finest tobacco leaves in Cuba (and thus in the whole world) are grown. Despite its tiny size, the most famous – and therefore the most photographed – field of all is the **Hoyo de Monterrey**.

Few travelers venture west beyond this point. Though the roads are reasonable and can be driven in any normal car, the effort rather outweighs the attractions. The Carretera Central leaves the hills for more monotonous terrain. You pass the planned city of **Sandino** – named after the Nicaraguan revolutionary hero and partially populated by Cubans forcibly transferred from the Escambray mountains in the '60s for supporting the counter-revolution – and then end up at the fishing outpost of **La Fé**.

From La Fé, you can continue west to **La Bajada**, where the road branches south to the **International Diving Center** of **Punta María La Gorda** ⓫. This place – Fat Maria's Point – was named for an obviously well-fed Venezuelan girl abandoned here after being kidnapped by pirates. The diving center is rapidly developing, and though the accommodation is still rather rough, a range of dive packages are available. For example, a 10-dive package costs around $200.

La Bajada marks the beginning of the **Península de Guanahacabibes**, a national park and the site of this doomed indigenous race's last stand against the Spanish. To enter, you must buy a $10 permit from the diving center at Punta María la Gorda. The roadway along the **Bahía de Corrientes** sparkles with fine, white-sand beaches, and dolphins can be seen swimming in the blue seas of the bay. Foreigners cannot drive beyond the lighthouse of **Cabo de San Antonio** ⓬, an area said to house a political prison. This is Cuba's most westerly point: beyond this, the Gulf of Mexico stretches into the distance.

A rustic "beach hut" on idyllic Cayo Levisa.

Cayos de San Felipe

Ten miles (16 km) south of Pinar province are these ten little cays. Entirely undeveloped, they are a haven for all kinds of wildlife including three species of lizard and a woodpecker that are unique to the islands. The wildlife thrives in the absence of humanity – there is just one tiny community who fish the warm seas. At present, the only way to get there is independently, by boat from **La Coloma** ⓭ on the mainland, or by taking an expensive trip with Alcona SA (tel: 222526), who feature them in a mountain and sea "eco-package" (around $800 for eight nights) at the Finca La Guabina mountain resort near the Viñales valley and the **Cayos de San Felipe** ⓮. ❑

BELOW: Cayo Levisa ferry captain.

SECRETS OF THE CUBAN CIGAR

Thanks to the ideal climate and soil, plus centuries of expertise in cultivating the tobacco crop, Cuba produces the world's finest smokes

The big fat Cuban cigar holds almost as important a role in the national identity as rum and salsa. Tobacco is grown on smallholdings in parts of eastern, central and western Cuba, but the most highly prized comes from the *vegas* (plantations) around the town of San Juan y Martínez in Pinar del Río province, in an area called the Vuelta Abajo.

It is this region's leaves – the most important of which are grown under cheesecloth to protect them from direct sunlight – that end up in Havana's cigar factories, to be made into world-famous brands such as Cohiba, Montecristo and Romeo y Julieta. Around 100 million cigars are exported each year, netting Cuba around $50 million a year. The industry is one of the island's chief hard currency earners.

BUYING CIGARS

The black market in counterfeit cigars is rampant. A box of Cohibas bought on the street may look like the real thing, with the packaging and cigar bands pilfered from a factory, but the tobacco may well be inferior. Unless you're an aficionado, it's best to buy from an official shop (the best are in tobacco factories), where prices are much higher but still only a fraction of what they are abroad.

If you get the chance to inspect the contents of a box before parting with your money, you should check that the cigars are of a similar color (the darker the color, the stronger the flavour), and that if you squeeze them they readily spring back into shape and don't crackle.

◁ **THE TOP BRAND**
The Cohiba, named after the Taíno Indian word for tobacco, was created in the 1960s as largesse for foreign diplomats.

◁ **SIZE MATTERS**
Cigar lengths vary from around 10–20 cm (4–9 inches). Thicker cigars tend to be fuller flavored and smoother.

▽ **GREEN TO BROWN**
Tobacco leaves are strung up with needle and thread on poles in wooden or thatched barns, where they are left to cure for up to two months.

△ **PAINSTAKING PROCESS**
The tobacco harvest, which takes place between February and March, is labor-intensive, with the leaves being picked in six phases.

◁ **PARTAGAS FACTORY**
Founded in 1845, this cigar factory is now the largest in the country, producing 5 million cigars a year.

▷ **UPMANN FOR DIRECTORS**
This brand is named after an old London bank, which at first imported cigars solely for its directors.

◁ **LABELS AND BOXES**
Colorful labels have adorned cedar cigar boxes since the 1830s. Cedar is used to keep the contents moist.

THE CUBAN CIGAR FACTORIES

Cigars for domestic consumption are made in small-scale factories across the country; those for export are produced in Havana's large, famous factories such as Partagás and La Corona.

The highlight of a factory visit is seeing a room full of *torcedores* (cigar-rollers) dexterously blending together the filler, binder and wrapper leaves. The best rollers can produce as many as 150 cigars a day. All rollers are allowed to smoke as many cigars as they want on the job. To help pass the time, every day a lector takes the podium to read from a newspaper or book.

Visitors are often allowed to look in on other parts of the cigar-making process, such as the sorting of leaves into their various strengths, and the color grading, banding and boxing of the final product. Before cigars can leave the factory, *catadores* (tasters) smoke random samples from selected batches.

▷ **REFORMED SMOKER**
Castro gave up smoking cigars in the 1980s, explaining: "They're good for the country, but not so good for my health."

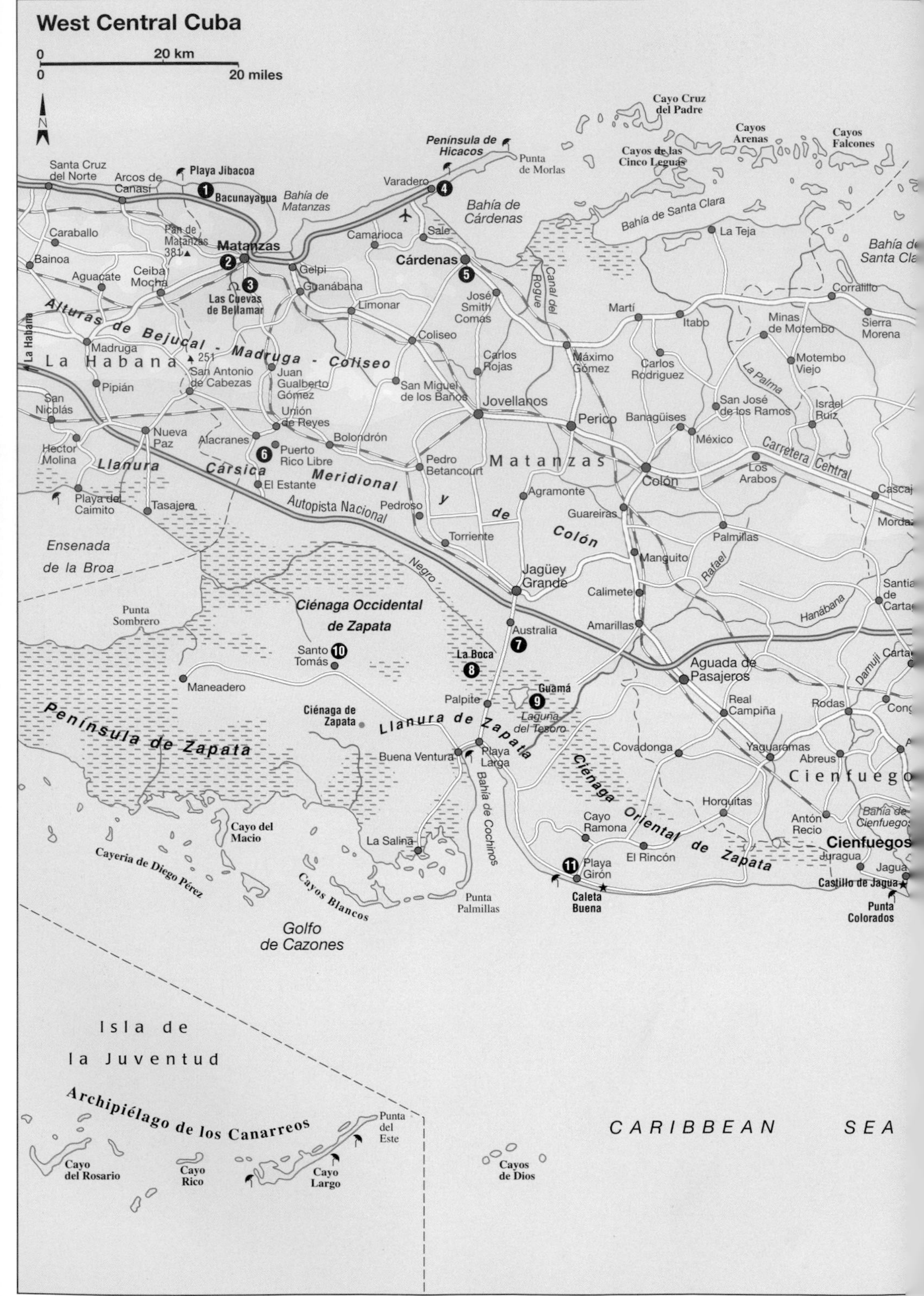
West Central Cuba
0 20 km
0 20 miles
N
Santa Cruz del Norte
Arcos de Canasí
Playa Jibacoa
Bacunayagua
Bahía de Matanzas
Península de Hicacos
Punta de Morlas
Varadero
Bahía de Cárdenas
Cayo Cruz del Padre
Cayos de las Cinco Leguas
Cayos Arenas
Cayos Falcones
Bahía de Santa Clara
La Teja
Caraballo
Pan de Matanzas 381
Matanzas
Camarioca
Sale
Cárdenas
Bainoa
Aguacate
Ceiba Mocha
Las Cuevas de Bellamar
Gelpi
Guanábana
Limonar
José Smith Comas
Canal del Rogue
Martí
Itabo
Corralillo
Minas de Motembo
Sierra Morena
Alturas de Bejucal - Madruga - Coliseo
Madruga
Coliseo
Carlos Rojas
Máximo Gómez
Carlos Rodriguez
Motembo Viejo
La Habana
251
San Antonio de Cabezas
Juan Gualberto Gómez
San Miguel de los Baños
Jovellanos
Perico
La Palma
San José de los Ramos
Israel Ruiz
Pipián
San Nicolás
Unión de Reyes
Banagüises
México
Hector Molina
Nueva Paz
Alacranes
Puerto Rico Libre
Bolondrón
Llanura Cársica Meridional y de Colón
Pedro Betancourt
Matanzas
Colón
Los Arabos
Carretera Central
Playa del Caimito
El Estante
Autopista Nacional
Pedroso
Agramonte
Cascajal
Tasajera
Guareiras
Mordazo
Torriente
Palmillas
Ensenada de la Broa
Negro
Manguito
Rafael
Jagüey Grande
Calimete
Santiago de Cartagena
Punta Sombrero
Ciénaga Occidental de Zapata
Australia
Amarillas
Hanábana
Santo Tomás
La Boca
Aguada de Pasajeros
Cartagena
Damují
Maneadero
Guamá
Palpite
Laguna del Tesoro
Real Campiña
Rodas
Península de Zapata
Ciénaga de Zapata
Llanura de Zapata
Covadonga
Yaguaramas
Abreus
Buena Ventura
Playa Larga
Bahía de Cochinos
Ciénaga Oriental de Zapata
Cienfuegos
Horquitas
Cayo del Macio
Cayo Ramona
Antón Recio
Bahía de Cienfuegos
La Salina
El Rincón
Cienfuegos
Cayeria de Diego Pérez
Juragua
Playa Girón
Jagua
Cayos Blancos
Caleta Buena
Castillo de Jagua
Punta Palmillas
Punta Colorados
Golfo de Cazones
Isla de la Juventud
Archipiélago de los Canarreos
Punta del Este
Cayo del Rosario
Cayo Rico
Cayo Largo
Cayos de Dios
CARIBBEAN SEA

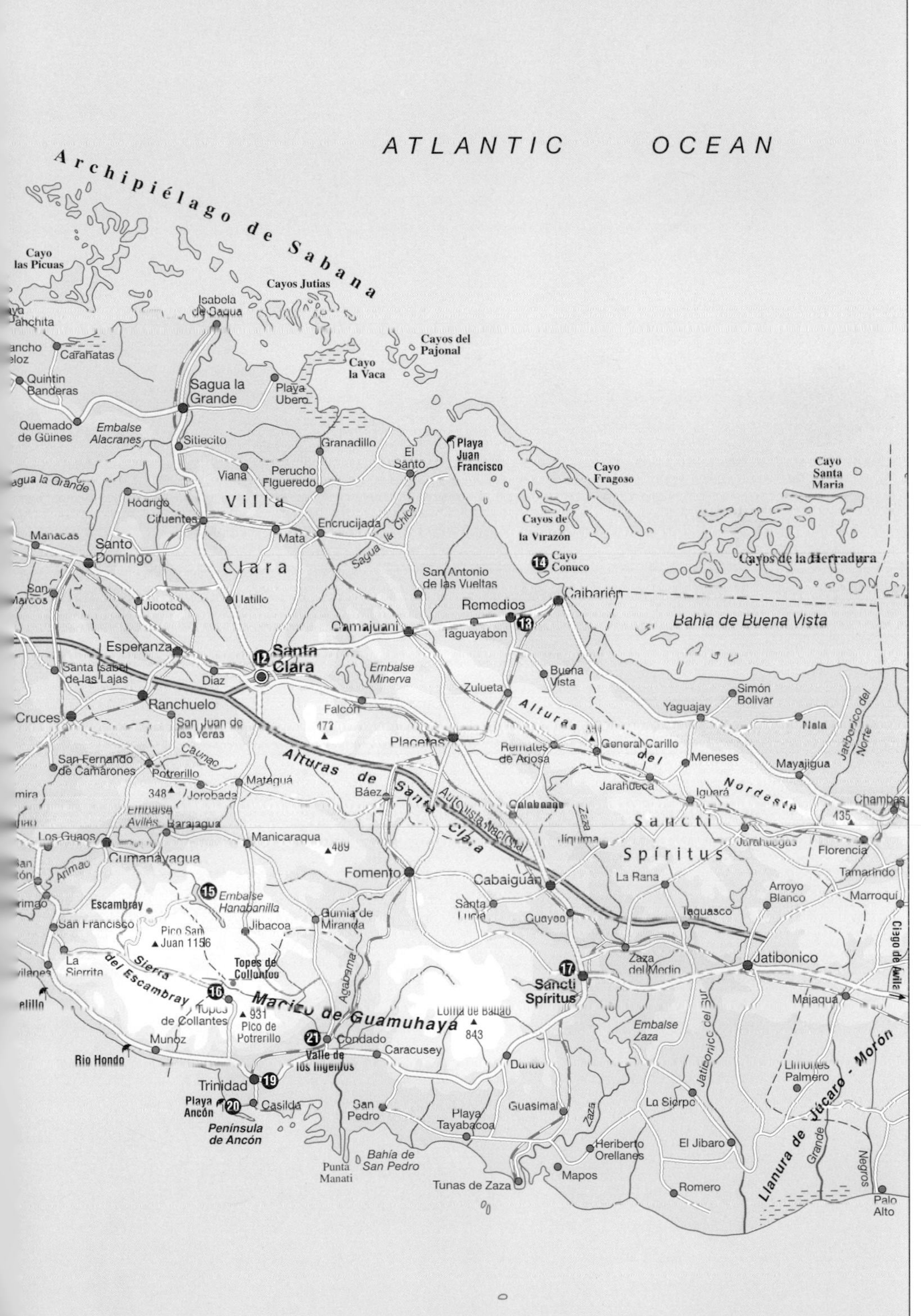
ATLANTIC OCEAN
Archipiélago de Sabana
Cayo las Picuas
Cayos Jutias
Isabela de Sagua
Carahatas
Quintin Banderas
Sagua la Grande
Playa Ubero
Cayo la Vaca
Cayos del Pajonal
Quemado de Güines
Embalse Alacranes
Siliecito
Granadillo
El Santo
Playa Juan Francisco
Cayo Fragoso
Cayo Santa Maria
Viana
Perucho Figueredo
Rodrigo
Villa Clara
Cifuentes
Encrucijada
Mata
Cayos de la Virazon
Cayo Conuco
Cayos de la Herradura
Manacas
Santo Domingo
San Antonio de las Vueltas
Caibarién
Bahia de Buena Vista
Jicotea
Hatillo
Remedios
Camajuani
Taguayabon
Esperanza
Santa Clara
Santa Isabel de las Lajas
Diaz
Embalse Minerva
Buena Vista
Zulueta
Ranchuelo
Simón Bolivar
Yaguajay
Cruces
Falcón
San Juan de los Yeras
Alturas del Nordeste
General Carillo
Nela
Placetas
Remates de Ariosa
San Fernando de Camarones
Potrerillo
Alturas de Santa Clara
Meneses
Mayajigua
Jarahueca
Mataguá
Báez
Autopista Nacional
Jorobada
Iguará
Chambas
Embalse Avilés
Barajagua
Calabazas
Sancti Spíritus
Los Guaos
Manicaragua
Jiquima
Jurahueca
Florencia
Cumanayagua
Fomento
Cabaiguán
La Rana
Tamarindo
Embalse Hanabanilla
Escambray
Santa Lucia
Arroyo Blanco
Marroquí
Guayos
Iguasco
San Francisco
Pico San Juan 1156
Jibacoa
Gumia de Miranda
Jatibonico
La Sierrita
Sierra del Escambray
Topes de Collantes
Zaza del Medio
Ciego de Avila
Macizo de Guamuhaya
Sancti Spíritus
Majagua
Pico de Potrerillo
Loma de Banao
843
Condado
Embalse Zaza
Munoz
Valle de los Ingenios
Caracusey
Rio Hondo
Banao
Limones Palmero
Trinidad
Playa Ancón
Casilda
San Pedro
Guasimal
La Sierpe
Llanura de Júcaro - Morón
Península de Ancón
Playa Tayabacoa
Heriberto Orellanes
El Jibaro
Punta Manati
Bahía de San Pedro
Mapos
Tunas de Zaza
Romero
Palo Alto

VARADERO AND MATANZAS PROVINCE

Cuba's prime resort for package tourism, Varadero is a world apart from the rest of the island – including even this area's own peaceful hinterland and the city of Matanzas nearby

The **Province of Matanzas** couldn't have a grander point of entry than the **Puente Bacunayagua** ❶. This impressive bridge spans the 370-ft (112-meter) deep gorge of the Bacunayagua river which divides the provinces of Havana and Matanzas. The Yumuri valley winds away to the distant mountains beyond. Turkey vultures wind lazy circles above the near silent gorge. cicadas sing. Few vehicles pass. There is a small restaurant and café here – an obligatory pit stop for coach parties, and deservedly so: the view is impressive.

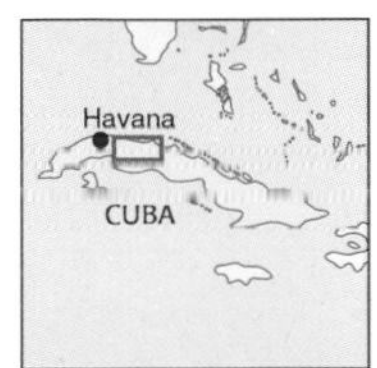

City of the slaughter

About 12 miles (20 km) east of here is the provincial capital of **Matanzas** ❷, founded more than 300 years ago. The highway passes right by the city's supertanker port, capable of receiving 150,000-ton oil tankers and linked by pipeline to the Cienfuegos Oil Refinery, 116 miles (187 km) to the south.

Matanzas Bay was first navigated by Sebastián de Ocampo in 1509, although the city itself wasn't established until October 1, 1693. On that day, Severino de Balmaseda, the provisional governor of Cuba, traveled from Havana to Matanzas with a team of surveyors to parcel out lots to newly-arrived settlers from the Canary Islands. The city's name, which means "slaughter," was originally thought to refer to a massacre of a local indigenous tribe, but recent study suggests it probably had more to do with the killing of herds of pigs kept near the bay to resupply ships.

Local farmers started out growing tobacco but by the end of the 18th century they had converted to sugar. Sugar and the slave trade made the city immensely rich, and during the 19th century the local aristocracy became a major patron of the arts. Matanzas developed a rich café society and many poets and artists made their home here. During Cuba's 1895–8 War of Independence, it was the center of a battle between Spanish general Arsenio Martínez Campos, and two of Cuba's most important national heroes, Máximo Gómez and Antonio Maceo. On January 1, 1899, the Spanish Army handed over the town in the **Plaza de la Vigía**, in the center of town – not to the Cubans, but to General J.P. Sanger of the US Army.

Vigía Square still boasts a reminder of that conflict, the **Statue of the Unknown Soldier** – erected in 1919 on the same spot where Matanzas was founded in 1693. Here too is the Neoclassical **Teatro Sauto** Ⓐ, which has glorious ceilings and acoustics – it is still open for regular performances and there are guided tours (Wed–Sun, 1pm–3pm; entrance fee). Adjacent to

PRECEDING PAGES: a bee hummingbird after its breakfast.
LEFT: Varadero beach.
BELOW: old cures in the Pharmaceutical Museum, Matanzas.

Matanzas Cathedral has some beautiful frescoed ceilings.

the square is the **Museo Histórico Provincial** in the **Palacio del Junco** **B** (open Tues–Sun, 10am–6pm; entrance fee), which houses hundreds of documents and artefacts relating to the history of Matanzas; the issue of slavery in the sugar plantations is given unusually detailed treatment.

To the south of the theater towards the river, you find the **Parque de los Bomberos** (Firemen's Square), with an elegant neoclassical fire station and a perfectly preserved vintage fire engine. On the same side of the street as the nearby **Galería de Arte Provincial** (open Mon–Sat, 9am–6pm; entrance fee), is **Ediciones Vigía**, which produces limited editions of marvelous handmade books: you can tour the workshops (Mon–Fri, 9am–6pm; entrance fee). The street crosses the Río San Juan at the rotating **Puente Calixto García**, a bridge built in 1849. A couple of blocks west of the Plaza de la Vigía on Calle 282 stands the **Catedral de San Carlos** **C** (open Mon–Sat, 8am–noon and 3–5pm, Sun am only), which has been partially restored with money given by a German tourist who fell in love with it on a visit to the city.

A healthy tonic

Perhaps the most important attraction in Matanzas overlooks the main square, **Parque La Libertad**: it is the **Museo Farmaceútico** **D** (Calle 83/Milanés 4951; open Mon–Sat, 10am–6pm and Sun 9am–1pm; entrance fee), housed in the three-story dispensary of two 19th-century doctors, Juan Fermín Figueroa and Ernesto Triolet. Considering the shortage of common medications in present-day Cuba, this may be the only well-stocked pharmacy in Matanzas. Among the most important pieces here are porcelain medicine flasks, hundreds of pharmacy books and a dispensary table that won a bronze medal at the 1900

BELOW: The caves at Bellamar outside Matanzas.

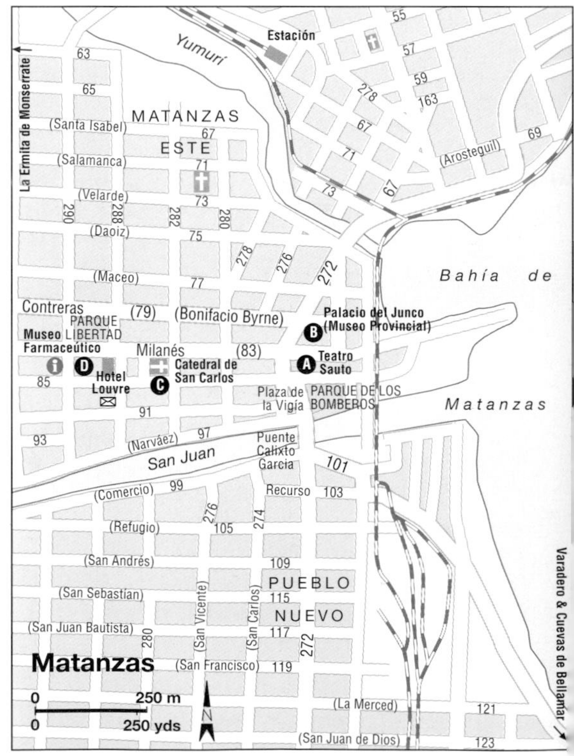

International Exposition in Paris. Displayed in an adjacent laboratory are ancient utensils, a wood-burning brick oven, and an *alambíque* or still, in which water, alcohol and essential oils were distilled for medicinal purposes.

Don't fail to pop into the **Hotel Louvre** next door – a shadow of its former self but with echoes of a glorious past. There is a leafy courtyard, a quaint dining room serving good, simple food, and bedrooms with grand old beds and tatty antiques. And don't leave town either without visiting the ruined **Ermita de Monserrate** sanctuary, at the northern end of Calle 306 (Domingo Mujica), which offers a panoramic view of the city and the Yumurí valley beyond.

A slave's cavern

Also in the region are many interesting caves. The most important are **Las Cuevas de Bellamar** ❸, 3 miles (5 km) southeast of downtown Matanzas. After a slave working an open lime pit in 1861 discovered the cavern, 1000 tons of rock had to be broken and extracted to clear the entrance; the work revealed one of the Caribbean's largest and most beautiful underground formations. According to an American traveler, Samuel Hazard, writing in 1897, anyone who hadn't visited the Bellamar Caves hadn't really seen Cuba. Perhaps this is a slight exaggeration, but the caves are still very impressive.

The Gothic Hall, 265 ft (80 meters) long and 80 ft (25 meters) wide, contains peculiar stalagmites with romantic names such as The Woman's Hand and The Codfish Tail. The Confessional Gallery, 570 ft (173 meters) long but only 10 ft (3 meters) high, has a crystallized vault covered by stalactites, while the Lake of Dahlias – a rocky area covered with water – is famous for the thousands of tiny calcite crystals covering its roof, walls and floor.

Map on pages 210–11

Mantanzas possesses two Casas de la Trova: one near the cathedral, the other at Calles 272 and 121, where the city's top stars sometimes play, including the famous rumba group, Muñequitos de Matanzas.

LEFT: Matanzas fire station.
RIGHT: searching for shells.

Key West, Florida, lies only 130 miles (210 km) to the north at this point. Tune in your radio to see just how close Florida is. It's a surreal experience passing sugar fields and an occasional 1953 Oldsmobile while listening to Miami traffic reports.

BELOW: soaking up the sun at Varadero.

The **Vía Blanca** highway powers 20 miles (32 km) eastwards from the caves to Cuba's most famous international beach resort, passing towering onshore oil rigs which proudly fly the Cuban and Canadian flags, representing another of the island's joint ventures.

Varadero

The resort of **Varadero** ❹ is the closest you'll get to finding Miami Beach in Cuba. It is flashy in a Cuban kind of way. Nowhere else on Cuban soil can you find such a high concentration of oceanfront restaurants, nightclubs and luxury hotels. Sadly, nowhere else is the island's "tourism apartheid" more obvious.

Indeed, Varadero is the ideal place to vacation if you don't want to meet too many Cubans. Take a leisurely stroll along its palm-fringed, white-sand beach, considered one of the finest in the Caribbean, and you're likely to encounter lots of Spaniards, Italians, Canadians, and Germans – but few locals. If you are looking for a straightforward beach vacation, relatively free of *jineteros*, in a good modern hotel with cable TV; with air-conditioning that works; a pool and a jacuzzi; a golf course left over from the 1950s; and restaurants serving pizzas and hamburgers, then this is the place for you. The seas are warm and crystal blue – and it is one of the few places in Cuba where women can sunbathe topless. Despite the very open sexuality of Cuba, topless bathing is, perhaps surprisingly, illegal, although it is tolerated in tourist-only resorts like Varadero.

Even before arriving at the hotels, you'll see evidence of the segregation of tourists from Cubans. Two government-controlled checkpoints along the road to the peninsula officially act as a toll (visitors must pay a small fee on entry and departure). However, they are really police checkpoints: any Cuban traveling to

Varadero is asked to show their identity card. If they are not natives of the resort and can show no official proof of needing to travel there, they will not be allowed in. This has all but killed the *jinetero* problem in town, simply by making it off-limits to Cubans; but whilst the policy has got rid of 95 percent of the prostitutes it has also affected the town's ambience. This is Varadero's biggest problem: because there are no Cubans, there is very little atmosphere.

Many package-deal tourists fly directly to Varadero and never leave, so almost the only Cubans they will encounter work on the hotel staff. Foreign hotel firms pay the Cuban government an average $400 a month per employee. The government pockets those dollars and pays the workers in nearly worthless pesos. Hotel jobs in Varadero are much sought after, however, due to the access to hard currency tips and better food they provide. An industrious waiter can make between $8 and $10 a day in tips which is more than the average monthly salary in Cuba.

The early years

As it turns out, Varadero has been something of a private preserve for much of its history. Local tribes once lived here, but the earliest historical mention of it dates from 1587, when the merchant Don Pedro Camacho began mining salt, both for local use and for Spanish fleets that dropped anchor in Havana.

Throughout the 1600s and early 1700s, pirates preyed on the few inhabitants of the 13-mile (18-km) **Península de Hicacos**, along which Varadero is located. In 1726, a certain José Antonio Gómez bought the peninsula and used it to produce livestock and salt. Thirty-six years later, the Varadero Hacienda – consisting of 2,800 acres (1,140 hectares) of land from Paso Malo to Hicacos

Map on pages 210–11

The poor-quality oil found along the north coast of Matanzas province contains high levels of sulphur and produces a foul smell during drilling. If the wind is blowing in the right (but wrong) direction, you can smell it from Varadero.

BELOW: Xanadú, Varadero's most famous mansion.

Most beers brewed in Cuba are light (clara). *Hatuey is one of the island's best, but look out also for the tasty Mayabe from Holguín province.*

Point – was sold to Bernardo Carrillo de Albornos, whose aristocratic heirs were still in possession of the land by the mid-19th century.

Varadero's tourist history started in the 1870s, when families from nearby Cárdenas began visiting. In that decade, they built the first palm-thatched frame houses on the northern coast, while the southern coast remained the preserve of fishermen. The beach's fame grew, however, luring visitors from Havana, who in those days arrived by ox-cart. The year 1915 marked the inauguration of the Hotel Varadero – the fledgling town's first resort. Three years later, the Cuban Congress passed a law authorizing annual rowing regattas at Varadero Beach, which soon became a highlight of the local social calendar.

Then in 1926, the chemicals magnate Alfred Irénée Du Pont (who had made his fortune making dynamite during World War I) scored a real-estate coup with the purchase of 1,265 acres (512 hectares) of prime Varadero property for as little as four centavos a square meter. The lavish vacation house he built, **Xanadú**, is still standing today – one of the few tourist attractions in Varadero worth visiting. Located right on the beach, the mansion was finished in 1930 at a cost of $338,000 – an astronomical sum back then. These days, it houses the **Restaurante Las Américas**, an overpriced seafood joint where lobster thermidor goes for an outrageous $35. Don't be intimidated – you can probably get a better-tasting lobster meal in a private home for half the price, and with better service.

But even if you don't eat here, you can still take a guided tour of the four-story Xanadú mansion for US$3, or see the ground floor yourself for free. The mahogany ceilings and banisters are all original, as are the Italian marble floors and the 1932 organ, one of the largest privately-built organs in Latin America. Don't overlook Coleridge's original poem ("*In Xanadu did Kubla Khan a stately pleasure dome decree...*") reproduced in full on the wall, or the beautiful terrace with a sweeping view of the Atlantic. There is also a golf course adjacent, but the small, predominantly flat area does not make for a tremendously satisfying game.

BELOW: Baywatch, Cuban style.

Foreign money: good and bad

Du Pont, who continued to buy up oceanfront property through the 1930s and 1940s, was not the only land speculator in Varadero. Others invested here, often with the complicity of corrupt Cuban officials and Mafia connections. The **Casa de Al**, which evokes those years, is a restaurant housed in a mansion once owned by Chicago gangster Al Capone.

In 1950, the **Hotel Internacional** was constructed for $3 million. That sparked a development boom that continued right up until the Cuban Revolution. Dozens of mansions arose from one end of Varadero to the other, along with golf courses, gambling casinos and hotels with links to the "Jewish godfather" Meyer Lansky and other figures of organized crime.

That all came to a screeching halt in 1959. A state-approved tourist pamphlet says that two months after Batista's overthrow, the Cuban government passed Law 270 "proclaiming the people's full right to enjoy all beaches." Even so, for many years the only kind of tourists Castro welcomed were solidarity brigades from the Soviet Union and other sympathetic countries. It was only with the end of aid from the USSR that Cuba began to court large-scale tourism from capitalist countries.

It was in Varadero that the first joint venture between the Cuban government and foreign capitalists was inaugurated in 1990 – the $26 million, 607-room **Hotel Sol Palmeras**. Since then the same firm, Spain's Grupo Sol, has built two more hotels, the **Meliá Varadero** and **Meliá Las Américas**. Varadero now has more than a third of Cuba's total hotel rooms, and is central to the government's plan to build Cuba into a world tourist mecca. Development has been swift and all-embracing, with 55 hotels along the beach: even the old "Campamiento Internacional," where Cuba's young pioneers once stayed alongside young foreigners from solidarity brigades, has been bought for development. There are investors here from across Europe, Latin America, the Caribbean, and even China, which has just opened a Chinese restaurant. Cuba's Ministry of Tourism intends to have 23,000 hotel rooms in Varadero by the year 2000.

Map on pages 210–11

One launch that isn't Miami-bound.

A break from the sun

Besides the Restaurante Las Américas and the beach itself, Varadero offers few sites of historical interest. Tourists with time to spare might like to check out the **Parque de Diversiones** (amusement park) at 3ra (Tercera) Avenida between Calles 29 and 30. There is a tiny **tobacco factory** on Avenida Primera and Calle 27, and an equally diminutive **Museo Municipal de Varadero** (open Tues–Sat) on Avenida Playa and Calle 57, which has interesting exhibits of local flora and fauna. Varadero's municipal park, **Parque Retiro Josone**, lying between 54 and 59 streets, has a pleasant flamingo lake where you can hire boats. It is the former estate of a local sugar baron, José Onclia, who lived here in the 1930s. At the far eastern tip of Varadero beach is the **Parque Natural de Varadero**. The most interesting feature of this reserve is the limestone caves which have aboriginal paintings, including the **Cueva de Ambrosio**, a small cave discovered in 1961, which contains about 50 of the best preserved prehistoric drawings. The rest of the park consists mostly of rather uninteresting dry scrub.

Into the "real" Cuba

It is an easy matter to hire a car in Varadero and head into northern Matanzas Province. While the physical distance is minuscule, the difference in lifestyles is astonishing. Only 9 miles (15 km) south of Varadero, across Cárdenas Bay, is the city of **Cárdenas** ❺, founded in 1828. In 1850, it was the subject of an unsuccessful annexation attempt by 600 US soldiers, mostly from Ohio and Kentucky. Later that year, Cuba's national flag was raised for the first time here. A plaque commemorating this event can be seen on the walls of the **Hotel Dominica** on Avenida Céspedes. On May 11, 1898, after Spain had already been defeated in the Spanish-American War, Cárdenas was shelled by US Navy ships under the command of Admiral William T. Sampson.

Today, over 100 years later, Cárdenas is an impoverished, drab-looking city of about 20,000 souls, with

BELOW: sugar refinery in Cárdenas.

none of the excitement or color of nearby Varadero. Like many other provincial Cuban towns, traffic here consists of horse-drawn carts rather than cars, which sit in driveways and backyards, immobilized by the lack of cheap gasoline.

Nonetheless, Cárdenas is home to the interesting **Museo de Oscar María de Rojas** (open Tues–Sat 1pm–6pm, and Sun 9am–1pm; entrance fee) – named for a local revolutionary hero. Located on the Calzada de Vives, this natural history museum has several exhibition halls devoted to Cuban coins, weapons, shells, butterflies, minerals, pre-Columbian objects and interesting documents from the various revolutions and wars of independence. At the end of Calle Céspedes is a small **fortress** (also named for Oscar María de Rojas), which is now a café and a popular meeting place for locals. At Calle Genes No. 240 is the **Casa Natal de José Antonio Echevarría**, the birthplace of the student who was killed in 1957 whilst leading the attack on Batista's Presidential Palace. The city has a fine **cathedral** on Parque Colón with a statue of Columbus from 1858, said to be the first erected in Latin America. Also in Cárdenas is a mausoleum in the **Plaza de la Independencia**, containing the remains of 238 patriots who fell fighting Spanish colonialism in the late 19th century.

The quiet hinterland

The province of Matanzas is almost totally dependent on sugar exports. South of the provincial capital, not far from Cuba's national motorway, is **Puerto Rico Libre** ❻ (pop. 1,200), a typical sugar-mill town. The town's name was chosen in 1960, when the newly triumphant Fidel Castro decided to adopt the cause of Puerto Rican independence and make it part and parcel of his revolution. Before that, the place had been known simply as Conchita, after the wife of the American industrialist who was responsible for building the sugar mill. Nearly all the adults here work at the mill, harvesting *caña* for processing and export. Their children go to schools where they learn a Cold War history very different from that taught in Puerto Rican schools.

RIGHT: the coast near Matanzas. **BELOW:** A countryside farewell.

Southeast of Matanzas the pot-holed Carretera Central offers an alternative route towards Santa Clara to that of the main *autopista*, passing by or through some pretty colonial settlements, like **San Miguel de los Baños** – a delightful old spa town set high in the rolling Matanzas hills. The spa has been forgotten for many years, but there are plans to resurrect it from its sad decay. A once elegant hotel, the Rincón del Baño still has a grand air, but is in dire need of restoration.

The Carretera continues through **Jovellanos**, an old slave town with a strong Afro-Cuban tradition, and on to **Colón**, another colonial settlement with a busy main street but otherwise sleepy squares, before crossing over into Santa Clara Province. Independent travelers may be interested to know that Jovellanos and Colón both have a Cupet gas station. Both also have peso hotels, but the Hotel Santiago in Colón is the most accustomed to dollar-paying tourists. Still, do not expect too much in the way of comfort or peace and quiet. The hotel overlooks the main street and the Cupet station (the social hub of the town). Don't miss a visit to the nearby cabaret if there's a show on. ❑

THE ZAPATA PENINSULA

Map on pages 210–11

The best-known of Cuba's wildlife havens, the Zapata Peninsula is a refuge for many bird and animal species. Nearby Playa Girón earned its place in history during the Bay of Pigs invasion

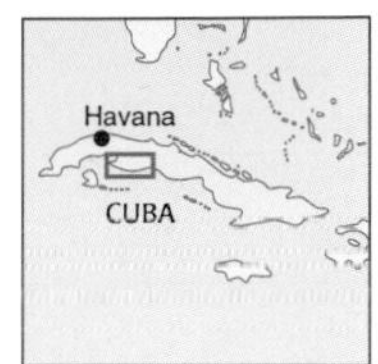

The half of Matanzas Province that lies to the south of the *autopista* from Havana is mainly low, marshy terrain that is primarily a destination for visitors interested in the rich Cuban wildlife to be found here. Passing the town of **Torriente**, you come to the main access town for the area, **Jagüey Grande**. This is the heart of the world's largest citrus operation – a 103,000-acre (40,000-hectare) grove of orange and grapefruit trees owned by the Cuban government and managed by a secretive Israeli firm. Here too, just south of the Zapata turnoff, is the **Finca Fiesta Campesina,** a tourist venture with a small zoo, shops, coffee bars, and a small cabin-style hotel, the **Bohío de Don Pedro**. It is an obligatory stop on the Zapata tour, and has surprisingly appealing gardens where you can sip fresh fruit *batidos* (milkshakes) in the 24-hour bar and inspect the coffee growing on the hillside. There is even an original kind of lottery where you are asked to bet on which hole a guinea pig will run into on its release. If you want to visit the Zapata nature reserve, you must organize a permit and compulsory guide here (*see overleaf*).

Don't be surprised if you see signs for "Central Australia" here: just east of the Finca Fiesta Campesina is the town of **Australia** ❼, dominated by its sugar mill (*central*). The mill here was Fidel Castro's headquarters during the battle at the Bay of Pigs, and part of it is now a museum (open Mon–Sat, 8am–noon and 1pm–6pm; entrance fee). The next long, straight stretch of road leads to the turn-off for the Zapata Peninsula, with monuments to the fallen of the Bay of Pigs all along the roadside.

LEFT: a flamingo (*flamenco*) strikes a pose.
BELOW: Indian village at Guamá.

Reptile refuge

Crocodiles are rare in Zapata. Two species exist – the widespread American crocodile, and the rarer Cuban crocodile, which can only be found elsewhere in the Lanier Swamp in the south of the Isle of Youth (and is under threat there from a small but aggressive cousin introduced from South America). At **La Boca** ❽, on the road from Jagüey Grande to Playa Larga, there is a **crocodile farm** (*criadero de cocodrilos*) where both species can be seen alive. Some years ago they were held together in the same pits, and hybridized so freely that the Cuban endemic nearly became extinct. They are now held in separate enclosures.

A boat carries passengers from La Boca on a 20-minute ride through a man-made canal to **Guamá** ❾, on the far side of the **Laguna del Tesoro** (Treasure Lagoon). The lake got its name because, it was said, the indigenous Taíno people of the area threw all their valuables into it rather than surrender them to the Spanish. Some artefacts have been found, but no gold – it seems that the Taíno had a different idea of treasure to that of the Spanish. Cabins, bridges and piers here are made of coarse wood, in a pleasant, supposedly Taíno-inspired style. Snail kites are abundant, as well as the endemic *manjuarí* (garfish or pike) – its teeth, snout and body are a crude parallel to those of a crocodile, and its lineage goes back some 70 million years.

TIP

If you value peace of mind or your complexion, ensure to take plenty of mosquito repellent to Zapata. Eating plenty of garlic beforehand reputedly reduces your appeal to the insects, but may have the same effect on your human companions too.

The Zapata Peninsula

The **Península de Zapata**, 97 miles (156 km) southeast of Havana, was named for its similarity to the outline of a shoe (*zapato* in Spanish). An enormous swamp, it has had a history of acting as a refuge, firstly for Taíno Indians, and later for buccaneers and charcoal makers.

The entire region is now a nature reserve, partly for military reasons; ever since the Bay of Pigs, the authorities have been to keep control of who goes in and out. There are just two points of entry to the reserve, and there is a Ministry of the Interior checkpoint at both; no unauthorised person is allowed access. To enter, you must obtain a **permit** from the Rumbos tourist agency desk at the Finca Campesina or the Bohío de Don Pedro. Access is not cheap – an obligatory guide costs around $50 for one person (slightly less per person for groups of more than one, with a maximum group size of seven).

It is well worth the cost. The scenery is spectacular: flamingos swoop across the milky lagoons, and crocodiles meander out across the dirt roads. The area is virtually uninhabited – there are just a dozen or so families scattered here and there who work in the reserve or fish for a living. The main entrance to the **Ciénaga de Zapata** (Zapata Swamp) reserve is gained through the tiny settlement of **Buena Ventura**, just to the west of Playa Larga, at the head of the famous Bahía de los Cochinos (Bay of Pigs).

BELOW: not all Cuban residents are hot-blooded.

Map on pages 210–11

Most of the peninsula is barely above sea level and is flooded every year during the rainy season. About 30 percent is slightly higher, supporting a wide strip of forest some 10 miles (16 km) from the southern coastline. Other elevated patches of terrain are scattered throughout the swamp, and clumps of trees grow on these patches like tiny islands. The western, triangular part of the Zapata Peninsula is entirely unpopulated.

Many narrow, linear canals are visible from the air, connecting lagoons with the surrounding shallow seas. These were all excavated by hand by the desperately poor charcoal makers a century or more ago, to facilitate lumber transportation. There are many hidden sink-holes, and it is not uncommon for a person walking off trails in knee-deep water to suddenly fall into deeper basins. Much of the swamp area is covered by a thick mat of peat that during the dry season behaves like a gigantic mattress. The underlying hard sediment of limestone frequently shows through, and, below ground, it is eroded into a network of caverns.

The Zapata's forests were once abundant in cabinet-quality hardwoods like ebony, mastic and mahogany. Regrettably, these virgin forests were thoroughly exploited in past centuries, and even the tallest trees today are only secondary growth. More recent logging has produced unsightly corridors through the forest. Moreover, feral pigs and the introduced white-tailed deer (the latter absurdly protected by a 1936 law) have devastated the plant life of the undergrowth and altered the balance of the forest species. As a result, species that you might expect to grace the forests – like orchids, ferns, bromeliads and vines – are rarities.

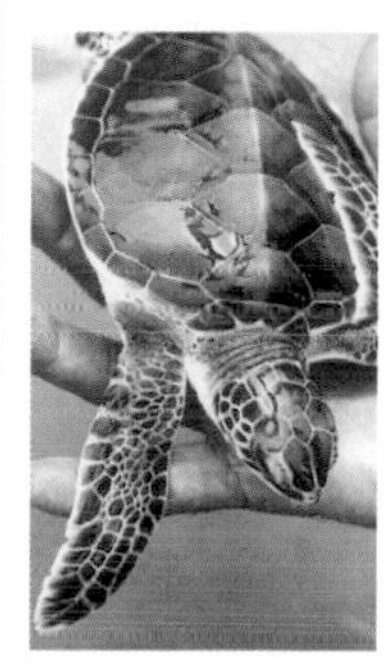

ABOVE: a sea turtle hatchling.
BELOW: an iridescent *zunzún* (hummingbird).

A birdwatcher's paradise

Birds are the main attraction in the peninsula, with a total count of 190 species. Most of Cuba's endemic species can be found here: the bee hummingbird, Cuban parakeet, Gundlach's hawk, blue-headed quail dove, Cuban tody, Cuban trogon, two species of blackbirds, two types of woodpeckers, and a couple of very small owls. Some species, such as the Zapata wren and rail, are unique to the swamp, whilst others can be found in few other places – the Zapata sparrow, for instance, is only found here, in Cayo Coco and the desert area of Baitiquirá, near Guantánamo.

The best place for the ornithologist is north of **Santo Tomás** ⑩ village. Always let your local guide show you the routes through the infinite, seemingly identical 6-ft (2-meter) clumps of sawgrass. The wren is a tiny, drab-looking bird, but an energetic songster; the sparrow isn't dressed to kill either, and barely buzzes or chatters. With some patience and luck, it's possible to hear the rail's ventriloquial calls – although unfortunately there is practically no chance at all of actually seeing one: this bird can pick its way through thickets of near-impenetrable grasses at speed, and only a handful of people have ever glimpsed one. Besides the resident native birds, many migrants show up at Zapata during the spring and winter, from October to April. These have flown down all the way from the US or even Canada. Most are warblers (more than

30 different species), but there are also herons, terns, rails, sparrows, swallows, and several birds of prey.

One particularly poignant shot in the Girón Museum shows the wall on which wounded infantryman Eduardo García Delgado scrawled the name "Fidel" in his own blood, just moments before his death.

The eastern side of the Bay of Pigs

From **Playa Larga** (one of the landing sites in the notorious 1961 invasion), the road skirts the edge of the Bahía de los Cochinos as it runs south towards Cuba's most famous beach of all, Playa Girón. Some wide man-made canals can be found slightly inland beyond **Los Hondones** (about 6 miles/10 km – from Playa Larga), where waterbirds abound: coots, gallinules, ducks, whistling ducks, herons, ospreys, jacanas, migratory buntings, and peregrine falcons.

Further along this stretch of road, look out for the many monuments to the Cuban dead of the Bay of Pigs invasion, and stop off at some of the beautiful sink-holes (*cenotes*) surrounded by forest, which are connected to the nearby sea by underwater tunnels. These flooded caverns in the limestone are full of tropical fish in all colors of the rainbow. The water is crystal clear even deep down, and surprisingly cold. You can snorkel in most of these *cenotes*, which is like swimming in an aquarium. One of the largest and loveliest, the **Cueva de los Pesces** (Fish Cave), has sadly been spoiled by over-development. It is well signposted, and there are two restaurants, a bar, and loungers for sitting by the lagoon and admiring the scenery. You can hire snorkeling gear, and though loud music ruins the ambience, the swimming and the fish are still lovely.

Remembering the Bay of Pigs

The small village of **Playa Girón** ⓫ holds an important place in Cold War history: this was the site of the Americans' disastrous 1961 Bay of Pigs invasion.

BELOW: veteran with captured American tank at Playa Girón, Bay of Pigs.

Not far from the palm trees and oceanfront tourist bungalows is a defiant billboard depicting a raised rifle and the words: "Playa Girón – the First Imperialist Defeat in Latin America."

Less than 300 ft (100 meters) from the landing spot, the **Museo de Girón** (open daily, 9am–noon and 1pm–6pm; entrance fee) has been built to commemorate the events of 1961, during which Castro first proclaimed his revolution to be of a "socialist" character. The rather drab-looking museum has some excellent exhibits commemorating the battle that began shortly after midnight on April 17, 1961, when the 2506th assault brigade – a CIA-trained force of some 1,500 mercenaries and Cuban exiles – landed to force the overthrow of Fidel. However, *El Jefe Máximo* was ready for them with Soviet-built T-34 tanks and T-33 fighter jets, and by the afternoon of April 19th, following two days of intense air and land battles, the 2506th surrendered. Of the invading force, 107 were killed and 1,189 were taken prisoner. Most of these men were later released back to the States, in return for a $53 million consignment of medicines and foodstuffs. Castro, who led the people's militia in the battle, lost 161 men and women, aged between 16 and 60 years old.

Outside the museum, you can inspect the remains of a B-26 bomber shot down by the Cubans, and a few captured American tanks. Inside are two rooms full of documents, photographs and weapons and an array of artefacts. Among the most interesting items on display here are a 12.7mm Czech-made anti-aircraft battery used to shoot down US planes, and a map showing how the mercenaries sailed from Puerto Cabezas, Nicaragua, to the southern Cuban coast. Their invasion was preceded two days beforehand by a bombing raid aimed at crippling the Cuban Air Force, but regrettably for the invaders, it failed in its objective, and only served to put Castro on full alert.

Map on pages 210–11

A trophy from the Bay of Pigs invasion outside the Girón Museum.

BELOW: treasures await beneath the waves.

Diving and snorkeling

The western side of Playa Girón is also a sanctuary for local fauna. Authorization is needed to pass through the gate and follow the old solid-fill causeway that has slowly killed all vegetation to the west. Flocks of rosy flamingos and spoonbills can be seen, feeding in the shallow salty lagoons, alongside other waders such as white ibises, black-necked stilts, sandpipers and plovers.

At Playa Girón itself, bathing and snorkeling is possible off the beach or at several spots along the shore where the seas are shallow. In addition, there are good opportunities for deeper scuba diving for those with the necessary experience, organized at the scuba center in the **Villa Horizontes Playa Larga** hotel. Further out to sea, the Caribbean shelf sinks vertically to hundreds of feet, and here you'll see rare black corals, spiny oysters,and ocean fish species like amberjack and little tunny.

A little further along the bay to the south is another good place to dive, the lovely cove of **Caleta Buena,** which also happens to be well blessed with spectacular sponges and red coral; there is a small entrance fee to the cove. Beyond here, a rough road best negotiated in a four-wheel drive vehicle heads east towards the city of Cienfuegos. ❑

THE RURAL HEARTLAND

As well as acres of sugarcane, Cuba's heartland has lovely towns, such as buzzing Santa Clara and the little-visited gem of Remedios, plus stunning landscapes in the Escambray mountains

East of Varadero begins a fertile green belt of land that produces enough sugarcane to sweeten the entire world. This is Cuba's agricultural backbone: orchards, rice fields, vegetable farms and enormous cattle ranches eat up the remaining terrain and feed much of the island's population.

From Havana or Varadero, the two-lane **Carretera Central** runs to the region's main cities and innumerable smaller towns: buses, trucks, tractors, carts, cars, bicycles, and animals all share the road, presenting a slow but picturesque parade of life in the countryside. The **Ocho Vías Autopista**, projected as an eight-lane highway all the way to the eastern tip of the island, is completed only as far as the other side of Sancti Spíritus. Along the way are a handful of dollar-only service stations. These offer gas, oil and air; rest rooms; drinks and food (proper meals in some cases); and usually one or two shops. The busiest are at Finca Fiesta Campesina (*see page 223*), at the turning to the Zapata Peninsula, and at **Aguada de Padajeros**, where the highway meets the road running south to Cienfuegos and Trinidad. If you have decided to join the locals and hitch, these are popular places to pick up a ride.

With a population of 800,000 people, the province of **Villa Clara** runs the gamut of rural backdrops. There are sleepy fishing villages, pretty coves and untouched offshore cays to the north; colonial towns and sugarcane plantations in its center; the rolling hills of the Alturas de Santa Clara to the east; and to the south, the majestic Escambray Mountains.

PRECEDING PAGES: "One lump or two?" – a coffee break in the cane fields
LEFT: steam trains still work the refineries.
BELOW: nanny goat and kids.

Santa Clara

The provincial capital of **Santa Clara** ⓬ (pop. 200,000), 171 miles (276 km) east of Havana on the *autopista*, is well worth visiting. Beyond the suburbs you'll find a buzzing place with streets lively with people going about their daily lives, and the city benefits from having a large student population. The center seems well looked after and relatively litter-free – a startling sight to anyone arriving from Havana.

Santa Clara was founded in 1689 by families from Remedios who had tired of pirate attacks and the legions of demons afflicting that settlement (*see page 235*). Set in the middle of the island, and being an important center for the sugar industry, the "gateway to the East" was of vital importance during many wars, including in the 1950s, when Che Guevara's seizure of the city in 1958 was the decisive victory in the war against Batista: this seminal moment is commemorated at sites across the town. But the city has far more to offer than simply Guevara memorabilia.

Santa Clara's main square is the delightful, leafy **Parque Vidal** Ⓐ, with a graceful central gazebo used for concerts. A monument marks the spot where rev-

olutionary hero Leoncio Vidal was killed, and benches line the promenades that cross and circle the park – in earlier days, an iron fence separated the inner promenade for whites from the outer area for blacks. The colonnaded buildings lining the square date from the late 19th and early 20th centuries, including the **Casa de la Trova**, the provincial **tourist information office**, and the **Hotel Santa Clara Libre** Ⓑ, distinguished by a façade riddled with shrapnel from the 1958 campaign.

On the plaza's north side is the **Museo de Artes Decorativas** Ⓒ (open Mon–Fri 9am–5pm; Sat 1pm–9.30pm; entrance fee), in one of the loveliest colonial buildings in the city. Rooms are sumptuously furnished with colonial pieces in many different styles, but dating mainly from the 19th century. On the nearby corner is **Teatro La Caridad** Ⓓ, which was financed by the philanthropist Marta Abreu de Estevez to bring culture to the poor of Santa Clara. Guilt-tripping on their fabulous sugar wealth, her parents had earlier established the city's first free clinic and primary school in 1878. The school, a block behind the theater, was used successively as a convent, a trade school and the incipient Ministry of Education in the early 1960s. Today it has been restored and reopened as the **Restaurante Colonial 1878**, with colonial furnishings to complement the date, and serves simple Cuban food.

Santa Clara's six-block long **Boulevard**, running along the Calle Independencia one street to the north of the plaza, is an enticing brick-paved mall with iron grilles, colonial lamps and conversational benches at each crossing. At the western end is the **Casa de la Ciudad** Ⓔ, an attractive old mansion with a motley array of exhibits, and the **Fondo de Bienes Culturales**, where local arts and crafts are sold. From the porches of small houses on any of the streets

TIP

The views from the rooftop bar and tenth-story restaurant of the Hotel Santa Clara Libre overlooking Parque Vidal are the best in town.

BELOW: a soldier guards Santa Clara's Revolution Square.

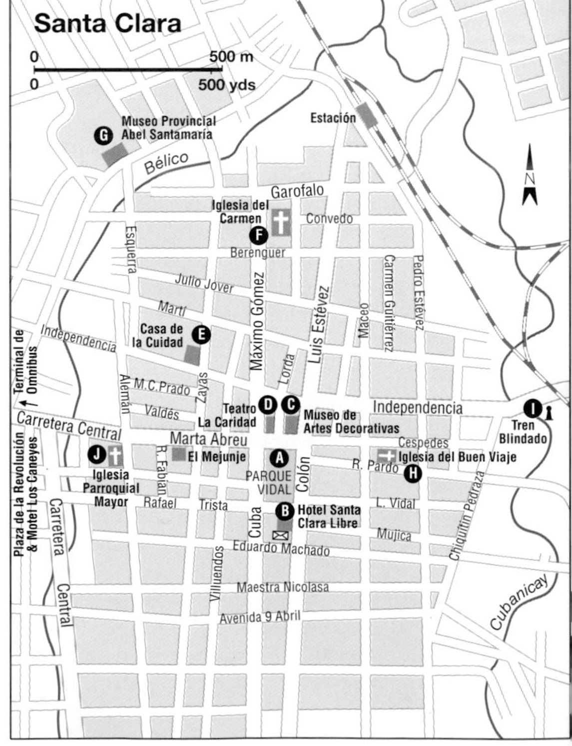

leading back to Parque Vidal, resident vendors offer flutes of freshly roasted *maní* (peanuts), squares of peanut candy or homemade guava paste.

Further north, up Máximo Gómez street, you come to an attractive church, the **Iglesia del Carmen** ❻, and to the west of here lies the **Museo Provincial**, in the **Escuela Abel Santamaría** ❼ (open Tues–Sat 1pm–6pm, and Sun 9am–1pm; entrance fee), with exhibits on natural history and the area's past.

The appealing **Iglesia del Buen Viaje** ❽, three blocks east of the plaza along Calle R. Pardo, is well worth visiting for its hybrid of architectural styles. And a short walk across the river, along Calle Independencia, will bring you to the famous **Tren Blindado** (Armoured Train) ❾ and museum (open Tues–Sun, 8am–noon and 3–7pm; entrance fee). This train, loaded with government soldiers and munitions sent from Havana to stop the Rebel Army's advance, was derailed at a critical moment during the battle for Santa Clara when it was attacked by rebels with guns and Molotov cocktails. To prevent the train's escape, Che himself ripped up the lines with a bulldozer, derailing the train, and winning the battle. Both bulldozer and train have been preserved in situ.

Artists' hangout

Two blocks west of Parque Vidal, on Marta Abreu, a handmade sign above a brick façade announces **El Mejunje**. Artists, intellectuals, and bohemians of all ages meet here to sip beer and *infusiones* (herbal brews), listen to a poetry recital or a musical group, dance and chat. The cultural potion is just right for laid-back Santa Clara, and there's no place quite like it anywhere else in Cuba.

A couple of blocks further along Calle Marta Abreu is the city's cathedral, the **Iglesia Parroquial Mayor** ❿, built in the early 20th century.

Map on pages 210–11

BELOW: Santa Clara's younger generations learn to look up to the heroic Che.

Homage to Che Guevara

Calle Marta Abreu joins the Carretera Central, which continues west to the *circunvalación* (ring road). Just south of the junction of the two roads is the **Plaza de la Revolución**, the usual place for Revolutionary gatherings. It is dominated by one of Cuba's finest revolutionary statues: a giant figure of Che Guevara, shown with his arm is in a sling – he broke it when he fell from a building during the battle for Santa Clara in 1958. The bronze statue bears the legend "*Hasta La Victoria Siempre*" ("Ever Onward to Victory"), a refrain which appears on many a billboard around Cuba.

Beneath Che's statue is the **Mausoleo** (open Tues–Sat 9am–6pm, Sun 9am–1pm; free), where the rebel's remains were interred in 1997. The mausoleum, low-ceilinged and made almost entirely of stone, has the look and feel of a cave. By Che's resting place, a lamp casts a light in the shape of a five-pointed star, and an eternal flame burns. Few visitors are not moved by the aura of reverence. There is also an interesting **museum** (same hours; free) featuring revolutionary memorabilia and some primitive broadcasting equipment used at Radio Rebelde, set up by Che at La Mesa mountain station.

Motel Los Caneyes, just off the ring road, not far from Plaza de la Revolución, is the best place to stay in Santa Clara. This hotel has conical thatched huts like the *caneyes* that native Cubans once built and the *bohíos* still seen today. See *Travel Tips* for details.

Villa Clara's northern coast

On the province's northwest coast, close to the border with Matanzas Province, is the town of **Corralillo**, famous for the **Baños de Elguea**, natural baths that spew sulphuric mud and carbonic water. The various springs and pools at this large spa help relieve rheumatism, neurological and circulatory pain, minor skin irritations and respiratory distress. Further east along the coastal road, you will reach the town of **Sagua La Grande**, which has a Cupet filling station, and

BELOW: pressing cane for *guarapo*.

THE TOWN OF COMANDANTE CHE

On December 28, 1958, Che Guevara's rebel troops attacked Santa Clara. Two days later, with the aid of townspeople (who braved air raids and snipers to help build barricades and mix Molotov cocktails), the rebels emerged victorious and cut Batista's communications with the east of the island, causing him to flee Cuba the next day. Many older Santa Clarans remember the battle well and will recount fascinating details of the events. To this day, the town remains Guevara's city: his wife, Aleida, is a native of the town; the names of institutions and numerous monuments attest to the affection in which he is held; and now he is even interred here.

When the handless mortal remains of this rebel icon were discovered after a lengthy search in Bolivia in 1997, they were brought to Cuba for burial. His flag-draped coffin lay in state in Santa Clara – the scene of his greatest triumph – for three days, and queues of those wishing to pay their final respects stretched back more than 3 miles (5 km). In the town's Revolution Square, on October 8, 1997, Fidel Castro made a speech as the coffin, and those of six companions from his Bolivian campaign (including one Bolivian and a Peruvian), were laid to rest in the specially-constructed mausoleum.

is close to the **Embalse Alacranes**, a freshwater reservoir renowned for its bass fishing. Simple accommodation and food is available at the Motel Amaro or Motel la Roca.

Map on pages 210–11

Remedios

Thirty miles (48 km) to the east of Santa Clara is **Remedios** ⓭, one of Cuba's most delightful colonial towns and the oldest settlement in the province of Villa Clara, dating back to 1578. There has been little recent urban development here, something the town has in common with Trinidad. While it may not be as picturesque as Trinidad, Remedios scores top marks for its lack of tourists.

Remedios did not enjoy an auspicious first hundred years, being ravaged during repeated raids by French, English and Portuguese pirates. If that were not enough, Remedios subsequently became occupied, according to one of the town's pious inhabitants, by "infernal legions of demons" (*see page 24*), and several families decamped to found the settlement of Santa Clara. However, most inhabitants ignored their wily cleric's warnings and stayed put. In the early 19th century, another tradition – that of misfortune – continued, and most of Remedios was razed by fire. It was rebuilt around what is now **Plaza Martí**, the town's pleasantly spacious central square.

Unquestionably the most stunning edifice in Remedios is the Iglesia de San Juan Bautista, more commonly referred to simply as the **Parroquial Mayor**, bordering the east side of Plaza Martí. The old church was severely damaged by a 1939 earthquake, but a millionaire penitent underwrote a 10-year renovation. The church is a religious treasure: Cuban artist Rogelio Atá carved the elaborate cedar altar in Moorish style and encrusted it with 24-carat gold. The decoration

BELOW: the Virgen del Buen Viaje church in the main square, Remedios.

You can stay overnight in Remedios in the delightful colonial Hotel Mascotte, in Plaza Martí. Máximo Gómez stayed here in 1899, when he met US President McKinley's representative to discuss the terms of discharge for Cuba's ragged independence fighters, who had been all but ignored by the Americans and Spaniards. A plaque commemorates the meeting.

continues along the edge of the mahogany ceiling – which is a breathtaking example of a *mudéjar*-style vaulted ceiling (*alfarje*), discovered only during the restoration work in the 1940s. The ceiling is particularly rare for its floral decoration. Also overlooking the square is the attractive church of the **Virgen del Buen Viaje**, though its interior seems very plain after a visit to the Parroquial Mayor.

On the north side of Plaza Martí is the splendid **Museo de la Música** (open Tues–Sat & Sun am; entrance fee), originally the home of Alexander García Caturla, a lawyer who devoted his life to music and became one of Cuba's most famous avant-garde composers. Caturla broke with the conventions of his class in every way. He married a black woman and, after her death, married her sister. His worst crime, though, was his incorruptibility as a lawyer and judge: in 1940, at the age of 34, Caturla was summarily assassinated after having refused a politician's bribe. The intimate museum exhibits Caturla's personal effects, scores, musical instruments, and tapes of some of his compositions.

The **Casa de Cultura**, in the former Spanish Casino just off the square, and the enormous mansion that is now the **Museo de Historia**, attempt to explain, with mixed success, the folk tales, religious traditions and superstition that mingle in Remedios's bizarre history.

A festival not to be missed

Remedios is famous for its strange and passionate street festivals, known as **parrandas**, which evolved from the percussion street bands, known as *repiques*, that processed through the streets to arouse people for the pre-dawn Mass held to honor San Juan de los Remedios on December 24. In the 19th century, this religious celebration developed into a street fair, with costumes, parades, music and food.

Below: a gilt San Francisco in Parroquial Mayor, Remedios.

The fascinating **Museo de las Parrandas** (open Tues–Sat), two blocks off the plaza at Máximo Gómez 71, displays the instruments heard during the celebrations, but it is of course only a static reflection of the real events, in which neighboring districts of the town (Carmen, identified by a sparrowhawk and a globe, and San Salvador, whose symbol is a rooster) spend the week between Christmas Eve and New Year's Eve competing for best parade float (*carroza*). For months beforehand, artists and engineers secretly plan and build a so-called *trabajo de plaza* – a great tower of light and imagination that represents their neighborhood; it can reach as high as 90 ft (28 meters). The *parrandas* start when night falls, with the unveiling of these incredible confections. The celebrations continue until dawn breaks with salutes by musicians playing traditional polkas; paraders carrying hand-made lanterns and banners; tableaux on dazzling floats; and fireworks as thrilling as they are menacing. Other towns in the area – including Placetas and Zulueta – maintain similar traditions.

The Northern Islands

Six miles (10km) northeast of Remedios is the rather run-down fishing port of **Caibarién**, where boats dot the harbor, and almost any local captain will take you out to fish. The wharves and warehouses along the waterfront recall the town's one-time importance as a shipping port. Caibarién has some mediocre beaches, on a promontory jutting out into the sea, and there is also a nautical base on the bay northeast of the port, where locals practise sailing, windsurfing and kayaking to compete in national and international competitions.

From Caibarién, you can take a boat for the 15-minute ride across to **Cayo Conuco** ⓮. A sagging wooden dock is the landing point on this 363-acre (145-hectare) islet, and a trail leads uphill to one of the most delightful campsites in Cuba. *Cabañas* nestle in the woods, and campers can swim, fish, ride horses, cook outdoors, and enjoy nature: they share the cay with numerous species of animals, including iguanas and *jutías* (a type of rodent), as well as 172 species of plants. On the coast east of Caibarién, a causeway runs out 28 miles (45 km) to **Cayo Santa María** and the smaller cays closer to shore. All these cays in the **Archipiélago de Camagüey** are, or soon will be, developed for tourism.

Into the Escambray Mountains

South of Santa Clara, the scenery of the province folds from pastoral farmland into the Escambray Mountains. At **Manicaragua**, the road splits, giving you the option to head straight on to Trinidad, east to Sancti Spíritus or west to **Embalse Hanabanilla** ⓯ – an enormous reservoir at the top of a 5-mile (8-km) climb from a turning after the village of La Moza. Perfectly situated in a gorgeous location by the lakeside, with hills all around, is **Hotel Hanabanilla**. You may decide simply to enjoy the views and the swimming pool, but you can also fish for largemouth bass, hike through the woods, visit nearby waterfalls, or take a boat across the lake. A boat trip is highly recommended for the glimpse it pro-

Map on pages 210–11

Fresh lobster is often available, illegally, in private restaurants near the coast.

BELOW: Cuban kids enjoying the sand on the north coast.

TIP

A boat takes people across the lake to the Río Negro Restaurant. From here the lake seems as placid as a pond, framed by green hills in the distance, with a foreground of gaudy bougainvillea. This feast for the eyes is matched by a feast for your tastebuds, as succulent spit-roasted pork is served beneath the shade of palm-thatched umbrellas.

BELOW: one of the Escambray's beautiful waterfalls.

vides of mountain life. Farmers who work small plots along the shore have their own animals, keep bees and grow most of their food – fruits, vegetables, and coffee. Bags of beans, jars of thick honey and other apiary products like royal jelly are sometimes for sale in the back patio. Coffee is considered a "state crop" and, legally, only the state can buy or sell the beans, but the farmers often conveniently ignore the law.

Jungle and struggle in the Escambray

The majestic Sierra del Escambray is Cuba's second most famous mountain range after the Sierra Maestra in the Oriente, with its heighest peak – the Pico San Juan – topping 3,700 ft (1,100 meters). Even at the height of summer, when temperatures in Trinidad or Santa Clara reach 100°F (40°C), you may still need a jersey here. Some of the heaviest rainfall in Cuba feeds the Escambray's lush jungle, where trees are laden with bromeliads and delicate waterfalls greet you at every turn; look out for the giant umbrella-like ferns, a prehistoric species. This is also an important coffee-growing region. On the lower slopes, jungle gives way to pastures and royal palms.

The Escambray provided a perfect hide-out for counter-revolutionaries in the 1960s. The number of anti-Castro guerrillas, who ranged from hardened CIA-trained fighters to farmers adversely affected by Castro's land reforms, had reached an estimated 3,000 by 1962, when the revolutionary government instigated a campaign to defeat the *bandidos* ("bandits"). Counter-insurgency units combed the area, driving the bands into more and more difficult terrain until they had no option but to surrender or fight. Even so, the last groups were not killed until 1966. (There is a museum about this struggle in Trinidad; *see page 254.*)

A health spa in the hills

From Manicaragua, the road twists and turns south through spectacular scenery, with every bend offering new views of tropical vegetation, interspersed with plantation forests of eucalyptus and pine. Parrots (*cotorras*) and other bird species abound, though casual observers are more likely to hear than see them.

Eventually you come to **Topes de Collantes** ⓰, a spa resort originally built in the 1930s as a tuberculosis sanitarium, and then developed for wider health tourism. The resort is conspicuously run-down, but is undergoing renovation to attract more foreign tourists, offering saunas, mineral baths, massage and herbal therapies. Three hotels accept foreigners: the monstrous-looking Kurhotel is better on the inside than out; the Hotel Los Helechos, which has a nice swimming pool; and the basic Motel Los Pinos.

For most visitors, however, the appeal of Topes lies in the walks and the exotic **waterfalls** nearby – especially **Salto Vega Grande** and the sweeping uniquely-shaped **Salto Caburní**, a 250-ft (75-meter) fall, which is a testing 2½-mile (4-km) hike from the Kurhotel. Local guides wait at the top of the trail, and the few dollars it costs to hire them is money well spent.

From Topes the road continues dramatically downhill to Trinidad, with some stunning views of the coastline. If you are driving, be sure to stay in low gear: brake pads can wear out quickly on a hot day

The Kurhotel sanitarium in Topes de Collantes.

Sancti Spíritus

The Carretera Central east from Santa Clara cuts through the central plains to reach the city of **Sancti Spíritus** ⓱ (pop. 87,388) – capital of the province of the same name. Although the city in no way rivals the splendor of Trinidad, on

BELOW: the Yayabo Bridge, Sancti Spíritus.

THE CITY: A HEALTH HAZARD?

The young Winston Churchill was a visitor to Sancti Spíritus in 1895. Riding with the Spanish army, he became involved in a skirmish with the mambí Cuban independence fighters at Arroyo Blanco, east of the city. He narrowly escaped being shot, and later recalled the experience in his memoirs: "There is nothing more exhilarating than to be shot at without result."

Arriving in the city itself, he was not in the least impressed, immediately dismissing it as "a very second-rate and most unhealthy place." Perhaps he had drunk from the River Yayabo, for years the city's only source of water, despite its impurities.

Nowadays things have changed, and Sancti Spíritus has a modern viaduct, which brings in fresh water from the nearby hills. In spite of this, there is still a tradition of drinking the river water, filtered of course, and served in a *porrón* – a small earthenware jug. Almost everyone who crosses the Yayabo Bridge stops at a public watering place called El Porrón for a welcome thirst quencher. Don't worry about Churchill's warning – you're unlikely to face even the danger of a stomach upset here now, let alone yellow fever or bullets. Yet if that had been the case back then, he would surely have complained that the town was too dull.

Map on pages 210–11

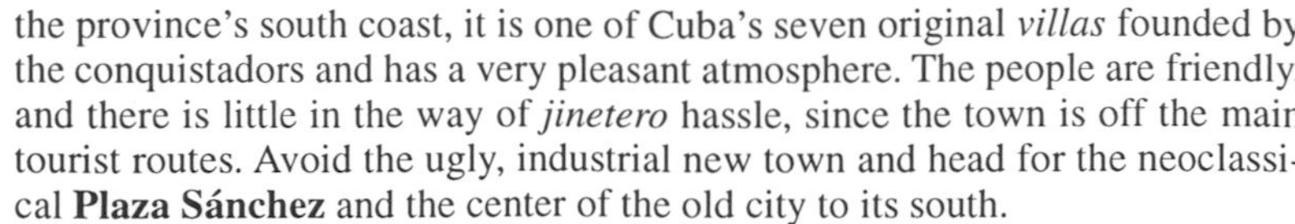

the province's south coast, it is one of Cuba's seven original *villas* founded by the conquistadors and has a very pleasant atmosphere. The people are friendly, and there is little in the way of *jinetero* hassle, since the town is off the main tourist routes. Avoid the ugly, industrial new town and head for the neoclassical **Plaza Sánchez** and the center of the old city to its south.

Sancti Spíritus had an unfortunate early history: it had to be relocated from its original site after the area's native inhabitants – a plague of stinging ants – decided to fight off the invaders; and then the new city was twice burned and destroyed by pirates. Therefore, none of this city's historic buildings is as old as those in Trinidad, though it does still have some delights. Chief among them, on the **Plaza Honrato del Castillo**, is a most enchanting church, the **Iglesia Parroquial Mayor del Espíritu Santo**. Originally built in 1522, it was rebuilt with the same materials in the 17th century after its destruction by pirates. The tower was added in the 18th century and the cupola in the 19th, giving it a classic Cuban feel. With its rich, burnished yellow exterior, and its peaceful location, this is one sight in the city that shouldn't be missed.

A statue of Christ in the grounds of Sancti Spíritus cathedral.

Also on the square is the small **Museo de la Esclavitud**, which relates the harrowing experiences of slaves brought to work on the sugar plantations. Just to the south is the **Museo de Arte Colonial** (open Tues–Fri 1pm–10pm, Sat 1–5pm, Sun 10am–4pm; entrance fee), housed in an attractive colonial mansion, and worth visiting for its original decor and furnishings alone. Along with the church, the nearby colonial houses of the cobbled Calle El Llano and the **bridge** across the **Río Yayabo** have all been declared national monuments. The bridge, built in 1522, is the only arched stone bridge left in Cuba. Beneath it is an excellent *paladar* on a houseboat, the **Merendero el Puente**, which seems to specialize in seafood.

RIGHT: Dolphins fan. **BELOW:** whiling away the day.

The sugar plains

Endless expanses of sugarcane surround Sancti Spíritus and supply the Uruguay sugar mill, the country's largest, east of the town. *Bagasse* (residue) from the cane is used in the modern paper mill in **Jatibonico** nearby.

Although cane cutting on the flat central plains is largely mechanized today, the *machetero* who fells the stalks with his sharp machete remains the Cuban work hero. Sometimes billowing black clouds can be seen rising from the cane, indicating that it has been burned in preparation for cutting. This process crystallizes the sugar and increases its yield, at the same time as polluting the atmosphere and blackening both the *macheteros* and the machinery.

Lakeside peace

Cuba's largest man-made lake, the **Embalse Zaza,** outside the city, is known for the size and quantity of its large mouth bass, while the surrounding woods harbor mourning and white-winged doves for seasonal hunting. There is a hotel here where sportsmen can stay, and an international fishing competition in September. The area is also popular with bird-watchers, as the mangrove-choked marshes of the River Zaza provide a habitat for copious quantities of waterbirds. ❑

Dolphins

CIENFUEGOS AND TRINIDAD

Two historic but very different cities and a splendid stretch of coastline, with one of Cuba's favorite beaches, provide a breath of fresh air after the sugar fields and mountains of the interior

Maps
Area 210
City 246

Havana
CUBA

Cienfuegos province, with 326,000 inhabitants, is dominated by green rolling country, peppered by small sleepy towns and *bohíos*. Palm-fringed fields of sugar run down to the Alturas de Santa Clara in the east and the distant blue Escambray mountains in the south. The 1959 Revolution brought change to what was once primarily an agricultural region and it has, around the city of Cienfuegos at least, become highly industrialized: home, even, to Cuba's notorious and still unfinished nuclear power station.

Cienfuegos

The road to Cienfuegos city from the *autopista* runs through the small town of Rodas: a pleasant but sleepy place, best known for its Ciego Montenero spring, the origin of most of Cuba's fine mineral water. **Cienfuegos** ⓲ (pop. 105,000), the "city of one hundred fires," is also known as the "Pearl of the South" – though this traditional name is kept alive primarily in Cuban tourist literature.

Europeans first sighted the area in 1494 during the second voyage of Christopher Columbus, but no settlement was established until 1819 when Louis de Clouet, a Frenchman who had emigrated to New Orleans, founded the colony of Fernandina de Jagua. It was renamed Cienfuegos the following year in honor of Cuba's then Spanish Governor General, who invited further settlers from Louisiana. In 1869, a group of Cuban nationalists led by Juan Díaz de Villegas rebelled against the Spanish government here, and years later, in October 1895, Major-General José Rodríguez organized the Cienfuegos Brigade, which later played a key role in the battle of Mal Tiempo during Cuba's second War of Independence.

Following the 1959 Revolution, Cienfuegos received massive investment from the Soviet Union, which turned the region into a major industrial center. Today, the province of Cienfuegos has 12 sugar mills which can grind 43,000 tons (39,000 tonnes) of raw *caña* daily. Likewise, its port – the only deep-water terminal on Cuba's south coast, and home to a sizeable fishing and shrimping fleet – handles around 30 percent of the country's sugar exports. Despite such developments, downtown Cienfuegos has not changed greatly over the years, and with a little imagination you can appreciate the attempt by its French founders to give the city a certain Parisian feel, with its parks, tree-lined boulevards, and colonnades.

The historical center of the city is the **Pueblo Nuevo** district, which, as the dollar increasingly takes over as the only usable Cuban currency, is rapidly becoming quite a pleasant shopping center. Most of the city's best buildings can be seen around **Parque José Martí** Ⓐ, the square where the first settlement

PRECEDING PAGES: view from Trinidad toward the sea.
LEFT: Trinidad's under-used cathedral.
BELOW: a gift to brighten someone's day.

was founded on April 22, 1819, under the shade of a *majagua* tree. The place where the tree stood is now marked by a bandstand. There are a series of statues to the city's illustrious citizens, including one to José Martí guarded by lions, and also a triumphal arch, inscribed with the date 20 Mayo, 1902 – commemorating the birth of the Cuban Republic.

Cienfuegos is built according to a strict grid system: even-numbered Avenidas *run east to west, while odd-numbered* Calles *run north to south.*

The **Cathedral**, dating from 1870, dominates the square and has an impressive interior, complete with marble floors. Nearby, on the north side, is the **Teatro Tomás Terry** (officially known as the Teatro de Cienfuegos), completed in 1895. It was named after a rich sugar baron who arrived in Cuba a poor Venezuelan emigré, and made a dubious fortune by buying up weak and sick slaves, nursing them back to health, and then reselling them at a profit. The ornate interior of the theater is made virtually entirely of precious Cuban hardwoods (a luxury now consigned to the past), with classical reliefs and nymphs providing some of the decoration. National and local performances are staged here, from the National Ballet to local comedy acts. Adjoining the theater is the pastel-painted, columned **Colegio San Lorenzo**, built in 1927.

On the opposite side of the square, the **Museo Histórico Provincial** (open Tues–Sun, 9am–5pm; entrance fee) focuses on the city's role in the War of Independence, but you may find more fun is to be had by climbing up the tower of the **Casa de Cultura**, which occupies the former home of a rich sugar baron on the west side of the square.

Also on the square are the **Primero Palacio**, apparently modeled on Havana's Capitolio and now the local government headquarters, and the **Mesón El Palatino**, a snack bar where weary tourists can cool off with lemonade, soft drinks, or imported beer.

BELOW: the tower atop the Casa de Cultura in Parque Martí, Cienfuegos.

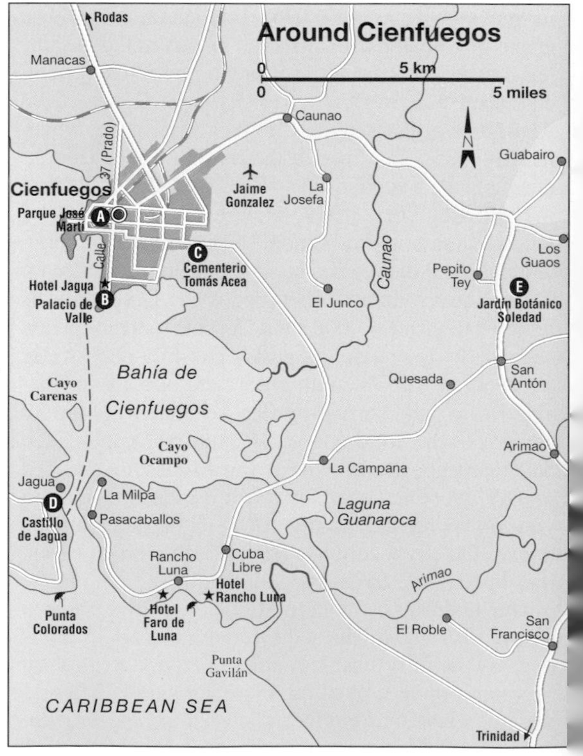

Map on page 246

The pedestrianized streets around the Plaza José Martí hum with activity: particularly **Boulevard San Fernando**, where food stalls, souvenir vendors, flower sellers, boot blacks, and other entrepreneurs cash in on Cuba's gradual return to capitalism. The main street, however, is the broad Calle 37, usually called the **Paseo del Prado** – a more befitting name for the longest boulevard in Cuba; south of Avenida 46, just before it hits the waterfront, the street is known as the Malecón. Always a busy street filled with traffic and gossiping crowds, it is the hub of the city's social life, and is lined with statues, busts and plaques to the place's most notable citizens.

Arabian nights

Cienfuegos's best known landmark, however, isn't in the center of town but at the very end of the Prado. At the south end of the Malecón, you reach Punta Gorda where once gracious French-style mansions and plantation houses can be found. You can't miss the vast **Hotel Jagua** – the city's only dollar hotel – which was once a notorious casino hotel run by Batista's brother, but the main attraction is the adjacent **Palacio de Valle** **B** (open daily).

This whimsical mansion, done up in Moorish Revival style with a few other styles mixed in for good measure, was commissioned by businessman Aciclio Valle. He brought in craftsmen from Morocco in 1913, and had the building finished by 1917. After the 1959 Revolution, the Valle family fled Cuba, and for many years the palace served as a government hotel school. Then, in 1990, the Hotel Jagua, situated across from the Palacio, converted it into an expensive Italian restaurant, which today serves delicious shrimp and lobster dinners and an exquisite *flan* (crème caramel). Watching the sunset over Cienfuegos Bay

A touch of the Orient at Palacio de Valle.

BELOW: detail of the Palacio de Valle.

from the third-floor balcony of the Palacio is unforgettable. So too is the resident pianist, the flamboyant Carmen, who wears glitter make-up and seems to know a song from every country on earth. If you decide to dine here, enjoy an after-dinner sing-along at Carmen's side and finish off the evening at the Hotel Jagua's hilarious drag-show cabaret.

Castillo de Jagua can be reached by ferry from the port in Cienfuegos or by boat from outside Hotel Pasacaballo, on the other side of the bay.

Around Cienfuegos

The sights of the bay south of Cienfuegos can be seen using a combination of buses and ferries. A ferry departs three times a day from a terminal south of the Parque Martí, serving the small communities around the bay and taking about an hour to reach the Castillo de Jagua. Alternatively, take the road that follows the eastern side of the bay. Leaving the city by this road, after about a mile (2km) you pass **Cementerio Tomás Acea** Ⓒ, an impressive neoclassical cemetery overlooking the bay. You will eventually end up at the ugly, Soviet-built **Hotel Pasacaballo**. This hotel is built directly across the bay from the Castillo de Jagua, but strangely all the rooms face the other way.

It does, however, afford excellent views of one of Cienfuegos's most curious tourist attractions: the concrete dome of Cuba's biggest white elephant – the Soviet-designed **Juraguá nuclear power plant,** known as "Nuclear City." Construction of the $2½ billion facility began in 1983, but the twin reactors were only 60 percent complete when the USSR collapsed, and plans for its completion are on hold until Cuba can secure additional financial backing.

For more traditional architecture, take a 15-minute boat ride across the mouth of the bay to the **Castillo de Nuestra Señora de los Angeles de Jagua** Ⓓ, the 17th-century Spanish fortress built to defend the area against pirate attacks.

BELOW: the beach at Rancho Luna.

The castle has a bar and restaurant inside, but there's not much to it otherwise. Along the water's edge beneath the castle lies **Perché**, a tumbledown fishing village founded by Spanish fishermen from Valencia and the Balearics.

Four miles (6 km) east of Pasacaballos, just where the road veers inland, is the **Hotel Rancho Luna**, a resort popular with Canadian tourists. It has a large pool and sun deck, and looks out on to the beach with its warm shallow turquoise sea. The nearby **Hotel Faro Luna** is smaller but has similar facilities. On the way back to town, you pass the **Comunidad Mártires de Barbados**, a collective farm named in memory of 73 Cuban athletes who died in 1976 when right-wing terrorists bombed a Cubana de Aviación jetliner over Barbados.

The **Jardín Botánico Soledad** Ⓔ (open daily, 8am–4pm; entrance fee), just north of San Antón about 10 miles (16 km) east of Cienfuegos, is well worth a visit. Founded in 1899, before the Revolution the gardens served as Harvard College's Botanical Station for Tropical Research and Sugar Cane Investigation. Now run by the Cuban Academy of Sciences, the vast gardens are home to around 2000 species, including over 300 types of palm tree.

Maps
City 246
Area 211

TIP

Guajimico, midway between Cienfuegos and Trinidad, is a lovely place to stay. A collection of *cabañas* are scattered prettily around a secluded cove, with its own small beach and harbor.

The road to Trinidad

You can reach Embalse Hanabanilla (*see page 237*) and Santa Clara by taking the scenic road via Cumanayagua to Manicaragua, across the foothills of the **Sierra de Escambray**, but the main road between Cienfuegos and Trinidad proceeds south, across a delightful hummocky landscape until it reaches the sea. Here, the road often hugs the shore, pushed close to the sea by the mountains, providing fleeting glimpses of hidden coves and beaches.

At **La Sierrita**, 20 miles (32km) east of Cienfuegos, cut inland into the Escambray for one of the most dramatic routes through the mountains to Topes de Collantes (*see page 239*), taking you close to **Pico San Juan**, the highest point. The road surface is poor in places, and the inclines are often steep, but the views are magnificent. (The most popular route into the mountains and to Topes runs north from Trinidad.)

Back on the coast road, you pass several small (and often deserted) beaches, the first of which is **Playa Inglés**, about 30 miles (48 km) from Cienfuegos. The second is **Playa Yaguanabo**, 3 miles (5 km) further east, where Villa Yaguanabo offers two-story cabins with basic facilities and a restaurant.

BELOW: the stately Botanical Gardens outside Cienfuegos.

Colonial sugar capital

Located in Sancti Spíritus Province, 50 miles (82 km) east of Cienfuegos, is **Trinidad** ⓳, Cuba's third-oldest settlement and one of the island's crown jewels. Its red-tiled roofs, pastel buildings, cobblestoned streets and historic museums make the town a must-see for any tourist interested in Cuba's colonial history.

Trinidad was founded in January 1514 by Spanish explorer Diego Velázquez, at a spot just inland from the Caribbean Sea near the mouth of the Río Arimao. From the outset, Velázquez and his men enslaved the local indigenous Taíno inhabitants, but when they died out due to disease and overwork, the colonists started importing black slaves from Africa.

By the census of 1795, there were 2,676 slaves in Trinidad. That year, the area's 82 sugar mills produced 60,000 arrobas *(750 tons/680 tonnes) of sugar, 1,000 barrels of* aguardiente *(a local liquor), and 700 urns of molasses.*

As the sugar industry grew, the area around Trinidad became known as the Valle de los Ingenios (Valley of the Sugar Mills), and fabulous plantation houses began to dot the countryside. Throughout much of the 1600s, the area's wealth sparked raids by pirates and corsairs, who destroyed the provincial capital of Sancti Spíritus but spared Trinidad itself. The town was also a thriving center for smugglers and the slave trade – the source of much of its wealth. When Cuba officially abolished slavery in 1880, the practice continued in more subtle forms for several years, even after the 1895 War of Independence. Throughout most of the 20th century, Trinidad has remained economically tied to sugar, though tourism is now becoming an increasingly important source of revenue for the town's 52,000 people.

A protected gem

In 1988, the United Nations declared Trinidad and its Valle de los Ingenios a World Heritage Site, but the town had already been recognized as a National Monument since the Batista years. There are no garish signs or souvenir displays in the town itself, as these are against the law.

It well deserves the praise heaped on it: painted mahogany balustrades run along the shady colonnades; massive ancient timber doors open to reveal cool green courtyards beyond; transport is mainly pony or mule driven; and life in the city moves sleepily along. At night, there is little sign of life – the town is dark, and lit by low lights or the eerie glow of black and white TVs as the inhabitants settle down to watch an evening soap opera or movie. The town's picturesque quaintness is in increasing demand by foreign companies as a TV and film location, and many magazines have shot fashion features here. However this is not

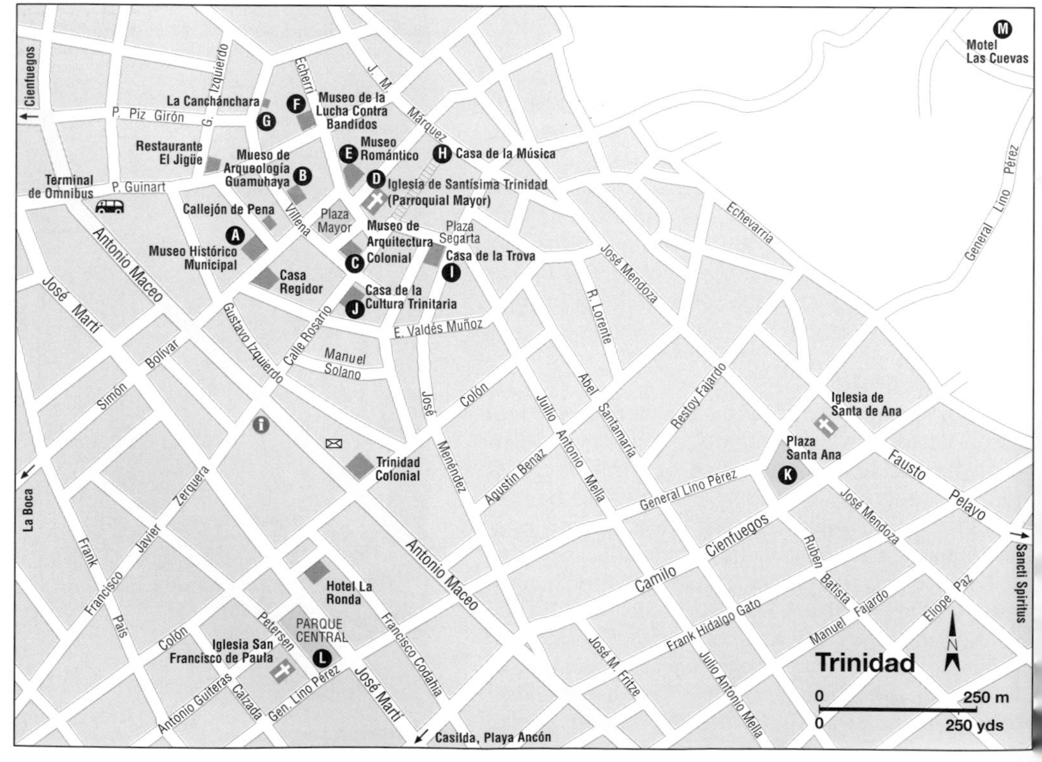

entirely a "museum city." The influx of the dollar has brought the usual scourges of "*jineterismo*" – though this is more on nearby beaches than in the town itself. In Trinidad, young children after change are as common as local youths offering to act as your "guide."

Exploring the city

Trinidad is divided into the old and new towns. The newer town is built on a grid system and is centered around the Parque Céspedes. **Old Trinidad** centers around the Plaza Mayor where the rich built their mansions. The sloping streets all have a central gutter to let the water flow easily away, though legend has it that the first governer of Trinidad had one leg shorter than the other and could therefore walk more easily through the streets by walking in the gutters.

Whatever the length of your legs, virtually the only way to explore Trinidad is on foot. The streets in the old town are closed to traffic and in other parts of the town they are generally old and narrow and difficult to negotiate by car unless you know them well. Following a simple walking tour takes three to four hours – museum and lunch stops included – although you might like to make it last a few days. Sightseeing is best in the morning, while it's still fairly cool and the streets are less crowded, or in the early evening, when the buildings are bathed in a delicious, pinkish light.

Colonial aristocrats financed their lavish lifestyles with the profits from sugar plantations.

If you're driving, park on **Calle Antonio Maceo**, where an attendant will guard your car (and give it a thorough washing too) for a dollar. Walking up Calle Simón Bolívar you pass several impressive colonial mansions, before reaching the **Palacio Cantero**, one of the city's most exquisite mansions, housing the city's **Museo Histórico Municipal** Ⓐ (open Mon–Fri, 10am–6pm; Sun 9am–1pm; entrance fee), with some fine pieces of colonial furniture and interesting exhibits on the slave trade. Once a Roman-style bath house, a fountain spouted *eau de cologne* for women and gin for men. However, the finest feature is the house's square tower, which provides an exceptional view of the whole town – a perfect introduction to the delights of Trinidad, especially in the late afternoon.

Within a few paces of the museum are the **Museo de Artes Decorativas** (on a site where the famous conquistador Hernán Cortés is said to have lived before departing for Mexico to conquer the Aztecs), the **Casa del Regidor** (formerly the Mayor's residence), and the **Callejón de Pena**, a street full of private merchants, and a good place to find excellent arts and crafts, but be sure to bargain.

BELOW: a stick helps over bumpy ground.

The heart of the City

One block further up, you emerge into the splendid, intimate **Plaza Mayor**, one of Cuba's most photographed sights. Immediately on your right, the attractive balconied building contains the **Galería de Arte Universal**, with many paintings for sale, although you will find prices cheaper if you buy from artists privately. To your left, another beautiful mansion houses the **Museo de Arqueología y Ciencias Naturales Guamuhaya** Ⓑ (open Sun–Fri, 9am–5pm; entrance fee). Here, you'll find some rather unap-

A pair of shapely bronze greyhounds guards Trinidad's Plaza Mayor.

pealing displays of stuffed animals and birds, but others are related to the more interesting history of the region's pre-Columbian peoples.

Cross the square from the Archaeological Museum, and enjoy the square, with its white wrought iron benches and small statues, including two bronze greyhounds. On the opposite side, at No. 83, is the former house of the Sánchez family, now the **Museo de Arquitectura Colonial** Ⓒ (open Sat–Thur, 8am–5pm; entrance fee), which tells the history of Trinidad's development with maps and models, showing how colonial craftsmen worked. Like many buildings in Trinidad, this 1735 house was painted yellow rather than white, because white was considered too harsh on people's eyes in the strong tropical sun. When the house was restored in the 1980s, sections of yellow were left as a reminder of its original color. The museum is crammed with interesting artefacts, including an exhibit of hand-carved doors and windows, gas-lit chandeliers and a stockade built to hold 12 slaves at once. In the shady courtyard is a sundial, an unusual multi-fauceted shower and even a 19th-century gas generator which was made in New York City. There is a delightful garden at the back of the museum.

The huge, cream-colored cathedral standing at the top of the square is the **Parroquial Mayor** Ⓓ, which was begun in 1868. This is the only church in Cuba to have hand-carved Gothic altars, and five aisles instead of three. It was fully restored in 1996, but the church is still said to be unfinished, since its niches remain empty, intended for Italian statues that never arrived.

BELOW: wedding photographs in Trinidad's main square.

A home of elegance and romance

A strong contender for Trinidad's best museum is the bold yellow building with marzipan arches on the same side of the square: the **Museo Romántico** Ⓔ

(open Tues–Sun, 9am–6pm; entrance fee), housed in a sumptuous mansion that for many years belonged to the Brunet family of Spain. The family, which bought noble titles with its sugar wealth, came to Cuba in 1857, and their 12 children lived in this mansion, along with a number of slaves.

In 1974, the house was turned into a museum, and its rooms were filled with period pieces collected from many mansions throughout the city. Here, for example, you can see a priceless 18th-century Austrian writing desk, covered with enamel painted scenes of mythology; a marble bathtub and wooden "throne" from 1808 used as a toilet; and, in the kitchen, a limestone water filter and a set of beautiful custom-made porcelain plates and dishes from 1823. The upstairs balcony has fine views over the square. Next door is an Artex store selling jewellery, arts and crafts and souvenirs.

Religion to revolution

Leaving the museum, walk down Calle Echerrí (also called Cristo) to the intersection with Calle Piro Guinart. Here are the **Archivos de la Ciudad** (City Archives), recognizable by the colorful coat-of-arms hanging on the façade. Directly in front is the tallest and most famous landmark in Trinidad: the **Convento de San Francisco de Asís**, parts of which date from 1731. The building was enlarged and embellished in 1809 by Father Valencia of Spain, but, after the construction of the nearby Parroquial Mayor in 1892, the convent ceased to function, and the building was made into a military barracks for the Spanish Army. Then, in 1984, in a perverse twist of history, the former convent was turned into the **Museo de la Lucha Contra Bandidos** Ⓕ or Museum of the Struggle against Counter-Revolutionaries (open Tues–Sat 9am–noon and

BELOW: a display of lace in a Trinidad home.

2pm–6pm; entrance fee), which concentrates on the campaign to weed out anti-Castro guerrillas in the nearby Escambray mountains in the 1960s. Inside is a boat in which Cuban exiles came from South Florida to destroy the oil tanks at the nearby port of Casilda, and a Russian truck used in the search for counter-revolutionaries in the mountains.

The real beauty of this building, however, has nothing to do with politics. Climb the 119 granite and wooden stairs to the top of the bell tower. Once you've caught your breath, enjoy the view: from here, all of Trinidad is clearly visible, as are the blue waters of the Caribbean and the distant, hazy peaks of the Sierra Escambray.

TIP

Two good areas for buying cheap street food with pesos in Trinidad are Calle Martí, off the Parque Central (Parque Céspedes), and Calle Piro Guinart, near the bus terminal.

Shake your tree

Walking to the end of Echerri, you reach the area called El Fortuno. In the 18th century it was home to several foreign pirates who were welcomed by the Trinidadians, many of whom, indeed, grew rich from smuggling and trading with these men. The house at Ciro Redondo No. 261 was said to have been built for a French pirate, Carlos Merlin, in 1754. At the foot of Redondo, turn left into Calle Martínez Villena, heading towards **La Canchánchara** **G**, a fun tourist-oriented bar with live entertainment, and its own house cocktail, the "Canchánchara" made from *aguardiente*, lime, honey and sparkling water, a good investment at $1.50.

On the parallel Calle Vicente Suyama (also known by locals as Calle Encarnación) is a makeshift gallery at No. 39 run by art professor Carlos Mata: it's typical of several private galleries that cater specifically to foreign tourists, and which have sprouted up around Trinidad since early 1994, when the government

BELOW LEFT: in-depth detail in the Museum of the Struggle Against Counter-Revolutionaries.

BELOW RIGHT: kids outside the church of Nuestra Señora de la Candelaria.

began tolerating certain limited forms of private enterprise. One block along from La Canchánchara to your right is the spot where, in the 16th century, Diego Velázquez conducted the first Christmas Mass in Trinidad under a stately old *jigüe* tree: the **Plazuela Real del Jigüe**, complete with one of Trinidad's best little restaurants.

The next stop, on your right at No.59, is definitely not for the average tourist; in fact, some will find this place downright spooky. This is an authentic Santería house, complete with Cuban revolutionary posters and an altar of a black Madonna. There's also a rock shaped like a perfect egg, inside a pot full of seawater; the whole contraption is covered with fine lace. If you'd like to enter, ask for Israel, the Santería priest, who'll explain everything.

Before reaching the Plaza, on your right, you'll notice a dirt yard, which, in the evenings, is one of the most enjoyable places to visit in the city. Here on most nights, dancers and musicians celebrate a *parranda* – best described as a jam session – under the magnificent old mango tree. Tourists are welcome to participate – cold beers or weak *cuba libres* can be bought from the house at the back – and don't forget to tip the musicians.

Map on page 250

When the original tree in the Plazuela Real del Jigüe reached the end of its life, a cutting was taken and replanted, a custom that has continued across the centuries. The present tree was planted in 1929.

East of Plaza Mayor

To the right of the Iglesia Parroquial Mayor, an ancient staircase marks the end of Calle Rosario. At No.3 is a house built in 1732 for Fernandez de Lara, Trinidad's chief inquisitor, who was responsible for upholding Christianity and burning at the stake anyone who disagreed with the Vatican's views. Several people accused of witchcraft and black magic were crucified nearby. At the top of the staircase, you will find the **Casa de la Música** **H**, with displays of old instruments. Here you can also buy a range of Cuban music on CD and tape. You may hear African tribal music floating down from a nearby terrace. This is the headquarters of the **Conjunto Folklórico de Trinidad**, which has performed Bantu and Yoruba dances all over Cuba and in France, Spain and Germany as well. Like many Cubans, the troupe's 27 members are believers in Santería. If you're interested in seeing a practice session, walk half a block east and on your left is the entrance to the Conjunto Folklórico. On your way out, leave a small donation.

Slightly further east is a triangular plaza – the **Plazuela de Segarta**, where some of the oldest houses in Trinidad are to be found. One of these is now the **Casa de la Trova** **I** (open Tues–Sun 11am–2pm, free; and Fri–Sun, 8pm–midnight; entrance fee), built in 1717 and decorated with murals. Many tourists visit during the day, but on weekend nights, the locals take over. Beer can be bought for dollars, or you can usually get shots of (rough) *aguardiente* for a couple of Cuban pesos.

One block down the hill and to your right, you come to **Calle Rosario** again. On the corner at No. 406 is a light blue house that once belonged to one of Trinidad's sugar barons. Today it is the **Casa de la Cultura Trinitaria** **J**, where dances, concerts, plays and other performances are offered. Back up the hill, notice the 18th-century walls made from rocks, bricks,

BELOW: behind one of Trinidad's typical *rejas* (grilles).

*Cockfighting (*la riña de gallos*) is very popular in rural Cuba, and about the best chance visitors will have to witness this controversial sport is at Finca Dolores, a mile west of Trinidad. Every Sunday morning hordes of locals gather for the fights, which kick off at around 8.30am.*

bones and bottles of all sizes and shapes, and kept together with clay, straw and plaster. The yellow house at No. 79 is the **Casa de los Curas**, residence of the Parroquial Mayor's priests for centuries.

Trinidad's other sights

There are two other areas worth visiting outside the heart of the Old Town. To the east, the **Plaza Santa Ana** Ⓚ has a beautiful restored church of the same name, which is now home to a bar, restaurant, gallery and shop. There is also a rare statue to Bartolomé de Las Casas, the Dominican friar who fought for indigenous rights in the 16th century. To the southeast of the Old Town, the **Parque Central** (also called **Parque Céspedes**) Ⓛ has no stunning architecture but is busy with local life – and has a rather more "real" feel to it. In November, the square is the focus of a week of cultural events and music.

One of Trinidad's most unusual attractions lies above town, near **Motel Las Cuevas** Ⓜ (the best hotel in town: *see Travel Tips*). Here, you can visit the literally cavernous Discoteca Las Cuevas – a series of impressive, lofty caves that have been converted into a spectacular nightclub. It rarely gets the numbers it needs, however, even at weekends, and you shouldn't bother going much before midnight, as the place will be empty.

Peninsula de Ancón

Some 8 miles (12 km) south of Trinidad lies a spectacular stretch of beach, accessible either by way of **Casilda** or the more scenic route via the small fishing village of **La Boca**, where Trinidad's river disgorges its waters into the sea. The beach here is popular with locals, who can't usually be found at the main

BELOW: Playa Ancón, a popular resort for package tourists.

tourist resort of **Playa Ancón** ⑳, further out along the peninsula. Playa Ancón has an excellent long beach with white powdery sand, lined with palm trees. The clear blue waters are warm and snorkeling is popular here. Bathers tend to gather on the beaches in front of the vast Hotel Ancón and the nearby Hotel Costa Sur, where they can be within easy reach of bars and restaurants.

Divers can take the trip to **Cayo Blanco**, south of Ancón, from either of the above hotels. The crystal seas and coral make for a fantastic dive (an initiation dive costs $9; a full dive for qualified divers costs $30, or $35 at night; costs include all equipment and instructor/guide).

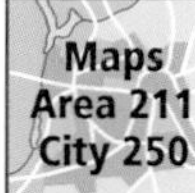

Enjoying a drink at La Boca, a beach dominated by local people, west of Playa Ancón.

Valle de los Ingenios and the road to Sancti Spíritus

As you leave Trinidad on Route 12, heading northeast to Sancti Spiritus, the road passes through the spectacular, lush **Valle de los Ingenios** ㉑ (Valley of the Sugar Mills) which, like Trinidad, is a UNESCO World Heritage Site.

At one point, when it was Cuba's most important sugar producing region, there were 43 working sugar mills in the valley. However, the valley's economy collapsed in 1880 when world sugar prices slumped. In the rest of Cuba, the more efficient *central* sugar mill was becoming the norm, and the valley's *ingenios* could not compete. Many of the magnificent plantation houses and mansions from those days are now in ruins, but some still stand, most notably the exceptionally beautiful farm of the Iznaga family.

You cannot miss the farm, splendidly signposted by the **Torre de Manacas-Iznaga**, 7½ miles (12 km) from Trinidad (entrance fee), which rears proudly out of the green cane fields. Legend has it that the tower was built after a bet between two brothers in the family, in which one had to build a tower higher than the other could dig a well deep. No-one knows the outcome, as no-one has ever found where the reputed well was dug. Step carefully. You're on safer ground with the tower (probably designed originally as a watchtower to keep an eye on the slaves working in the fields), from where there is a magnificent view. Birds of prey circle on the thermals, and a refreshing wind cools you as you climb up above the valley floor. The immaculate Hacienda below is an excellent place for a meal or a drink of *guarapo*, the freshly-pressed sugar cane juice that is milled by Cuba's only original *trapiche* (sugar press) remaining in situ.

BELOW: graceful Manacas-Iznaga Tower, in the Valle de los Ingenios.

If you are bound for Santa Clara, you should take the road running north from the Manacas-Iznaga tower to **Güinia de Miranda**. This is a little used but beautiful route. Be warned that the paved road surface is bumpy and potholed in places, but not difficult.

The road towards Sancti Spíritus curves and dips across lovely landscape, passing the heights of the **Alturas de Banao**. Turn left (north) off the highway at La Güira to stay at the **Hacienda Los Molinos**, an old timber house where you can rent rooms and horses to follow the various forest trails. A little further northeast, turning off at Banao, you can visit an eco-tourism center, the Casa del Guardabosques in the protected reserve of **El Naranjal** – a diverse mountain forest with 722 species of flowering plants, including over 60 types of orchid, and rich birdlife. ❑

EASTERN LOWLANDS

Map on pages 260–61

This region's economic mainstay is agriculture not tourism. While not full of obvious attractions, it is worth visiting the colonial city of Camagüey, and there are fine beaches along the north coast

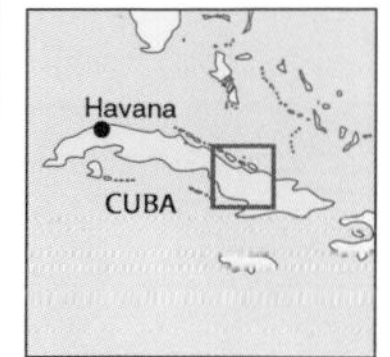

The Carretera Central highway continues east from Sancti Spíritus through **Ciego de Avila Province** (pop. 370,000). With its fertile soils and abundant water, this is Cuba's fruit bowl, producing citrus, bananas and pineapple, in the most productive plantations on the island.

Pineapple town

The provincial capital, also called **Ciego de Avila** ❶ (pop. 89,000), has little to recommend it apart from the friendliness of its inhabitants. The town's original name, San Jerónimo de la Palma, fell out of use long ago, and the present one comes from a 16th-century rancher named Ávila, who cleared the original dense forest here to make a clearing, or "*ciego*" in Spanish. Often known as the "Pineapple Town" to other Cubans, its nickname is well-deserved: the **Empresa Piña**, outside the city, covers fields golden with the Queen of Fruits. Here, a single variety of pineapple, the sweet and juicy Española Roja, is grown in vast quantities that still fall short of demand.

Traffic in the town is almost all horse-driven, and the longest possible journey should only cost a few pesos by pony trap. The town is built on a strict grid system centered on **Parque Martí**, but there are few buildings of note. A popular meeting place on the square is the **Casa de Agua** (Water House), which serves free glasses of the local mineral water, as well as homemade *refrescos* (soft drinks) and fruit juices. The most interesting building is the **Teatro Principal**, just south of the square. This was built by a rich socialite, Angela Hernández Vida de Jiménez, who battled to create a cultural mecca in her home town. Between 1924 and 1928 she spent 250,000 pesos building this remarkable baroque confection, but though the theater is still used, her dreams of cultural supremacy for the place have come to nought.

LEFT: harvesting pineapples.
BELOW: a stark bank interior.

A Cuban Maginot Line

During the first War of Independence in the 1860s, the Spanish colonial government built a string of 43 forts – called **La Trocha** – across the island at this point, so as to cut the rebellious East off from the rest of the island. One of the few remaining forts, the **Fortín de la Trocha**, can be found across the railway lines on Calle Máximo Gómez. It now houses an unremarkable restaurant.

Island pearls

South of Ciego de Ávila lies **Júcaro** ❷, a pleasant fishing village on the coast, and also the point of embarkation for the enchanting island chain of **Los Jardines de la Reina** (The Gardens of the Queen).

This delicate necklace of coral cays is accessible only by boat. Fishermen will sometimes take passengers from the marina here, and the Cuban state enterprise Puertosol (tel: 332–83126) offers day trips from the same place to **Cayo Caña** and **Cayo Chocolate**, as well as diving trips aboard their yacht lasting several days. For the moment at least, the Jardines remain reasonably untouched. Almost every one of these tiny desert islands has a beautiful white sand beach where flamingos wade and turtles swim.

Morón: no jokes, please

A mascot for Morón. English speakers, ignoring Spanish accents, can't resist making a joke about the name of this town.

Morón ❸, a real country town where people get around on foot, on bicycles or in horse-drawn carts, lies to the north of the province. Since its foundation, the town's symbol has been a crowing cock, representing the people's triumph over arrogant officialdom. Until the 1950s, the image was all in the mind, but then the local citizenry raised money to have Morón's cock sculpted in bronze as a public monument. As the project neared completion, dictator Fulgencio Batista got into the act and decided to unveil the statue in what would be known as Batista Park. The outraged residents saved their rooster from humiliation by boycotting the inauguration, but regrettably the bird was subsequently kidnapped and destroyed by misguided guerrillas.

In the calmer 1980s, Morón's cock was born anew and placed in the **Parque del Gallo** (Rooster Park), at the entrance to the town's new hotel, Hotel Morón. There it stands, perched victoriously at the top of a small mound on a dry branch. In the adjacent tower is a clock, and an amplified recording of jubilant crowing is electronically set to go off twice a day at 6am and 6pm.

North of Morón are popular places for fishing, hunting and boating: **Laguna**

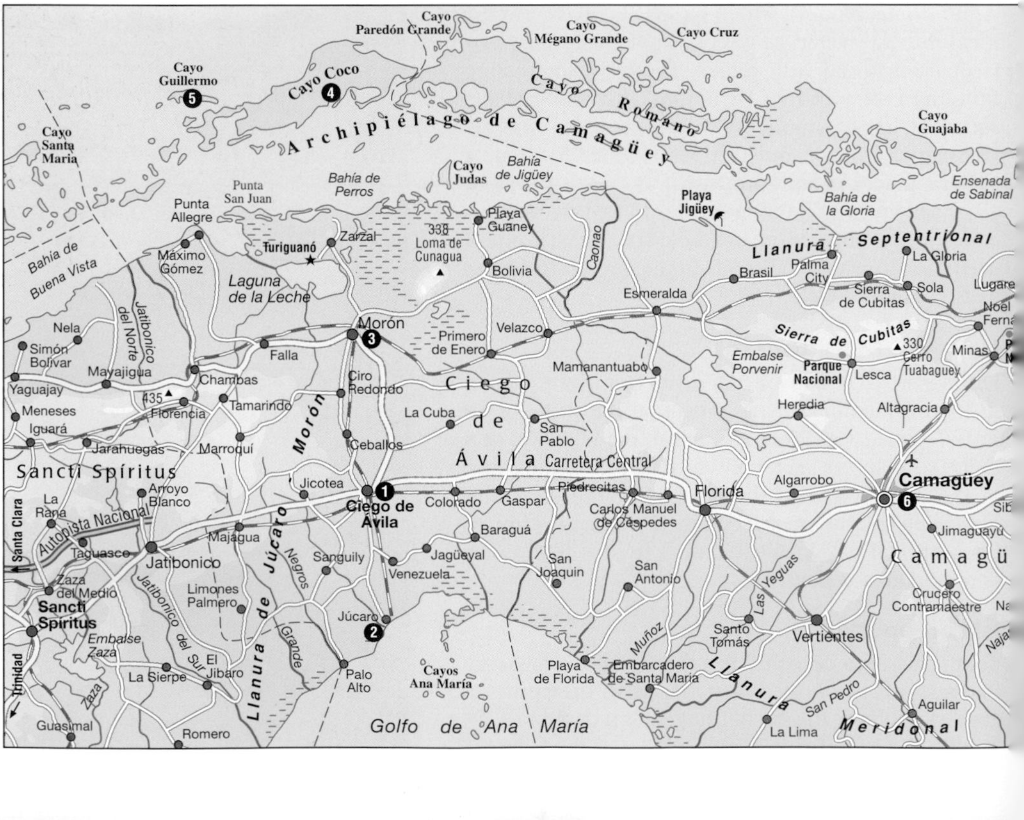

La Redonda, where bass abound; **Aguachales de Falla**, a hunting reserve inhabited mainly by mallards and fulvous tree ducks; and **Laguna de la Leche**, a lagoon milky-white from sodium carbonate deposits that seem to nourish snook and tarpon. The lagoon is Cuba's largest natural reservoir, and because of its size and central location, it was strategically important during Cuba's 1895 War of Independence: Cuban *mambí* fighters crossed it on numerous occasions to deliver munitions from Camagüey to Villa Clara, thus evading the string of fortifications the Spanish had erected from Júcaro to Morón (*see page 259*). On the coast north of the lagoon is the **Isla de Turiguanó**, completely devoted to the herds of ruddy St Gertrude's cattle that graze there.

The northern islands

Covering an area of 230 sq. miles (595 sq. km), **Cayo Coco** ❹ is larger than several Caribbean countries and much bigger than Varadero Beach, Cuba's main resort. A 17-mile (27-km) causeway that shoots straight through a mirror of water links the cay to the mainland. It is named, not for abundant coconut groves, as one might suppose, but for a long-legged wading bird, the white ibis – known locally as a *coco*; this, along with the rosy flamingo, is one of the island's more striking inhabitants. Since the cays in this area were only recently settled, wildlife – including 156 other bird species – had a chance to thrive, and the area is a legally protected zone. The wild cattle and boar that now roam the cay were imported at some point in history, perhaps by passing pirates, but the indigenous iguanas and *jutías* were there before them. So were the insects: if you are visiting, it's best to stock up on insect repellent, as the mangrove swamps provide a good breeding ground for the more irksome forms of wildlife.

Cayo Coco was a favored hangout of Hemingway, who sailed and camped here when it was still a deserted wilderness. He pursued German U-boats off the coast in his boat, the Pilar *– a time he was later to write about in* Islands in the Stream.

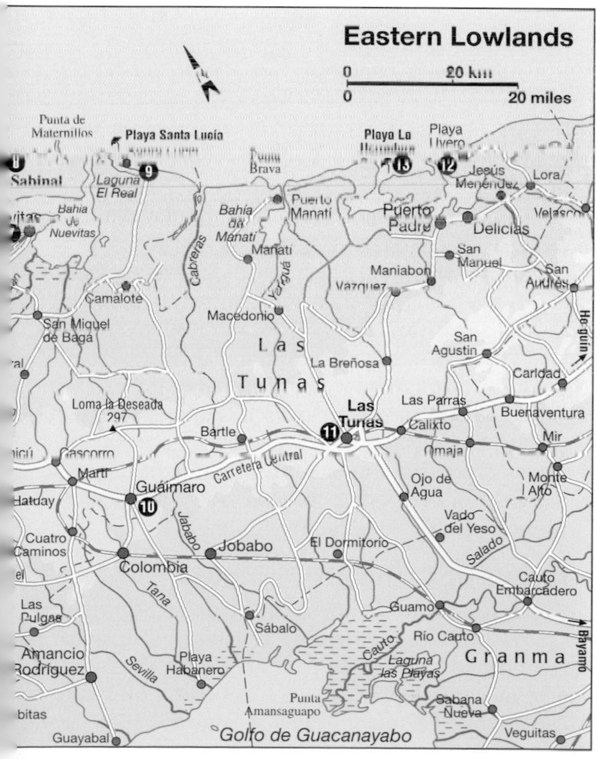

BELOW: waves lap the shore of Cayo Coco.

Conchs are heavily exploited as a source of food.

Tourist developments are proliferating these days, and it is to be hoped that the rare fauna can be protected. Hotels have nature trails, and visitors are welcome at the **Institute for Coastal Research** where a team of scientists monitors the effects of tourism and agriculture on the local environment. Many Cuban ecologists profess to being concerned about the long-term effects of development, especially the way the causeway has obstructed the free flow of currents, leaving the lagoon deficient in some of the essential nutrients required for a healthy ecosystem.

There are nine beaches of varying sizes on the cay's northern coast. Separated by escarpments, they add up to 13 miles (22 km) of white sand and crystalline water. A hundred yards in from the shore is a large hotel complex that has been modeled as a simulated colonial township, the **Hotel Tryp Cayo Coco**. Aimed at the package tour market, it often falls short of tourists' expectations, and its five-star billing seems over-generous.

The causeway connecting the cay to the mainland continues west to **Cayo Guillermo** ❺ – also open to tourism as a base for scuba diving and fishing – and east to nearby **Cayo Romano** and **Cayo Paredón Grande**, as yet much less developed, with empty, white sand beaches.

Heart of the Heartland

The province of Camagüey (pop. 749,000) has its fair share of cane fields, but far more important are its cattle pastures, supporting both dairy and beef cattle. *Vaqueros* (the local cowboys), wearing broad-brimmed hats and dangling machetes, can be seen herding stock from astride their horses, lassos flying.

The capital of the province, **Camagüey** ❻, is Cuba's third largest city (pop. 286,000). It was one of the seven original settlements of Diego Velázquez, founded as the Villa of Santa María del Puerto Príncipe and dating from 1514. It was twice moved, and then razed by Henry Morgan and his crew of pirates in 1668 (*see page 24*). It was rebuilt soon after, with a street plan that seems designed to help ambush future invaders: it is a web of unexpected turns and cul-de-sacs.

Unlike the raw farm towns that are the capitals of the adjacent provinces, Camagüey is a place of beauty, culture and tradition. The entire old town is a delight: narrow, twisting streets wind from the river, lined by rows of small, rainbow-colored, stuccoed houses, with lush courtyards set back from the street that can be glimpsed through open, ancient timber doors. Don't come here expecting to find another Trinidad: Cienfuegos is a large city, whose inhabitants are by no means dependent on tourism. Lacking the chocolate box prettiness of other colonial cities, Camagüey is still left off many tourist itineraries.

BELOW: a rural worker in the sugar fields.

A tour of Camagüey's sights

The city's most famous son, Ignacio Agramonte (1841–73), was the fighting general of Camagüey's rebel forces during the first War of Independence (he died in action in 1873). The **Casa Natal de Ignacio Agramonte** Ⓐ (open Mon and Wed–Sat 1pm–7pm, Sun 8am–noon; entrance fee) is a museum in the hero's birthplace – a lovely 18th-century mansion in the center of the city, sumptuously furnished with period pieces. A prominent feature are the *tinajones* – round, wide-mouthed earthenware jugs which were modeled on the big-bellied jars which came from Spain filled with wines and oils. Cuban versions were created by local potters to solve a pressing problem: Camagüey had almost no water sources, and rainfall, while abundant, was seasonal. The water supply is more reliable these days, but you still see *tinajones* in the shady courtyard of many Camagüeyan households. Ranging in size from large to enormous, some of those still in use were made more than a century ago.

Near the Agramonte museum, on Calle Príncipe, is the birthplace of a more recently famous Camagüeyan, the **Casa Natal de Nicolás Guillén** ❸ (open Mon–Fri 8am–4.30pm, Sat 8am–noon). The world-renowned writer (*see page 110*) was born here in 1902, and this pleasant little home celebrates his life. There is a large bronze portrait of the poet at the front of the house.

North of here sits the splendid **Teatro Principal** ❸, which draws the biggest audiences when the Ballet de Camagüey or the local symphony orchestra perform. Calle Padre Valencia brings you back to the attractive 18th-century **Iglesia de La Merced** ❹, across from Agramonte's birthplace on the **Plaza de los Trabajadores.** Considered one of the most splendid churches in the country when it was first built, La Merced has benefitted from recent restoration: the decorated ceiling is particularly striking. Avenida Agramonte leads you to another important church, also dating from the 1700s, **Iglesia de la Soledad** ❺. Its red-brick exterior looks unpromising, but inside you are greeted by glorious decoration on the arches and pillars, topped by a splendid vaulted ceiling. Before continuing south to the heart of the city, you can make a diver-

Map Area 260 City 265

Camagüey's layout is unusual, not just for the lack of a grid pattern, but also for the lack of a central square acting as a focus for the city. A useful reference point is Avenida República – which runs north to south through the center of Camagüey.

BELOW: *vaqueros* (cowboys) at work.

sion north along Avenida República (which becomes Avenida de los Mártires beyond the train station) to the **Museo Provincial Ignacio Agramonte** Ⓕ, with an eclectic collection ranging from stuffed animals to archaeological finds.

Continuing on our route south, you reach **Parque Ignacio Agramonte** Ⓖ, the nearest thing Camagüey has to a main square, though it is too small to really fulfil such a role. The dramatic mounted figure of Ignacio Agramonte is overshadowed by the **Catedral** Ⓗ, which is not as impressive as La Soledad or La Merced, but is still worth a peek. Its wooden ceiling is its best feature.

Another splendid, if dilapidated, church is the **Iglesia del Carmen** Ⓘ, which lies several blocks west of the square along Calle Martí. While you are in this area, you should walk the few blocks south to the church of **Santo Cristo del Buen Viaje** Ⓙ. The interest here lies not so much in the 19th-century church but in the adjacent **cemetery**, one of the finest graveyards in the country.

However, surely the loveliest place in Camagüey is the restored, 18th-century **Plaza San Juan de Dios** Ⓚ, south of Parque Agramonte. Now a national monument, the square is beautifully peaceful, and is usually completely deserted at night. Surrounded by brightly colored houses with elegant wooden *rejas* (grilles), tall doors and windows, the plaza is dominated by the **Iglesia San Juan de Dios**, a small, intimate church with a fine mahogany ceiling and altar. Adjacent, in the old hospital, is the local heritage office and a small **museum**. Two of the finest buildings are now restaurants, **La Campaña de Toledo** and the **Parador de los Tres Reyes**, popular with day-trippers.

The farmers' market or **Agromercado** Ⓛ, on the banks of the river, is a great place to appreciate the Camagüeyans renowned love of good food. In addition to stalls selling fresh produce are simple kitchens serving up piping hot meals.

TIP

The best place to hear traditional music is in the Casa de la Trova, overlooking Parque Agramonte. It is open daily except Tuesday, and has a small bar. On the other side of the square, try La Volanta for a simple *criollo* meal in a lovely old colonial mansion, where you'll have local people for company.

BELOW: at play in a colonial back street in Camagüey.

Exploring the province

The city of Camagüey is a cultural oasis in an otherwise arid province, where cows seem to outnumber people. Second in size is **Nuevitas ❼**, the Atlantic seaport located on the Bahía de Nuevitas. Despite its run-down appearance, Nuevitas is an important trading center for the rural heartland, and it's now being spruced up for tourism – based primarily on its location close to the bridge across to **Cayo Sabinal ❽**, a cay to the northwest with over 20 miles (30km) of beaches. More hotels are planned, but for the moment the best place to head for is Playa Los Pinos, with basic accommodation and a rustic restaurant.

Boats link Cayo Sabinal with nearby **Playa Santa Lucía ❾**, to the east, but the most common route is by road from Camagüey – a journey of 65 miles (105km) through cattle country. At Santa Lucía, the 12 miles (20 km) of dazzling white sands are still relatively quiet, largely due to the area's isolation. There are half a dozen hotels but not a great deal else. The area is becoming well known for the quality of the diving. Scuba buffs recommend the area for the sheer

Map Area 260
City 265

King Ranch, 15 miles (24km) south of Santa Lucía, gives tourists a taste of cowboy culture. Top of the bill are the rodeos, but you can also organize horseback rides, and their are rooms to rent too.

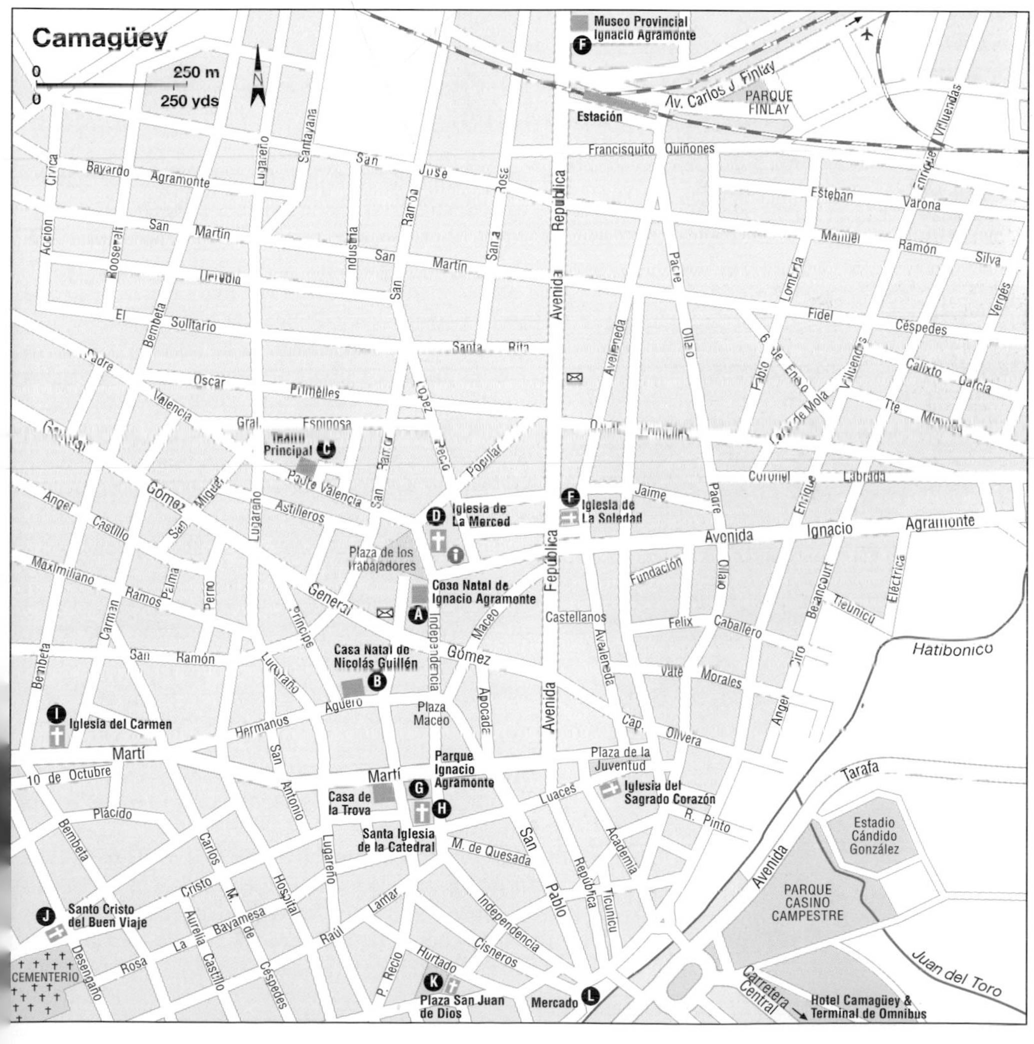

Map on pages 260–61

variety of underwater sites. The International Scuba Center rents diving equipment, and guides are available from the hotels.

Divers also recommend the coral reef off **La Boca**, a tiny fishing village 5 miles (8km) west of the main resort. One of the most lovely spots in Cuba, La Boca is impossibly picturesque, with a glorious crescent of sand that knocks spots off the strip at Santa Lucía. There are several *paladares* specializing, not unnaturally, in seafood. Behind is a lagoon where flamingos gather.

Cattle and more cattle

The tuna *or prickly pear, after which the province of Las Tunas is named.*

Traveling eastward from Camagüey along the Carretera Central, you can be in no doubt how the local people make their living. The vast, almost treeless grasslands are virtually empty except for cattle, numerous ranches (*ganaderías*) and the attendant cowboys. The only town before you cross into Las Tunas province is **Guáimaro** ⑩, whose main claim to fame is that it was the site of the assembly which drew up Cuba's first Constitution in 1869.

South of Guáimaro, near the town of **Najasa**, the Sierra Guaicanama-Najasa is the site of a little visited reserve of **Hacienda La Belén**; the birdlife is especially rich, with many species of parrots. There is a limited amount of accommodation available.

A whistle-stop destination

There is not a lot to stop you driving through province of Las Tunas without stopping. It is sparsely populated, and the provincial capital does not have a great deal going for it as a tourist destination. Flying saucer-shaped water towers are perhaps the most distinguishing feature of the city of **Las Tunas** ⑪. Burned to the ground in both wars of independence, it has no colonial landmarks. The main square, **Parque Vincent García** is not unpleasant but is spoilt by traffic on its way through town. Located here is the former home of the Cuban fencing champion Carlos Leyva González, who was killed with 72 others when a Cuban plane bound for Barbados was sabotaged in 1976, is now a museum dedicated to those who died.

BELOW: a colonial façade in Camagüey.

The region's most famous son is El Cucalambé, the pseudonym of the poet Cristobal Nápoles Fajardo, whose 19th-century *décimas* (10-line rhyming topical songs) are honored at the annual Cuculambeana Fair, when troubadours, poets and singers from all over Cuba come for a feast of local music and food. The town has a popular traditional dish, a nutritious *caldosa* (stew) made of meat and root vegetables, which is served in tasty form at **Quique Marina**, a family-style restaurant on the Carretera Central on the western outskirts of the town. Finally, look out for terracotta ceramics dotted about the town – Las Tunas is famous for them.

There is nothing much south of Las Tunas other than mangrove coast and rice farms. On the north coast, near the town of Jesús Menéndez, are two fabulous beaches, **Playa Uvero** ⑫ and **Playa La Herradura** ⑬, both of which are, at present, completely unspoiled. There are, however, two hotels which are in the process of conversion to the dollar market. ❑

The Guajiro

A *guajiro* is a Cuban peasant – the traditional, mythic version of the *campesino*, or rural worker. The true guajiro must be country-born and bred, devoted to the land, fiercely independent and set in his ways. By tradition and preference, he lives in a *bohío.* These rustic thatched-roof cottages can still be seen throughout the countryside, with rocking chairs tipped up on the front porch, horses tethered at the door, a TV aerial atop the roof, chickens cackling in the patio and pigs penned outside.

The stereotypical guajiro is taciturn and mistrustful of outsiders, especially city slickers and farming bureaucrats – the ones who set quotas and prices for whatever they've told him to plant. In recent years, more and more guajiros – persuaded by their wives and the state – have joined their land to larger cooperatives. Even so, he's still a guajiro, guiding his ox-pulled plough through the fields, dressed like his predecessors in old boots, baggy pants, long-sleeved shirt and straw hat; breaking his dawn-to-dusk work day with a big midday meal; relaxing with a cigar and a shot; and occasionally feasting on pork and music.

The first guajiros were the tobacco farmers of western Cuba, sons of Spaniards who revolted against the Spanish tobacco monopoly in 1717. Although plantations based on slavery soon dominated Cuban agriculture, they always co-existed with small farms owned and worked by free men. No matter the crop or where they grew it, these farmers had little in common with the plantation owners, who operated on a totally different scale, with a large workforce of slaves.

Though unsophisticated, the guajiro has made his contribution to Cuban fashion with the *guayabera*, a cotton shirt he donned for a down-home *guateque*, or party. In the 1800s, Cubans rebelling against Spain adopted the guayabera for dress parade; in the early 20th century, Havana bohemians brought the look into their clubs. The guayabera is still Cubans' favorite dress shirt.

The guajiro enlivens the *guateque* with a dance that expresses his exuberant energy: the *zapateo*, a toe-and-heel jig that keeps couples hopping between shots of *aguardiente* (raw rum) and hunks of roast pork.

Despite lacking formal education, the guajiro brought poetry to the Cuban countryside in the form of the *décima*, which originated in 16th-century Spain. The décima consists of 10 octosyllabic rhymed lines, improvised and usually sung in counterpoint, accompanied by three main instruments – a guitar, a *tres* and a lute – with *claves* and a dried gourd for percussion. The songs describe the guajiro's life of joy and pain, trust and deception, success and failure; or they may be a witty polemic on some current problem.

Perhaps most typical of rural Cuba is the *guajira* ballad, first sung by roving troubadours and later commercialized for radio. The most famous guajira is Joseito Fernández's tune *La Guantánamera*, sung in praise of the guajiro and using verse written by José Martí: "I am a sincere man from the land where the palms grow... Guantánamera, guajira, Guantánamera..." ❑

RIGHT: The "*hombre sincero*" of *guajiro* folklore.

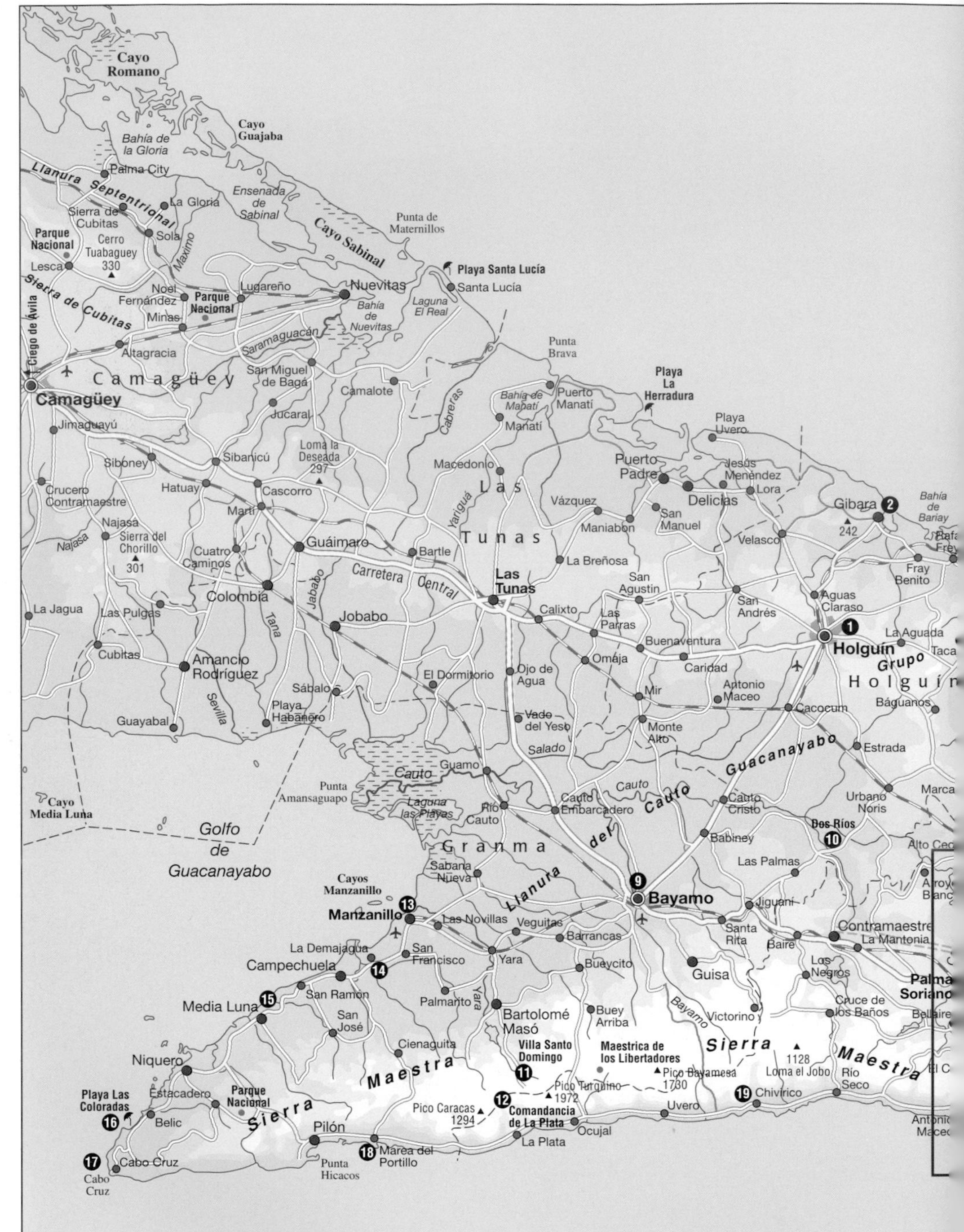

Cayo Romano
Cayo Guajaba
Bahía de la Gloria
Palma City
Llanura Septentrional
La Gloria
Sierra de Cubitas
Sola
Parque Nacional
Cerro Tuabaguey 330
Lesca
Ensenada de Sabinal
Cayo Sabinal
Punta de Maternillos
Playa Santa Lucía
Santa Lucía
Maximo
Noel Fernández
Parque Nacional
Lugareño
Nuevitas
Bahía de Nuevitas
Laguna El Real
Sierra de Cubitas
Minas
Ciego de Avila
Altagracia
Saramaguacán
Camagüey
Camagüey
San Miguel de Bagá
Camalote
Punta Brava
Bahía de Manatí
Puerto Manatí
Playa La Herradura
Cabreras
Jimaguayú
Jucaral
Manatí
Playa Uvero
Siboney
Sibanicú
Loma la Deseada 297
Macedonio
Puerto Padre
Jesús Menéndez
Crucero Contramaestre
Hatuay
Cascorro
Las Tunas
Delicias
Lora
Gibara
Bahía de Bariay
Martí
Yariguá
Vázquez
San Manuel
242
Najasa
Sierra del Chorillo 301
Maniabón
Velasco
Najasa
Cuatro Caminos
Guáimaro
Bartle
La Breñosa
Fray Benito
Carretera Central
Las Tunas
San Agustín
Colombia
Jabobo
Aguas Claraso
La Jagua
Las Pulgas
Tana
Jobabo
Calixto
Las Parras
San Andrés
Holguín
La Aguada
Cubitas
Buenaventura
Grupo Holguín
Amancio Rodríguez
Omája
Caridad
El Dormitorio
Ojo de Agua
Antonio Maceo
Sábalo
Mir
Cacocum
Báguanos
Guayabal
Sevilla
Playa Habanero
Vado del Yeso
Monte Alto
Salado
Guacanayabo
Estrada
Guamo
Cauto
Cayo Media Luna
Punta Amansaguapo
Laguna las Playas
Río Cauto
Cauto Embarcadero
Cauto
Cauto Cristo
Urbano Noris
Marca
Golfo de Guacanayabo
Llanura del Cauto
Dos Ríos
Babiney
Alto Ced
Granma
Sabana Nueva
Las Palmas
Cayos Manzanillo
Bayamo
Jiguaní
Manzanillo
Las Novillas
Veguitas
Santa Rita
Contramaestre
La Mantonia
La Demajagua
San Francisco
Barrancas
Baire
Campechuela
Yara
Buey cito
Guisa
Los Negros
San Ramón
Palmarito
Yara
Cruce de los Baños
Media Luna
San José
Bartolomé Masó
Buey Arriba
Bayamo
Victorino
Sierra
Maestra
Cienaguita
Villa Santo Domingo
Maestrica de los Libertadores
1128
Niquero
Pico Bayamesa 1730
Loma el Jobo
Río Seco
Maestra
Playa Las Coloradas
Estacadero
Parque Nacional
Pico Turquino 1972
Chivirico
Pico Caracas 1294
Comandancia de La Plata
Uvero
Belic
Sierra
Pilón
Ocujal
La Plata
Marea del Portillo
Cabo Cruz
Cabo Cruz
Punta Hicacos
CARIBBEAN SEA

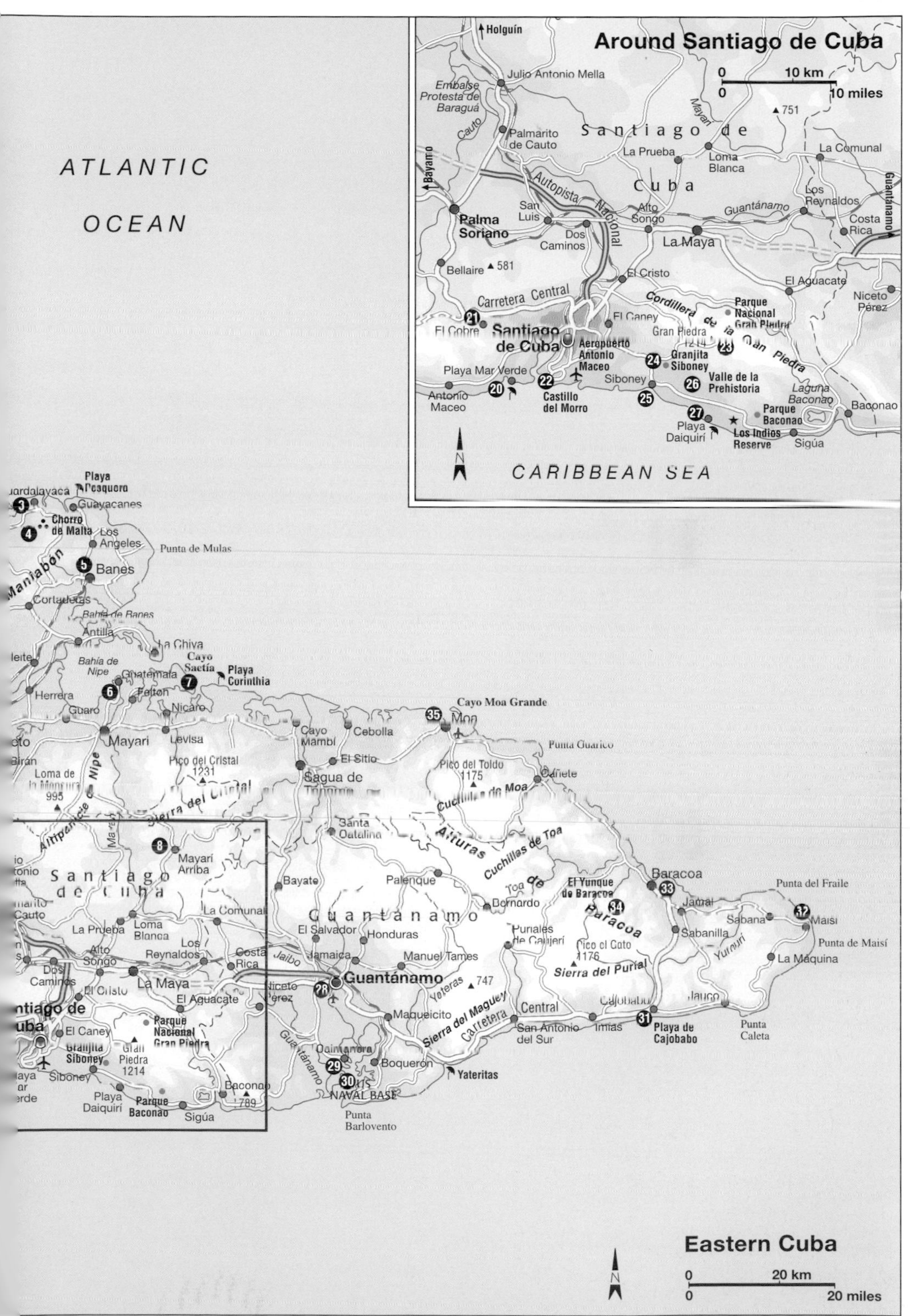

Around Santiago de Cuba
0 10 km
0 10 miles
CARIBBEAN SEA
ATLANTIC OCEAN
Eastern Cuba
0 20 km
0 20 miles
Holguín
Julio Antonio Mella
Embalse Protesta de Baraguá
Palmarito de Cauto
Santiago de Cuba
La Prueba
Loma Blanca
La Comunal
Palma Soriano
San Luis
Dos Caminos
Alto Songo
La Maya
Los Reynaldos
Costa Rica
Bellaire
El Cristo
Carretera Central
El Aguacate
Niceto Pérez
El Caney
Parque Nacional Gran Piedra
Gran Piedra 1214
Cordillera de la Gran Piedra
El Cobre
Santiago de Cuba
Aeropuerto Antonio Maceo
Granjita Siboney
Playa Mar Verde
Siboney
Valle de la Prehistoria
Antonio Maceo
Castillo del Morro
Laguna Baconao
Baconao
Parque Baconao
Playa Daiquirí
Los Indios Reserve
Sigúa
Autopista Nacional
Guantánamo
Playa Pesquero
Guardalavaca
Guayacanes
Chorro de Maltá
Los Angeles
Punta de Mulas
Banes
Cortaderas
Bahía de Banes
Antilla
La Chiva
Bahía de Nipe
Cayo Saetía
Playa Corinthia
Guatemala
Felton
Herrera
Nicaro
Guaro
Mayarí
Levisa
Cayo Moa Grande
Moa
Cayo Mambí
Cebolla
Punta Guarico
El Sitio
Pico del Cristal 1231
Pico del Toldo 1175
Sagua de Tánamo
Cañete
Loma de la Mensura 995
Cuchillas de Moa
Sierra del Cristal
Altiplanicie de Nipe
Santa Catalina
Alturas
Cuchillas de Toa
Mayarí Arriba
Bayate
Palenque
Baracoa
Punta del Fraile
Bernardo
El Yunque de Baracoa
Jamal
Maisí
Sabana
Guantánamo
El Salvador
Honduras
Sabanilla
Punta de Maisí
Punales de Cajujerí
Pico el Gato 1176
Jaibo
Jamaica
Manuel Tames
La Máquina
Sierra del Purial
Guantánamo
747
Central
Cajobabo
Jauco
Maqueicito
Sierra del Maguey
San Antonio del Sur
Imías
Playa de Cajobabo
Punta Caleta
Caimanera
Boquerón
Yateritas
US NAVAL BASE
Punta Barlovento

FLo.1028
CARINA

HOLGUÍN AND GRANMA

From the island's top archaeological site to the rugged mountains of the Sierra Maestra, this region has much to offer. Even so, it attracts surprisingly few tourists

Map on pages 270–71

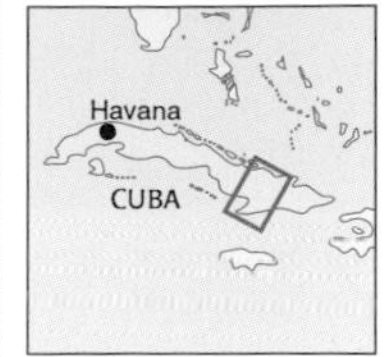

Often called the "Granary of Cuba" because of its agricultural wealth, the province of Holguín has some million people living within its borders, making it second in population only to Havana Province. Its capital city, also called **Holguín ❶**, is the fourth largest city in Cuba, with a population of 233,000. Along with its agricultural importance, it is a relatively active industrial center and has grown rapidly in recent decades.

Holguín is a city of squares. The colonial center of the city is marked by **Parque Calixto García**, an expansive square built around the monument to Holguín's most famous independence fighter, General García, who was born in Calle Miró nearby – the house, of course, is now a museum. Fronting the square are, among other things, a striking Art Deco movie house, the local Casa de la Trova, the provincial library, bookstores and art galleries. Most noteworthy is the building known as **La Periquera** or "Parrot Cage" – so named ever since Spanish soldiers, in their blue, yellow and green uniforms, took refuge behind the barred windows during a *mambí* attack in 1868.

This building now houses the cavernous **Museo Provincial** (open Mon–Sat, noon–7pm; entrance fee). The museum's prized possession being the *hacha de Holguín* or Holguín Ax, a 12-inch (30-cm) pre-Columbian figure of an elongated man carved in polished rock; found in 1860, it has been adopted as the symbol of the province. There are also interesting displays on slavery, and all kinds of historical memorabilia. There is plenty to fascinate even the non Spanish speaker.

Half a block south of the square, on Calle Maceo, is the **Museo de la Historia Natural Carlos de la Torre** (open Tues–Sat 8am–6pm, Sun 8am–noon; entrance fee), with a fine collection of *polymitas*, the brightly-banded snails indigenous to eastern Cuba. Around the corner, **Parque San Isidoro**, a rather neglected square, is the site of the city's **cathedral**, dating from 1720. Its rough brick arcades harbor birds and figures carved by a local artist; other treasures include the original baptismal font.

Three blocks north of Parque Calixto García, leafy **Plaza San José** is the most picturesque square in Holguín, centered on a ruined church, the Iglesia San José. You'll usually find bicycle rickshaws (*bicitaxis*) parked in the square offering you a ride to **La Loma de la Cruz** (The Hill of the Cross), Holguín's most visible landmark and a place of pilgrimage. It's not far to walk, in fact, but when you get there you must tackle the 468 steps leading up to the cross – erected in the 18th century.

On the eastern edge of the city is the enormous **Plaza de la Revolución**, as soulless as most such squares in Cuba. Its main feature of interest is the

PRECEDING PAGES: view from Santiago's Morro fortress toward the Sierra Maestra.
LEFT: shrimp boats off Manzanillo.
BELOW: Holguín church tower.

Part of the moving monument which commemorates the historic landfall of Christopher Columbus at Bariay.

Mausoleo de Calixto García which is decorated with a vast frieze representing the struggle of the Cuban people from the Conquest to the Revolution. The city's two main dollar hotels, the **Hotel Pernik** and the **Hotel El Bosque**, are both located nearby – in the ugly Lenin District, once described as "Moscow with palm trees." A more scenic but less convenient alternative, located near the airport, is **Villa El Cocal**, a pleasant villa in lovely gardens. Further afield, in the middle of nowhere, 6 miles (10km) southeast of the city, is the **Motel Mirador de Mayabe**, a collection of cabins on a hill overlooking the valley.

Gibara, a colonial gem

The further north you go, the better Holguín Province gets. **Gibara** ❷ – on the coast, 22 miles (36 km) north of the capital – exudes maritime charm and colonial grace. Hollyhocks line the road to an old iron bridge that crosses the **Río Cacoyoquin** where it empties into the sea. The bridge leads into the town along a shady, seaside drive with a **statue of Christopher Columbus** and a small ruined garrison at the end. A fishing cooperative, the shipyards and a spinning mill sustain Gibara's population of more than 16,000.

With its terracotta roofs, flowering patios, weather-beaten church, cobblestoned streets and harbor fishing boats, Gibara is endlessly photogenic. The restored **Teatro Colonial**, which dates from 1889, is a diminutive masterpiece, but the *pièce de resistance* is the **Museo de Artes Decorativas** (open Tues–Sat 8am–5pm but closed for lunch, noon–1pm; Sun 8–noon; entrance fee), housed in the second floor of a magnificent 19th-century mansion. Besides gorgeous *mediopuntos* – Cuba's characteristic, fan-shaped stained-glass windows – and *mamparas* (decorative saloon-style doors), there is a fine collection of furniture

BELOW: enjoying the view above Gibara.

that the museum has done well to hold on to; there are many Art Nouveau pieces too. You can climb up to the roof terrace for a view of the town.

There are no dollar hotels, but one of the handful of peso hotels should accept your money. Eating out is easier: the **Miramar** and **El Faro**, both on the waterfront, offer meals for dollars and normally have a good choice of seafood.

Map on pages 270–71

A controversial monument

There is a long-standing debate between Gibara and Baracoa about the exact place where the Europeans first landed in Cuba (*see page 21*), but historians seem to agree that the first landfall was made actually in **Bariay Bay**, east of Gibara. A **monument**, erected in 1992 to commemorate the 500th anniversary of Columbus's discovery of America, sits on the tip of Cayo Bariay, within sight of what is almost certainly the flat-topped mountain mentioned by the explorer. The monument, set in a delightful palm grove, consists of a collection of columns and idols designed to symbolize the meeting of European and aboriginal civilizations. If traveling by car, you can reach the site by driving 4 miles (7km) north of Fray Benitos, but boat trips are also arranged from Guardalavaca.

Burial of a defeated race, at Chorro de Maita's indigenous cemetery.

Guardalavaca

Further east, beyond the **Rafael Freyre** sugar mill, with its ancient steam locomotives, lies northeastern Cuba's main resort area, where the sea is a diaphanous blue and the beaches creamy white, fringed by tropical foliage. First you reach the powdery white sand beach at **Playa Esmeralda**. A prime attraction here, as well as the beach, is the marina where you can swim with the dolphins ($20). There is an excellent seafood restaurant and bar, too, as well as a hotel.

Beyond, **Guardalavaca ❸** is a quiet resort with a stunning stretch of beach. It has never really taken off despite great efforts by the Ministry of Tourism, so is greener and less hurried than Varadero. But, as in Varadero, there are few locals other than those who work in the hotels. The resort may be too low-key for some people, but it has the advantage of being well placed for exploring some interesting sights in the area. You can rent cars, bikes and mopeds, as well as organize boat or bus trips through the hotel.

BELOW: the special sands of Guardalavaca.

Chorro de Maita and Banes

Just south of Guardalavaca, the hilly road passes **Chorro de Maita ❹**, the largest pre-Columbian burial ground known to exist in the Antilles. Archaeologists have revealed skeletons of the indigenous Taíno people who inhabited the area from about 10,000 BC to the end of the 16th century. A section of the graveyard has been excavated to show how the skeletons were buried. Two of the children wear European jewelry, and the presence of a Spaniard indicates that there must have been cross-cultural relationships in the early years of the conquest.

Some of the finds from Chorro de Maita are on display at the excellent **Museo Indocubano** (Tues–Sat noon–6pm, Sun 2pm–6pm; entrance fee) in nearby **Banes ❺**. The utensils and jewelry are made of delicately carved and shaped shells, rocks,

Former president Batista was born in Banes, the son of poor cane-cutters. The richest family in the area were the Castros, and local people still remember when Fidel and his brother Raúl came to dances in town. Some also recall Fidel's wedding to Mirta Díaz Balart (daughter of the mayor of Banes) on October 12 , 1948.

bones, ceramic, wood and metal. The gold idol of a woman wearing a headdress and offering a bowl is, arguably, a joint Indian-Spanish effort.

Banes is a sleepy colonial town and a fascinating relic of US involvement in Cuba. It was once right at the center of the American United Fruit Company's lands and many of the town's wooden buildings show an unmistakable US influence, with their zinc roofs and broad verandahs. Many Jamaicans came here to work in the 1930s, and some people here still speak English.

South of Banes, the road runs around **Bahía de Nipe**. There is a turnoff to **Cueto**, a wild west sort of town where ancient steam locomotives chug right up the main street and *guajiros* trot around on their ponies. In theory, you can get a bus from here to **Birán**, the birthplace of Fidel Castro, but in fact the bus rarely runs. The old Castro house still stands in this tiny community – a lacy, elegant, wooden house by a rippling river. A long avenue of royal palms sweeps up to the front of the blue and yellow house, which is not open to the public.

Birán itself has been entirely reconstructed since the Revolution: the old thatched *bohíos* have gone. The village looks like a second-rate holiday camp, with rows of identical concrete houses, each one built and furnished by the state. Just one old farmer still has his original house – a thatched timber building where pigs scratch around under the mango trees. There is nowhere to stay in Birán, though the friendly local people are happy to put strangers up in their homes, and older people love to tell stories of the Castro family.

Slave town

Back towards the Bahía de Nipe, **Mayarí** is an industrial town with little to interest travelers. **Guatemala** ❻, an old slave town right by the bay, however,

BELOW: tilling the rich soil.

is a gem. The sugar mill still dominates the town, but there are plenty of gingerbread cottages, all built by the slaves themselves out of palm timber and driftwood. Each one is charmingly individual, and each a work of art: some have carved wooden gargoyles, others elaborately worked gables, and every house is a different color from its neighbor; the gardens are lush and colorful. The locals proudly show their bar – once an exclusive "whites only" country club but now open to all – selling shots of rough *aguardiente* spirit for a peso.

At the mouth of the Bahía de Nipe is the island of **Cayo Saetia** ❼, once the exclusive resort of top Communist Party officials; locals say Raúl Castro used to be a regular visitor. This tiny reserve (16 sq. miles/42 sq. km) has ostriches, zebra, antelope and many other exotic species – specially imported, not as a novel way of letting them enjoy the fruits of paradise, but to be shot at. Hunting is still allowed for those so inclined.

Map on pages 270–71

A city of strong passions, Bayamo produced 22 of the country's generals in the wars of independence.

The central highlands

The impressive **Sierra Cristal** mountain range, reaching a height of 4,000 ft (1,200 meters) at Pico del Cristal, rolls through Holguín and Guantánamo provinces. The best place to get close to nature is the research center and hotel at **Pinares de Mayarí**. The center was established in 1988 to study the mountain ecology of the region.

Cuba's great hero from the first *mambí* independence struggle, Carlos Manuel de Céspedes, established his revolutionary government at nearby **Mayarí Arriba** ❽ in 1868. The area is covered with coffee plantations established by French planters who fled here in the early 19th century after the slave rebellions in Haiti. From here, a precarious and twisting road descends to Cuba's second city of **Santiago de Cuba** *(see page 285)*.

Visiting Granma province

Granma Province was carved out of the old *Oriente* or Eastern Territory historically controlled by Santiago de Cuba. The peculiar name, of course, comes from the cabin cruiser Fidel, Che and their comrades used to sneak into the country from Mexico in 1956 before they took up their arms in the mountains. The stunning scenery of the Sierra Maestra is one of the area's main attractions, but so too are the numerous sites linked with the 1950s guerrilla campaign, and also with the 19th-century struggle for independence.

Bayamo

Bayamo ❾ (pop. 128,000) was founded in 1513 by conquistador Diego Velázquez, the third of Cuba's seven original *villas*. The site was ideal: located far enough inland to be safe from pirate attacks and set on the navigable Río Bayamo. This flowed into the **Río Cauto**, the longest river in Cuba and the major transportation route for the eastern end of the island during the age when coastal trade was faster than rustic overland trails. (It wasn't until 1902 that eastern and western Cuba were linked by rail through the center of the island, and the Carretera Central roughly paralleling it wasn't finally finished until 1932, in the era of the dictator Gerardo Machado.)

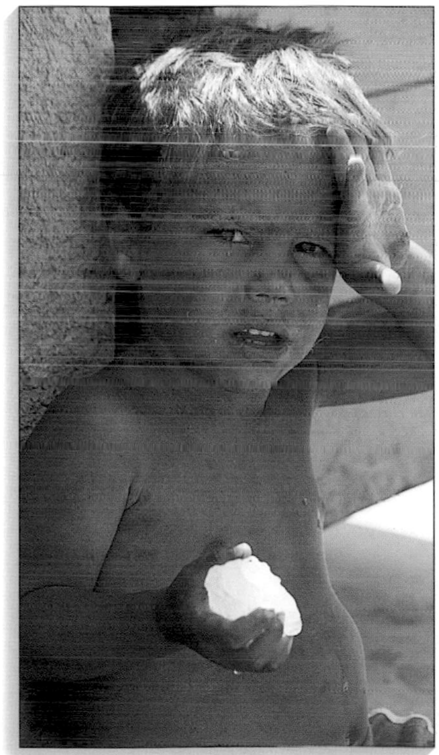

BELOW: cooling off on a hot day.

Granma
INTERNATIONAL

The Communist Party's newspaper (named, like the province, after the yacht used by the rebels in 1956) is the country's main source of news.

North of the city, swampland and lakes provided Bayamo's settlers with abundant game and fish. Even today this area, **Los Caneyes de Virama,** is a hunting and fishing reserve where sportsmen can catch duck, ibis, quail, *jutía*, or rabbit one day and fly-fish for bass the next. The city's location was so strategic that Bayamo became Cuba's smuggling center in the 16th and 17th centuries. Bayamo is, however, most famous for its role in the Cuban independence struggle.

Although it was torched during the war, Bayamo today retains its colonial street plan, as well as the main urban transportation of yesteryear, the horse-drawn buggy. These *coches*, immortalized in a popular song, follow regular routes from bus and train stations and the civilized **Hotel Sierra Maestra**. Not surprisingly, the city is dotted with monuments to the independence struggle. In the main square, **Parque Céspedes**, is the **Ayuntamiento** (Town Hall) where Carlos Manuel de Céspedes, the rebel president, signed the document abolishing slavery in the liberated zones. This was the first city that the rebels took, but with the defeat of the independence forces, it was not until 1888 that abolition truly came into effect throughout Cuba, by decree of the Spanish queen.

Across the plaza is the **Casa Natal de Céspedes** (open Tues–Sun), the house where the independence campaigner was born in 1819. Built of marble left over from a building in Havana, it emerged unscathed from the independence wars and was for years the local post office. Now a museum, this ambient colonial mansion houses documents and photos on the ground floor, with period furnishings and family memorabilia above. It recounts Céspedes's life in detail, from his days as a law student to the rebel presidency. It seems appropriate that a descendant, Onorio Céspedes, should be Bayamo's historian and director of

BELOW: a reminder that the Revolution has its roots in the past (*ayer*), but is relevant today (*hoy*), and tomorrow (*mañana*).

La Casa de la Nacionalidad Cubana (House of Cuban Nationality), recently opened in a beautifully restored colonial mansion to further historical and cultural research in the city.

Map on pages 270–71

A battle cry and anthem

A block from the central square, the **Iglesia San Salvador** was the church where Bayamese patriot Perucho Figueredo – like Céspedes, a lawyer and poet – first performed a stirring march for the independence fighters that later became Cuba's national anthem. It was aired during the Corpus Christi ceremonies four months before the war began. Bayamo's colonial governor listened in silent fury to the provocative words: "To battle, Bayamese patriots, pride of your country…" The church was burned down when Spanish troops retook Bayamo, and residents – mostly women – decided to torch the city and flee to the hills. They did, however, save the laminated wooden altar to the Virgen de Dolores, with its baroque sculptures of Cuban fruit, and the stone font at which Céspedes and Figueredo were baptized. Both of these artefacts can now be seen in the rebuilt church.

San Salvador Church, Bayamo.

Northeast of Bayamo, **Dos Ríos** ⑩ is one of Cuba's most revered, and least visited sites. It was here that Cuba's greatest hero, José Martí, met his death fighting for Cuban independence, just a month after his arrival at Cajobabo. Dos Ríos was his first battle, and he died without having fired a shot. Surrounded by a green lawn scattered with stately royal palms, a stone wall holds a bronze bust of Martí with the inscription; "When my fall comes, all the savor of life will seem like sun and honey." A simple white obelisk marks the spot, proclaiming: "He died in this place on 19th May, 1895."

BELOW: The bell that launched Cuba's first war of independence, at Demajagua.

CÉSPEDES AND CUBAN REBELLION

On the morning of October 10, 1868, Bayamo-born Carlos Manuel de Céspedes rang the great bell at his sugar plantation La Demajagua, south of Manzanillo. With that stroke he emancipated his slaves and, in the resonant "Grito de Yara" (Cry of Yara), he declared open rebellion against Cuba's colonial rulers, thus beginning the first War of Independence against Spain. As with the US Civil War of a few years previously, the issue of emancipation was not the main reason for the war, but it was always an important subsidiary one, and became an increasingly necessary weapon in the struggle. Other landowners were soon to begin freeing and arming their slaves for battle.

Céspedes's bold action climaxed 15 years of conspiracy during which he and his friends used Masons' lodges and chess tournaments in Bayamo and Manzanillo as a cover for anti-colonialist plots. He led the rebel forces as President of the Republic in Arms until October 1873, when factional infighting forced him from power. By now almost blind, he accepted his removal with equanimity and retired to San Lorenzo in the Sierra Maestra to teach letters and chess. He had just finished a chess game one afternoon in March 1874, when Spanish troops raided the town and ordered him to surrender. He refused and was shot down.

Into the Sierra Maestra

To experience fully the rugged beauty of the southeastern mountains, the best base is the **Villa Santo Domingo ⓫**, in the hills south of the road linking Bayamo and Manzanillo on the coast. The mountain road veers off at **Yara**, passing through the small town of **Bartolomé Masó**, on to the **Embalse Paso Malo**, and up the steep road into the heart of the Sierra. During the guerrilla war, Santo Domingo was a rebel camp with a mess hall and workshops. Today, these have been adapted for feeding and entertaining campers. Partially hidden in this woody setting are new cabins housing two to four persons each. The Yara river is at hand for clear-water swimming and there are horses for exploring the mountain trails. Castro's old rebel headquarters in the mountains are at **La Comandancia de La Plata ⓬**, just to the south (not to be confused with the small village of La Plata at the foot of the mountains on the coast).

Celia Sánchez: Fidel Castro's assistant in the Sierra Maestra, and the "First Lady" of the Revolution.

Guides accompany visitors to the area through the wilderness and lead hikes up Cuba's highest mountain, **Pico Turquino** (6,470 ft/1,970 meters), 10 miles (16 km) away. The trail is exciting and beautiful: between outcroppings of mineral and volcanic rocks, deep green conifers stand alongside precious cedar, mahogany and trumpetwood trees. The slopes are dotted with delicate wild orchids and graceful ferns. Although it can be cold and windy, the temperature rarely drops to freezing and there's never any snow. The view from Turquino is magnificent, looking out over the Caribbean – on a clear night, the lights of Haiti are visible. Note that Pico Turquino itself is not always open to tourists, but there are other paths which can be followed.

BELOW: a rural *casita* in the sierra.

Other trails and narrow roads link the isolated villages and houses of the sparsely populated mountains. The people of the Sierra Maestra are typical *campesinos*: they keep a couple of cows, a gaggle of chickens and a few pigs and goats; grow a little coffee and some vegetables for their own use; scrub the laundry on smooth stones (*piedras chinas*) in the nearest stream; cook with wood or kerosene; and watch television at night (though not everyone has electricity). Rationed staples are brought in monthly. The family doctor makes regular rounds, usually on horseback. In an emergency (and when there's fuel), a jeep ambulance speeds the patient to the nearest clinic or hospital, but pregnant women are checked into special mountain maternity houses.

Map on pages 270–71

The symbolism of the Demajagua Bell was exploited by Castro in his student years: it was brought to the University of Havana campus and used in a demonstration against the corrupt government of President Grau.

Liberty bell

Overlooking the Gulf of Guacanayabo, 30 miles (48 km) west of Bayamo, **Manzanillo** ⓭ is the second largest city in the province. Its fine harbor has also made it the main fishing center and principal shipping terminal for the sugar brought in by truck or rail from the little mill towns further south.

Like Bayamo, Manzanillo is steeped in rebellion, early on as a smuggling port, then during the wars of independence. Cuba's first communist cell was organized in Manzanillo in the 1920s, and the only communist mayor, Paquito Rosales, was democratically elected there in the 1940s. In the same decade, Jesús Menéndez, the incorruptible leader of the sugar workers' union, was assassinated on Manzanillo railway station platform after collecting workers' grievances in the area. During the 1950s, Celia Sánchez organized an underground campaign here in support of the 26th of July Movement.

Manzanillo seems to turn its back on the port, and the seafront Malecón is often deserted. Attention is focused instead on the large **Parque Céspedes**, where several colonial buildings show a marked Moorish influence – particularly the delightful, brightly colored *glorieta* or bandstand in the center of the square. In one corner of the square is a small stage where local groups sometimes perform. You still see people play the *organo oriental*, a type of hand-operated organ originally brought from France in the 19th century. Take the time also to stroll through the dusty backstreets of Manzanillo, which has a pleasantly spacious feel. It is also worth seeking out the **Celia Sánchez memorial**, with its colorful tiled murals of sunflowers and doves, located seven blocks southwest of the main square along Calle Martí. On a hill overlooking the city is **Hotel Guacanayabo**, another Soviet-inspired eyesore which has little more to offer than a spectacular view.

La Demajagua ⓮, on the coast just south of Manzanillo and connected to the city by a rail spur, is where Céspedes rang the bell – once used to call slaves to work – to call for independence and abolition in 1868. The plantation is now a park, with the great bell now firmly anchored in a stone wall and a small museum with displays of local archaeological relics and some of Céspedes' personal effects.

Past La Demajagua, the road follows the coast through **Media Luna** ⓯, the little town where Celia Sánchez was born in 1920. The house – now a community center – is somewhat more affluent than others along the main streets, for Celia's father was the

BELOW: the *glorieta* adds a Moorish flavor to Manzanillo's main square.

local doctor. He was also a follower of Cuba's national hero, José Martí. In 1953, to commemorate the 100th anniversary of Martí's birth, he and Celia placed a bust of the Apostle on Pico Turquino. A more explosive commemoration at the time was the attack in July on the Moncada Garrison in Santiago. In the years that followed, Celia Sánchez became a prominent underground organizer and was the first to make contact with Fidel after the landing of the *Granma*. Eventually, she joined the rebel forces and was a part of the revolutionary leadership up to her death in 1980.

Of the 82 men who disembarked from the Granma, *only 16 survived an attack by Batista's troops at Alegría de Pío.*

The guerrilla war began here

Heading south along the coast, **Playa Las Coloradas** ⓰ lies in the middle of nowhere, halfway between the port of **Niquero** (which has some interesting French-style plantation houses) and the isolated tip of Cabo Cruz. The beach's only significance is as the starting point of the Rebel Army trail: a wooden pathway now crosses the muddy terrain that Fidel, Raúl, Che and their band waded through after disembarking from the cabin cruiser *Granma* in December 1956 to begin the guerrilla war (*see page 44*). A monument roughly marks their landing place. The rebels were quickly surrounded by Batista's troops, and were nearly annihilated at Alegría de Pío, a tiny village surrounded by cane fields, reached by road from Niquero.

Far more interesting than Las Coloradas is **Cabo Cruz** ⓱, in the **Parque Nacional Desembarco del Granma**, marked by a lonely 19th-century lighthouse and relics from the 5000 year-old civilization of the indigenous Siboney. There is a tumbledown fishing village here, marking Cuba's most southerly point: a pretty place with gardens overflowing with bouganvillea. The marine terrace is replete with caverns eroded by the sea. Fissures in the rocky surface expose drops of up to 240 ft (70 meters) with vertical walls that open into enormous underwater chambers. Fascinating coralline formations and one of the country's largest collections of the coveted queen conch hug the rocky shore. Further out lies the hull of a ship sunk in the 19th century.

BELOW: wherever you are, you will never be far from a monument to Che.

The dry surface of the terrace reveals sturdy cacti poking through the rocks. Lizards scuttle underfoot, while cormorants, egrets, and gulls wing overhead. The Siboney once lived and stored their provisions in the caves along this coast. Their diet consisted of fish, small animals, and native plants; they collected shells and stones to make tools, utensils and weapons, and crushed rocks into colored powder for painting. Clearly visible on the walls of several caverns are black and red (sometimes blue and brown) drawings of enigmatic lines, circles and figures.

The dramatic south coast

Southeast of Niquero you drive through sugar cane plains and the foothills of the Sierra Maestra before coming to the beautifully-sited town of **Pilón**. From here the road hugs the coast, sandwiched between mountains and the Caribbean, all the way to Santiago de Cuba, with some of Cuba's most dramatic scenery along the way. **Marea del Portillo** is a small fishing village set in rather uninteresting, scrubby landscape by a protected inlet, with a black-sand beach fringed by coconut palms. There is still some local flavor, with horsemen mounting their steeds and riding up into the Sierra Maestra. You can rent a car at one of the three hotels that cater mainly to Canadian package tourists.

The drive along the south coast to Santiago is one of the most memorable on the island, as you pass through some of the most beautiful countryside in Cuba, with the mountains descending right to the shore. The journey used to be hazardous due to the terrible condition of the road, but the route has now been resurfaced. There are rock falls, however, so watch out for boulders in your path – particularly if you are driving after dark – and always keep an eye out for cows, goats, and other animals. Lastly, there is little in the way of roadside facilities, so fill your tank and take plenty of water and food for the journey.

La Plata (not to be confused with the Comandancia de La Plata inland) is the site of the rebels' first attack on Batista's army on May 28, 1957. A museum (open Tues–Sat, 9am–5pm) in the town focuses on this battle and other aspects of the guerrilla campaign. Nearby, **Las Cuevas** has a pleasant beach, and at **Ocujal** the road passes beneath Cuba's highest mountain **Pico Turquino**.

Uvero, 15 miles (24 km) further east, is another place where the guerrillas won an important victory. Beyond, the little fishing village of **Chivirico** ⓳ is famous for its bat-filled caves, **Las Cuevas de los Murciélagos,** and also its **international scuba center**, based at the Hotel Delta Los Galeones. This hotel and the Hotel Delta Sierra Mar nearby are two of the island's best resorts; both are rather isolated, but Santiago is within easy reach. Rental cars are available here if you're intending to drive the coastal route in reverse. ❑

Break up the last stretch on the road east to Santiago by stopping off at one of several small but beautiful beaches, such as Caletón Blanco, Buey Cabón, or Playa Mar Verde.

BELOW: the dramatic route along the south coast to Santiago.

SANTIAGO DE CUBA

Cuba's second city has a heroic revolutionary past, beautiful squares, and a vibrant musical tradition which includes the country's most vigorous carnival

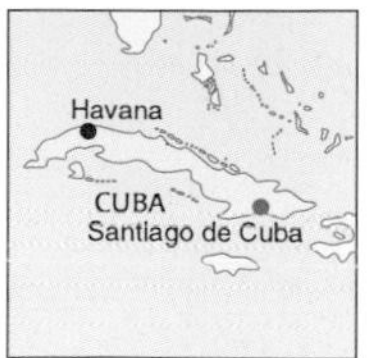

Nestled alongside a sweeping bay at the foothills of the Sierra Maestra mountains, **Santiago** is Cuba's most exotic and ethnically diverse city. More Caribbean than Cuban, it is where many Haitians, both white and black, settled after fleeing the slave uprisings of their country at the end of the 18th century, bringing with them the cachet of their French culture. Isolated and remote, it is Cuba's second largest city with a population of almost 400,000.

Surrounding the city are vast rural slopes covered with sugar cane and coffee plantations. The city itself has its share of structural decay, yet it's not nearly as run-down and dilapidated as Havana, nor as intense, imposing or congested. It is undergoing the same process of renovation as Old Havana: large areas are being pedestrianized, and museums, galleries, bars, and restaurants are emerging from *ciudadela* slums. This process is beautifying much of the colonial architecture – you'll see plenty of graceful hanging balconies, gingerbread latticework and wrought-iron gates throughout the city – but Santiago suffered greatly from the privations of the Special Period. There is a lot of poverty here and visitors have to put up with harassment from hustlers and beggars. For the same reason, crime is on the increase, and there is more need for care, especially when walking through the town alone at night.

LEFT: Santiago's cathedral rises above the rooftops. **BELOW:** José Martí's tomb in Santiago's Santa Ifigenia cemetery.

Santiago is renowned for producing much of Cuba's most important music, and this rich musical tradition, mingled with the remnants of French customs, gives the city a sensual, somewhat sleazy, New Orleans-like atmosphere. Wandering around can be confusing at times because some of the city's streets have two or three names, but Santiago is still ideal for walking and deserves several days to explore.

Bastion of nationalism

Founded by the Spaniards in 1514, Santiago was Cuba's capital from 1524 until 1549. Because of its deep, natural harbor and Caribbean coastline, it also served as the center of the island's prosperous slave trade in the 1700s and 1800s. In 1898 Spain's surrender to the US took place in Santiago, and then the city slowly slipped into second-class status after the government centered itself in Havana.

Today, Santiago is the island's only official "Hero City," revered for being a bastion of Cuban nationalism and the cradle of the revolution. It was here, on July 26, 1953, that the revolution began with the failed assault on the Moncada garrison by Castro and his rebels. It was also here that Castro accepted the surrender of Batista's army in 1959.

Formerly Cuba's second largest military post, the **Antiguo Cuartel Moncada** Ⓐ (open daily 8am–6pm, Sun 8am–noon; entrance fee) now serves two separate

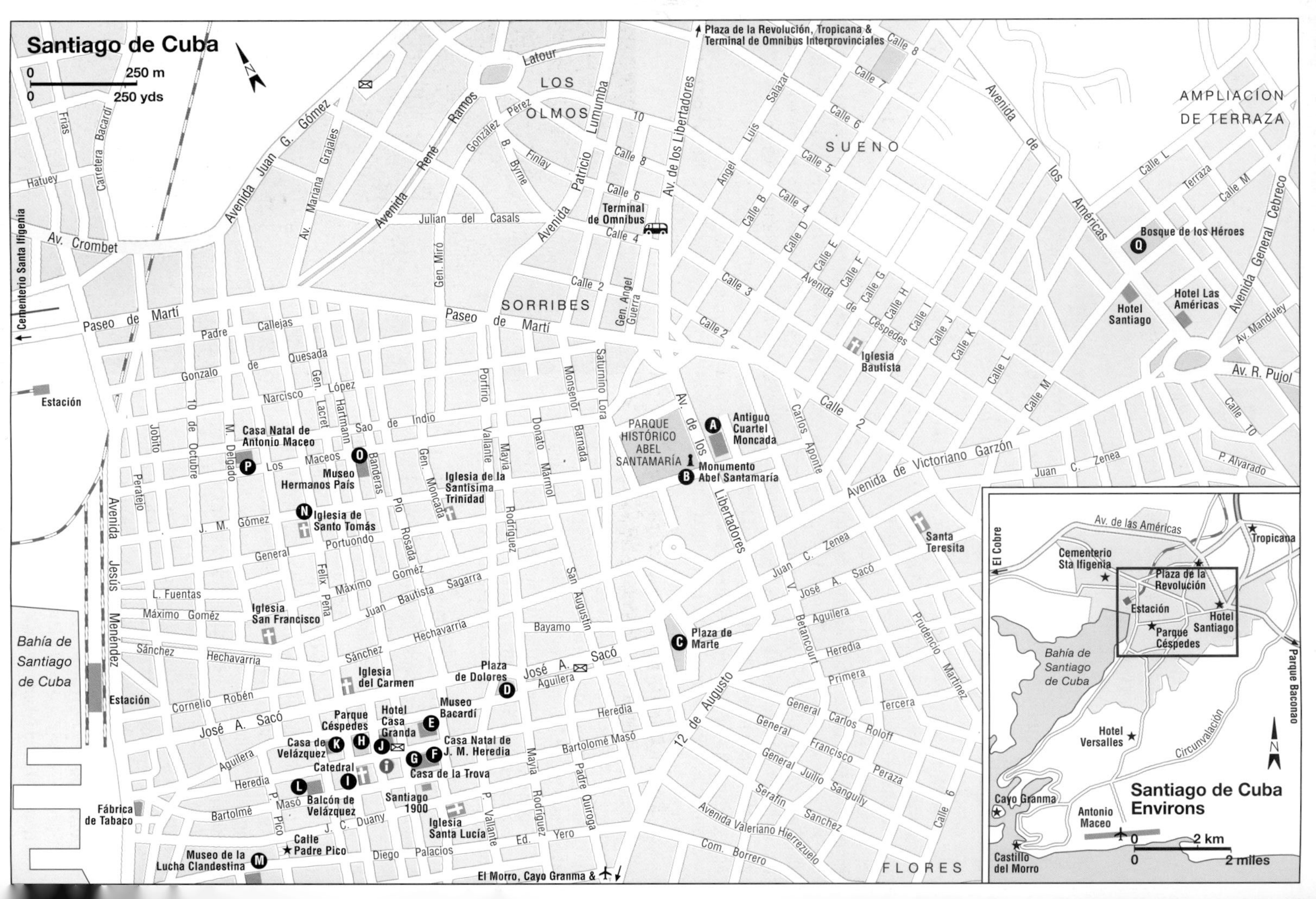
Santiago de Cuba
0 250 m
0 250 yds
A Antiguo Cuartel Moncada
B Monumento Abel Santamaría
C Plaza de Marte
D Plaza de Dolores
E Museo Bacardí
F Casa Natal de J. M. Heredia
G Casa de la Trova
H Parque Céspedes
I Catedral
J Hotel Casa Granda
K Casa de Velázquez
L Balcón de Velázquez
M Museo de la Lucha Clandestina
N Iglesia de Santo Tomás
O Museo Hermanos País
P Casa Natal de Antonio Maceo
Q Bosque de los Héroes
PARQUE HISTÓRICO ABEL SANTAMARÍA
Iglesia de la Santísima Trinidad
Iglesia del Carmen
Iglesia San Francisco
Iglesia Santa Lucía
Iglesia Bautista
Santa Teresita
Santiago 1900
Calle Padre Pico
Fábrica de Tabaco
Estación
Terminal de Omnibus
Hotel Santiago
Hotel Las Américas
Bahía de Santiago de Cuba
Plaza de la Revolución, Tropicana & Terminal de Omnibus Interprovinciales
El Morro, Cayo Granma &
Cementerio Santa Ifigenia
AMPLIACIÓN DE TERRAZA
LOS OLMOS
SUENO
SORRIBES
FLORES
Paseo de Martí
Avenida de los Américas
Av. de los Libertadores
Avenida de Victoriano Garzón
Avenida Jesús Menéndez
Avenida Juan G. Gómez
Avenida René Ramos Latour
Avenida Patricio Lumumba
Avenida General Cebreco
Av. R. Pujol
Av. Crombet
12 de Augusto
Santiago de Cuba Environs
0 2 km
0 2 miles
Tropicana
Parque Baconao
Plaza de la Revolución
Estación
Parque Céspedes
Hotel Santiago
Cementerio Sta Ifigenia
Hotel Versalles
Antonio Maceo
Cayo Granma
Castillo del Morro
El Cobre
Circunvalación
Av. de las Américas

purposes: one half is a school for young children, while the other is a museum dedicated to Cuban history, but with most attention paid to the Revolution. Inside its bullet-ridden brick walls are revolutionary memorabilia such as guns, grenades, documents, photographs, Castro's khaki uniforms and Guevara's muddy boots. The museum is very strong visually, so non-Spanish speakers can still have an enjoyable visit.

A block away is the impressive **Monumento Abel Santamaría** Ⓑ, a tribute to one of the leaders of the 1953 attack on Moncada. It was Santamaría's job to create diversionary fire at the nearby hospital – a task he performed too well, in fact: unaware that the main assault had failed, he and his men continued firing until the hospital was surrounded. Despite pretending to be patients, the unfortunate rebels were caught, and then summarily tortured.

Towards the colonial center

Walking southwest towards the old town from here, you reach Avenida Garzón. Look out for **Hotel Rex**, on the left just before you reach **Plaza de Marte** Ⓒ. Now a very basic peso hotel (which does, nevertheless, take tourists), the Rex is where Fidel Castro and his fellow guerrillas ate their last meal before the Moncada barracks attack in July 1953 – and some even stayed overnight. From Plaza de Marte, a pleasant square where private taxis often gather and where goat-pulled carts take children for rides at weekends, head down Aguilera to **Plaza de Dolores** Ⓓ. There are several bars and restaurants here, including Cafeteria La Isabelica, a local institution, and Taberna de Dolores, housed in a cavernous colonial mansion and attracting a young Cuban crowd.

Continuing down Calle Aguilera, you come to the imposing Provincial Government building on your right and, opposite, the **Museo Bacardí** Ⓔ (open Tues–Sat 9am–8.30pm, Sun 9am–3.30pm; entrance fee), Santiago's top museum, and the country's oldest. It was founded in 1899 by Emilio Bacardí Moreau, a Cuban writer and the first mayor of Santiago, but more famous for his Caney Rum distillery, which was moved to Puerto Rico after the Revolution to produce the re-named Bacardi Rum.

The museum contains some first-rate Cuban art (including works from the talented Tejada Revilla brothers), colonial European art, memorabilia from Cuba's wars of independence, historic documents, flags, maps, and weapons. There is also an easily-missed basement section, with native Indian artefacts and an out-of-place Egyptian mummy.

From the Bacardí Museum it is just a short walk to one of old Santiago's most important streets, **Calle Heredia**, which has a couple of museums worth a quick visit. The most interesting is the small **Museo del Carnaval** (open Tue–Sun, 9am–5pm; entrance fee), which gives a bit of background to the city's famous summer festival, mainly in the form of rather faded photographs. The nearby **Casa Natal de J.M. Heredia** Ⓕ (open Tues–Sun, 8am–5pm; entrance fee) is the birthplace of José María Heredia, one of the first Cuban poets to speak out in favor of national independence.

Map on page 286

The old Bacardí rum distillery, an enormous building opposite the railway station near the port, produces some fine post-revolutionary brands. There is a shop and bar attached, and it is sometimes possible to go on a tour of the factory.

BELOW: welcome to the city.

Music on Calle Heredia

Calle Heredia is a good venue for the arts. The local office of the **Unión de Escritores y Artistas de Cuba** (Cuban Writers' and Artists' Union) is here and stages regular poetry readings, art shows, lectures, and literary discussions. Another venue is the **Artex** shop, which sells various crafts and works of art, but also hosts bands at night in the relaxed atmosphere of the courtyard at the back.

Heredia is most famous for its live music, and you may well witness some of the finest musicians of your stay in Cuba here. The most famous venue is the renowned **Casa de la Trova** **G**. This dates back to the 18th century, but underwent a misguided "refurbishment" in the mid-1990s. The place is much less smoky and atmospheric now, but it is still considered an honor by musicians to play here – treading as they do in the footsteps of a string of Cuban greats – and so it continues to attract some very accomplished artists. All week long, local musicians perform acts that range from somber Spanish guitar classics to vibrant Afro-Cuban drumming, solo acts to 12-piece bands, trained professionals to talented amateurs. Not too long ago, most of the musical instruments used by the performers were older than the performers themselves, and many were held together with tape, wire and clothes pins. Things have improved of late – especially with the money that tourism brings in – even if quality instruments are still in short supply. The venue's clientele consists primarily now of tourists, but is still an essential part of any trip to the city. Tape recorders are not allowed.

On Saturday and Sunday nights three blocks of Calle Heredia are blocked off from traffic and turned into a mini street carnival where musicians, mime artists, magicians, and dancers entertain the crowd. Street vendors supply the crowds with drinks and snacks.

The central square

In the center of the city is **Parque Céspedes** **H**, a leafy colonial square with a bust of Carlos Manuel de Céspedes at its center. The nucleus of the city, this is

BELOW: the Moncada Garrison, now home to a museum and a school.

where you'll find young, old, rich and poor gathering to exchange news or simply watch the world go by. Teenagers mingle beneath the trees and young couples sit entwined on park benches. Dominating the park is the **Catedral de Santa Ifigenia** ❶, a vast, mainly 20th-century church on the site of the original cathedral built in 1528. It contains an ecclesiastical museum and, it is said, the remains of conquistador Diego Velázquez, though these have never been located.

Next door to the cathedral is the **Hotel Casa Granda** ❶. Once a high-society spot where the Cuban elite gathered on the rooftop terrace to sip rum, dance and smoke cigars, the Casa Granda during the 1950s was a sinister place that teemed with both American spies and Cuban rebels. One of the hotel's former guests was author Graham Greene who used the setting for a scene in his book *Our Man in Havana*. The restored interior is splendidly grand, and suites have been decked out in golden silk. Breakfast and dinner are taken on the hotel's front patio restaurant, which has plenty of character, even if there is a problem with the large quantity of *jinetera* working girls that congregate outside.

Bust of Céspedes in the main square.

Cuba's oldest house

In the northwest corner of Parque Céspedes is the **Casa de Velázquez** ❶, which houses the **Museo de Arte Colonial** (open Mon–Sat 9am–4.40pm; entrance fee) and should not be missed. A solid stone structure with Moorish screened balconies, floor-to-ceiling shutters, and glorious cedar ceilings (*alfarjes*), the house was built between 1516 and 1530 and is said to be the oldest home in Cuba. In the 16th century, Governor Diego Velázquez used the ground floor as his office and the upper floor as his residence. Before being turned into a museum, the historic home was used as a hotel. Among its collection are

BELOW LEFT: this little piggy went to market.
BELOW: peppermint colonial façade.

European tapestries, crystal, paintings, ceramics, and antiques that once belonged to Santiago's colonial settlers. Nearby is the **Balcón de Velázquez** Ⓛ, a small park on the site of an earlier Spanish fort with good views of the harbor.

The streets that radiate from the main square are filled with theatrical displays of everyday life. Men walk along with live chickens under their arms and scrawny pigs on a leash, women wait in long lines at the food markets, and children scurry to school. Most of the streets are dotted with large, colonial homes that have been turned into overcrowded apartment buildings. Music, both live and from radios, pours out on to the sidewalks from windows left wide open for the breeze. Above the narrow streets are a tangle of out-of-order neon signs that once beckoned shoppers during more prosperous times.

Entrance to Santiago Cathedral, whose façade dates from the 1920s.

BELOW: a poster beckons visitors to Santiago's version of Havana's Tropicana cabaret.

South and west of Parque Céspedes

One of the oldest of these thoroughfares is **Bartolomé Masó**, a cobblestoned street lined with antique gas lamps. Look out for **Restaurante 1900**, housed in a grand colonial home that once belonged to Emilio Bacardí. Furnished with 19th-century antiques and crystal chandeliers, the restaurant effectively retains some of its original elegance. Each evening a piano trio performs nostalgic Cuban music during dinner. The street leads all the way down to Avenida Jesús Menéndez and Parque Alameda, flanking the harbor.

The broad, dusty promenade by the seafront is not particularly scenic, but you may want to venture down here to visit the cigar factory, the **Fábrica de Tabaco Cesár Escalante**, the rum factory (*see page 287*) or one of the transport terminals. You must also cross this district en route northwest to **Cementerio Santa Ifigenia**, though on a hot day you are advised to pick up a cab or a horse and cart. Once segregated by race and social class, the cemetery has both massive mausoleums and unpretentious graves. Carlos Manuel de Céspedes, Emilio Bacardí and Cuba's first president, Tomás Estrada Palma, are amongst the famous figures buried here. The tomb to receive most visitors, though, is that of the patriot José Martí, whose marble tomb has six women carved around the outside bearing the symbols of Cuba's provinces. The national flag is reverently draped over Martí's sarcophagus, which is so positioned as to catch the sun throughout the day.

One of the prettiest streets in the city is **Padre Pico**, which climbs to the top of a steep hill southwest of the main square, in the so-called Tivolí district. The streets here are lined with 16th-century houses that were once home to French refugees fleeing the slave rebellion in Haiti. At the corner of Padre Pico and Santa Rita is the **Museo de la Lucha Clandestina**, or Museum of the Underground Struggle, Ⓜ (open Tues–Sun; entrance fee), a former colonial mansion now dedicated to the heroes of the 26th of July Movement. In 1956 one of Castro's guerrillas firebombed the office of the Batista police headquarters that was housed here, but it has now been beautifully restored. There is a fine view of the city from outside the museum.

North of Parque Céspedes

Santiago's main shopping street, **Calle Saco** (also known as the Enramada), lies one block north of the main square. Beyond here, though, the streets become suddenly quieter and can be fun to explore. **Calle Félix Peña** runs down a gentle slope to Placita Santo Tomás a charming colonial square overlooked by the 18th-century **Iglesia Santo Tomás** Ⓝ. Also well worth a visit is the **Iglesia de**

Map on page 286

TIP

One block north of Parque Céspedes on Calle Saco is a small, helpful shop owned by Egrem records, the major Cuban record label. Here you can listen to a broad range of CDs or tapes before you buy.

BELOW: counting out the pennies.

CARNAVAL IN SANTIAGO

Every summer, in the intense heat of July, a Rio-style carnival envelops Santiago and the city is overrun with colorful floats, frenzied street dances and conga lines that snake their way through the town. The potent smell of rum saturates the air as revelers with supple spines are swept away by the rhythm of African drums, cowbells, brassy horns and maracas. Unlike in other Latin American countries, Cuban carnival does not take place during Lent.

Everyone agrees that Santiago's festival is far superior to its Havana counterpart, and it is also more traditional and folkloric. The custom dates back to the 18th century when French culture was influential, and neighborhood dance groups regularly paraded through the city. These elegant yet earthy dance groups, known as *carabalis*, have been a part of Santiago ever since. Some have a very Afro-Cuban character, others are more Spanish and wear costumes of 18th-century Spain.

Groups can be seen practising throughout the year for the annual event. Carabali Izuama, one of the oldest groups, practises on Pío Rosado; La Tumba Francesca, a Haitian group founded in 1852 and named after a Haitian dance, rehearses on Calle Los Maceo.

la Santísima Trinidad, five blocks east, though you'll be lucky to find it open.

On Calle General Banderas is another monument to two of Santiago's revolutionary heroes, the **Museo Hermanos País** O (open Mon–Sat 9am–5pm; entrance fee), dedicated to the País brothers. Frank País was a poet, teacher and army rebel who led the Santiago uprising in 1956. His younger brother, Josue, was also active in the 26th of July Movement. Both were gunned down in 1957, and their boyhood home is now a national shrine.

Antonio Maceo rides on in Santiago de Cuba's Plaza de la Revolución.

The great Antonio Maceo, hero of Cuba's wars of independence, was also born in a modest house nearby. The **Casa Natal de Antonio Maceo** P (open daily; entrance fee), on a street now called Los Maceo, includes photos and personal possessions, along with exhibits on Maceo's military battles.

East of the old town

Heading east of the old town, along Avenida Garzón, you come to one of the city's most modern and wealthiest areas, with the landmark red, white and blue **Hotel Santiago**. Nearby is a buzzing farmers' market, and, next to the **Hotel Las Américas**, a small, rather neglected park, the **Bosque de los Héroes** Q, which has more monuments dedicated to those who led Cuba's revolution in the 1950s.

Just east of here, flanking Avenida Manduley, is the attractive **Vista Alegre** district. North along Avenida de las Américas, you'll find a very different atmosphere in the **Plaza de la Revolución**, at the junction of Avenida Los Libertadores. The square is dominated by the vast **Monumento Maceo**, which is connected to a museum containing holograms of various famous revolutionary items. Further out of town in this direction is Santiago's **Tropicana**, not perhaps as grand as its famous Havana counterpart, but a fine show, nevertheless. ❑

BELOW: the modernist architecture of the Hotel Santiago.

Los Autos

They haunt the roads of Cuba like ostentatious ghosts of American capitalism: big old Buicks, Packards, Chevys, Chryslers, Studebakers, Hudsons, Edsels, and Fords. It's not known exactly how many antique cars there are in Cuba, but their numbers are estimated in the thousands. Since the US trade embargo began in 1961, no new American cars have been exported to the island, and the old ones from the 1940s and 1950s now share the roads with the Hungarian buses and boxy Russian Ladas of more recent years.

These flashy American behemoths could once cruise at 100 mph (160 km/h) without a hint of strain. With back seats big enough for six, leather interiors, and jazzy two-tone color schemes, they are some of the most powerful cars ever produced by the US automobile industry, the ultimate in conspicuous consumption. In most other countries they would be garage-kept prized possessions, but in Cuba they are everyday transportation work-horses. Many of these gas-guzzlers have been turned into black market taxi cabs in order to earn their keep.

Riding on mismatched tires, they are coaxed into running order by tree-shade mechanics who represent the epitome of Cuban ingenuity. They barter chickens for parts, transplant carburetors from Russian jeeps, and turn water-filled pickle jars into makeshift filters.

Some are in perfect shape: soaring tail fins that glisten in the sun, sturdy running boards, gap-tooth grillwork and jazzy hood ornaments polished to perfection. Others are sorry heaps of metal: bodies wavy from too many putty patches, coated with layers of house paint, electric windows frozen open, and fenders rusted out from the salt air.

During the late 1980s, the Cuban government began selling some of the old cars to foreign investors. Cuban owners were offered a new Lada or cash for trade. However, following the collapse of the Soviet Union, the Ladas became difficult to get hold of, and Cuba's classic car racket faltered. In fact, many Cubans had proved reluctant to part with their old, much-loved vehicles.

Although a blatant symbol of Yankee imperialism, these antique autos are very much part of Cuban history. During his first few years in office, Castro cruised around in a luxurious Oldsmobile, and Batista before him did the same. A museum in Old Havana (*see page 152*) is dedicated to famous old cars (including Che's Chevy), with another located in Baconao Park, east of Santiago.

One car in particular became a very hot item – the 1955 Chrysler convertible once owned by Ernest Hemingway. Most recently owned by Augustín Nuñez Gutiérrez, a former policeman, the car cost Hemingway $3,924 new. Today it is worth a fortune. The Cuban government offered Gutiérrez a Lada for trade, but knowing the value of his treasure, he demanded a house. Frustrated by the bureaucracy surrounding the trade, and life in Cuba in general, Gutiérrez hid the car, hopped on a raft, and went to Miami. Somewhere, tucked away in the countryside, the Chrysler is waiting to become a collector's dream. ❑

RIGHT: one of the thousands of ancient cruise-mobiles, made in the US but forever Cuban.

AROUND SANTIAGO

Several day and half-day trips can be made from Santiago de Cuba, including to the spectacular Morro fortress, the island's most holy Catholic shrine, great beaches and a dinosaur fantasyland

Map on pages 270–71

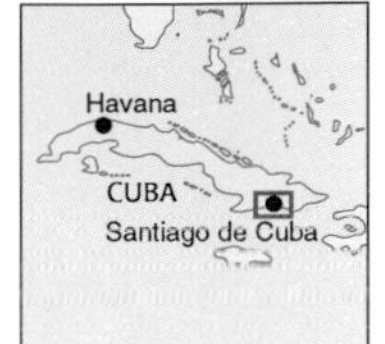

Within easy striking distance of the capital of the Oriente are several sights that shouldn't be missed. A rental car provides the most convenient way of exploring these, but they are also accessible either on public transport or by hiring a taxi for the day – just ensure you strike a deal and an itinerary before you set off. Most sights are located east of Santiago. West of the city you'll find a scattering of pleasant beaches, such as **Playa Mar Verde** ⓴, not to mention the stunning drive along the coast into Granma Province.

Virgin or Goddess?

Of all the monuments in the Santiago region, the most famous is the shrine to the **Virgen de la Caridad del Cobre**, 12 miles (19 km) northwest of the city. **El Cobre** ㉑ is named for the first open copper mine in the Americas, which supplied the ore for Havana's artillery works, the largest in the New World, in around 1600. Although the mine still produces copper, the place has long been identified with a far more precious object that three young men found floating in the Bay of Nipe off Cuba's northern coast, in 1608: a 1-ft (30-cm) tall wooden statue of a mestizo Virgin carrying the infant Christ on her left arm, and holding a gold cross in her right hand. At her feet was the inscription, *Yo soy la Virgen de la Caridad* ("I am the Virgin of Charity"). Legend has it that she had been floating for almost 100 years, since an indigenous chieftain – who had been presented with the statue by the conquistador Alonso de Ojeda in 1510 – had set her adrift to protect her from the evil intentions of other less Christian native *caciques* (chiefs).

LEFT: the Basilica of the Virgin at El Cobre, Cuba's holiest site.
BELOW: the view from Santiago's El Morro fortress.

During every struggle in the town or at the mine after her arrival in El Cobre, the Virgin seemed to side with the people and ensure their victory. Through the years, she has been invoked to protect freedom, perform miracles, offer consolation and heal the bitterness of battle. In 1916, at the petition of veterans of the War of Independence, the Pope declared her patron saint of Cuba. The Virgin's sanctuary, Cuba's only basilica, was inaugurated on her saint's day, September 8, in 1927.

From a distance, the cream-colored church, surrounded by bougainvillea, looks stunning against the wooded slopes behind. Inside, the nave rises in arched vaults above stained-glass windows set high on the side walls. Above and to the right of the altar is the air-conditioned niche holding the diminutive figure of the Virgin, dressed in a yellow, gold-encrusted satin gown and wearing a replica of the valuable coronation crown presented on her saint's day in 1936.

Behind the main altar is the Shrine of Miracles, where grateful believers leave braces, crutches, clods

of earth from foreign lands, flags, armbands, coins, medals, locks of hair and other *ex voto* offerings. There is even a piece of the Berlin Wall, and the athletic shirt of the famous Cuban 800-meter Olympic gold medallist, Ana Quirot. From here, stairs lead up to the altar and the image of the Virgin itself.

When Pope John Paul II visited Cuba in January 1998, he bequeathed a gold rosary to the Virgin of El Cobre and crowned her in a ceremony in Santiago witnessed by vast crowds.

Thousands of worshippers flock to the church on her saint's day every September, for the Virgin is also worshipped in Afro-Cuban religions as the mulatto Ochún, the magnetic and sensual goddess of love and rivers in Santería. It was on her saint's day in 1993 that the Conference of Catholic Bishops of Cuba issued a fervent call to the Castro government to seek real, lasting solutions to the poverty that was then afflicting Cuba.

A Spanish fortress

To the south of the city, perched above the scraggy banks of Santiago Bay, is the Spanish fortress known as **Castillo del Morro** ㉒. This stunning fortress was built in 1633 according to the design of a specialist Italian architect, Giovanni Batista Antonelli, who had also designed the Morro in Havana. It was destroyed by the English pirate Henry Morgan in 1682 and rebuilt between 1690 and 1710. It has an elaborate labyrinth of drawbridges, moats, passageways, staircases and barracks, all executed with marvellously precise angles and a geometric beauty. Its dark, dank inner cells, complete with built-in iron shackles, once housed African slaves in transit, and its small chapel still contains a wooden cross carved by a 16th-century Spanish artist. Look out for the contraption that was used to haul mighty stone balls up from the store to the cannon above. Inside the fortress is a history of Caribbean piracy, beginning with the bearded scoundrels of the 1500s and ending with the Yankee imperialists of the 1900s.

BELOW: Cayo Granma and Santiago Bay.

Map on pages 270–71

The local ferry boat to **Cayo Granma** – a small island community that lies just inside the mouth of the Bay of Santiago – departs from a pier a mile along the coast from the small beach at the foot of El Morro. Costing only a few centavos, ferries depart roughly every forty minutes throughout the day, and follow a roundabout route linking the island with several little communities on the shores of the bay. Ferries also depart about once every hour from Santiago harbor. Formerly called Cayo Smith for the wealthy English slave trader who once owned it, the island's name was changed after the Revolution.

Cayo Granma today has about 4,000 residents, some of whom still fish and build boats for a living, but most commute by ferry to factory and office jobs in Santiago. Since there are no cars or hotels on the island, it still has a very tranquil and old-time atmosphere. It has a beautiful beach, a small park where locals gather for games of dominoes, a few schools, shops, and plenty of private *paladar* seafood restaurants overlooking the sea. Many local residents offer rooms, and, indeed, the island makes a pleasant, relaxing place to spend a night – and feels a thousand miles away from the bustle of Santiago.

The intricate pattern on the walls of the Morro fortress is not one of its more defense-minded features.

Gran Piedra

The highway east of Santiago which follows the Caribbean coastline is a marvellous road that slips between the sea and a rocky, cacti desert with the blue green mountains beyond. A 200,000-acre (80,000-hectare) area here, the **Parque Baconao**, has been recognized as a biosphere reserve by UNESCO.

Eight miles (13 km) into the mountains there is a well-marked turnoff to **Gran Piedra ㉓**, taking you from dry and dusty desert into cloud-capped mountains shrouded in rainforest, up a long access road that looks like a testing site for land mines. Each twist and turn in the road reveals a new vista across the mountains, and local people gather by the road to sell delicious fruit and scented flowers. At 4,300 ft (1,300 meters) above sea level, you come to the Gran Piedra ("Big Rock") itself with fabulous uninterrupted views across the mountains and out to sea, even as far as Jamaica – if there's no cloud, that is; sadly, there usually is. It's ideal for what Cubans call *montañismo* or climbing. Most people visit for the day, but visitors can stay at the **Villa Gran Piedra Cubanacán**, an "eco-lodge" with comfortable rustic cabins along the edge of the mountain ridge and unbeatable views.

Near to Gran Piedra, the **Jardín Ave de Paraíso** (Bird of Paradise Garden) is essential viewing. First planted in 1960 to provide flowers for hotels, celebrations and formal presentations, nowadays they mainly supply Interflora, who opened a Cuban branch in 1997. The gardens are beautifully landscaped and the flowers are breathtaking.

In a lovely spot a mile or so along a dirt road east of La Gran Piedra, **La Isabelica** (open Tue–Sun, 8am–4pm; entrance fee) is one of the area's few relics of the plantation era, when coffee was a major crop. La Isabelica, a 19th-century plantation home, gives some insight onto what life on such an estate was like. The house originally belonged to a family of French descent, refugees from Haiti's slave rebellion.

BELOW: relief from the tropical heat up in the hills.

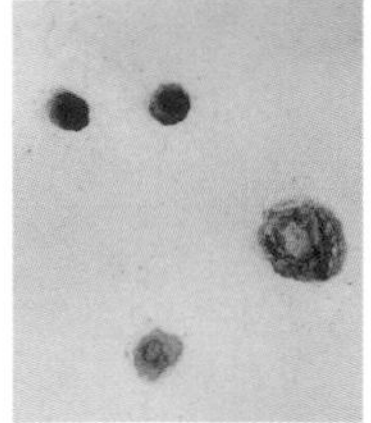

Bullet holes from shots fired by Batista's troops in the walls of Granjita Siboney. Not the originals, but they look authentic.

Down the mountain, and back on the main highway is **Granjita Siboney** 24 (open daily, 9am–5pm; entrance fee), the farmhouse where Fidel Castro and other rebels planned the 1953 attack on the Moncada barracks in Santiago (*see page 285*). It has been converted into a museum, with some classic examples of revolutionary hagiography – the most sacred relic may be the check from the Santiago restaurant where the *compañeros* had their last supper before the failed assault, but there is also the usual collection of bloodstained clothing. A well in the garden is where the weapons were hidden.

Nearby, the village of **Siboney** 25 has a pleasant beach, as yet undeveloped and much used by friendly locals. **El Oasis** a little further on is an artists' colony with a shop just off the road. Just after El Oasis, another excellent small beach, **Playa Bucanero**, is now well developed as a tourist resort. The **Hotel Club Amigo Bucanero** caters mostly to Germans and Canadian package tourists. The next turn off heading inland brings you to **La Poseta**, a large natural pool fed by an underground spring. Rather soiled by tourism, it has a barbecue and bar, whose loud music spoils the atmosphere.

One unmissable site for students of Cuban kitsch is the dinosaur theme park, the **Valle de la Prehistoria** 26 nearby, located some 16 miles (24km) east of Santiago. The park was created in 1983, but the collection of life-sized models of brontosauri, tyrannosauri and other dinosaurs has certainly attracted more visitors since the worldwide success of the film *Jurassic Park*. Children and adults alike cannot fail to be amused by the park, and the campy snapshots you can take make great keepsakes. Inevitably, if you pick up hitch-hikers in the region, you'll find someone who likens the dinosaurs to Cuba's leadership. There is no entrance fee as such, but you are expected to pay to park your car, with

BELOW: a prehistoric day dawns.

extra charges for cameras. There is also a very good museum here – the **Museo de Ciencias Naturales**, full of interesting facts on local flora and fauna.

The **Museo Nacional de Transporte** (open daily; entrance fee), up a left-hand turning a little further to the east, is also definitely worth visiting for its collection of vintage cars – including the Cadillac of the renowned Cuban singer, Beny Moré – and the display of over 2,000 miniature cars, which illustrate the development of transport from the early years to the present day.

History was made on the coast, south of here. Not, for a change, the history of political movements or ideologies, either. The name says it all: **Villa Daiquirí**, for the *daiquirí* was invented here (originally as a type of anti-malarial tonic for local miners), even if it was "perfected" in Havana's El Floridita bar (*see page 159*). Unfortunately, when you sit by the beach and sip on the watery drinks they make now, you can understand why it needed the Floridita's contribution. You'll do better to stroll down to the beach – called **Playa Daiquirí** ㉗, of course – and enjoy snorkeling or scuba diving in the clear water. There is one more historical connection to this site: it was on Daiquirí beach that Teddy Roosevelt and his Rough Riders came ashore during the Spanish-American War of 1898.

Beyond lie a string of other beaches and mostly rather unappealing resorts. **Playa Bacajagua** is pleasant, but the best place to aim for is **Playa Cazonal**, though the shallow water makes for limited swimming. There are a couple of German-run hotels, here, the best of which is **Los Corales**. Just beyond lies **Laguna Baconao**, in a lovely spot surrounded by hills. There's a restaurant, a couple of boats and a crocodile farm, but few signs of activity.

The paved road ends by the lake. If you don't mind a rough ride, you can continue along a dirt track to Guantánamo, but most people return to Santiago. ❑

Map on pages 270–71

No love-bite this.

BELOW: Playa Daiquirí, and time for a drink.

YUMURI-BARACOA

THE FAR EAST

The US military base of Guantánamo is one of the planet's most vivid reminders of the Cold War era, and the eastern reaches of Cuba can also offer some of the island's wildest landscapes

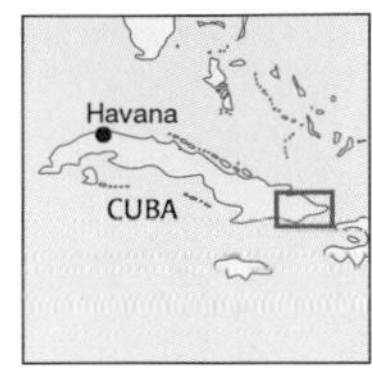

Cuba's state-run tour agencies are always glad to tell you about La Moncada and the rest of the must-see sites in Santiago de Cuba, the cradle of the revolution, but they have far less in the way of practical information on the area to the east of the city. There are few regular buses for tourists heading in this direction, so sightseeing generally means renting a car. However, the region has, of late, been opening up to tourism and, despite the obstacles involved, it is definitely worth making the effort to spend at least a couple of days here.

The terrain east of Santiago is mostly hilly countryside dotted with lakes and pastures, like an ever-unfolding landscape by Tomás Sánchez, the great Cuban painter now in exile. It is possible to travel for hours on end without spotting a foreigner – until you reach the lookout point over Guantánamo, from where you can make out US soldiers across the barbed-wire fences, and across what the *norteamericanos* call "Castro Barrier Road." It's where visitors can see one of the very last vestiges of the Cold War.

PRECEDING PAGES: deforested hills in eastern Cuba.
LEFT: on the Yumurí river near Baracoa.
BELOW: the city of Guantánamo is not an obvious tourist attraction.

Uneasy capital of a province

More than one visitor has remarked on the broad stretch of highway approaching **Guantánamo** ㉘. It is perfectly level, and paved so smoothly it looks suitable for a bowling tournament. But why a modern, four-lane highway when there are next to no cars?

Residents answer with a wink: it's a landing strip in the guise of a road, in case the Cuban Air Force has to repel a US attack. And sure enough, as you drive you'll see regular exit ramps cut into the hills, ramps that lead nowhere. They're for storing planes. The more you drive along that empty blackness, the more the Guantánamo highway looks like a deserted aircraft carrier dropped into the middle of cattle pastures.

There's no immediately obvious reason to make the 85-mile (136-km) trek from Santiago to Guantánamo. The city is not particularly pretty to look at, nor is it a great cultural center. The city seems to have two rather unfortunate unofficial emblems. One is a depot crammed with rusting buses that have no fuel. The other is an apartment tower that was to be a showcase of efficient, prefabricated architecture. Eighteen stories of apartment units were to be built in Santiago, then assembled in Guantánamo. But the locals had to lower their expectations, along with their building: there was a shortage of cement and of diesel for trucks carrying the few prefab pieces being made, so the would-be landmark has been topped off at 12 stories.

Not everything is so grim, however. City life revolves around **Parque Martí**, a pleasant leafy square shaded by laburnum trees (glorious in March), and with an attractive golden-colored church, the

Iglesia Parroquial de Santa Catalina. It's worth at least spending an hour exploring some of the streets around the main square. There are some attractive old houses on Calles Pérez and Calixto García, north of Parque Martí, while Los Maceo, one block east, is buzzing with shoppers. You should seek out the unusual **market**, a neo-classical structure occupying an entire block.

An evening in Guantánamo would not be complete unless you hear someone playing "Guajira Guantanamera" – the song composed by Joseito Fernández with words by José Martí paying tribute to the farmer-peasants of Guantánamo Province.

Caimanera: one view of the US base

Travel agents often don't explain that the city of Guantánamo itself offers no views of the controversial US naval base, which actually extends to the south of the city. For a glimpse of it, there are two options open to visitors.

The first and most difficult option is to pass through marshland and two Cuban military checkpoints, to **Caimanera** 29. You need a pass, however, to get through the military checkpoint – all local residents have to carry a pass, and their relations from outside who wish to visit must also obtain permission to enter. The necessary papers can be obtained – in principle – from the Ministry of the Interior (or MININT) office on Calle José Martí in Guantánamo. Here, though, they usually tell you to apply via the Ministry of Foreign Relations in Havana. This is a shame, because the Hotel Caimanera is comfortable and pleasant. And where else could you find a hotel with a three-story observation tower for monitoring the **US Naval Base** 30, complete with the history of Yankee oppression in Cuba? A billboard in the town proudly proclaims "Caimanera: The First Anti Imperialist Bunker of Cuba".

From far away, it is hard to believe the world came close to nuclear war over Nikita Khrushchev's project to put nuclear missiles in Cuba in 1962, with Castro grumbling about "Cuba, the little sardine" and "the satiated shark, the United

BELOW: low-tech transport in Guantánamo.

States." But from the balcony of Caimanera's public school, the closest observation point, it can all begin to seem real. Looking at the no-man's land and watching the jeeps and troops on the move beyond, you can almost hear Kennedy saying: "It shall be the policy of this nation to regard any nuclear missile launched from Cuba as an attack by the Soviet Union on the United States, requiring full retaliatory response on the Soviet Union."

On a sultry afternoon, nowadays Caimanera hardly looks like it's on a state of alert. Families spill out of their small cinder-block houses on to narrow sidewalks to play dominoes on folding tables. Even the occasional North American tourist is offered a glass of rum. But look up: on all sides of town are the omnipresent tunnels where residents are to go in case of an emergency.

So is there any way across from the Cuban Guantánamo to the American? One way, of course, is by swimming, avoiding sharks and, some say, gunshots; the US State Department has declared that Cuban troops have endangered, and even killed, swimmers by shooting at them. The Cuban Foreign Ministry countered that it was *soldados norteamericanos* who have done the shooting. A handful of trusted Cuban workers make the daily journey by land from the Cuban to the American side, but for others the safest route – because of the peculiarity of the Cold War – is by US military plane from Norfolk, Virginia, 1,300 miles (2,100 km) away. Only journalists and academics may do this, with plenty of paperwork in advance.

Los Malones: another view of the US base

For the average visitor, the best view they are going to get of the US base is from the Los Malones lookout point, off the Baracoa road about 15 miles (24km)

Map on page 270–71

TIP

It's best to heed the barbed wire and warnings in the area not to trespass: the coast around the US base is one of the most heavily mined areas in the world – though it is said that some of the mines are now being dismantled.

BELOW: an eastern desert garden.

US Guantánamo

It sits inside the southeast corner of Cuba, an enclave of American military might, occupying 45 sq. miles (116 sq. km) of Cuban territory. This Naval Base has for decades been one of Uncle Sam's most-favored ports. Affectionately called Gitmo by sailors, it has a casual, country-club atmosphere where off-duty officers play golf, relax in the sun, and ride horses by the shore.

Founded in 1898 after 600 US Marines landed here to fight in the Spanish-American War, the base was formally established in 1901 by a Cuban constitutional document known as the Platt Amendment. Until 1959 it was a good-time assignment where sailors over-indulged in cheap rum and accommodating women. Saloons and brothels dotted the streets of nearby Guantánamo city.

During the late 1950s, some prostitutes who worked in the town reputedly requested guns and grenades from the sailors as payment for their services. These they passed on to Castro's guerrillas in the nearby Sierra Maestra. Following Castro's takeover, the brothels and bars were shut down, commerce between the Americans and Cubans was forbidden, and security on the base was tightened considerably.

Surrounded by barbed wire, Gitmo is an isolated installation guarded by 500 Marines. About 8,000 people live on the base, including civilians and families. Like other US bases, it contains housing, a school, health spa, movie theater, shopping center, and a McDonald's restaurant – the only one on the island. Children watch Saturday morning cartoons picked up by satellite from US television networks, and twice a week a military plane flies in with supplies.

Servicemen stationed on the base conduct defense exercises, maintain warships and monitor Cuban airspace. Rifles slung over their shoulders, they patrol the perimeter, which is mined with explosives. Though neither the US nor the Cuban government will confirm the figure, it is estimated that about 100 Cubans a year illegally enter the base by swimming through the shark-infested waters or jumping the fence. Since 1960, dozens of these asylum-seekers have died attempting to escape. In 1994, Gitmo was turned into a temporary refugee center for thousands of Cuban rafters who had been picked up at sea by the US Coast Guard.

Since 1960, Castro has not cashed any of the annual US$4,085 rent checks issued by the US Treasury Department, since to do so would acknowledge the legitimacy of the base. Guantánamo, according to Castro, is "a dagger plunged into the heart of Cuban soil." A dagger that earns the paltry sum of about 15 cents per acre.

Gitmo meanwhile costs the US government $36 million a year to operate. Since Cuba poses little military threat to the US, and there are other American bases in the Caribbean, it has almost no strategic value other than as a thorn in the side of Castro. According to the agreement, Guantánamo remains in US hands until the expiry of a 99-year lease signed in 1934. From the looks of it, Uncle Sam will likely remain a stubborn tenant who ignores his landlord's wishes to move out for some time to come. ❑

LEFT: The US base, as seen from Caimanera.

east of Guantánamo. You can arrange a visit through the Hotel Guantánamo (tel 36015) in town, ideally a couple of days in advance. For a reasonable fee (note that if you do not have a car, you will have to fork out the money for a taxi), a guide will accompany you into the Cuban military zone which surrounds the naval base and then along a very bumpy dirt track to the lookout point. First, you will be shown a model of the base, and given a few vital statistics, and are then free to climb the stairs for the view over the base. Through the telescope you can pick out vehicles and people moving around, and spot the US and Cuban flags flying by the perimeter fences. That tourists could visit such a spot would have been unthinkable a decade ago. Now there is even a bar.

Map on pages 270–71

The Cuban flag flies defiantly within view of the US naval base.

Up into the mountains

Driving into the mountains northeast of Guantánamo, towards Palenque, the village of **Boquerón** is home to the famous **Zoológico de Piedra** (Stone Zoo) of Angel Iñigo, a former coffee farmer who has carved over 100 animals out of the limestone on his land. Some large sculptures are carved in situ from outcrops or large boulders, others from smaller rocks lifted into position, and all stand amidst a beautiful garden. Amazingly, all were carved from pictures in books: Angel has never seen most of the animals he has so faithfully sculpted. A rough road from here continues through the mountains towards Baracoa.

Along the coast

The road east out of Guantánamo passes pleasant little farming communities and beaches at **Yacabo Abajo** and **Imías**. **Playa de Cajobabo** ㉛, next along the coast, is a place of great historical importance as it was here that José Martí and

BELOW: one of Angel Iñigo's creations in his Stone Zoo near Guantánamo.

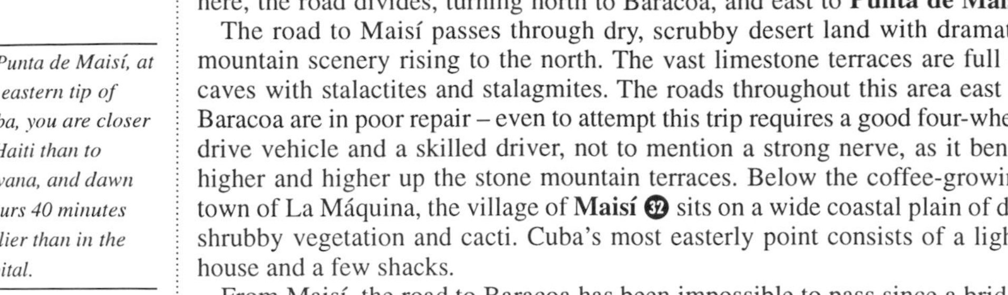

Máximo Gómez came ashore to begin the fight against the Spanish in 1895. From here, the road divides, turning north to Baracoa, and east to **Punta de Maisí**.

At Punta de Maisí, at the eastern tip of Cuba, you are closer to Haiti than to Havana, and dawn occurs 40 minutes earlier than in the capital.

The road to Maisí passes through dry, scrubby desert land with dramatic mountain scenery rising to the north. The vast limestone terraces are full of caves with stalactites and stalagmites. The roads throughout this area east of Baracoa are in poor repair – even to attempt this trip requires a good four-wheel drive vehicle and a skilled driver, not to mention a strong nerve, as it bends higher and higher up the stone mountain terraces. Below the coffee-growing town of La Máquina, the village of **Maisí** 32 sits on a wide coastal plain of dry shrubby vegetation and cacti. Cuba's most easterly point consists of a lighthouse and a few shacks.

From Maisí, the road to Baracoa has been impossible to pass since a bridge over the Yumurí river was swept away in a flood (though it would be worth asking if it has been repaired). Boats take people across the river at the village of **Yumurí**, but if you are in your own vehicle, you will have to go back the way you came. Beyond the river is a natural stone arch, the **Túnel de los Alemanes**, and **Playa Bariguá** locally famous for its palm-fringed, silvery-white sands.

The route via Cajobabo is, in fact, by far the most dramatic route to take to Baracoa – along the hair-raising but well maintained road over the mountains. This road, known as **La Farola** ("The Beacon"), twists through some fearsomely acute bends. The crash barriers are disconcertingly broken through in places and warning notices appear regularly – "Caution: 72 Accidents on this Bend So Far." The wonderful scenery, of course, compensates for the risk – magnificent mountain vistas, wild jungle, coconut groves, and coffee and cocoa plantations. The drive to Baracoa takes a careful driver at least three hours.

BELOW: statue of the "Discoverer" of the Americas in Baracoa.

The Admiral's first landing?

One of the great trivia questions of the Caribbean has to do with the outpost of **Baracoa** 33 and with Columbus, who may have landed there on October 27, 1492 and stayed a week. In addition, if he *did* land here, specifically what did or didn't he leave behind? Columbus was in fact looking for the Orient, but no matter. He found the *Oriente* (East) of Cuba. "A thousand tongues would not suffice to describe the things of novelty and beauty I saw," he later recalled. The town nestles beneath El Yunque – a flat anvil-shaped mountain which some people like to believe is the one described by Columbus in his log (*see page 275*).

Baracoa certainly was Cuba's first town, founded by Diego Velázquez in 1512, and was also both the first capital of Cuba and the starting point for the Spanish conquest of the rest of the island. Three years later, Santiago and finally Havana took over the role as capital. Baracoa then remained an isolated town right up until La Farola was built in 1962; prior to that, access was possible only by sea.

Baracoa's magnetic charm

Even the most rigid travelers can find themselves staying for more than a week in Baracoa, as they succumb to the gentle, old-world atmosphere of this Caribbean frontier town, with its neat lines of one-story houses with red-tile roofs and lush vegetation. The streets, impossibly picturesque in the late-afternoon light, are heaven for photographers.

This laid-back air is a result primarily of Baracoa's isolation – face to the sea and back to the mountains, with Havana 670 miles (1,070 km) away. Some things are changing, however. While Baracoa is still well away from the main tourist trail, word is spreading that the town's combination of friendly people, attractive scenery, and a distinctive cuisine make it a great place to spend some time. The Cuban tourist industry has finally taken note of the constant stream of visitors to Baracoa, and new hotels are being planned.

Life in Baracoa revolves around leafy **Parque Independencia**, where the indigenous chief Hatuey was burned alive by Spanish conquistadors (*see page 21*): the spot where he died is marked by a bust in his honor, right opposite the entrance to the **Catedral de Nuestra Señora de la Asunción**. The church was built in 1805, replacing the original which was destroyed by pirates in 1652. Columbus's famous Cruz de la Parra is kept inside, in a glass case.

At weekends, there is sometimes live music or a disco in the square. You should also investigate the small **Casa de la Trova**, nearby at Antonio Maceo 149, which normally gets going at about 10pm. In neighboring **Plaza Martí**, you can sometimes catch soap operas and movies being shown on open-air TV.

The **Malecón**, Baracoa's seafront boulevard, sees surprising little action, though there are a couple of restaurants and a small farmers' market. At the western end is **La Punta** fortress, now a restaurant, while at the eastern end is the small but well-preserved **Fuerte Matachín** (1802), one of the region's best **museums** (open daily, 8am noon and 2pm–6pm; entrance fee). It has a minimum of Revolutionary Wonders, offering instead a mixture of displays on the

Map on pages 270–71

Baracoa's mysterious Cruz de la Parra – the oldest cross in the New World.

BELOW: pensive at sunset in Baracoa.

A Cross Debate

In Baracoa almost every resident over the age of six can, and will, tell you the story of the **Cruz de la Parra** (Cross of the Vine), fashioned from hardwood, which Columbus reputedly brought from Spain and planted on reaching Baracoa. It vanished until it was found amid the backyard brambles of a colonizer's house in 1510. This historic cross survived pirates, fires, vandals and other hazards, although relic-hunters have chipped away at the edges. Standing 3½ ft (1 meter) tall, it is now kept safe in the cathedral, with its edges encased in metal.

That, at least, is the story. The question that has turned amiable scholars into enemies is: did the cross really belong to Columbus? The church maintains it did. So does Alejandro Hartmann, director of the **Museo Matachín** of local history in Baracoa. But a host of scholars in Havana pooh-pooh the tale. Everybody has a conflicting notion – and everyone can back it up with data. For the best anecdotes, read *Cuba Before Columbus* and the more recent *Trading with the Enemy* by Tom Miller.

Carbon dating seems to back the tale, dating the cross to the late 15th century, but – less convincingly for Baracoa – tests also revealed it was not from Spain: the cross is made of a hardwood native to Cuba.

One of Eastern Cuba's brilliant polymita snails.

indigenous Taíno peoples, local natural history, and on a few Baracoan characters. One of these was **La Rusa**, founder of a well-known hotel on the Malecón.

La Rusa was a Russian woman who abandoned the Soviet Union in the 1950s, came to Cuba and ended up supporting the rebels. Fidel and Che both stayed here, and guests fight over the rooms where they are said to have slept. La Rusa is popular among independent travellers, but the best hotel in town is, in fact, **El Castillo**, on a cliff overlooking the town. The castle was originally built in 1770 to keep out the British; it later became a prison, and then a hotel. It has a pool, an excellent restaurant serving local specialties, and the best views in town. Another good hotel is the **Porto Santo**, also with a pool, but some may find its location across the bay, near the airport, a little inconvenient.

Past the Anvil and into the wilds

Baracoa's horizon is dominated by **El Yunque** ㉞ or The Anvil (1,800 ft/560m). Archaeologists have found ceremonial shells and skeletons left by the Taínos, who, during the conquest, took advantage of the mountain's protective cliffs and natural lookout points – as did anti-Spanish rebels during the 19th century. Many other caves in the mountains contain pre-Columbian indigenous paintings. It is said that in the rugged terrain inland from Baracoa there are remote villages where indigenous features can still be detected in the faces of the local people. Some villages in these hills began as *palenques*, founded by runaway slaves.

The mountains are cloaked in virgin rainforest, part of which is protected by the rarely-visited **Cuchillas de Toa** mountain reserve. This is one of the wildest regions in all Cuba, with excellent potential for hiking. Hotel Castillo runs excursions here, including white-water rafting trips on the River Toa.

BELOW: keeping the pot boiling at La Punta Fortress.

A Regional Cuisine

Near Plaza Martí you can buy local specialties like *tamales* – made not of boiled corn, as in the rest of Cuba, but mashed plantains, stuffed with spiced meat, wrapped in a banana leaf and roasted over a fire. Baracoan food is very different to that of the rest of Cuba, with a greater use of spices and native specialities like coconut and chocolate. Food is cooked in coconut oil and *lechita* (coconut milk), giving the whole town a heavenly smell when the cooking starts in the evening.

Other local dishes include *bacón* (a plantain tortilla filled with spicy pork), and *tetí* – a bizarre type of small red fish that are caught in the river estuaries between August and December. They are surrounded by a gelatinous protective wrapping, which dissolves upon reaching fresh water, and are tasty when eaten raw or in omelettes. Rice is colored yellow with annato seeds and "Indian bananas" are boiled in their pink skins and dressed with garlic and lime juice. *Cucurucho* (shredded coconut mixed with sweet orange, papaya and honey) is a typical sweet, and don't miss the opportunity to try the local chocolate drink – made with cocoa, sugar, vanilla, cloves and salt – in the **Casa del Chocolate** at Antonio Maceo No. 121.

Map on pages 270–71

You can climb El Yunque in a couple of hours. It is not difficult to tackle on your own (the path runs from Campismo El Yunque, near the base of the mountain), but you can also hire horses and guides for the trip at **Finca Duaba**, just outside Baracoa along the Moa road. The Finca has a restaurant serving local food, and organizes demonstrations of how local crops, such as cocoa and bananas, are cultivated.

Legend says that those who sleep in Baracoa's **Bahía de Miel** (Bay of Honey) will never want to leave. Disappointingly, the city beach is gritty and grey, and the sea rather muddy. Most people prefer to swim in the cool mountain rivers or in the sea northwest of Baracoa. The best beach, and one of the finest in Cuba, is **Playa Maguaná**, 12 miles (20 km) from the town; **Villa Maguaná** has a few rooms here, but these must be booked through Islazul – either at La Rusa in town or another Islazul agent. Closer to Baracoa is **Playa Duaba**, near the mouth of the Duaba river; you can swim in either fresh or salt water.

From beaches to belching chimneys

The road northwest from Baracoa takes you back into Holguín Province, along a dramatic route which skirts between green mountains and the sea. It is rough going in the early stages, with many bumps and potholes, so you should allow about three hours for the drive to **Moa** ㉟.

Unless you are a metallurgist, you probably won't want to spend much time in Moa. This is mining country, with possibly the world's largest reserves of nickel and cobalt. Cuba ranks fourth in the world league of nickel-producing countries. An important industry, but one which results in belching chimneys and polluted seas and rivers washing up against blackened, terraced hills. ❑

The Indian chief who died in Baracoa and whose profile adorns every bottle of Hatuey beer.

BELOW: washing in the river, outside Baracoa.

SOUTHERN ISLANDS

Most important are the Isle of Youth, with good diving, caves with indigenous paintings and the prison where Castro was once incarcerated, and Cayo Largo, with its sugar-white beaches

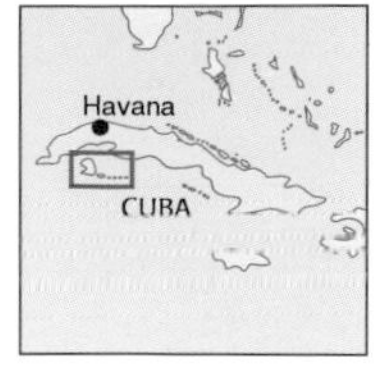

Located off the main island's south coast, the islands of the Archipiélago de los Canarreos each have their own distinct personalities. **Isla de la Juventud** (Isle of Youth) is relatively undeveloped and cheap, with a colorful history as a pirate refuge, home for American settlers, and prison camp for revolutionaries; **Cayo Largo**, on the other hand, is one of the most pricey and commercialized places in all of Cuba, while other cays, like Cayo Rosario, are just virgin specks of sand wallowing in the blue Caribbean.

The real Treasure Island

Isla de la Juventud, the largest by far of Cuba's subsidiary islands with an area of 1,180 sq. miles (3,020 sq. km), lies to the south of the mainland, and is reached either by plane from Havana or by the ferries and hydrofoils that depart from the port of Surgidero de Batabanó (*see page 191*). Accommodation for visitors is focused in Nueva Gerona, the capital, although the **Hotel Colony** on the southwest coast, is a popular base for divers.

LEFT: repairing the nets in Nueva Gerona. **BELOW:** harbor scene.

Over the centuries, the island has seen immigrants from Spain, England, Scotland, China, Japan, Jamaica, the Caymans and even America, and it has had a similarly varied history in terms of the names it has been given. Local Indians called it Camarcó or Siguanea, but Christopher Columbus renamed it La Evangelista when he landed here in 1494, on his second voyage to the New World. By the 17th century, it was known as Isla del Tesoro ("Treasure Island"), because of the pirate treasure allegedly buried there (thus inspiring at least the name of Robert Louis Stevenson's classic adventure tale). When the Spaniards finally got around to colonizing the island in the 1840s, they renamed it Colonia Reina Amalia. Other, later names include: the Isla de los Deportados, when it became a dumping ground for criminals and rebels deported from the mainland; La Siberia de Cuba, in recognition of the isolated prison where Castro and others spent several years in the 1950s; Isla de las Cotorras (Parrot Island), as the habitat of the bright-colored birds that are still the trademark of the island's bottled spring water; and, until recently, Isla de Pinos (Isle of Pines). Finally, it acquired its present name in the 1970s, a symbol of the influx of young people to the island.

In 1971, Cuba began taking students from Third World countries and educating them for free on the island, thus hoping to spread solidarity for the Cuban revolution across the undeveloped world. At its height, the program included 60 boarding schools with 150,000 students. In recent times, the flow of foreign students has dwindled, due to economic difficulties in Cuba and political changes in their own countries.

The last foreign students completed their studies in 1996, and returned home. Today, 77,000 people live on the Isle of Youth, about half of them in the capital.

Nueva Gerona's boat and hydrofoil terminal is on the Río Casas, at Calle 31 between Calles 22 and 24, a few blocks northeast of the Parque Central.

Town with a *yanqui* touch

The point of arrival is invariably **Nueva Gerona** ❶, which looks for all the world like a small village in America's West at the turn of the century: the older houses are wooden, with spacious, columned verandas, shuttered windows and carved doors with brass knockers. The similarity is no accident, since many of the town's first pioneers came from the US in the early 1900s, lured here by unscrupulous American land dealers. It was these midwesterners who planted the island's first citrus groves, which now cover some 62,000 acres (25,000 hectares). Along the riverside road is a wooden bungalow built by a Swedish-American family whose last surviving member lived there for 60 years before finally returning to the US. Her parents, like hundreds of other Americans, believed the Isle would soon become another state in the Union by vote of the US Congress. They built houses and planted orchards in places they named McKinley, Columbia, Westport, and San Francisco Heights. They spoke English, worshipped a Protestant God and were buried in the **Cementerio Americano**, a grassy park maintained today as a historical site. The starkly simple headstones – most of them dating from 1905 to 1925 – contrast sharply with the mausoleums, statues and vaults that decorate the **Cementerio Católico** in town.

Cayman and Jamaican islanders added their Caribbean English to that of the Americans in those early years, whilst a sizeable group of Japanese settled as farmers. This mix, together with Spanish merchants, Chinese storekeepers and Cuban landowners, provided a lively diversity in island life.

Below: a student on the Isle of Youth.

Today, downtown Nueva Gerona consists of an eight-block grid, so everything is within easy walking distance. This area has stores, eateries (mostly snack places, though both **El Corderito** and **El Cochinito** restaurants serve decent meals) and the main community and cultural centers. There are also a couple of night spots: **Los Luceros**, by the river, is a popular open-air cabaret that attracts a mostly young crowd; and **Disco Calle 24**, an indoor spot with dim lights and loud music that also appeals mainly to the young.

Calle 39, the main street of downtown Gerona, has been radically refurbished with pretty pink tiles and fresh coats of paint on every building. The street runs south from the always empty La Cubanita Hotel – which still denies access to foreigners despite the lack of a Cuban clientele – and along one side of **Parque Central** (also called Parque Guerrillero Heróico on some new maps). The square holds the island's oldest church, **Nuestra Señora de los Dolores**: a typical Latin colonial church, even though it was built only in 1929.

The church of Nuestra Señora de los Dolores in Nueva Gerona.

Opposite the church is the **Ayuntamiento** or Town Hall, formerly the Spanish military commander's HQ. During the 1895–8 War of Independence, the square was the scene of a thwarted uprising led by a beautiful young rebel girl. She was later imprisoned in Havana, rescued by an American journalist and then smuggled to the United States to promote Cuba's freedom – along with the interests of the Hearst press.

The **Academia de Ciencias y Planetario** on Calle 41 (open Tues–Sun; entrance fee) covers natural history and archaeology, and is worth visiting for the replica of the Punta del Este cave paintings (*see page 318*) if you don't have the time to see the real thing. On the corner of Calles 24 and 45 is the local **Museo de los Clandestinos** (open Tues–Sun; entrance fee), devoted

BELOW: the steamer that took Fidel to the mainland.

The Presidio Modelo, these days bereft of inmates.

mainly to the underground campaign in the run-up to the Revolution. **El Pinero**, the ferry boat that carried Fidel Castro and his fellow revolutionaries back to the mainland after their release from prison, is permanently moored on the riverbank between Calles 26 and 28, and the nearby statue of a cow is dedicated to **Ubre Blanca** (White Udder), a local heifer who broke world milk production records.

Memories of Cuban Siberia

A few miles east of town, on the road to Bibijagua Beach, you can't miss the **Presidio Modelo** (Model Prison) ❷. It was built in the early 1930s using the plans from a prison in Joliet, Illinois, to keep Cuba's hardest cases – most famously Fidel Castro and other revolutionaries after the failed attack on the Moncada Barracks in 1953. As political prisoners, Castro and company fared a good deal better than the common inmates. They were housed in the hospital wing, where they studied, trained and imposed their own group discipline without much interference from the Batista-appointed prison officials. The prison closed in 1967. An impressive **museum** (open Tues–Sat, 9am–5pm and Sun, 9am–1pm; entrance fee), which includes Fidel Castro's (rather comfortable) old cell, recounts the prison's grim past. Photography is forbidden inside.

Cuba's 19th-century revolutionary hero, José Martí, also spent time on the island in 1870, when he was awaiting deportation to Spain for expressing anti-colonial ideas. For a few months between his gruelling prison labors and his exile, Martí stayed at the farm **Finca El Abra** (open Tues–Sun, 9am–5pm; entrance fee), where the Sardá family nurtured him back to relative health. The farm is located just off the road to the Hotel Colony, near marble quarries that are the source for the floors, façades and carved objects seen all over the Isle.

BELOW: the Presidio Modelo, a prison with a stormy past.

La Fé ❸, southeast of the island capital, used to be the market town for the surrounding farmlands. The shady main plaza is no longer a farmers' market, but the radio station, public library, post office and telephone company make this an important point of communications. The ruins just off the square are what is left of an old hotel. Earlier this century, La Fé was a well-known spa resort: the **medicinal springs** are nearby, near a deteriorating hotel and baths.

As a town, La Fé is far more attractive than Nueva Gerona, with green parks and tree-lined streets (although, of course, they eventually lead out to barren-looking prefab housing blocks). Not far from the center of town is **La Cotorra spring**, in a perfect little park enclosed by an iron fence with a tile parrot (*cotorra* in Spanish) at the gate. This is the spring that supplies the island's bottled drinking water. It is also the best place on the island to have a close look at some brilliantly colored parrots, who screech at visitors from cage perches until their keeper intervenes with a calming voice.

Map on page 314

Dive signs at the Hotel Colony.

Pirates' Coast

From La Fé and Nueva Gerona, roads lead west to the **Hotel Colony** ❹ on **Ensenada de la Siguanea** (Siguanea Cove). For years the only luxury hotel on the Isle, the Colony was completed at the end of 1958, just in time for the rebels to take it over. The bay here is picturesque but too shallow for swimming – the pool is the place for that.

Across the bay, though, is **Cabo Francés**, where the spectacular scuba sites of the **Costa de los Piratas** (Pirates' Coast) begin. At more than 50 marked sites, divers can see coral in every shape, size and color, giant sponges, tropical fish and crustaceans, underwater caves, tunnels, and rock formations. One

BELOW LEFT: Punta del Este beach. **BELOW RIGHT:** ancient Siboney pictographs.

famous coral feature is the **Catedral del Caribe** (Caribbean Cathedral), reputedly the tallest column of coral in the world. The site is of particular interest as it contains the sunken remains of a great sea battle between the pirate ships of Thomas Baskerville and the Spanish fleet. And near Punta Francés are three Spanish galleons lying together. The International Scuba Center at the Hotel Colony provides the boats, scuba gear and monitors for diving – usually an all-day trip, moving from site to site and with a buffet lunch aboard. It also provides special diving packages to the Pirates' Coast. There is an international marina here, too, as well as plenty of opportunities for deep-sea fishing trips.

The south coast of the island, from **Punta Pedernales** to **Punta del Este**, is breathtakingly beautiful and practically uninhabited except for the little town of **Cocodrilo** ❺, settled by English-speaking Cayman islanders at the beginning of the 20th century. Their descendants speak a lilting Caribbean English, though this is beginning to die out as younger generations slowly adopt Spanish. There are numerous magnificent beaches, as yet untouched by tourism and development, but accessible on day trips. However, the entire area inland of Cocodrilo and nearby **Caleta Grande** is a military zone and definitely off limits.

The blue-green water and fine white sand along this coast are backed by thick forests of pine and hard woods. The region is separated from the north by the mosquito-ridden **Ciénaga de Lanier** (Lanier Swamp) – and this geographical isolation once made the area a plunderers' paradise, especially for lumbermen who felled trees and shipped logs to all the ports of Cuba and the Caribbean. Reafforestation has fortunately been a priority since the early 1960s.

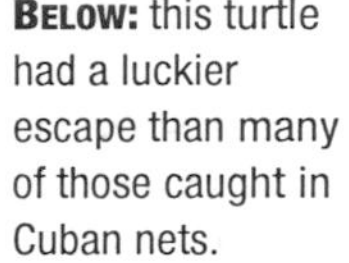

BELOW: this turtle had a luckier escape than many of those caught in Cuban nets.

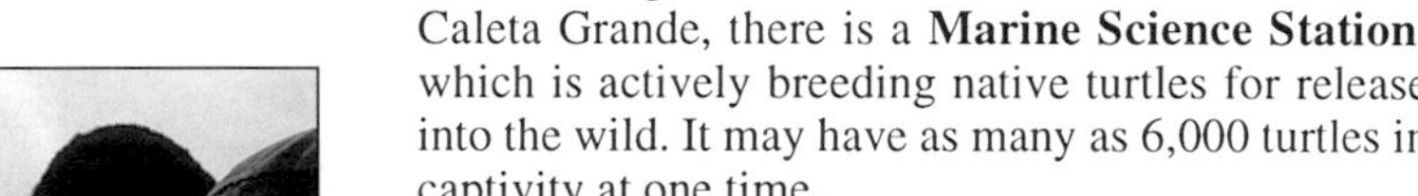

The Isle of Youth and the Zapata Peninsula (on the mainland) are the only places in the world where the endangered Cuban crocodile can be found. At Caleta Grande, there is a **Marine Science Station**, which is actively breeding native turtles for release into the wild. It may have as many as 6,000 turtles in captivity at one time.

Indigenous cave paintings

Punta del Este ❻, in the southeast corner of the island 37 miles (60 km) from Nueva Gerona, is awe-inspiring. Except for the ferocious mosquitoes, it is altogether magnificent, and is so far mercifully free of intrusive tourist development.

Alongside a sparkling, pristine beach are a series of mysterious **caves** where the indigenous Siboney inhabitants painted pictographs around 3,000 years ago. The caves are one of the most important archaeological finds in the Caribbean, first explored by the famous Cuban anthropologist Fernando Ortíz in 1922. The main cave is considered the Siboneys' Sistine Chapel. It is a single spacious chamber with a fairly low ceiling containing seven natural vaults: sunlight spotlights more than 200 drawings of circles, arrows, triangles and serpentine lines. The whole is a great red and black mural believed to represent a lunar calendar, including human figures and animals in the world the Siboney knew and imagined.

From the top of the headland above the caves, a long coral reef is visible about 2 miles (3.5 km) offshore. The blue waves crash against the coralline wall in a spray of foam that rolls onto the inner lagoon. The calm, nearly transparent water affords a marvelously clear view of the seabed – a clean sandy plain rippled in undulating zigzag crests like tiny drawn-out dunes.

At some points, a fine celgrass carpets the sea floor, revealing Queen Conch shells, with their shiny pink mouths, large King Helmuts shaded from dark brown to lustrous cream, and conical Top Shells. Perfectly symmetrical starfishes adorn the sandy bottom, on which white coral appears in a thicket of gorgonians, with delicate hands and multiple fingers swaying in the water.

Snorkelers can explore this far, but full diving gear is needed to swim through the coralline wall into the extraordinary reef garden, formed of the most varied green, white, yellow, violet and pink corals surrounded by a nearly transparent liquid mass. These corals are found only where the sea is less than 330 ft (100 meters) deep and where the temperature never drops below 68°F (20°C). At a deeper level, squirrelfish, hogfish, barracudas and sharks may be spotted.

Most Cuban travel agencies offer package trips to Cayo Largo. Day trips are fairly popular, but you can arrange to stay for longer if you are after a thoroughly inactive holiday.

Cayo Largo: Cuba's answer to Waikiki?

East of the Isle of Youth, a myriad of tiny cays lies scattered in a wide arc. Most are uninhabited and inaccessible from the mainland. All have delicious beaches of white powdery sand and magnificent diving amongst the coral and the shipwrecks: the Nueva España treasure fleet that went down in 1563 on the reefs somewhere between Cayo Rosario and Cayo Largo provides just a fraction of the more than 200 known wrecks in this area. So far, all but one of these dream islands are undeveloped and only accessible by boat. Plans are afoot to develop Cayo Rico, just west of Cayo Largo, but nothing has happened there yet.

The only cay currently geared to tourism is **Cayo Largo**, accessible by plane from Havana or Varadero. Back in 1985, before Cuba plunged into schemes to attract international tourism, the slogan for this once pristine island of 150 sq. miles (384 sq. km) was "Thus it all began." Then came the building boom, the package tours, and the airport disco reception with watery rum cocktails. Even the boat trip to swim and lunch at lovely **Playa Sirena** has been over-commercialized, and tourists are charged a fortune every step of the way.

Still, Cayo Largo remains popular with travelers looking for sun and sea and not much else – anyone at all interested in Cuba or Cubans would be better off going elsewhere. There is, however, escape: from Cayo Largo, you can take day trips to nearby islets that have no tourist installations at all.

One of these is **Cayo Iguana**, inhabited by hordes of these friendly reptiles (which can also be seen on the main island anyway). Another is **Cayo Rosario**, west of Cayo Largo and almost as big. Rising to high dunes, a crescent beach is enclosed by a sandbar that forms a natural lagoon of clear blue water over fine pearly sand, with minuscule shells of deep pink piled in the ridges of the sea bed, creating a wavy texture. The calm water is lovely for gentle swimming. Miraculously, the cay also has a fresh water river. For the time being at least, the only inhabitants are the large iguanas and other, more elusive wild animals and birds that exist in this sensitive environment. ❑

BELOW: everyone hangs out at the beach on Cayo Largo.

INSIGHT GUIDES

Travel Tips

CONTENTS

Getting Acquainted

Planning the Trip

Practical Tips

Getting Around

Where to Stay

Where to Eat

Culture

Nightlife

Shopping

Sport

Further Reading

Getting Acquainted

The Place

Area: 42,827 sq. miles (110,992 sq. km).
Population: 11 million.
Language: Spanish.
Religion: Catholicism; Santería and other Afro-Cuban religions.
Time Zone: Like the entire east coast of North America, Cuba is on Eastern Standard Time (Daylight Saving applies during summer). When it's noon in Havana, it's 5pm in London, 6pm in Madrid and Rome, 2pm in Buenos Aires and 11am in Mexico City.
Currency: the national currency is the peso, but US dollars are widely used; there is also a "convertible peso," which is pegged to the dollar (*see page 324*).
Weights & Measures: Officially, the metric system is used, but see page 330.
Electricity: 110 volts, as in the US, is the most common, but some new hotels operate on 220 volts.
International Dialing Code: 53

Geography

The Republic of Cuba, the largest archipelago in the Western Hemisphere and the most important in the Greater Antilles, lies like a somnolent crocodile sunning itself in the Caribbean. Over 775 miles (1,250 km) long, the body tapers from 118 miles (190 km) wide at its eastern head to 19 miles (30 km) at its western tail. Including the Isle of Youth and some 1,600 islets and cays, Cuba has an area of 42,827 sq. miles (110,992 sq. km). The Bahamas float along its dorsal; other island neighbors are Haiti, 48 miles (77 km) east; Jamaica, 87 miles (140 km) south; and Key West, Florida, 90 miles (148 km) north.

Nearly 300 beaches ring the island, and Cuba even has its own desert, where a wide variety of cacti can be identified, in Guantánamo Province.

Mountain Ranges Cuba's geography is made up of extensive and fertile plains broken by several mountain ranges. The most spectacular of these is the Sierra Maestra in the southeast, where Pico Turquino, Cuba's highest peak, rises to 5,928 ft (1,794 meters). In the center of the island, the beautiful Escambray mountains rise from the plains and stretch across Sancti Spíritus Province to fall precipitously to the Caribbean on the southern coast.

Western Cuba has the Cordillera Guaniguanico, encompassing the unique rocky outcrops or *mogotes* that rise up from the flat floor of Viñales Valley. An hour's drive westward from Havana, the gentle slopes of the Sierra de los Organos and Sierra del Rosario mountains cradle trails, streams, waterfalls, a resort, a campsite and a botanical garden devoted entirely to orchids.

National Tree

Presiding over the Cuban landscape is the royal palm, which appears on the national coat of arms as a symbol of strength.

The People

Cuba has a total population of around 11 million, with a median age of 22.

Although the economy is based on sugarcane and other agricultural products, nearly 8 million Cubans are urban dwellers – living in Havana (2.1 million), Santiago de Cuba (420,000), Camagüey (286,000), Holguín (233,000), and the smaller provincial cities.

The ethnic mixture on the island is basically of Spanish and African descent, but Chinese and other Caribbean islanders have also made a significant contribution to the Cuban melting pot. The indigenous population of some 100,000 was effectively decimated during the Spanish conquest and only a few families in eastern Cuba retain traces of their Indian past. Historically, Cubans have identified themselves as *criollos* or creoles (those born on the island of European descent), negros or *morenos* (descendants of black or dark-skinned African slaves), and *mestizos* or *mulattos* – people of every skin tone and hair texture, as well as any other person of mixed blood. The influx of Chinese (*asiáticos*) came at the turn of the century, adding arresting features to the racial mixture.

Climate

Cuba has a subtropical climate, with a mean annual temperature of 77°F (25°C). The mean relative humidity is 77 percent during the dry season (November–April) and 82 percent during the wet season (May–October).

The sun seems to shine all the time in Cuba, but temperatures are most definitely higher during the rainy "summer" season than in the drier "winter" months. Those who are not accustomed to melting temperatures, would do well to avoid visiting the island in July and August – when most Cubans spend every spare moment either by the beach or in the shower.

While the rain of the wet season is not often more than an inconvenience, the summer is also hurricane season.

Therefore, the best time to visit Cuba is from November to April, after the hurricane season is over and before the hot, muggy summer months arrive. To avoid high season prices and crowds, visit in November or from February.

The Economy

For years, the Cuban economy was artificially sustained by enormous **credits** and **imports** from the Soviet Union and other eastern European socialist countries. With the demise of the socialist bloc, 80 percent of Cuba's trade went down the drain; there was suddenly no oil to keep the economy moving, no products to resell for hard currency that could buy medicine and high-tech equipment. The sugar harvest dropped to a low of under 5 million tons and food became so scarce that nutrition-related illnesses reached epidemic proportions. The **US trade embargo**, in force since the early 1960s, was tightened to block foreign-owned ships from docking in US ports for six months after visiting Cuba.

As a way out of the crisis, Cuba began counting heavily on **tourism** and tourism-related **joint ventures**. Tourism is now Cuba's number one industry, bringing in more hard currency than sugar. In 1997, the numbers of tourists visiting Cuba exceeded 1 million for the first time (1.2 million), with Italians making up the largest number of visitors. Other joint ventures with foreign countries have led to oil prospecting off the north coast.

In the 1990s, as the US tightened its trade embargo, many foreign investors, notably Canada, relishing the lack of competition, significantly increased their trade with Cuba. The number of Canadian tourists visiting Cuba exceeded 120,000 a year.

As far as **exports** are concerned, Cuba lacks a viable marketing network even for such traditional products as rum and cigars, while its pharmaceuticals – much touted as a promising new industry – have been unable to meet world standards and competition.

The only sector of the state economy that operates at a profit is **retailing**, based on the chain-store concept of offering cheap imported consumer goods for a quick profit – and even this is done in US dollars, possession of which was legalized only in 1993 (the Cuban peso is for all intents and purposes worthless). Prices vary quixotically from store to store in Havana, sometimes for the same product or brand name.

Outside the state network is a flourishing **black market** that sells all goods much cheaper. Relaxation of restrictions on private enterprise in 1993 have led to dozens of individuals providing goods and services that haven't been around in years. Private enterprise is in and the dollar is king, but a lot more of both are needed to keep the island afloat economically.

Government

Cuba is administered by the **Municipal, Provincial** and **National Assemblies of People's Power** (or *Poder Popular*), whose delegates are nominated in coordination with the neighborhood **Committees for the Defense of the Revolution** (CDR) and "elected" by popular ballot from a single voting list.

The National Assembly elects the **Council of State**, the supreme governing body, which in turn selects the **Council of Ministers**. Fidel Castro Ruz is President of both these Councils and head of the **Communist Party of Cuba** (PCC), the country's highest policy making body. The PCC sets economic and political guidelines and determines how they should be implemented through the organs of People's Power.

There's little room for organized opposition in this highly authoritarian top down system. Police investigation, vigilante raids, house arrest and imprisonment are among the tactics used to intimidate and punish political dissidents and protestors. However, when disaffection is apparent among such a significant group as the student élite, the government often opts for appeasement and concessions rather than confrontation.

Planning the Trip

General

The vast majority of tourists to Cuba travel in some organized or semi-organized tour group. Such trips can work out cheaper than purely independent travel, and also overcome the considerable logistical problems of getting from the airport, finding a room, and getting from one city to another.

It is, however, perfectly possible – and is becoming easier – to travel independently in Cuba (and nobody who books a tour is forced to follow its movements). It helps to be able to speak some Spanish, since outside the tourist net many will attempt to communicate in English, but few succeed.

First-time travelers to Cuba should check out itineraries and prices with experienced travel agents (*see page 326*), since options are changing and expanding every day on the island. The nearest Cuban consulate may be helpful if you don't know where to start; and some tourism enterprises in Cuba have offices abroad (*see page 329*).

Passports and Visas

All visitors entering Cuba must show a passport (which must be valid for at least six months beyond the date of your arrival in Cuba). In addition, most visitors must show a **tourist card** (*tarjeta de turista*), issued by the Cuban consulate directly or, more commonly, through a travel agent. This will be valid for the length of your planned visit, but can be extended (once) up to the date shown on your return plane ticket – as long as the total number of days you are in the country does not exceed 60 days. Tourist cards can be extended in certain dollar hotels, including the Habana Libre in the capital.

Those planning to stay with a Cuban family must apply some time in advance for a **tourist visa**, while any commercial travelers must apply for a **business visa**. Ask at the local Cuban consulate for more information.

Visas for US citizens

These are handled by the Cuban Interests Section in Washington, DC. United States Treasury Department regulations prohibit US citizens from spending money in Cuba unless they qualify as journalists, researchers, or relatives of Cubans living on the island.

Americans who oppose their government's trade and travel blockade against Cuba regularly evade or purposely violate these restrictions, and some do so just out of curiosity: many fly in via Mexico or Jamaica. Although they could theoretically be prosecuted, they generally aren't.

Customs Regulations

Tourists may bring in, duty-free, personal effects – including medicine for their own use or as gifts – cameras, tape-recorders, personal computers, cellular phones, sports and camping equipment. All of these items should in theory be listed on a customs declaration form on arrival. Actual customs inspection is random.

Visitors importing electrical items as gifts – TVs, kitchen equipment, etc. – should note that 100 percent duty is payable. Certain items, mainly video-recorders, modems and photocopying equipment and supplies, are restricted: you may bring them in only for accredited people such as journalists and approved organizations. Such items will be confiscated by customs until the necessary paperwork from the Ministries of Foreign Relations and Communications are presented.

Money Matters

The **Cuban peso**, divided into 100 **centavos**, is the official currency, but US dollars are widely used and are the only currency generally used by foreigners. Most people, however, find it useful to change a few dollars into Cuban pesos for use on public transport, in cinemas, when shopping for fresh fruit at the farmers' markets, and when buying food and drink from street vendors.

Changing Money

You can change your dollars into pesos legally at Government licensed CADECA booths. These are fairly widely scattered – in Havana, there is one outside the Coppelia ice-cream gardens in Vedado, and one in Plaza de San Francisco in Old Havana. Many farmers' markets have a CADECA attached. Every sizeable provincial town has at least one CADECA – ask at the hotel.

You can also change money on the street, illegally, with black-market vendors. There are always large numbers of these around the farmers' markets hissing "change" or "*Compra dollar*" ("I buy dollars"). The rate is usually the same as at the CADECA – fluctuating at around 20 pesos to the dollar. Oddly, the black-market price is usually a peso or so less than the official price as there is usually a long queue at the CADECAS. DON'T be tempted to try to change dollars for pesos at the bank, as the rate here is 1 peso to 1 dollar.

The Cuban Government also issues *pesos convertibles*, or "convertible pesos" (both as bank-notes and coins). These are equivalent to the US dollar and can be used as such anywhere on the island, including paying your airport tax. Don't take them home with you except as souvenirs, since they are not, in fact, convertible currency.

Other hard currencies may be exchanged for US dollars through the Banco Financiero Internacional S.A. in Havana, or any foreign bank, but all visitors are strongly advised to bring only US dollars with them to Cuba.

Travelers' Checks

All brands of travelers' checks can be cashed at the front desk of most dollar hotels – except for American Express, which is not accepted because of the US economic embargo. You should, in theory, be a guest at the hotel, but not all reception staff enforce this rule. The cashier at the Hotel Inglaterra in Havana, for example, will cash checks for non-guests.

Credit Cards

Access/MasterCard, Diners Club, Visa and other credit cards are welcome at all hotels, and at most dollar restaurants and shops – provided they have been issued outside the US (again, because of the embargo). So, American Express is no use on the island.

Credit-card operations in Cuba do not always run smoothly. The centralized computer system often fails, going down for hours at a time; this affects every credit card machine in the land, and you will not be able to use your card at all while the system failure lasts.

A credit card can also be a useful back-up if you need cash in an emergency: cash can be withdrawn against a credit card at branches of the Banco Financiero Internacional, but be warned that this is best done in Havana and Santiago.

Cash

While travelers' checks are a safe way to carry money, you should always try to have a good supply of cash with you, particularly if you head out of the city. Not all provincial hotels will be able to cash travelers' checks for you.

Getting change from big bills is often difficult, so it is worthwhile keeping a stock of $10s, $5s and single notes in your wallet. Try to bring with you as many small denomination bills as possible, and always try to break big bills when you are staying at city hotels, where they are more likely to have a better supply in their tills. If your hotel can't help, you may have to resort to a bank; most banks will change big bills for you. You will normally have to show some ID (a passport is preferred) if you produce a $50 or $100 bill in a Cuban shop.

You may also want to have a few 20-centavo coins for callboxes, though many old peso phones are now being replaced with new, dollar phones which take only cards (*see page 328*). If you want to take the bus, you will need some Cuban change – most routes cost 40 centavos to a peso (but, if you're stuck, few drivers would be adverse to taking some dollar change).

Asistur

Asistur offers tourists insurance, and also acts as an emergency center – though, arguably, it's not great in a crisis. They can also change Amex travelers' checks at 10 percent commission. The Havana office is at Prado 254, but there are branches in tourist centers all over the island.

What to Bring

Clothes

Casual, comfortable clothes are appropriate anywhere on the island, especially light cottons that can be put on and taken off in layers as the temperature changes.

As far as many Cubans are concerned, the less you wear the better. Shorts, even bathing suits, are accepted at all seaside resorts, though more coverage is expected for dining out. Unless you're coming for business, you won't have much use for a suit and tie.

A waterproof jacket is optional – you can usually wait out a tropical shower; and if there is a real downpour, a waterproof jacket will be of minimal use.

You shouuld take comfortable walking shoes and dark glasses for protection against the harsh tropical sunlight. Straw and cloth sunhats can be bought in any tourist shop.

Electrical adapters

Most appliances run on 110 volts, 60 cycles, as in the US, but be warned that some hotels operate on 22 volts. Electric outlets take two, flat-pronged plugs, again, as in the United States.

Camera Film

You can buy color film in many tourist hotel shops, though not all will stock film for slides. For this, you may have to look for a special photo shop (usually known as *photoservice*). These dedicated outlets also offer quick development of prints in several sizes. Generally, however, developing and printing facilities are poor: film may come back scratched, or the color quality of the prints may be less than perfect. Ideally, you should wait until you get home. One place where the quality of developing is good is at the *Photoservice* on Calles 23 and O in the Vedado district of Havana.

Most types of video tape are also available. However, as a general rule, supplies of anything to do with normal or video cameras are variable in Cuba, plus prices are almost always higher than those at home. In conclusion, it is always safer to bring important items with you from abroad.

Medical Supplies

Travelers to Cuba should bring their own medicines, vitamins, adhesive bandages, contraceptives and sunburn lotion – none of which is readily available. And if you do locate them in a hotel dollar store, you are likely to pay more than you would at home.

No health certificate is required of visitors unless they are arriving from areas where cholera, smallpox or yellow fever exist, in which case they must show a certificate of vaccination against those diseases.

Emergency treatment in Cuba is free, while follow-up treatment and medicines are payable in dollars. If emergencies arise, you will, as a foreigner, be treated in a dollar-only hospital. Health costs at these hospitals are akin to those in the US, and you are strongly advised to take out **health insurance** before leaving home.

Getting There

Some people visit Cuba by private yacht – the Marina Hemingway in Havana, plus other marinas dotted about the island, can provide docking and services. Most people, however, arrive on one of the growing number of scheduled and charter flights.

Banks

Banco Financiero Internacional

Open: 8.30–3pm, Mon–Fri.
You can get cash on your credit card here. In **Havana**, there are branches inside the Hotel Habana Libre; at the corner of Línea and O, Vedado (near Hotel Nacional), also open on Sat, 8.30am–noon; at the Plaza de la Revolución; in Old Havana at Oficios #200 (near Plaza de San Fransisco); and at Calle 18 #111. In **Santiago de Cuba**, there is a branch on Felix Pena (also called Santo Tomás) #365, north of Parque Céspedes.

Other branches in Cuba:
Camagüey: on Independencia.
Guardalavaca: at Hotel Atlántico.
Holguín: at Calle Libertad #56.
Matanzas: on Calle Medio, at the corner of 2 de Mayo.
Varadero: Avenida de la Playa and Calle 32.

Banco Metropolitano SA

The branch on the corner of Línea and M, in Vedado, Havana, deals in foreign currencies (cash on credit cards, travelers' checks, etc.), and has shorter queues than the Banco Financiero).

Banco Nacional

The branch next door to the Cubana office on La Rampa (Calle 23) in Havana, cashes travelers' checks and also gives cash on a credit card.

Cubana de Aviación, the national airline, flies scheduled and charter routes between Cuba and other cities in the Americas and Europe, serving primarily Havana. The airline does not have the best safety record in the world, and most flights are positively no-frills, but for many visitors Cubana flights provide the cheapest, quickest and easiest route into Cuba.

From Europe

Cubana has scheduled flights to and from London (Gatwick) and Manchester; Brussels; Paris; Berlin and Frankfurt; Lisbon; Moscow; Madrid, Barcelona, and Santiago de Compostela; Rome; and Basle. There are charter flights to and from: Vienna; Cologne and Frankfurt; Milan; Lisbon; Madrid; Paris; and London.

Other airlines also fly to Cuba from Europe. There are various charter flights from Gatwick and Manchester, in the UK, to Havana, Varadero and Holguín; Air UK flies direct to Camagüey from Gatwick.

Airline Offices

In Havana, international and domestic airline offices, as well as some tour operators, are all located on "La Rampa" – a stretch of Calle 23 between Calle M and the Malecón.

British Airways is also expected to start direct scheduled flights from London in 1999. Other scheduled flights already in operation from Europe include daily services with **Iberia** from Madrid and regular flights with **KLM** from Amsterdam.

The holiday airline, **LTU International Airways**, has four weekly flights from Düsseldorf and Munich to Havana, and three weekly flights to Holguín. The Dutch charter airline **Martinair** flies from Amsterdam to Holguín and Varadero.

From Latin America and the Caribbean

Cubana has sheduled flights from: Buenos Aires; São Paulo and Rio de Janeiro; Santiago de Chile; Kingston, Jamaica; Mexico City; Caracas; Panama City; Bogotá; Lima; and San José, Costa Rica.

Cubana also has charter flights from: Nassau, Bahamas; Santo Domingo, Dominican Republic; Guayaquil and Quito, Ecuador; Guadalajara, Mexico City, Veracruz, Cancún and Mérida, Mexico; Buenos Aires; Gran Cayman, Cayman Islands; Montego Bay, Jamaica; Montevideo, Uruguay; and Chile.

Many Latin American and Caribbean airlines also serve Cuba, with both scheduled and charter flights available. **Mexicana** flies daily between Mexico City and Havana, and there are also frequent flights from Cancún and Mérida in Yucatán. There are regular connections between Havana and San José on the Costa Rican airline, **Lacsa**.

From Canada

Cuba is accessible by air from Montreal, Toronto and Ottawa.

UK Tour Operators

A growing number of UK operators offers Cuba in their brochures:

Cosmos Holidays, Cosmosair, Tourama House, 17 Homesdale Road, Bromley, Kent BR2 9LX, tel: 0181-464 3444; fax: 0181-290 0714; telex: 896458. Offers mainly all-inclusive properties in Varadero and Ancón (Trinidad).

Cox and Kings Travel, St James Court, London SW1E 6AF, tel: 0171-873 5001; fax: 0171-630 6038; telex: 23378; e-mail: cox.kings@coxandkings.co.uk. Cultural tours and tailor-made vacations.

First Choice Holidays, Astral Towers, Betts Way, Crawley, West Sussex RH10 2GX, tel: 01293-560777; fax: 01293-588680. All-inclusive to budget apartment accommodation in Varadero.

Gane & Marshall International, 98 Crescent Road, New Barnet EN4 9RJ, tel: 0181-441 9592, fax: 441 7376, e-mail: holidays@ganeandmarshall.co.uk Tailor-made trips, including to Cubamar campsites.

Interchange, Interchange House, 27 Stafford Road, Croydon, Surrey CR0 4NG, tel: 0181-681 3612, fax: 0181-760 0031; telex: 928059. Study tours mainly for professionals or special interest groups. Tailor-made vacations, too.

Journey Latin America, 14–16 Devonshire Road, Chiswick, London W4 2HD, tel: 0181-747 8315; fax: 0181-742 1312; telex: 925068. Cultural tours and twin-center vacations with other Latin American countries.

Kuoni Travel, Kuoni Gardens, Mill Road, South Holmwood, Dorking, Surrey RH4 1DX, tel: 01306-742222; fax: 01306-744222. All-inclusive hotel package in Varadero combined with a stay in Jamaica.

Regent Holidays, 15 John Street, Bristol BS1 2HR, tel: 01179-211711; fax: 01179-254866; e-mail: regent@regentholidays.co.uk. Specializes in itineraries for independent travelers. Also offers itineraries for special interest groups and cultural tours. Has operated to Cuba since 1975.

Saga Holidays, The Saga Building, Middelburg Square, Folkestone, Kent CT20 1AZ, tel: 01303-711111; telex: 9666331; e-mail: http://www.saga.uk. Organizes cultural tours.

South American Experience, 47 Causton Street, London SW1P 4AT, tel: 0171-976 5511; fax: 0171-976 6908. Itineraries tailor-made to individual requirements.

Sunworld, Devonshire House, 29–31 Elmfield Road, Bromley, Kent BR1 1LT, tel: 0181-218 3300; fax: 0181-218 3367. Sends people to the beach resorts of Holguín, Santa Lucía and Varadero. Also twin-center vacations at Varadero–Cayo Largo. Weekly charter operation all year round.

Cubana runs scheduled flights from Montreal, while **Air Canada** and **Royal Airlines** fly from Toronto to Varadero. There are charter flights from Ottawa.

Flights from the US

In 1998, the US State Department announced the resumption of daily charter flights between Miami and Havana (these were suspended in February 1996).

The flight is intended only for Cubans visiting relatives and for US citizens who meet Treasury Department requirements (such as accredited journalists and special guests). Those with their visas already in order can buy air tickets from **Marazul Tours** in New York, tel: (212) 582 9570. There is often a long waiting list to travel on this flight, and US currency restrictions usually apply.

Health Tourism

Cuba has various health tourism programs involving combinations of treatment for specific illnesses and disabilities at specific hospitals, spas and health resorts. Hotels and transportation are not generally designed to cater for disabilities, though wheelchairs can be rented.

Women Travelers

Foreign women traveling alone may opt to visit Cuba within some planned framework: such as a package beach vacation, or a cultural tour, with Cuban specialists guiding and animating most of the action. However, Cuba is not a difficult place to travel as a single woman.

Cubans out in the hinterland may regard a foreign woman traveling alone as something of a freak, but they'll normally be very friendly and helpful. Women are safer in Cuba than almost anywhere else in the world. For example, this is one of the few places in the world where hitch-hiking is a safe option: hitch-hiking is a common way to get around for many people, and is controlled by state officials (*see page 68–9*).

Rape is almost unknown (although foreign women should be aware that the Cuban definition of "rape" is not the same as at home; a woman who takes a man up to her hotel room or indulges in public heavy petting will not be taken seriously if she later claims rape).

Cuba is in Latin America, after all, so women can expect a lot of male attention: this may be in the form of whistling, hissing (this is not perceived as rude in Cuba) or comments whispered or shouted in the street. This is rarely intended to be aggressive, and is just something a woman (whether native or foreign) has to get used to in such a macho country. Ignore the perpetrators, and they will normally leave you alone. On the other hand, any kind of acknowledgement – a smile, even a glance – is likely to be taken as a come-on.

Language Courses

The University of Havana, the University of Santiago de Cuba and the Central University in Santa Clara offer intensive Spanish-language programs for foreigners and a range of specialized courses and seminars for Spanish-speaking foreigners. Low-cost lodgings and meals as well as field trips are usually part of a student package. Travel agents dealing with Cuba have these schedules, as do Cuban consulates.

Traveling with Children

Cubans love their own kids and take them everywhere with them, so they are fascinated by foreigners who do the same. Your children will be pampered guests at any hotel and the employees will quickly learn their names and interests. The beach resorts all have supervised activities for them, and family rates are offered during the low season.

Practical Tips

Media

NEWSPAPERS AND MAGAZINES

The printed media of Cuba is extremely limited due to paper shortages and governmental control. Newspapers are posted on kiosks for the general population to read, and you sometimes see vendors wandering the street with copies to sell. The only daily paper is the Communist Party organ, *Granma*, which offers mainly an update on solidarity, trade and agriculture and provides interesting rather than scintillating reading. Tourists are more likely to find the international edition of *Granma* in hotel shops: this is published weekly in Spanish, English, French, German and Portuguese.

The long-established magazine *Bohemia* offers general features, and there are various other specialized Cuban publications on sale at dollar news-stands in hotels and airports. In response to the growing number of tourists visiting Cuba, four- and five-star hotels (particularly in Havana) often now carry foreign publications from *Time* to *Cosmopolitan*.

TELEVISION

Cuban national television is broadcast on two local channels (2 and 6), with approximately six hours of programming a day, beginning at 6pm. National and international **news** is reported on two half-hour programs. **Sports** events – especially baseball and boxing and increasingly soccer – are often covered live. Other shows include officials and specialists speaking at length and **music** of all kinds in concerts or videos. Foreign **movies** (usually American), seven a week, are shown on Thursday, Friday, Saturday and Sunday. Action movies are most popular, but a recent crackdown on violence and sex has resulted in an increase of "family" movies. **Soaps,** usually Brazilian, Mexican and Cuban, are highly popular: there are normally two on the go at any one time, one being shown in the afternoon and one in the evening.

Tourist hotels all have satellite TV with more than 20 channels, some of which are pulled into private homes via inventive roof-top parabolas that pick up signals from a hotel satellite dish.

RADIO

Just about everybody has a radio-cassette recorder, and loud music is a constant background sound everywhere. Apart from local stations, radios pick up waves from Miami, Jamaica and the American Forces Network at Guantánamo Base. **Radio Reloj** (Clock Radio) gives round-the-clock news on AM, to the infuriating background noise of a ticking clock; **Radio Havana Cuba** broadcasts news and features on short wave, where the **BBC** also comes through, though the reception is poor (early morning on 6195, 8am–10am on 15220, 10am–1pm on 17840, and mid-afternoon till late on 5975).

Voice of America, VOA, broadcasts from 6pm on 7070, short wave. **Radio Marti**, VOA's Spanish-language propaganda service from Miami, changes its frequencies often to avoid jamming, without much success.

Stamp collecting

Cuban stamps are inexpensive and attractively designed. Collections can be purchased at the postal shop in Havana's main post office just off Plaza de la Revolución. There is also an excellent stamp museum nearby (*see page 175*).

Postal Services

Every rural town has a post office, and major cities have a central post office with municipal branches. You can buy stamps here for pesos. In hotels, you will be charged the same price, but in dollars.

Postcards and letters to Europe cost 75 cents. Domestic delivery is slow, but usually faster from city to city than within the same city. Postcards and letters to friends in Europe and the Americas arrive a month or more after mailing, even via airmail.

Mother's Day (second Sunday in May) is the one day of the year when cards and telegrams are delivered on time all over Cuba. For a week or so ahead of the mailing deadline, cardboard boxes labeled by province are stacked in the lobby of the larger post offices so senders can drop in their addressed and stamped cards. The boxes are flown to the provincial capital to be sorted and then dispatched – and they are sure to reach mother on her day.

Telecommunications

The Cuban **local telephone service** is in the middle of a complete overhaul. It is possible to make crackle-free calls without wrong numbers across Havana (except Vedado) and as far east as Camagüey. By 1999, the entire island should have a modern, digitized service.

Certain exchanges have been set up for satellite communications and are rented in dollars. These work fairly efficiently.

International and local calls can be made from your hotel room (see page 329). Most hotels also have a **telex** service.

Given the unpredictability of postal services, many Cubans use **telegrams**, also sent from the post office, as a fast and fairly inexpensive way of communicating to other parts of the island. Dollar payment is now the general rule.

Telephone Calls and Faxes

Local and international telephone calls and faxes can be made through the operator from your hotel room (or sometimes through reception). International calls can also be made from any dollar phone (prefixed 33, 24 or 66). For direct dial, key in 119, followed by the country code and the number.

Payphones

Many street phones in Havana are being replaced by dollar phones that take phone cards (*tarjetas*), which can be bought at hotels or at branches of Photoservice and cost from $10 to $50. These phones can be used for local and international calls, more cheaply than in a hotel. You still find old peso phones, which use 5, 10 or 20 centavo coins. There are also a few street kiosks that were first set up to sell newspapers but now offer a phone service (usually for just local calls.) Most payphones outside Havana still use pesos.

Reversing the Charges

Reverse-charge calls can be made from a regular Cuban line (as found in most homes) to the US, Canada, Argentina, Colombia, Brazil, Chile, Mexico, Dominican Republic, Puerto Rico, Italy, Portugal, Spain, Italy, and the UK. For the US dial 661212, for other countries dial 09. Most operators speak English. You cannot make a reverse-charge call from an international (33, 24, 66) line.

Charges

International calls are expensive: to the US $2.50 per minute; the rest of the Americas and the Caribbean $3.50 per minute; the rest of the world $5.85 per minute.
Local calls cost 5 cents per minute, but hotels often charge 25 cents, sometimes even more.

Tourist Offices

All hotels have at least one **tourism information desk**, where hotel and restaurant reservations can be made, sightseeing tours booked, etc. More complicated queries should be addressed to your guide (if you have one) or to the hotel public relations manager.

General tourist information offices do not really exist in Cuba. Instead, there are a whole range of tourism enterprises, whose services sometimes overlap and which concentrate on offering packages or other specific services rather than telling visitors the opening hours of a museum and so on. If you are on a package tour, you should make a note or which company is responsible for you.

Most of Cuba's tourism organizations have improved greatly in recent years as regards helpfulness and efficiency. Most specialize in a particular field, so you should try to decide which agency suits your needs.

Cubanacán

Cubanacán promotes and arranges conventions and package tours, mainly in eastern Cuba, and such specialties as health tourism. Its main office is in Havana, at Calle 136 between Calles 11 and 13 (tel: 33-6006, 21-9448) near the International Conference Center.

Cubanacán Overseas has offices in Sao Paulo, Brazil; Toronto, Canada; Santo Domingo, Dominican Republic; Milan, Italy; Mexico City, Mexico; Rijswijk, Netherlands; Madrid, Spain; and London, UK. US travellers should contact the Cubanacán office in Toronto.

Cubatur

For years, Cubatur was the only commercial subsidiary of the Ministry of Tourism (INTUR), the state umbrella organization for tourism. Nowadays, Cubatur sells excursions through the tourism bureaux in most of the hotels in western Cuba. Its headquarters and individual tourism office in Havana are located at 156 Calle 23, Vedado (tel: 53-7-334 155, 334160, 334161.

There are Cubatur offices in most Latin American and European cities and in Montreal and Toronto, Canada. There is an officer in the Ministry of Tourism based at the Cuban Embassy in London.

Gaviota

Gaviota (owned and run by the Cuban armed forces, or FAR) has fewer and more specialized tourism interests, focused in Varadero, Havana and in eastern Cuba. Its head offices are on Calle 16 between Avenidas 5 and 7 in Miramar, tel: 230977, fax 241879.

Havanatur

Havanatur organizes land arrangements for the clients of its tour operators abroad. Its headquarters are on Calle 2 between Avenidas 1 and 3 Avenues in Miramar, tel: 332877, 332121, fax: 332877. Its **Tour & Travel Havanatur** can be contacted at tel: 249074, fax: 242547.

Publicitur

Publicitur, on Calle 19 #60 between Calles M and N in Vedado (at the back of the Focsa Building), tel: 334334/5/6; fax: 333422, organizes specialist tours of Cuba, and arranges publicity for Cuban tourism. If you are writing a book, making a film or TV program, or anything that might be good for Cuban tourism, you should contact Publicitur for reduced costs and help with the organization of the trip.

Embassies and Consulates in Havana

Argentina: Calle 36 #511, e/ 5ta y 7ma, Miramar, tel: 242110, 242549.
Austria: Calle 4 #101 esq. a 1ra, Miramar, tel: 242394, 242825.
Belgium: 5ta Ave #7408 esq. 76, Miramar, tel: 242410, 242561.
Brazil: Calle 16 #503 e/ 5ta y 7ma, Miramar, tel: 242139, 242786.
Canada: Calle 30 #518 esq. a 7ma, Miramar, tel: 242516, 242517, 2422527.
Chile: Avenida 33 #1423 e/ 16 y 18, Miramar, tel: 2421222, 21223.
Colombia: Calle 6 #106 e/ 1ra y 3ra, Miramar, tel: 241246, 241247, 241248.
Denmark: Paseo de Martí #20, apto. 4, Centro Havana, tel: 33-8128, 33-8144.
Germany: Calle 28 #313 e/ 3ra y 5ta, Miramar, tel: 33-2539, 33-2569, 33-2460.
Great Britain: Calle 34 #708 Miramar, Havana, tel: 241771, 241772.
Greece: 5ta Ave #7802 esq. a 78, Miramar, tel: 242995, 242854.
Italy: Calle Paseo #605 e/ 25 y 27, Vedado, tel: 33-3334, 33-3356, 33-3378, 33-3390.
Mexico: Calle 12 #518 e/ 5ta y 7ma, Miramar, tel: 242142, 242634, 242498.
Nicaragua: Calle 20 #709 e/ 7ma y 9na, Miramar, tel: 241025.
Netherlands: Calle 8 #307 e/3ra y 5ta, Miramar, tel: 242511, 242512, 242534.
Peru: Calle 36 #109 e/ 1ra y 3ra, Miramar, tel: 242477, 242632.
Poland: 5ta Ave #4407 e/ 44 y 46, Miramar, tel: 242610, 272964.
Portugal: 5ta Ave #6604 e/ 66 y 68, Miramar, tel: 242871.
Russia: 5ta Ave esq. a 66, Miramar, tel: 336398, 333617.
Spain: Zulueta #2 esq. a Cárcel, Centro Havana, tel: 33-8029, 33-8030.
Sweden: Ave 31 #1411 e/ 14 y 18, Miramar, tel: 242563, 242831, 242971.
Switzerland: 5ta Ave #2005 e/20 y 22, Miramar, tel: 242611, 242729, 242989.
United States (Interests Section): Calzada e/ L y M, Vedado, tel: 33-3551 to 59, 33-3543 to 47, 33-3700.
Venezuela: Calle 36A #704 e/ 7ma y 42, Miramar, tel: 242662, 242612, 242497, 242631.

Security and Crime

Crime is undoubtedly on the increase in Cuba, but it is still low by Latin American standards. Indeed, in comparison with most of the countries from which they come, tourists will find Cuba reassuringly safe. However, bag-snatching is not uncommon, particularly in the poorer sections of Havana. Leave as much as you can in the hotel – including travel documents, large banknotes and ostentatious jewelry – and keep a firm grip on your camera and on any bag you decide to carry.

Violent crime is rare, but there have been some incidents that have landed tourists in hospital. Most of these occured when people tried to fight off muggers. DON'T!

Havana is still safer than the majority of cities in the world, and it is highly unlikely you will be robbed. However, some areas – such as the darker streets of Old and Central Havana – should be avoided after dark, even if you are in a group. Take the sorts of precautions you would take in any large, unfamiliar city: at night, keep to busy and well-lit streets (admittedly, not always easy with constant blackouts).

There's much less crime outside the capital, but in Santiago you must take the same precautions as you would in Old or Central Havana.

Loss of belongings

In case of theft, you should report the crime to the nearest police station immediately. Make sure you ask for the case report (*denuncia*), to back up any insurance claim on your return home. The Cuban firm **Asistur** (*see page 325*) handles tourism insurance for losses on the island.

You should report lost or stolen passorts to your embassy or consulate, which can issue emergency papers to get you home.

Health

Common medicines – such as aspirin and basic stomach remedies – can be bought in hotels. More specialized items can usually be bought over the counter without prescription from dollar pharmacies, but these outlets are uncommon outside the capital. In Havana, there are good ones at the **Camilo Cienfuegos Hospital** on Línea and Calle L, and at the **Cira García Hospital** in Alamar (in Habana del Este). Of course, if you use prescripton medicines, it is best to bring a supply with you.

To avoid upset stomachs and diarrhoea – the two main illnesses suffered by tourists – drink bottled water and eat lightly. Naturally, be sensible about over-exposure to Cuba's strong, tropical sun.

Medical services

All hotels have a first-aid post of sorts, and the larger hotels will have a resident doctor or nurse, plus transportation to take a patient to the nearest clinic or hospital. Unless you fall ill in a remote rural area, as a foreign visitor you will be treated in a dollar-only hospital or a special tourist clinic (run by Servimed).

Most doctors and some nurses speak at least a little English, but hardly anybody is multilingual. The Cuban health-care system is free and readily available to all Cubans, but medicines and supplies are in short supply except in facilities that cater to dollar-paying foreigners.

Business Hours

Most **bank** branches open from 8.30am to 3pm Monday to Friday. Most Cuban **offices** open around 8.30am and close at 5 or 6pm, often with a break at lunchtime. But it is not rare for offices, even those serving the public, to close early because of blackouts, shortages and transportation problems.

Farmers' markets open early, from around 7am or even earlier, and close when traders decide to leave – usually between 4 and 6pm. **Neighborhood markets** selling rationed food in pesos are generally open from 8am to noon and again from 5 to 7pm – if they have any merchandise to sell.

New **dollar retail stores** are opening up all over the country; most open daily (except Sunday) from 10am to 5pm.

Dollar supermarkets usually open 9am–6pm Monday–Saturday and 9am–1pm Sunday. Tourists may be asked to show their passport at the so-called **diplomercado**, near the Russian embassy in Havana's Miramar suburb. One of the city's original dollar supermarkets, always popular with expats, the "diplo" sells food (including fresh meat and vegetables) and household supplies in dollars. It is open 9am–7pm Monday–Saturday, but not on Sunday.

Weights & Measures

Officially, Cuba uses the metric system, but you'll find that goods offered at stores that deal with mostly Cuban shoppers, such as the farmers' markets, use imperial pounds (*libras*) – a hangover from the days when America provided almost all of Cuba's imports.

You may find the following conversion formulas useful:

Temperatures

To convert Centigrade into Fahrenheit, multiply by 1.8 and then add 32; for Fahrenheit to Centigrade, subtract 32 and multiply by 0.55.

Metric to Imperial

1 cm	=	0.39 inch
1 meter	=	3.28 ft
1 km	=	0.62 miles
1 gram	=	0.035 oz
1 kg	=	2.21 lbs
1 liter	=	0.22 Imp. gallons
1 liter	=	0.26 US gallons

Imperial to Metric

1 inch	=	2.54 cm
1 ft	=	0.30 meters
1 mile	=	1.61 km
1 oz	=	28.35 grams
1 lb	=	0.45 kg
1 US gallon	=	3.79 liters

BRITISH AIRWAYS
TRAVEL CLINICS

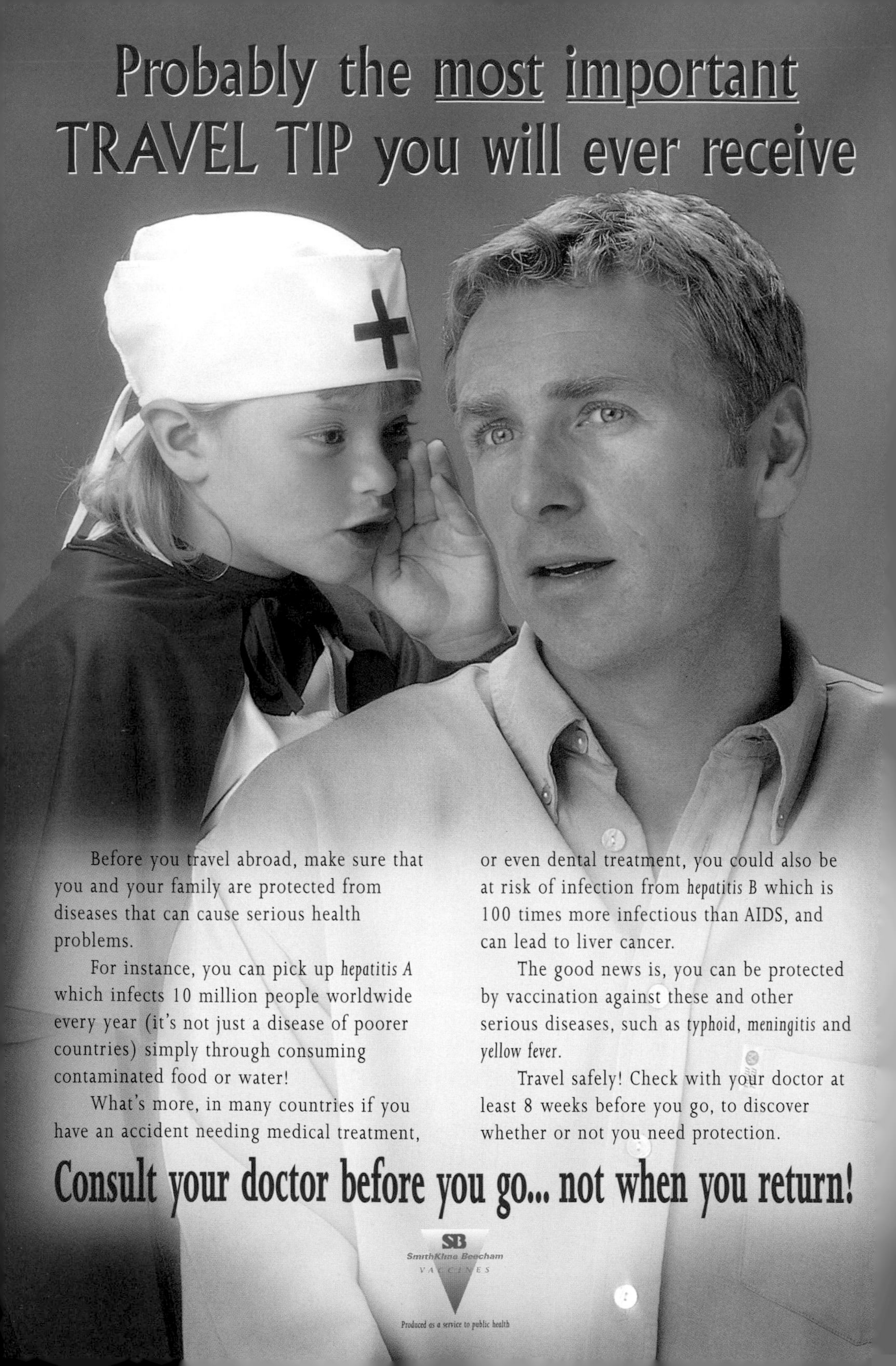

Probably the most important TRAVEL TIP you will ever receive

Before you travel abroad, make sure that you and your family are protected from diseases that can cause serious health problems.

For instance, you can pick up *hepatitis A* which infects 10 million people worldwide every year (it's not just a disease of poorer countries) simply through consuming contaminated food or water!

What's more, in many countries if you have an accident needing medical treatment, or even dental treatment, you could also be at risk of infection from *hepatitis B* which is 100 times more infectious than AIDS, and can lead to liver cancer.

The good news is, you can be protected by vaccination against these and other serious diseases, such as *typhoid*, *meningitis* and *yellow fever*.

Travel safely! Check with your doctor at least 8 weeks before you go, to discover whether or not you need protection.

Consult your doctor before you go... not when you return!

Produced as a service to public health

Tipping

Taxi drivers, waiters and hotel staff expect tips in dollars: 10 percent is adequate for taxis and restaurants. You should leave a dollar or more (depending on the length of your stay) for the hotel chambermaid.

Religious Services

The hotel tourism bureau can direct you to the church of your choice, but may not know precisely when services are held.

In Havana, Mass and baptism services at the **Cathedral** in Old Havana are posted at the entrance. The **Jewish Synagogue** at Línea and Calle M holds services and has a library. The **Methodist Church**, a block away from the Habana Libre hotel at Calles 25 and K, programs social activities as well as services and has a small guest house attached. **Catholic churches** are open all over the island and anyone can walk in any time to have a look or attend a mass.

Public Holidays

January 1 Liberation Day, commemorating the guerrillas' triumph over Batista.
May 1 Labor Day, celebrated with workers' parades.
July 25–27 A three-day holiday celebrating July 26, 1953, the date of the attack on the Moncada Garrison in Santiago, recognized as the start of the Revolution.
October 10 Celebrating the start of the War of Independence against Spain in 1868.

In addition to these official public holidays, there are innumerable other important dates which are commemorated, including:

- **January 28** The death of José Martí (1895).
- **April 19** The victory at the Bay of Pigs (1962).
- **October 8** Death of Che Guevara.
- **December 25** Christmas Day

Getting Around

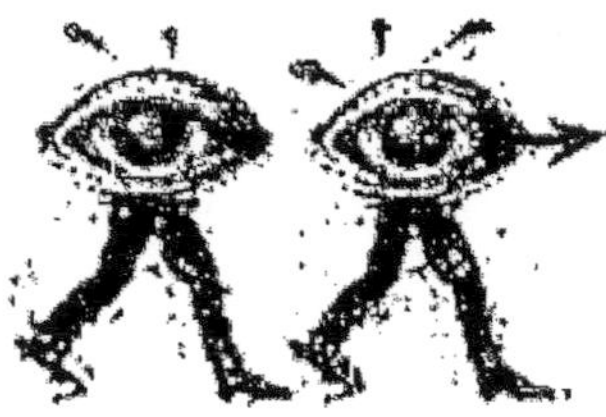

From Havana Airport

Havana's **José Martí International Airport** has three terminals:

- Terminal 3, opened in 1998, for international flights.
- Terminal 2, for flights from Miami.
- Terminal 1, for domestic flights.

If you are on an organized trip, then you should be met at the airport and accompanied on the transfer from the airport to the hotel. Individual travelers will need to arrange their own transportation.

Tourist taxis are always available at the airport: the fare runs from around $12 with Panataxi or Havanataxi to $18 with Turistaxi; other companies – such as OK and Gaviota – charge somewhere in between. Drivers from the various taxi companies gather at the terminal and hustle for your custom. It is illegal for **unlicensed cabs** to drive tourists to or from the airport, and the police keep an eagle eye on offenders. But while it is not always possible to locate unlicensed taxis hanging around the airport, it is easy to find illegal cab drivers downtown prepared to take you.

On Departure

If you are not being escorted to the airport, you may be brave enough to pin down a local bus service, one of which runs through the Parque Central, in Habana Vieja – but you should allow plenty of time for the wait and the journey. If you pick up a tourist taxi or an unlicensed cab, you should allow about 30–40 minutes for the journey from Old Havana.

If you are traveling independently, you must remember to reconfirm your ticket, ideally 48 or 72 hours prior to departure.

Airport departure tax is $15. You can pay with dollars or *pesos convertibles.*

By Air

Flying is currently the most convenient way to travel for anyone with limited time and a desire to see various corners of the island. Note, however, that most services originate from Havana. The national airline, Cubana, has regular scheduled flights to 10 Cuban cities from the capital.

Recent departure times and prices for domestic flights are as follows:

Baracoa: $156. Tuesday and Friday 6am, Sunday 6.30am.
Bayamo: $118. Every Monday and Thursday at 8am, every alternate Friday at 1.35pm, and every alternate Saturday and Sunday, at 8.30am.
Camagüey: $120. Monday at 3.10pm, Tuesday at 9.30am, Wednesday at 12.20pm and 6pm, Thursday at 9.30am, Friday at 6pm, and Saturday and Sunday at 9.30am.
Ciego de Avila: $88. Friday only, at noon.
Guantánamo: $120. Monday 6am, Tuesday 7.35am, Wednesday 9.30am, Thursday 6am, Friday 7.35am, Saturday and Sunday 6am.
Holguín: $158. Monday 2.30pm, Tuesday 12.20am, Wednesday 3.30pm, Thursday 12.20pm, Friday 3.30pm, Saturday 2.30pm and Sunday 1.55pm.
Nueva Gerona (Isle of Youth): $40. Twice daily at 7.15am and 7.55pm, plus additional flights on Monday and Friday at 9.30am, and Tuesday and Thursday at 6.15pm. Demand always outstrips supply, so always check in at least two hours before departure – latecomers lose seats to those on the waiting list.
Santiago de Cuba: $160. There are always three, and sometimes four or more flights per day – some flights are diversions from Holguín or Bayamo that make the extra stop when they have spare seats. For up-

to-date information, it is best to call Cubana at José Martí airport in Havana, tel: 335177, or in Santiago, tel: 226-41061 and 226-86184.
Trinidad: $70. Monday and Friday 7.30am.
Varadero: $60 with the charter airline Aero Caribbean. On Saturday morning (but subject to schedule changes, tel: 334543 in Havana). The Aero Caribbean office is on the Rampa #113. In Varadero, tel: 05-6676096). You can fly to Varadero from other tourist destinations – Cayo Coco, Santiago, Guardalavaca and Baracoa via Cubana. Tel: 334446/7/8 and 705961.

Ongoing air transportation can be arranged from Santiago or Holguín to Manzanillo/Bayamo, Guantánamo and Baracoa, and to lesser points of interest such as Las Tunas and Moa. Return flights should be confirmed on arrival. **Aero Caribbean** and **Aero Gaviota**, two smaller lines, fly charters to Cayo Largo, Cayo Coco and other popular tourist destinations.

By Train

The Cuban Railroad, the first in Latin America, may be the last in efficiency and comfort today. Trains are crowded and services have been reduced – almost all are now locals that stop at every station. All are achingly slow and prone to breakdown. Except on the so-called Havana-Santiago Express (which averages 18 hours traveling time), little or no food or water are to be had, so remember to take provisions with you.

Seats on Cuban trains are always booked well in advance with long waiting lists. There are always seats reserved for those paying in dollars, however – usually a whole car. For peace of mind, you ought to try and book your ticket a day in advance, and you should arrive at least one hour before departure to check in: unassigned seats will be re-allocated to those on the waiting list if you have not confirmed that you are traveling.

Dollar-paying passengers buy their tickets from the offices of LADIS (still often known by its old name of "Ferrotur"), which is usually situated inside the station or nearby. In Havana, LADIS is outside the main station on Calles Arsenal and Cienfuegos. At many provincial LADIS offices the staff are not really accustomed to dealing with foreigners and tend to take the same unhelpful (or downright rude) attitude they inflict on their fellow Cubans. Persist if you are told that there are no seats: it is unlikely that there are no seats if you are paying hard currency. Unfortunately, it is only too common in Cuba today that a firm "No hay" is simply a way of asking for a bribe: $5 will usually do the trick.

Public Transportation

Fuel shortages have prompted drastic cuts in inter-urban and inter-provincial public bus services. Many Cuban cities rely on horse-drawn carts that use the same urban routes buses once used to follow.

In Havana, thousands of Chinese-made bicycles have been introduced, but there are many more non-cyclists who wait two hours or more for a bus every day. In some places, it is mandatory for cars and trucks to pick up hitchhikers; but the further you go into the countryside the fewer vehicles you see. See pages 68–9 for a look at how people get around in Cuba.

By Bus

Buses, known as **guaguas**, are often slow, crowded and uncomfy, but are nevertheless a cheap way to get around the island, as well as a good way to meet Cubans.

Especiales are faster and more comfortable than **regulares**, but less common. When using provincial bus services, turn up as early as you can on the day – it is not always possible to reserve a seat in advance. If you have a reservation, still try to arrive at least an hour before departure: when the bus arrives, the names of those with reservations are read out, and those not present will have their seats allocated to those on the waiting list. Some bus stations are now issuing tourists with tickets for dollars, making the whole process a great deal easier.

Provincial buses traveling between small towns make frequent stops. Just stick out your hand; the fares are usually a few centavos. These buses are, however, infrequent, and you might wait many hours before a bus turns up – if at all. Hitching is quicker and more reliable, which is why so many people do it (*see page 69*).

It is possible to buy bus tickets for dollars at the **Empresa Omnibus Nacionales**, Avenida Independencia #101, in Havana. Only one-way tickets are sold in advance, and you usually find the waiting list for return journeys is sold out a month in advance. Travel light, as luggage space is severely restricted.

Tour Buses

Travel by local bus in Cuba is only for the patient and hardy. Of course, dollar-carrying tourists can also use tour buses. All hotels can book reasonably priced excursions to all the main tourist destinations. Travel is on modern, comfortable, air-conditioned buses. If you are short of time – or unused to roughing it – these trips are definitely worth considering. You can sometimes pay less if all you want to do is travel from A to B.

Driving

Increasingly, tourists are getting around Cuba by car. This gives the greatest degree of independence, and allows you to reach corners of the island that otherwise would be hard to reach in a short time.

Cuban highways and secondary roads are fairly well maintained, except for a range of potholes. Otherwise, driving is safe and Cubans are ever helpful with directions – even though they are often vague when it comes to distances.

Car Rental

The cost of a rental car starts at around $50 per day for the smallest model, such as a Peugeot 205, plus insurance ($10–15 daily) and gas at $1.20 per liter, as well as a deposit. The rental charge plus extras is paid in full in advance, but it is possible to use a credit card.

Be sure to check the car carefully for damage and scratches. Draw attention to anything you find, and insist any damages are noted on the paperwork. Be warned that car rental agents have all kind of ruses for not returning the full deposit. Whatever you do, be sure to take out the maximum insurance cover possible.

Cars can be rented through major hotels in Havana, Varadero, Cienfuegos, Trinidad, Camagüey, Holguín and Santiago de Cuba. The main rental companies are Havanautos, Transautos and Cubanacán.

Gas

Buying gas used to be a nightmare in Cuba. It still is for most ordinary Cubans, at least for those who have no access to dollars. Tourists and anyone else with hard currency, however, can now make use of the **Cupet** filling stations, which you will find in all the main towns and even in some smaller provincial towns, as well as scattered at (infrequent) intervals along the six-lane highway (*autopista*), which runs east from Havana (and eventually peters out in central Cuba).

Cupet stations normally offer minimal mechanical back-up.

Puncture Repairs

The nearest petrol station (be it dollar or peso) may be able to help if you have a flat tyre. Otherwise, ask around for the nearest *ponchera*. Since self-employment was legalized, many Cubans have set up puncture-repair workshops. Most of these deal mainly with bicycle tyres, but some can handle car inner tubes.

Private Cars & Taxis

You may prefer to let someone else do the driving. One way Cubans are making dollars now is by driving visitors around. Some charge a flat rate for a half or a whole day of sightseeing or for an excursion, for example from Havana to Varadero and back. The price should be considerably less than the cost of an organized tour with a state agency. Private taxis are a good way to see Havana. The day rate within the city is $25–40 (big American gas guzzlers charge more) and it is the same for excursions outside the city. Set a price before you go.

It is even possible to organize a car and driver for a week – as long as you are prepared to pay for all their food and lodging.

It will not always be apparent, but some private taxis are licensed and some are not – depending on whether the driver pays the hefty license fee-cum-tax imposed by the government.

It is supposedly illegal for private taxis – both legal or illegal – to ferry passengers to any airport or to Varadero, the Eastern Beaches (Playas del Este) or any other tourist resort. A Cuban caught doing this will be heavily fined and may lose his license – even his car, if it's not a first offence. Hence, some "street" taxis will now refuse to take you to these destinations. Note that if you find a private driver willing to take the risk, and are stopped by the police, you too could end up spending several hours at a police station while the paperwork is done – though it will be the Cuban who suffers in the end.

Official taxis Several state companies provide a taxi service, the main ones being Turistaxi and Havanataxi. These are easiest to pick up outside a hotel – rather than hailing them in the street. The cabs run by **Panataxi** can be summoned only by phone but charge a cheaper rate. If you feel uncomfortable using a private taxi, Panataxi is the next best option.

Where to Stay

Choosing a Hotel

Many of Cuba's tourist lodgings have been, or are in the process of being, upgraded – and so are their prices. Foreign tour operators and hotel chains marketing Cuban tourism pay about half the listed price for groups of 15 or more, giving them space for the attractive packages that the vast majority of tourists travel on.

Some hotels are **peso hotels**, which are not supposed to accommodate foreign tourists, and so cannot be booked through a tour operator. As Cuba promotes tourism more heavily, however, the better peso hotels are being refurbished and reopened as **tourist hotels.** At the middle and low end of the price scale are **apartment hotels** and **villas** (an arbitrary designation that usually means small and modest); **campsites** (outside the cities); and **private rooms**. In provincial areas, Cubans pay in pesos but tourists still pay in dollars, and at higher rates.

Tourist hotels are run by a variety of tourist enterprises, and it is possible to ascertain the standard of the hotel from the name of the enterprise that manages it. For example, hotels run by **Islazul** and **Horizontes** tend to be two-star or three-star, while those run by **Gran Caribe** are often four-star. In the popular tourist resorts, there are often many hotels run by foreign companies, such as Tuxpán and Meliá (both from Spain).

Facilities Most Cuban hotel rooms have private bathrooms, but even a three-star hotel may not have running hot water all the time. Bedrooms are expected to be air-conditioned (and a working machine is important since windows are often sealed shut), however in a two-star establishment you may have to be happy with just a fan (*ventilador*).

CAMPSITES

Campsites are operated by **Campismo Popular** in every province, and may charge as little as US$5 per person per night. Some of the sites are beautiful, on hidden beaches, clear lakes or mountain streams. Campers sleep more often in a hut (*cabaña*) than in a tent, equipped with cots (usually for two or four persons). Most camps have a food store and a cafeteria or snack bar, but supplies may be scarce. Group showers and latrines prevail.

The majority of these campsites are designed for Cuban tourists only, and are empty or closed out of the peak holiday months of July and August. However, a few sites are used for international tourism and are open all year round. These places also have better amenities, such as flush toilets and hot water. These international sites include:

- **El Abra** by Playa Jibacoa, beyond Playas del Este, east of Havana.
- **Aguas Claras**, near Pinar del Río.
- **Guajimico**, between Trinidad and Cienfuegos.
- **Villa Santo Domingo** in the Sierra Maestra, in Granma Province.

Reservations can be made directly with **Cubatur** on arrival or, even better, booked from abroad through a specialist tour operator.

PRIVATE ROOMS (*CASAS PARTICULARES*)

For many years, it was illegal to rent private accommodation in Cuba, but this was, none the less, widely practised and universally tolerated. The government decided to legalize the practice in 1996, but imposed rules which are fairly strictly enforced.

- It is illegal for a Cuban to rent an entire apartment – but people do.
- It is illegal to let unless you register with the government and pay hefty taxes ($250 per registered room, let or not) – but people do.
- If tourists stay in family accommodation they must sign official paperwork, which must be taken to the local Communist Party office (less sinister than it sounds!).

Note that you can put a legally registered *casa particular* on your tourist card as official place of residence in Cuba.

Costs The high taxes have pushed up the cost of living with a family – you should not expect to find a legal let for less than $30–35 a day in Havana, usually less than that elsewhere. Bigger, luxury apartments charge more. The price usually includes two meals a day, but you should check this before you move in. Of course many people are still letting illegally. Such rooms are much cheaper, $10–15 a day.

Finding a Let On the street, you may be approached by agents for people with a room or rooms to let (they take a commission from the owner). Otherwise, ask around: taxi drivers, black marketeers and the money-changers who hang around outside farmers' markets are good sources of information.

Not everyone who lets rooms is honest, and you should be careful with money and valuables. Be aware that since it is prohibited to take Cuban "guests" (i.e. prostitutes) to hotel rooms, many *casas particulares* have been doing a roaring trade as clandestine bordellos. These are often more expensive than the norm – many even charge by the hour. The best way to find a good *casa particular* is, of course, by recommendation from a fellow traveler.

Havana

Casa de Aurora Ampudia, Calle 15 #58 between M and N Vedado, tel: 537-321843. The house is awkward to find, being on a small spur of Calle 15 off Línea, a block from the Malecón. Ask taxis for the Japanese Embassy – the house is next door. Right in the heart of Vedado, this place is noisy but convenient. Aurora is friendly and seems to know everyone in Havana. She welcomes everyone and loves British guests (she is a Beatles fan). Her's is a bustling house, with always something going on. The daily rate includes meals on the terrace.

The Casablanca, house of Jorge Luis Duany, Calle 13 #197 between 6 and 8, Vedado, tel/fax: 537-35697. A tranquil house, with nice rooms in a quiet, green, leafy part of Vedado. The daily rate excludes breakfast and dinner.

Trinidad

Casa Colonial Munoz, house of Julio Cesar Munoz Cocina. José Martí #401 between Fidel Castro and Santiago Escobar, tel: 53419-3673. A lovely, breezy colonial house, built in 1800 right in the centre of Trinidad. There's hot water and Julio speaks English.

Casa de Irrael Ortega López, Calle Gustavo Izquierdo No.124a between Calles Simón Bolívar and Piro Aguinar, right opposite the bus station. A warm and hospitable family who'll serve you meals and do your washing.

Hotel Listings

Hotels are listed by region (in the same order as in the Places section) and then alphabetically by town. In Havana and Varadero, hotels are listed by price category.

The price categories cover the price of a double room in high season.

HAVANA

In Havana, hotels are being built and refurbished all the time. The biggest project on the go is the **Hotel Parque Central** – a new hotel with an old façade – in the Parque Central, due to open in 2000, while another is due to open in an 18th-century mansion on Plaza Vieja. The **Gran Hotel** on Brasíl (also called Teniente Rey), on the corner of Bélgica, is due to reopen in 1999 after major restoration.

Information Line

For information about the latest developments (including hotels) in Havana, call the helpful tourist line on 33-3333.

Price Guide

The following price categories indicate the cost of a double room in high season:
$$$$: Very expensive: $150–250.
$$$: Expensive: $90–150.
$$: Moderate: $50–90.
$: Inexpensive: under $50.

Very Expensive

Hotel Meliá Cohiba
Paseo and 1era, Vedado.
Tel: 33-3636.
Fax 33-4555.
Cuba's first five-star hotel, opened in 1995, on the seafront. Filled to bursting with restaurants, cafés, bars, nightclubs and shops. Spanish-run. Luxurious.

Hotel Nacional
Calle O and 21, Vedado.
Tel: 33-3564/5/6/7.
Fax 33-5054.
Once Havana's number one hotel. The rich and famous of the city's golden age in the 1940s and 1950s used to stay here; see their pictures in the Bar of Fame. Two pools, tropical gardens, tennis courts. So-so food and service and occasionally dodgy plumbing, but lovely views along the Malecón and undeniably elegant. The Cabaret Parisien is the next best thing to the Tropicana.

Hotel Santa Isabela
Calle Baratillo, Plaza de Armas, Habana Vieja. Tel: 612952.
Opened in 1997, in a beautiful, newly renovated former colonial palace, right in the heart of Old Havana. A vision in turquoise and stone, with a lovely courtyard. Five-star, popular with the business market. Excellent restaurant.

Expensive

Hotel Ambos Mundos
On Obispo #153, at the corner of Mercederes.
Tel: 669529.
Elegant, nicely renovated, old-style hotel (where Ernest Hemingway once stayed). The lovely views are lost to many guests since most rooms are windowless (although they are air-conditioned). Wonderful piano bar.

Hotel Comodoro
Calle 84 and 3ra, Miramar.
Tel: 225893, 292931.
Home of the popular Havana Club Disco, this seaside hotel is favoured by tour groups. Rooms and bungalows are airy and luxurious. Excellent swimming pool, but remote from the heart of Havana.

Copacabana
1ra #4404 between 44 and 46, Miramar.
Tel: 241027.
This 172-room seaside hotel is constructed in three low wings connected by galleries, gardens and a big pool with a terrace café. A natural pool runs the full length of the hotel to its boat dock, and there is a large conventional pool, too. Restaurants, snack shops, disco. The National Aquarium is just next door. Rooms are small but pleasant and some have balconies. Some distance from Old Havana, but relaxed and friendly.

Hotel Habana Libre Tryp
Calle 23 and L, Vedado.
Tel: 33-4011, 33-3141.
Fax 33-3145.
Having been a time capsule of 1950s design for many decades, the Libre is now – after a $20 million refurbishment – just another modern hotel. It is, however, far more pleasant and comfortable than before. Rooms are spacious. The higher up you go, the more expensive the room because of the views. It has several decent bars (including the rooftop Bar Turquino) and restaurants, and a branch of the Banco Financiero Internacional, and a whole range of shops.

Hotel Habana Riviera
Paseo and Malecón, Vedado.
Tel: 33-3986, 33-4051.
Fax 33-1345.
Recently refurbished but still needing a lot of work, the Riviera feels overpriced and is rather overshadowed by the Meliá Cohiba next door. However, it has an excellent swimming pool and has the city's hottest music venue, the "Palacio de Salsa." The lobby retains a pleasant 50s feel, if you like that kind of thing.

Hotel Iberostar Neptuno-Triton
3ra Avenida, corner of Calle 70, Miramar.
Tel: 24-1606, 24-1377/8/9.
Recently refurbished, the Triton now has a green lobby full of art and interesting shops. The twin Hotel Neptuno is closed for refurbishment until late 1998. They share a very large swimming pool and an artificially created private beach. The hotel is in a rather bleak and remote location, right by the Diplo-store and Russian Embassy.

Marina Hemingway
5ta Avenida and Calle 248, Santa Fe.
Tel: 246815.
Private yachts dock at this marina on the western outskirts of the capital. It is also a take-off point for shoreline cruises. Visitors are accommodated in a 60-room apartment-hotel, 20 two-story cabanas on the east side of the marina, and long-term house rentals on a connected island west of the marina. The complex has two specialty restaurants in addition to hotel facilities and a shopping center with a food market. Don't expect much atmosphere, and you're well away from the action.

Hotel Plaza
Agramonte #207, Parque Central.
Tel: 33-8583/84/85.
Fax 33-8592.
Favored by European tour groups, the Plaza has a grand columned lobby, while the café bar on the ground floor boasts a fountain, and is full of parrots and palms. The hotel has three rather mediocre and over-priced restaurants (the Italian restaurant being particularly bad), but breakfast on the roof terrace is undeniably pleasant, and the bar serves decent sandwiches. Rooms are on the poky side, looking out to the street or inner courtyards. All have delicate stained-glass windows and tasteful prints.

Hotel Sevilla
Prado #255 (corner of Trocadero).
Tel: 338560, 338566/7/8/9.
Beautifully restored in 1994, the Sevilla has a wonderfully Spanish ambience. Cool, tiled lobby with an

antique feel, and delightful blue-tiled patio café complete with fountain. The ninth-floor restaurant has spectacular views.

Hotel Victoria
Calle 19 #101, corner of M, Vedado.
Tel: 33-3510, 33-3625.
Fax 33-3109.
A quiet, unassuming, classically elegant hotel in a good position, but with only 32 rooms the Victoria is usually well booked up. There is a small pool. The restaurant is so-so, favoring seafood. There is a snug and comfortable bar which serves excellent coffee and ice-cream fruit shakes at moderate prices.

Moderate

Hotel Capri
Calle 21, corner of N, Vedado.
Tel: 33-3571/2, 33-3747.
Fax 33-3750.
Virtually untouched since it was built in 1957, and desperately in need of refurbishment. Popular with tour groups, it has a splendid rooftop pool and bar (where there is a cabaret most nights) and a good Italian restaurant. But avoid the basement restaurant.

Chateau Miramar
1era between Calles 60 and 62, Miramar.
Tel: 33-0224, 33-1952/3/4/5/6.
A moderately luxurious seafront hotel with saltwater pool and its own beach. Good restaurant.

Hotel Colina
Calle L between 27 and 27th November, Vedado.
Tel: 33-4071, 33-4103, 32-3535.
Magnificent views from the higher floors, especially of the university next door. Rooms are comfortable, but ageing equipment tends to fail. Very noisy. Great-value buffet breakfast.

Hotel Deauville
Galiano and Malecón, Centro Habana.
Tel: 33-8812.
Long used by tour groups, the Deauville is decidedly faded – rooms are comfortable but things (TVs, bedside lamps, showers, etc.) tend not to work. There is, however, a wonderful rooftop pool. The hotel itself is situated on the fringe of a rather rough part of Central Havana, but it is pleasant to wake up to the sound of the sea crashing onto the Malecón.

Hotel Inglaterra
Parque Central (Prado #416).
Tel: 33-8593, 33-8254, 33-8597.
As popular with independent travelers as with tour groups. A cool, gold and white lobby, a lovely 24-hour café bar, with live music from the grand piano or a (rather deafening) *mariachi* band. The restaurant next door is beautiful, gently lit by chandeliers and stained glass, but the food is awful. The small rooftop bar holds a salsa cabaret every night except Tuesday (entrance fee). The interior rooms tend to be rather stuffy but are at least quiet, while those with balconies looking out over the Parque Central or the Gran Teatro, next door, are light but noisy. You should try to specify what kind of room you would like when you book. The rooms are all the same price.

Hotel Presidente
Calzada and Avenida de Presidentes, Vedado.
Tel: 33-4075, 33-4394, 33-4395.
The lobby is impressive, filled with priceless antiques, while the rooms are somewhat poky. The pool is beloved by *jiniteras* and the music tends to be loud. It was recently closed for renovation.

Hotel St Johns
Calle O between 23 and 25, Vedado.
Tel: 33-3740, 33-3561.
Budget, but pleasant with a good pool. Well situated off the Rampa (Calle 23), a stone's throw from the Malecón.

Hotel Vedado
Calle O #244 corner of Humboldt, Vedado.
Tel: 33-4072.
Virtual twin to the nearby Hotel St Johns.

Inexpensive

Hotel Bruzón
Calle Bruzón #217, between Pozos Dulces and Boyeros.
Tel: 70-3531.
Comfortable, but basic rooms. Near the Plaza de la Revolución and convenient for the bus station.

Hotel Caribbean
Prado # 164.
Tel: 33-8210, 33-8233.
The traditional travelers' hotel, with about the cheapest rooms in the city. No-frills rooms with minimal natural light, and no-frills food in the bar-café downstairs, though the place has been improved by recent renovation. There have been reports of burglary, so you are advised to use the safe deposit boxes in reception.

Casa del Cientifico
Prado #212, on the corner of Trocadero.
Tel: 33-8527, 33-8950.
Fax: 338087.
The former Academy of Sciences is now an elegant hotel with a sweeping marble staircase, stained-glass windows and frescoed ceilings. There is a café and restaurant in the marble courtyard surrounded by classical statues. The hotel offers budget accommodation on the second floor (usually reserved for Cubans paying pesos), with shared bathrooms and cold water only. Third-floor rooms have private baths and hot water.

Hotel Kohly
Ave 49 and Calle 36, Kohly.
Tel: 29-6098, 22-6021.
A prefab structure that has been pleasantly refurbished, with wicker and flower-printed cushions, located in a quiet neighborhood not far from Tropicana Nightclub and a 10-minute drive from Old Havana.

Hotel Lido
Consulado #216, Centro Habana.
Tel: 33-8814, 62-0653.
The hotel vies with the Caribbean for budget travelers' custom. It

Price Guide

The following price categories indicate the cost of a double room in high season:
$$$$: Very expensive: $150–250.
$$$: Expensive: $90–150.
$$: Moderate: $50–90.
$: Inexpensive: under $50.

loses out due to its location, a block away from the Prado, in one of central Havana's rougher areas. The rooms are basic with fans and radios. Bad reputation for theft from rooms.

Hotel Lincoln
Galiano and Virtudes, Centro Habana.
Tel: 33-8209, 62-8061.
Faded grandeur and unpredictable plumbing. Pleasant friendly atmosphere. Rooftop bar.

Hotel Morro
3ra and D, Vedado.
Tel: 32-0530, 32-3740.
Small and basic, but one of the few very cheap hotels in Vedado. Just a block from the Malecón.

Hotel New York
Dragones #156, near the Capitolio.
Tel: 62-3071, 62-7001.
Basic, windowless rooms. The cheapest hotel in Havana, but not particularly accustomed to putting up foreign tourists.

Hotel Universitario
Calle 17, corner of N, Vedado.
Tel: 33-2964, 33-2128, 33-3403.
Basic, unassuming and well situated, near the Focsa Building.

Hostal Valencia
Oficios and Obrapía, just south of Plaza de Armas.
Tel: 62-3801.
The hotel has just 10 rooms and one suite, in a beautifully restored colonial mansion, centered around a glorious vine-draped courtyard with a pleasant café bar. There is also a decent Spanish restaurant. Rather noisy in the early morning, but the rooms are delightful, with original colonial features. The hotel is popular and usually booked up well in advance.

AROUND HAVANA

Playa Jibacoa

El Abra Cubamar
Playa Jibacoa, Santa Cruz del Norte.
Tel: 692-8 3612.
Basic accommodation in cabins, but there is a vast swimming pool and a glorious beach nearby. $

Villa Jibacoa Loma
Via Blanca Km 65, Playa Jibacoa, Santa Cruz del Norte.
Tel: 338252.
Pleasantly renovated with good facilities. $

Venta Club Villa El Trópico
Via Blanca Km 60, Playa Jibacoa, close to El Abra.
Tel: 338004.
Fax: 337585.
An all-inclusive resort hotel catering mainly to Italian tourists. $$$

Playa El Salado

Villa El Salado Cubanacán
Carretera Panamericana Km 16, Playa Salado, Baracoa.
A pebbly beach, but a pleasant cabin motel, west of Havana. $

San Antonio de los Baños

Hotel Cubanacán Las Yagrumas
Calle 40 y Río Ariguanabo, San Antonio de Los Baños.
Tel: 3352438/9.
Fax: 335011.
In a lovely spot by the Río Ariguanabo, just north of the town. In the middle of nowhere, but fine for a peaceful break from the bustle of Havana. Pleasant rooms gathered around a pool. Good sporting facilities. $$$

Playas del Este

There are many hotels here. The following are only a selection, but none is outstanding.

Las Brisas Horizontes
Calle 11, between 1 and 3.
Tel: 687-2469, 3384, 3390.
Modest self-catering apartments in lush gardens, located up the hill about 1 km from the beach. $$

Hotel Gran Vía Islazul
5ta Avenida, corner of 462, Guanabo, Habana del Este.
Tel: 687-2271.
Modest, but airy rooms, by the main road. $

Hotel Itabo
Laguna Itabo between Santa María del Mar and Boca Ciega.
Tel: 687-2580, 2550.
The best of the Eastern Beaches' poor choice of hotels. Red-tiled cabins sit on an island amid mangroves slightly back from the beach. There is a huge pool, pleasant gardens, a thatched-roof bar/restaurant. Modest rooms. Excellent value. $

Hotel Los Pinos Gran Caribe
Avenida de Las Terrazas, between 4th and 5th, Playa El Mégano.
Tel: 2617, 2691–6.
Another of the better choices, offering reasonable privacy in pre-revolutionary villas. $$$

Hotel Miramar Islazul
Calle 480, corner 9, Guanabo.
Tel: 687-2262.
Modest but pleasant rooms, with balconies that face the sea. $

Hotel Tropicoco Beach Club
Avenida Sur and Avenida de Las Terrazas, Santa María del Mar.
Tel: 33-8040.
Fax: 33-5158.
A recently renovated concrete blot on the landscape popular with tour groups. The hotel is very close to the beach, with 188 rooms, all air-conditioned with telephone and radio. It has a noisy disco. $

PINAR DEL RIO PROVINCE

Candelaria

Hotel la Moka
Autopista Habana-Pinar del Río, Km 51.
Tel: 80269.
Fax: 335516.
A beautiful modern hotel in traditional Cuban style. Live forest trees pierce its split levels and patios. Swim in the waterfall fed pool, hire a bicycle or spend time in the nearby artists' colony. $$

Cayo Levisa

Villa Cayo Levisa
Tel: 33-1162.
Fax: 33-1164, 33-5042.
Resort and diving center, with 20 rustic cabins gathered beside the beach. Watersports, bar, excellent "international" restaurant (mainly buffets). Beauty salon. $$

Maspotón

Club Maspotón Horizontes
Maspotón, Los Palacios.
Tel: Horizontes in Havana 33-4142.
Fax: 33316.
Depressing concrete cabins amid mosquito-infested mangroves, but said to be a hunter's paradise. 34 rooms with air-conditioning. Swimming pool. Full board. $$$

Pinar del Río

Villa Aguas Claras
Carretera de Viñales Km 7.5, just north of Pinar del Río.
Tel: 2722.
Pleasant cabins grouped around a swimming pool in acres of garden and woods – with at least one example of virtually all of Cuba's fruit trees. Horseback riding and hiking. 50 modest cabins. $

Hotel Globo
Martí #50, at Calle Isabel Rubio.
Tel: 82-4268.
A former peso hotel right in the center of town. Dark, tiled foyer with an amazing mosaic. 42 rooms. Basic accommodation. Noisy. $

Hotel Italia
Gerardo Medina #215 and Isabel Rubio.
Tel: 82-3049.
A no-frills, former peso hotel with 27 rooms with air conditioning. $

Hotel Pinar del Río
Calle Martí, at the eastern entrance to the town.
Tel: 82-5070–5.
Friendly staff but don't expect a particularly appealing ambience in this concrete monolith. There are 136 rooms and 13 cabins, fairly simple. Mediocre food and shops. The pool is popular with locals (when it's full). $

San Diego de Los Baños

Hotel El Mirador
Tel 33-5410.
A lovely canopied hotel on a hill by a rolling river and virgin rainforest. Serves the spa next door which offers medical and cosmetic treatments using its volcanic, mineral-rich waters and muds. Pleasant restaurant. $

Soroa

La Caridad Campismo
On Arroyo Manantiales, 1 mile (2 km) southeast of Villa Soroa.
Very basic cabins designed for Cuban tourists. $

Villa Turística Soroa
Carretera de Soroa Km 8, northwest of Candelaria.
Tel: 85-2122, 85-2041.
Has 49 pleasant cabins and 8 villas (*casitas*) with good facilities in stunning landscaped gardens. Olympic-sized pool. The houses are well equipped with everything from kitchens to VCRs. Three restaurants, two mediocre, including the hilltop Castillo de Las Nubes, and one good (serving *paladar*-style food). An hour's drive from Havana, Soroa is a pleasant daytime excursion (there are lockers for changing clothes). $

Viñales

Hotel Horizontes La Ermita
Carretera Viñales, Km 2.
Tel: 82-93204, 33-4238.
Just above the town of Viñales, nicely situated at the edge of the valley. La Ermita is a modern hotel in Spanish colonial design, with 62 rooms ranged around a swimming pool. Decent restaurant, bar, snack bar and recreation hall. Balcony rooms are the nicest, but there are great views from almost all rooms, especially at dawn and sunset. $

Hotel Horizontes Los Jasmines
Carretera Viñales, Km 25.
Tel: 82-33404, 82-93205/6.
Fax: 335042.
A handsome, pre-revolutionary colonial style hotel in a magnificent setting at the top of a hill above the town, with the Viñales valley unfolding beneath. Vine-draped gardens, large deep swimming pool and periodic poolside cabaret, children's playground and recreation hall. There are rooms in the main building and also in the annexe – most with balconies offering gorgeous views. Horseback riding and other excursions available. $

Hotel Horizontes San Vincente
Carreterra Esperanza Km 38.
Tel: 82-93201.
Fax: 33-5042.
This recently renovated hotel, 4 miles (7 km) north of Viñales, has 29 rooms and 34 cabins in a pleasant landscape. Spa treatments available, but no sweeping views. Restaurant, cafeteria, bars, table games, video room. $

MATANZAS PROVINCE

Cárdenas

Hotel Dominica
On Avenida Céspedes, near the statue of Christopher Columbus.
Tel: 521502.
A basic ex-peso hotel. $

Jagüey Grande

Bohío de Don Pedro
A small family hotel which has big log cabins with palm-thatched roofs and an excellent family-run restaurant. Just down the road the state-run restaurant is also good, serving *criollo* food. $

Matanzas

Canimao Hotel
Carretera de Varadero Km 3.5, east of the town.
Tel: 61-1014.
Located on a picturesque bend of the Canímar river, with rooms gathered around a swimming pool. Spacious lobby, with bar, comfy chairs and birds in cages. Comfortable rooms, hot water but normally no water at night. Two restaurants, poolside bar, evening entertainment ranging from salsa lessons to Mr Canimao contests. $

Hotel Louvre
Parque Libertad.
A crumbling old colonial mansion in the main square, which has still yet to be modernized for foreign tourism. Instead of great comfort, you can expect bags of atmosphere in the airy, antique-furnished rooms. $

Price Guide

The following price categories indicate the cost of a double room in high season:
$$$$: Very expensive: $150–250.
$$$: Expensive: $90–150.
$$: Moderate: $50–90.
$: Inexpensive: under $50.

ZAPATA PENINSULA

Boca de Guamá

Villa Guamá
Reached by boat from Boca de Guamá.
Tel: 59-7125, 59-2979.
Mosquitoes are a big problem and the disco is very noisy, but when the last tourist leaves it becomes a

place of peace and loveliness here. It is a replica of a pre-Columbian Indian village, with thatched-roof *bohíos* built on wooden bridges over a lake to lodge guests. Cabins have modern amenities and the facility has restaurants and a pool.

You can watch flocks of wild parrots descend to feed on the nectar of the bottlebrush trees. The village was Fidel Castro's original idea and he was once a regular visitor. Staff say that he always used to sleep in cabin #33. $

Playa Larga

Villa Playa Larga
Tel: 59-7224/5.
An unenthralling tourist facility with large but basic cabins, by a small beach on the eastern edge of the village. It is popular with locals during the hot summer months. The restaurant has a very limited menu and there is little to do, though well placed for exploring the Zapata Peninsula. $

Playa Girón

The beach and the facilities here are much better than at Playa Larga. There is a scuba center, which offers initiation dives. The diving is superb, with sponges and red coral.

Villa Horizontes Playa Girón
Tel: 59-4118, 4110, 4195.
A beach resort with 200 rooms in ugly concrete cabins and a couple of equally unprepossessing blocks, known as "motels." There's a pool, and a bar and restaurant offering the usual fare. $

VARADERO

With over 15,000 rooms and more on the way, there is no shortage of accommodation in Varadero: ranging from budget hotels, like the attractive colonial Hotel Pullman, to the luxurious Melía Las Américas, with its fabulous pool and own private beach, and resorts like Club Med Varadero. At the top end of the range, there is little to choose between the accommodation.

There are several self-catering apartments, but few places to shop for food. It is illegal for Cubans to rent space in their homes to foreigners in Varadero. A few still do at the risk of heavy fines, or even losing their house.There are also campsites.

It is easy to find your way around Varadero, occupying the thin Hicacos Peninsula. Most of the expensive hotels are at the eastern end of town, along Avenida Las Américas, which branches off Avenida 1era, east of downtown.

Very Expensive

Arenas Doradas
Avenida Las Américas.
Tel: 66-7810, 66-8150-6.
Fax: 66-8159.
A recently completed 316-room, two-story resort hotel, east of the Sol Palmeras.

Club Varadero
Avenida Las Américas, Km 3.
Tel: 66-7030/1.
Fax: 66-7205.
A rather pretentious, all-inclusive resort, with 100 rooms and 170 suites. Beautiful gardens, and facilities include a gym, aerobics classes, watersports and a complete scuba program. Not for families.

Meliá Las Américas
Tel: 66-7600.
Fax: 66-7625.
Not far from the Du Pont mansion (Xanadú). Has a fabulous lobby with art, palms and colored glass, pleasant sun deck and its own private beach. With 225 rooms, and 25 suites.

Meliá Varadero
Tel: 66-7013/3.
Fax: 66-7012.
Another Spanish-run hotel in the Meliá chain, with a spectacular 7-story spiraling atrium with parrots and trailing vines, and even glass elevators. Has an impressive 483 rooms and 7 suites, all with balconies.

Life in Varadero

Varadero has changed a lot since its first inception as an international tourist mecca in the early 1990s. Several major crackdowns on the huge numbers of prostitutes and hustlers gathering at the resort culminated in 1996 in street battles between the *jineteros* and police. Strict new laws were introduced as a result.

There are now two government-controlled checkpoints along the road to the Varadero peninsula. Foreign visitors must pay $1 on entry and departure, while Cubans are asked to show their identity cards. If they are not natives of Varadero, and they can show no official proof of needing to travel there, they will not be allowed to proceed.

Natives of the town now charge hundreds (or even thousands, apparently) of dollars to Cubans who want to marry them in order to get a Varadero identity card. While the policy has got rid of most of the prostitutes and *jineteros*, it has damaged the town's atmosphere: the streets at night are often empty and dark. Hotel managers reportedly pay their Cuban staff dollar bonuses to stay late and dance in the discos – to try to give the place some life.

However, if all you are looking for is a straightforward beach vacation, with minimal contact with *jineteros* and prostitutes (and any other Cubans, for that matter), in a good modern hotel with cable TV, a pool, and a jacuzzi, then Varadero is the place for you. The beach is beautiful, with miles of white sands and warm, shallow crystal blue sea – and it is one of the few places in Cuba where women can sunbathe topless. Despite the very open sexuality of Cuba, topless bathing is illegal – but tolerated in tourist ghettoes like Varadero.

Expensive

Barlovento Iberostar Gran Caribe
Avenida de la Playa between Calles 13 and 14.
Tel: 667140.
Fax: 667218.
Located on the seaside promenade in downtown Varadero, the Barlovento has 171 attractive rooms and a large pool, and does a great breakfast (complete with hot croissants). Convenient for downtown restaurants, cafés and shops.

LTI Bella Costa Cubanacán
Avenida Las Américas.
Tel: 66-7210.
Fax 66-7205.
Now one of the older joint-venture hotels in Varadero, but still the height of luxury, complete with a presidential suite. Vast, six-story complex, with 330 rooms. Shares sports facilities with the Tuxpán next door, run by the same German hotel group, LTI.

Club Med Varadero
Avenida Las Américas Km 3.
Tel: 66-8288.
Fax: 66-8340.
Predictable all-inclusive resort, with well-guarded entrances and a no-kids-please policy.

Cuatro Palmas Gran Caribe
1er Avenida and Calle 61.
Tel: 667040.
Fax: 667583.
The complex, managed by Oasis International Hotels, consists of a hotel on the beach side of 1era Avenida, and villas across the road. The villas provide less expensive accommodation. Both are designed with Spanish-type arcades and galleries that offset the blight of the Atabey and Siboney hotels up the hill.

Resort Internacional Gran Caribe
Avenida Las Americas.
Tel: 66-7038/9.
Fax 66-7246.
A classic luxury hotel built in the 1950s, as the splendid entrance, elegant lobby and spacious rooms verify.

Offers all the conveniences and a little nostalgia. Check out the top-floor open-air ballroom and the nine-hole golf course.

Sol Club Las Sirenas Hotel
Avenida Las Américas.
Tel: 66-8070.
Fax: 66-8075.
Spanish-run, all-inclusive upscale resort, west of the Bella Costa.

Sol Palmeras Sol Meliá
Autopista del Sur.
Tel: 667009.
Slightly less expensive than the Melía Vardero next door, Sol Palmeras is run by the same chain and was Varadero's first venture with Spanish investors, dating from 1990. There's a touch of the jungle, complete with tropical birds, in the lobby, and a thatched bar on an island in the middle of the swimming pool. This is Cuba's largest hotel, with 375 rooms, 32 suites, and 200 bungalows.

Hotel Tryp Paradiso Puntarenas
Reparto Kawama.
Tel: 66-7120/29.
At the "unfashionable" western end of the beach. Twin hotels built in the early 1990s are operated as a joint resort complex with a total of 518 rooms on the upper seven floors, above the recreational and service facilities. The complex is managed by Tryp Hotels of Spain. There are swimming pools, and an enormous sun deck.

Hotel Tuxpán
Avenida Las Américas.
Tel: 66-7560.
Fax: 66-7561.
LTI's first hotel in Varadero boasts the highest room occupancy in the country. With 235 rooms, attractive Mexican decor (design is based on Mayan pyramids) and an informal atmosphere, the hotel is known for its fitness facilities: it has an enormous swimming pool, massage and gym, and what is claimed to be the biggest jacuzzi in the Americas – in addition, of course, to the beach. The bars, restaurants and outdoor grill offer good food and service.

Villa Cuba Resort
Avenida 1ra and Calle C.
Tel: 61-2975, 61-2952.
Fax: 66-7207.
Tourists now rent rooms in the residences where wealthy Cubans summered in pre-revolutionary days. Not all rooms have private baths. Conveniently located, on the eastern fringe of downtown.

Price Guide

The following price categories indicate the cost of a double room in high season:
$$$$: Very expensive: $150–250.
$$$: Expensive: $90–150.
$$: Moderate: $50–90.
$: Inexpensive: under $50.

Moderate

Caleta
1era Avenida, between 17 and 18.
Tel: 66-7080.
Fax 66-7018.
Gaviota's downtown villa is small, consisting of 30 rooms overlooking a pool, and a cluster of five bungalows. Secluded but lively.

Los Delfines Horizontes
Avenida de la Playa and 39.
Tel: 66-7720.
Fax: 66-7737.
Small resort, with under 50 rooms, right on the beach in downtown Varadero.

Hotel Gaviota
Avenida 1 between Calles G and J, Reparto La Torre.
Tel: 66-7280/4, 66-7012/3.
Fax: 66-7194, 66-7018.
Consists of three beachfront hotels, the Caracol, the Caribe and the Cascada, all run by Gaviota. Contain a total of 228 rooms, surrounded by gardens and mangroves. Adults' and children's pools, recreational facilities, conference room, unisex beauty parlor, art gallery.

Kawama Punta Blanca
Calle 0, Reparto Kawama.
Tel: 66-7155/6.
Fax: 66-7254.
This older bungalow facility has doubled its room capacity to 207 and expanded its recreational facilities, but services are somewhat lethargic. Located in the western part of town.

Mar del Sur Aparthotel
Avenida 3ra, corner of 30.
Tel: 61-2246, 66-7481/2.
Fax: 66-7482.

Comfortable accommodation in a series of blocks, with a good-sized swimming pool to make up for the location – three blocks from the beach.

Hotel Oasis
Western tip of Hicacos Peninsula.
Tel: 66-7380.
Fax: 66-7004.
Not a convenient location, about 2 miles (4 km) from downtown Varadero, and the beach is not great. Ideal if you're desperate.

Inexpensive

Hotel Acuazul
Avenida 1era and Calle 13.
Tel: 66-7132.
Fax: 66-7229.
Located a couple of blocks from the beach. Has a pool, bar and disco.

Hotel Bellamar
Calle 17 between 1ra and 3ra Avenidas.
Tel: 61-3014, 66-7490.
Fax: 66-7247, 66-7733.
A downtown highrise with 145 two-bedroom apartments and 290 double rooms. Two blocks in from the beach and surrounded by other buildings, there is not much to recommend it other than the view from the top-floor bar and the excellent breakfast. Nice pool, lively, and the outdoor grill restaurant serves decent food.

Villa Caribe Horizontes
Avenida de la Playa and Calle 30.
Tel: 61-3310, 61-3397.
A 124-room complex of villas with a pool, beach bar, game room, moped and bicycle rentals. Located next to the beach, in downtown.

Club Herradura Horizontes
Avenida de la Playa between Calles 35 and 36.
Tel: 61-3725.
An apartment-hotel that curves around the sea like a horseshoe. It has 33 apartments with living room, dining room and fully equipped kitchen (there is a food market off the lobby).

Not as good as it sounds: rentals are by bedroom and tenants share the other apartment facilities, which can be uncomfortable or miserable. Rooms have fridges, but only some have TVs.

Hotel Dos Mares
Corner of Calle 53 and 1era Avenida.
Tel: 61-2702.
A comparatively old and pleasant building in downtown Varadero, one block from the beach. It has just 36 rooms, with two suites for families with children. It has a seafood restaurant and a solarium. Room rates a little over the odds probably because the Dos Mares is not the usual Varadero hotel.

Hotel Pullman
1era Avenida between 49 and 50.
Tel: 61-2575.
Fax: 66-7495.
An older establishment that still feels like a real hotel, with a handsome lobby, and cosy dining room and bar. There are just 15 rooms so book well ahead.

Villa Sotavento
Avenida de la Playa between Calles 12 and 13.
Tel: 66-7133/4.
Fax: 66-7229.
A complex of villas, with 255 air-conditioned rooms. Private bathroom but other facilities are generally shared. Accommodation basic but the beach is very close.

Villa Tortuga
Calle 7 between Avenida 1era and Camino del Mar.
Tel: 61-2622, 66-2243.
A pleasant complex of scattered villas, with 139 rooms (no TV or telephone), close to the beach. Tennis court, bicycles, mopeds and cars for rent.

Aparthotel Varazul
1era Avenida between 14 and 15.
Tel: 66-7132.
Fax 66-7229.
Located downtown, one block from the beach. Apartments have one or two bedrooms, living room and kitchen (food market in basement). Guests at the Varazul share the reception and facilities of the nearby Hotel Acuazul.

VILLA CLARA PROVINCE

Corallilo

Horizontes Elguea Hotel and Spa
Circuito Norte, Corallilo.
Tel: 66-8020.
Somewhat run-down, but under-going renovation. Has 139 air-conditioned rooms with bath, TV, telephone and refrigerator. $

Embalse Hanabanilla

Hanabanilla Hotel
Southwest of Manicaragua.
Tel: 8-6932, 4-9125.
A concrete Soviet creation, but has a breathtaking setting on Lake Hanabanilla, at the end of a 5-mile (8-km) hill, in the Escambray mountains south of Santa Clara. The lake is stocked with large-mouth bass and the hotel has its own dock and boats. There are 127 comfortable rooms, a disco, well-stocked games room, 24-hour bar, and lovely big pool. The restaurant specializes in lake-caught fish and will gladly serve up your own catch. Good base for hiking, boating and horseback riding, and there are waterfalls and caves nearby. $

Remedios

Hotel Mascotte
Parque Martí.
Tel: 39-5481.
Wonderful 19th-century mansion offering no-frills accommodation and food, but bags of nostalgia. $

San José del Lago

Motel San José
A spa resort, located 37 miles (60 km) east of Caibarién, along route 123. The motel is meant for Cubans, but if you are in the area and need a place to sleep you may be allowed to stay if there is room. $

Santa Clara

Hotel Santa Clara Libre
Parque Vidal 6.
Tel: 66-8007.
Fax: 66-2771.
Fairly basic accommodation: the 159 rooms have a shower and radio, but not all come with air-conditioning. Nice location on the main square, but it is not always easy to park nearby. There are good views from the top-floor restaurant, which also serves a decent breakfast. The hotel was home to Che Guevara and many of his men after the battle of Santa Clara; its façade is still pock-marked by shells fired during the 1958 battle. $

Hotel Horizontes Los Caneyes
Circunvalación and Eucalyptus.
Tel: 422-4512, 422-4212.
Fax: 33-5009.
On the main *autopista* a mile or so west of town, this motel was designed to resemble an Indian settlement. Whether it does or not, the conical thatched-roof huts contain very comfortable, spacious rooms, with hot water, TV, refrigerators and air-conditioning.

The garden setting is delightful. The pool provides the focus, with a bar, disco, and an excellent restaurant overlooking it.

There is also a hairdresser and a few shops. There are buses and taxis into town. Excellent value. $

Hotel La Granjita
On Carretera Maleza, Km 2.5.
Tel: 422-26051, 26052, 26059.
Cubanacán's villa in the northeastern outskirts of Santa Clara has 34 thatched cabins in a garden setting, with bars and a pool with kiddy area. $

SANCTI SPÍRITUS PROVINCE

Presa Zaza

Hotel Horizontes Zaza
At Finca San José, Km 5, Carretera Central.
Tel 66-8001.
The usual concrete monstrosity with air-conditioned rooms, all with TV and shower. $

Sancti Spíritus

Hotel Colonial
Maximo Gómez Norte 23.
Tel: 2-5123.
Central location, 20 rooms. $

Perla del Sur
Parque Serafín Sánchez.
Simple rooms in a lovely, refurbished colonial mansion. $

Hotel Plaza
Parque Serafín Sánchez.
Tel: 41-2 6940, 7102.
Basic, Islazul-run accommodation, overlooking the main square. $

Villa Rancho Hatuey Cubanacán
Carretera Central Km 383.
Tel: 66-8000.
A modern complex on a hill north of town. Rooms, cabins, and self-catering apartments around a pool and sun deck. All rooms have TV, air-conditioning, bath. $$

Hotel Las Villas
Bartolomé Maso 13.
Tel: 2-3958.
Located next to the Sancti Spíritus bus terminal, this is a peso hotel, but will normally take foreign tourists too. $

Topes de Collantes

At present, only three of the resort's hotels accept foreigners.

Kurhotel Topes de Collantes
Tel: 42-4 0288, 4 0304.
Fax: 33-2780.
This 210-room sanitarium is gigantic and monstrous outside, but pleasant inside with plant-lined passages and columned airy lobby. The light rooms have bath and satellite TV. $

Price Guide

The following price categories indicate the cost of a double room in high season:
$$$$: Very expensive: $150–250.
$$$: Expensive: $90–150.
$$: Moderate: $50–90.
$: Inexpensive: under $50.

Hotel Los Helechos
Tel: 42-41180–9, 40227.
Fax: 40288.
Less well appointed than the Kurhotel, but more pleasant. Has 48 rooms, a gym, and thermal swimming pool. $

Motel Los Pinos
Tel: 42-4 0117, 4 0330.
Generally open to Cubans only (you will normally be told to try the other hotels), but Los Pinos serves decent meals and cocktails.

CIENFUEGOS

There is only one dollar hotel in Cienfuegos, the Hotel Jagua. There are a handful of peso hotels, but they are always reluctant to take foreign tourists. You could try the **Ciervo de Oro**, on Calle 29 between Avenidas 56 and 58 or the **Perla del Sur** on Calle 37 at Avenida 62.

If you don't fancy the Jagua, you'll be left with the clutch of hotels across the bay, south of town.

Hotel Faro Luna
Tel: 61162/5/8.
Fax: 35059.
A Cubanacán motel by a rocky beach across the bay. It has 14 terraced rooms, a pool, shop, taxis, plus a baby-sitting service. $

Hotel Jagua
Calle 37 between 0 and 1a, Punta Gorda.
Tel: 24-5011, 432-3021–6.
The only dollar hotel in downtown Cienfuegos – though, in fact, it is 2 miles (3 km) south of the heart of the city. It was once a notorious casino hotel run by Batista's brother. The 145 large, airy rooms have air-conditioning, TV and good bathrooms. There's a large pool, and also a tacky cabaret show if you feel so inclined. $$

Hotel Pascaballo Islazul
Carretera Rancho Luna, Km 22.
Tel: 9 6212, 9 6280.
The bluff at the mouth of the harbor, opposite the Jagua fortress, deserves better than this rather ugly concrete block, whose 180 rooms actually face away from the bay. Facilities include a cafeteria, bar, salt-water pool, medical post and shop, but no beach. The hotel is popular with Cubans in summer, and the disco draws crowds from Cienfuegos at weekends.

The hotel is 15 miles (25 km) southeast of Cienfuegos. There is a ferry from the harbor downtown, and the hotel has its own boats. Otherwise the most reliable transport into town is by taxi. $

Rancho Luna Hotel
Carretera Rancho Luna, Km 15.
Tel: 24 5057.
Set on its own small beach 10 miles (16 km) southeast of Cienfuegos, Rancho Luna has motel-type cabins with a total of 255 rooms. There is a large pool and sun deck, and it looks out on to a small beach with shallow water. There is a choice of restaurants, cafeteria, bar, medical post and shop. The keep-fit classes are optional. Rancho Luna runs the rental car agency for Cienfuegos. $

TRINIDAD

There are plenty of excellent **casa particulares** in Trinidad. One that is often recommended is the **Casa Colonial Muñoz** (*see page 334*), but there are many more. Ask around in Parques Martí and Céspedes.

Hotel La Ronda
Calle Martí #238 (Parque Central).
Tel: 419-9 2248.
Colonial peso hotel offering cheap, basic rooms. $

Motel Las Cuevas
Finca Santa Ana.
Tel: 419 9 2340.
Fax 2302.
A Horizontes-run hotel, in a lovely spot overlooking the town. Individual, simple but clean cabins, with private bath, phones and radios. There is a swimming pool and bar, and a disco/nightclub with live entertainment most nights in a nearby cave – hence the hotel's name. $

Playa Ancòn

Hotel Ancón Gran Caribe
Tel: 419-9 4011, 419-9 3155, 66-7424.
Fax: 66-7424.
Identical in design to – but much better than – the Pasacaballos in Cienfuegos. The four-star Ancón has been renovated, and now boasts an annexe with more comfortable rooms than in the main block. There are excellent recreational facilities (including bikes for hire), but best of all is the beautiful beach alongside. It has a pleasant swimming pool, games room, cabaret and no less than seven bars. Rooms are air-conditioned with bath and radio. $$

The Hotel Costa Sur
Tel: 419-3810, 3419, 4010, 6100
The three-star, Horizontes-run Costa Sur is smaller and cheaper than the Ancón, but has its own private beach and offers scuba diving. There is a swimming pool and rifle range. Air-conditioned rooms and cabins with bath and radio. $

CIEGO DE AVILA PROVINCE

Cayo Coco

Hotel Tryp Cayo Coco
Tel: 33-5388.
Fax: 33-5166.
Modeled as a simulated colonial township, this large 458-room complex is just a hundred yards in from a glorious, white-sand beach.

At the center is the airy Town Hall, with a colonnaded portico, tiled floors and a central patio where the (sporadically) computerized reception facilities are located. Accommodation is in terracotta tile-roofed buildings of two or three stories, and named for the flower planted in front of each one: such as *azucenas* (madonna lilies) *mariposas* (butterfly jasmine), *claveles* (pinks), and so on. The hotel is geared to the mass tourism market, but sadly is not geared *up* for it – especially at busy times, when the facilities do not match the demand. Trips offered by catamaran to outlying islands are not always well organized.

Italian, continental, seafood, buffet, barbecue and *criollo* specialties are served in six pleasantly designed restaurants. There are facilities for all the usual water sports. $$$$

Cayo Guillermo

Villa Cojímar
Tel: 30-1012
Fax: 33-5554.
A lovely Italian-run, 200-room hotel, consisting of attractive bungalows set among lawns and gardens, with mainly Italian guests. Lovely beach and excellent diving. $$$

Villa Vigía
Tel: 301760, 301748.
The latest hotel to appear on the island. Not dissimilar to the Cojímar, catering mostly to Canadians. All-inclusive. $$$

Ciego de Avila

Hotel Ciego de Avila
Carretera de Ceballos, Km 2.5.
Tel: 33-28013, 28440.
The usual Soviet-designed monolith, but with 136 good rooms and a pool. Three stars, located 2 miles (3 km) north of the center. $

Hotel Santiago-Habana
Independencia and Honorato del Castillo.
Tel: 33-2 5301, 2 5305, 2 5703.
A former peso hotel in the center of town, but overpriced given the facilities. $

Morón

Hotel Morón
Avenida de Tarafa.
Tel: 5-3901/2/3/4.
The hotel is run by Cubanacán as a tourism training school. Service is sometimes haphazard but usually enthusiastic. There are 136 rooms and a handful of cabins, plus, of course, a pool $$

CAMAGÜEY PROVINCE

Camagüey

Hotel Camagüey
Carretera Central Km 4.5.
Tel: 322-72015.
Fax: 33 5699.
Inconveniently located 2 miles (4 km) southeast of the city center, this usual Soviet-designed concrete block has 136 good rooms with cable TV. There are also six cabins. The swimming pool is splendid, the food less so. Rental cars also available. $

Hotel Colón
Avenida República 472.
Tel: 322-83346, 83368.
A small but elegant colonial hotel in downtown Camagüey, with a lovely columned lobby, old, wood-topped bar and a stained-glass window picturing Christopher Columbus landing in Cuba. Rooms are simple but they have TV and air-conditioning. $

Gran Hotel
Calle Maceo 67.
Tel: 322-92093/4.
A restored hotel right in the heart of Camagüey. The elegant Salon Caribe restaurant on the fifth floor offers the best views in town. $

Hotel Isla de Cuba
Oscar Primelles and Popular.
Tel: 322-91515, 92248.
Basic. $

Villa Maraguán
Camino de Guanabaquilla, Circunvalante Norte.
Tel: 7-2017.
Cubanacán's villa, off the Carretera Central 3 miles (5 km) from downtown, near the airport. This

former country club has 32 comfortable rooms and three suites. There's a pool, abundant vegetation, a games room, and rental cars available. $$

Hotel Plaza
Van Horne 1.
Tel: 322-8 2413, 8 2445.
By the railway station, this is a large and atmospheric old hotel, but it can't compete with the other hotels downtown. Rooms are simple and, if you face the station, noisy. $

Hotel Puerto Principe
Avenida de los Mártires 60.
Tel: 82403.
Useful as a last resort. $

Florida

Florida
Carretera Central Km 536.
Tel: 5-3011.
Located 30 miles (48 km) northwest of Camagüey. Convenient if you want somewhere to stay late at night, and don't have the energy to continue to Camagüey itself. It has 74 rooms, and surprisingly can normally offer better food than the Hotel Camagüey. $

Santa Lucía

This resort is so small that it's not hard to find any of the following places. They are all located right on the beach.

Cuatro Vientos
Tel: 32-36493.
Fax: 32-335433.
A Cayo Coco style, low-level development, generally more pleasant than the other Santa Lucía resorts. Spanish-run, with 214 rooms. Full-board arrangements are offered. Transautos car rental desk. $$–$$

Golden Tulip Villa Coral
Tel: 32-36429, 36265.
Fax: 32-365153.
Efficient, Dutch-run beach villa with 246 rooms and 40 suites. Good food. $$–$$$

Golden Tulip Caracol
Tel: 32-36402/3.
Fax: 32-365153.
Offers similar facilities to the Coral. There are 150 rooms and four suites, and good recreational facilities – including fitness and dance classes. $$–$$$

Hotel Mayanabo
Tel: 32-36184/5.
All-inclusive hotel with 213 rooms and 12 suites contained in two blocks between pool and beach. Poolside snack bar, grill and open-air cabaret. Games room, shops and so on in street-side block. $$$

Villa Tararaco
Tel: 32-36222.
At the far end of the hotel strip, close to the public beach. Used to be dismal, but has improved since refurbishment. There are 55 rooms, 1 suite, with large games area downstairs. Still, aimed at the lower end of the market. $$

LAS TUNAS PROVINCE

Las Tunas

Hotel Las Tunas
Avenida 2 de Diciembre.
Tel: 31-4 5014, 4 3893, 33 5301.
Standard, Soviet-style hotel outside the center, but in need of renovation. Cold water only on a recent visit. $

HOLGUÍN PROVINCE

Holguín City

Motel El Bosque
Ave XX Aniversario, Reparto Pedro Díaz Coello.
Tel: 24-481012.
Fax: 24-481140.
Lodgings in 67 cabins in pleasant, leafy grounds, but otherwise nothing special, and there have been reports of theft from rooms. $

Villa El Cocal
Carretera Central, 6 miles (10 km) south of the city.
Tel: 24-461902.
Close to Holguín airport, this is a pleasant villa in lovely gardens hung with bougainvillea. Accommodation consists of 20 reasonable doubles and 20 triples in cabins. $$

Motel Mirador de Mayabe
Loma de Mayabe.
Tel: 24-423485, 422160.
Fax: 425347.
Cuban honeymooners often stay at this attractive, Islazul-run villa, in a rather isolated spot 6 miles (10 km) southeast of Holguín. Accommodation is in cabins scattered among trees. There is a splendid view of the valley from the terrace pool and rustic restaurant. $

Hotel Pernik
Avenida XX Aniversario and Plaza de la Revolución, Reparto Nuevo.
Tel: 24-481011, 481081.
Fax: 33-5301.
With 200 rooms, a good restaurant, large pool and even larger lobby, the four-star Pernik is the biggest and best place to stay in Holguín. There is a car rental desk. $

Sierra Cristal

Villa Pinares de Mayarí
20 miles (32 km) south of Mayarí.
Tel: 24-4007/8.
Health tourism villa, run by Cubanacán, between Holguín and Moa. Offers anti-stress treatment with massages and aerobics, and a steam room. Pleasant cabins, or rooms in the main building. There are many sporting facilities including horseback riding. $$

Guardalavaca

As in Santa Lucía, the hotels in Guardalavaca are all strung out in a line along the beach. You won't have any trouble finding them.

There are also a couple of hotels by Playa Estero Ciego, 4 miles (6 km) southwest of Guardalavaca, where the beach and surroundings are arguably better than in the main resort.

For greater isolation, try the Villa Don Lino, near Rafael Freyre.

Hotel Atlántico
Tel: 24-30180/1.
Fax: 30200.
Cubanacán-run resort in the center of Guardalavaca, with 136 rooms and 36 *cabañas* right on beach. Complete with diving center. $$

Las Brisas Club resort
Tel: 33-6336 (book through Havana).
Managed by the Canadian hotel chain, Delta. Probaby the best of Guardalavaca's resorts, with 230 rooms, good facilities, including watersports center, pool, disco, tennis courts, bikes for hire, and several restaurants and bars. $$$

Hotel Guardalavaca
Tel: 24-30180/1.
Fax: 30265.
Confusingly, Hotel Guardalavaca consists of a moderately priced conventional hotel (with 225 rooms)

and a clutch of budget *cabañas* down the road. $/$$

Villa Don Lino
5 miles (8 km) north of Rafael Freyre and about 15 miles (24 km) west of Guardalavaca.
Tel: 24-4977.
Simple cabins overlooking a small beach, with another beach – Playa Blanca – nearby. There's also a saltwater pool. Fine for a spot of isolation. $

Rio de Luna Resort
Playa Estero Ciego.
Tel: 24-30030/34.
Fax: 33-5571; 30035.
A medium-sized hotel with good facilities, particularly for watersports.
The adjacent Río de Mares Resort offers similar fare, and also has a diving center. $$

Villa Turey
Tel: 335301.
Good-value Cubanacán resort hotel, offering accommodation in small villas. $$

Cayo Saetía

Villa Cayo Saetia
Tel: 425350.
A hunting lodge, filled with trophy heads and skins. $$$

Gibara

This maritime city of colonial charm and good seafood has only peso hotels. The **Bellomar**, on Calle General Sartorio, normally takes tourists for dollars, while the **Gibara Hotel** and the **Río Luna** are generallly reluctant.

GRANMA PROVINCE

Bayamo

Villa Bayamo
Carretera de Manzanillo.
Tel: 23-42 3102.
A good choice if you don't mind being slightly out of town. This attractive hotel, in a former holiday center for the military, has a garden and a nice pool. $

Hotel Royalton
Parque Céspedes.
Recently renovated but still simple. Good location, though, in the heart of town. $

Price Guide

The following price categories indicate the cost of a double room in high season:
$$$$: Very expensive: $150–250.
$$$: Expensive: $90–150.
$$: Moderate: $50–90.
$: Inexpensive: under $50.

Sierra Maestra
Avenida General Manuel Cedeño.
Tel: 23-48 1013.
A mile or so northeast of town on the Carretera Central, this is in the tradition of all the other faceless concrete hotels in Cuba – bad service and so-so rooms. There are 200 rooms, a reasonable restaurant, a large pool and other amenities. $/$$

Hotel Telégrafo
Saco 108.
Tel: 42-5510.
Rather seedy old hotel, but cheap. $

Manzanillo

Most people stay in the Hotel Guacanayabo, but more interesting (if also more basic) options are the **Hotel Paris** and the **Hotel Venus**, on Avenida Valuendos, in the heart of the town near the main square. Both are former peso hotels.

Guacanayabo
Avenida Camilo Cienfuegos, southwest of the town center.
Tel: 23-5 3590, 5 4012.
Yet another Soviet-inspired concrete nightmare, with 112 rooms, but at least has a spectacular hilltop view of the fishing port. $

Marea del Portillo

A black-sand beach on the south coast, with two hotels catering for package holiday-makers. All-inclusive deals, with facilities for horseback riding and hiking in the mountains, diving, sport-fishing, boat trips, etc. Cars and mopeds can be rented and there is plenty of evening entertainment.

Hotel Farallon del Caribe
Tel: 23-59 4032.
This excellent 140-room resort hotel, owned by Cubanacán, is popular with Canadian tourists. Lovely views of the mountains. All-inclusive. $$

Hotel Marea del Portillo
Tel: 23-59 4201-3.
Fax: 59 4 134.
A low-key 70-room beach facility built in the 1980s, with bungalows added more recently. All meals provided. $$

Pilón

Other places to stay along the scenic southern coast route are a couple of hotels in the vicinity of Pilón. Neither is designed for a long stay, though.

Villa Punta Piedra
Tel: 23-59 4421.
A 12-room Cubanacán villa by a small beach 6 miles (10 km) east of Pilón. Has its own pool. $

Motel el Mirador
Tel: 23-59 4365.
Simple thatched cabins. $

SANTIAGO DE CUBA PROVINCE

Parque Baconao

This park east of Santiago is dotted with beach resorts of varying design and size, most constructed using on site rocks and sand. Many of those geared to Cubans are strictly no-frills, while those for foreign tourism all have air-conditioned rooms with private baths, restaurants and swimming pools. Most operate for inclusive package programs.

Balneario del Sol Club Resort
Playa Larga, Carretera de Baconao km 44.
Tel: 0226-86209.
Run by Canadian company, Delta, this resort has 125 rooms, with balconies and ocean views. The sea is rough here, crashing against the rocks, but there is a man-made seawater lagoon by the hotel to swim in as well as a pool. Scuba diving and plenty of activities. Bike, moped and car rental available. $$

Hotel Club Amigo Bucanero
Arroyo de la Costa, Carretera de Baconao Km 4.
Tel: 22-5 224, 9 1484.
Fabulous 200-room, all-inclusive

resort, with three swimming pools across a coral terrace above the sea. Set on a rocky beach promontory with no sand, but the lovely, sandy Arroyo de la Costa beach is nearby. Activities center around the swimming pool. Restaurants, bars, watersports, excursions available. Caters mostly to Germans and Canadians. $$$

Los Corales
Playa Cazonal, Carretera Baconao Km 54.
Tel: 226-27191.
Fax: 335429.
This, and the nearby (but inferior Carisol) are run as joint ventures with the German company, LTI. It is used primarily by German and Canadian tour operators, but Los Corales does not impose all-inclusive deals. There are 100 rooms in pleasant, leafy surroundings, close to one of Parque Baconao's best beaches, though the water is shallow. There is also a pool. $$

Hotel Daiquirí
Daiquirí, Carretera de Baconao Km 25.
Tel: 226-86177, 24849, 24735.
Run-down and probably due for a facelift, rather dismal out of the peak season. Has 94 rooms, 62 cabins. good sporting facilities, two pools on a plateau near a very pleasant, palm-fringed beach. $$

Chivirico

A village on the lovely coastal route running west from Santiago de Cuba. A pair of comparatively new resorts in the vicinity are a good place to get away from it all.

Hotel Los Galeones
Chivirico.
Tel: 022-29110, 26160.
Small, all-inclusive hilltop villa overlooking Chivirico village and the sea, with a small beach below. Just 34 rooms. It takes scuba groups for organized dives, and others if there's room. $$$

Hotel Sierra Mar
Playa Sevilla, 40 miles (65 km) west of Santiago de Cuba.
Tel: 022-29010, 29007.
Inaugurated in 1994 by Fidel Castro himself, this four-star Delta resort is located on a lovely (but man-made) sandy beach at the foot of the Sierra Maestra mountains. It consists of single-story buildings that barely rise above the dunes, a hotel and bungalows of various sizes: 200 rooms in total. Multiple eateries, a fitness center, a shopping mall, a fresh-water pool, an art gallery, games room, video room, disco and cabaret cover most needs on the spot; the hotel also has a regular minibus service. $$$

Price Guide

The following price categories indicate the cost of a double room in high season:
$$$$: Very expensive: $150–250.
$$$: Expensive: $90–150.
$$: Moderate: $50–90.
$: Inexpensive: under $50.

Gran Piedra

Villa La Gran Piedra
Tel: 226-5 1154, 51205.
An "eco-lodge" with comfortable rustic cabins along the edge of the mountain ridge. The views are wonderful. There is also a café, restaurant and souvenir shop on the road beneath the rock. $–$$

Santiago de Cuba

Hotel Las Américas
Avenida de las Américas and General Cebreco.
Tel: 226-42011, 86075.
Opposite the highrise Hotel Santiago de Cuba, Las Américas has 68 rooms. Its restaurant is mediocre and pool very small, but there's usually a pleasant, buzzing atmosphere; and the disco is at least popular. $

Balcón del Caribe
Km 7 Carretera del Morro.
Tel: 226-9 1011, 91506.
In a nice spot by the sea next to Santiago's Morro Castle, 6 miles (10 km) from the center of town. The hotel, with 72 rooms and 24 *cabañas*, is largely unmodernized but has a pleasant atmosphere. Handy for the airport, but it's also under the flight path. $

Hotel Casa Granda
Parque Céspedes.
Tel: 226-53021/2.
Overlooking the main square, this landmark hotel was once Santiago's top hotel. After years of neglect, it has finally been completely renovated, and is the only dollar hotel in the center of town. It has 55 rooms. The interior is splendidly grand, with suites decked out in golden silk. Breakfast and dinner are taken on the broad balcony. The fifth-floor bar offers fine views over downtown Santiago. $$

El Rancho
Km 45 Alturas de Quintero.
Tel: 226-33202, 33280.
Located near the university, El Rancho has 30 *cabañas* and a magnificent view from the thatched-roof restaurant. $

Villa Gaviota
Avenida Manduley 502 and Calle 19, Vista Alegre.
Tel: 226-41598, 42612, 42656.
A complex of 10 villas (30 rooms) in the quiet, leafy district of Vista Alegre, not far from Santiago and Las Américas hotels. You can rent just one bedroom or a complete house. There's a pool up the road for use by residents. $

Imperial
José Antonio Saco 361.
Tel: 8917, 8918.
A couple of blocks north of Parque Céspedes, this peso hotel has 47 basic rooms, with fans and no air-conditioning. $

Hotel Rex
Avenida Victoriano Garzón 10, just off Plaza de Marte.
Tel: 226-26314.
Recently refurbished, but still a basic, peso hotel. Tall ceilings, narrow rooms. Noisy. revolutionaries including Raul Castro slept here prior to the Moncada attack. $

Hotel Santiago de Cuba
Avenida de las Américas and M.
Tel: 226-42612, 42656, 86170, 86270.
Fax: 41756.
Spectacular red, white and blue modern building with glass-front lifts, but rather soulless inside.

270 spacious rooms and 34 suites. Popular with business visitors. $$$

Villa San Juan
Km 5 Carretera de Siboney.
Tel: 226-86602, 42478, 86070.
Fax: 226-86137.
A mile farther out than Las Américas and the Santiago, this motel is set in lush gardens on historic San Juan Hill – the scene of the final battle in the War of Independence. Pleasant rooms, good restaurant, large pool. $

GUANTÁNAMO PROVINCE

Guantánamo

Hotel Guantánamo
Calle 13 norte, between Ahogado and 1 Oeste.
Tel: 21-326015, 335011.
The standard provincial monstrosity, run by Islazul, north of downtown. Has 124 rooms, which are at least comfortable and inexpensive. $

Hotel Martí
Calle Calixto García.
A peso hotel, half a block north of the Parque Central and happy to rent rooms for dollars to tourists. $

Villa la Lupe
5km north of Guantánamo, on the road to El Salvador.
Tel: 21-326112.
Attractive cabins in a rural setting. Nice pool, noisy poolside disco. 50 well-appointed rooms. $

BARACOA

Hotel El Castillo
Off Calixto García.
Tel: 21-42103, 42125.
High on a cliff overlooking the town, this castle was built in 1770 to keep the British out, and later became a prison, then a hotel. It is hard to resist staying here: it offers the best views of the town and El Yunque mountain, has a gorgeous pool, lovely gardens and an excellent restaurant. 35 rooms. Great value. $

Villa Maguaná
30 km northwest of Baracoa.
Tel: 33-4142 (Havana).
A lonely villa with just 4 rooms by a spectacular white sand beach. The house comes with a cook and a maid. Rooms must be pre-booked through Islazul. $

Hotel Porto Santo
Carretera Aeropuerto.
Tel: 21-43578, 43590.
Fax: 226-86074.
Two miles (4 km) from town, close to the airport. Beautiful location on a terraced hill with lush foliage, winging birds and steps leading down to a small private beach across the harbor from Baracoa. 60 rooms, small but pleasant pool. $

Hotel La Rusa
Máximo Gómez 161.
Tel: 21-4 3570, 4 3011.
An aristocratic Russian who fled the revolution in her own country and lived to see another on her adopted island founded this 12-room hostelry near the waterfront. Now run by Islazul, La Rusa is popular among independent travelers. Fidel and Che once stayed here. $

ISLE OF YOUTH

Hotel Colony
Km 46 Carretera de Siguanea.
Tel: 61-98181/2.
On the southwest coast, 25 miles (40 km) from Nueva Gerona. Around 80 air-conditioned rooms, some in individual cabins. Good pool, mediocre restaurant. Facilities are good but the complex is ugly and run-down. The only reason to come to this hotel, which is miles from anywhere and surrounded by swamp and mangrove, is to dive. There is an **International Scuba Center**, and the hotel also provides diving packages. There is also an **International Marina**, which also provides deep sea fishing trips. $$

Motel Los Cordonices
Carretera a La Fe Km 4.5, 3 miles (5 km) southeast of Nueva Gerona.
Tel: 61-24 981.
Really a peso hotel intended for Cubans but accepts foreigners. There is a passable restaurant, a pool with bar and cabaret most nights. A reasonable standby if the Rancho del Tesoro (below) is full. $

Villa Gaviota
Autopista Gerona-La Fe, Km 1.5.
Tel: 61-3256, 4486.
Fax: 245425.
The best place to stay, just over a mile south of town, with pleasant, well-furnished rooms, TV air-conditioning, hot water. There is a nice pool that is popular with locals, hence noisy at weekends. $

Hotel Rancho del Tesoro Islazul
Carretera La Fe Km 1.5, on the way to the airport, less than 2 miles (3 km) south of Nueva Gerona.
Tel: 61-2 3637, 2 4069.
Has been recently refurbished and offers comfortable, if basic, accommodation in bungalows. 60 rooms. Run by Islazul. $

CAYO LARGO

All the hotels on the island flank the beach on the south side of the island. Reservations are best made as part of an inclusive package from the mainland.

Complejo Isla del Sur
Tel: 05-4 8159, 4 8111–118.
Fax: 05-4 8201, 4 8160.
A hotel complex comprising the former Villas Capricho, Iguana and Coral, with shops, restaurants, ice cream parlour. Everything from spartan cabins to very luxurious suites. $$-$$$

Villa Capricho: wood and stone thatched cabins right on the beach. Peaceful, and all cabins have terraces and hammocks, and satellite TV.

Villa Coral: has a lovely pool with a "swim up" bar. The thatched cabins are on the beach and have all facilities including satellite TV.

Villa Iguana: has bungalows and hotel rooms with all facilities.

Hotel and Villa Pelícano
Playa Lindamar.
Tel: 5-48 3336, 48165.
Fax: 48166/7.
The island's largest resort, with 324 rooms in a sprawling building or adjacent bungalows. Only "deluxe" rooms have fridges and satellite TV. Plenty of restaurants, bars, nightclubs etc.

Where to Eat

Choosing a Restaurant

While the locals are on strict rations, dollar-spending tourists have access to almost any type of foodstuff in pricey Cuban restaurants. Nevertheless, most **state-run restaurants** tend to serve bland, international fare rather than Cuban creole cuisine. Menus can seem monotonous within a short time. Fried chicken (*pollo frito*) turns up all the time, while the most common lunch snack served in dollar cafés and restaurants is the ham and cheese sandwich (*sandwich de jamón y queso*).

For an authentic Cuban meal (*see pages 120–21*), you will usually do best to eat at the private restaurants or ***paladares***, which traditionally consist of just a few tables in somebody's home (legally, they can have a maximum of just 12 covers), and have a much more congenial atmosphere than state-run restaurants. Havana obviously has the best choice, but even the smallest, most remote corners of Cuba seem to have at least one. Ask local people for advice.

Most large **hotels** have a restaurant which serves food buffet-style: you pay a fixed amount and then help yourself to as much as you want. There is often a small, à la carte restaurant too. **Breakfast** is often the best meal served in hotels: you can usually choose from a whole array of cakes, bread, meat, cheese, salad and eggs, as well as luxuries such as fresh fruit juice, cereal and yogurt.

The quality and choice of food in state-run restaurants depends on where you are in Cuba. For example, **Havana** has hundreds of restaurants in and outside the hotels, nowadays catering to most budgets. **Varadero** also has a good choice of restaurants, and the quality of the food in the large resort hotels is often excellent (but don't expect too much Cuban cuisine). Of the provincial cities, only **Cienfuegos**, **Trinidad** and **Santiago** have a reasonable range of places to eat. Beyond these centers, your choices quickly become more limited – in fact, you may well find that your hotel is the best option.

Booking

If you are planning to go to a very popular restaurant, such as the Bodeguita del Medio in Old Havana or El Tocororo in Miramar, you would do well to make a reservation at least a day ahead (the hotel tourism bureau can do this for you). On the whole, however, you don't have to worry about booking.

Prices

In expensive restaurants – such as those intended for foreign diplomats and businessmen and women in the Miramar district of Havana – a meal with wine can run to well over $50 a head, much more if you opt for lobster. At most restaurants, however, you are more likely to end up paying nearer $20 a head.

Paladares are much better value than state-run restaurants. The average price ranges from $8 to $15 a head for a full meal including beer or soft drinks.

Opening times

Most restaurants open for lunch at noon and for dinner at 7pm. Don't expect service after 10pm.

Restaurant Listings

Restaurants are listed area by area, in the same order as they appear in the Places section of the book. Only restaurants in the main cities have been included.

Havana restaurants are listed according to the type of food served, while elsewhere they are listed alphabetically.

The price categories are for a meal for one without drinks:

$$$$	Over $40
$$$	$20–40
$$	$10–20
$	Under $10

HAVANA

International Food and Seafood

La Cecilia
5ta Avenida between Calles 110 and 111, Miramar.
Tel: 22-6700.
Surrounded by green foliage, this relaxing garden restaurant serves everything from *ajiaco criollo*, a tasty soup of meat and vegetables, to sirloin steak grilled to your taste. The fish is fresh and prepared with subtle seasonings. Open noon–midnight. $$$

El Conejito
Calle M and 17, Vedado.
Tel: 324671.
A supposedly "English" restaurant, though the architecture and decor is more of a strange mix of English and Swiss styles. It specializes in rabbit (*conejo*) when it's available, but serves a wide range of international dishes. $$

La Divina Pastora
San Carlos de la Cabaña fortress.
Tel: 62-3886.
Located on the site of the old magazine at the foot of the Cabaña fortress (if driving, take the first right-hand turn after the tunnel), La Divina Pastora offers a stunning view of the Havana skyline. A good place for a meal or a drink before the 9 o'clock *cañonazo* (*see page 186*). Among the seafood specialties is fillet of red snapper stuffed with shrimp. Open noon–midnight. $$$

La Ferminia
5ta Avenida between 18207, between 182 and 184, Miramar.
An elegant, chandeliered mansion with individual dining rooms and a patio. Chicken and fish dishes. $$$

El Floridita
On the corner of Obispo and Monserrate, Old Havana.
Tel: 63-1060, 63-1063.
Havana's most fabled dining spot, and Hemingway's favorite for his daiquiris, is elegant but rather dark

and overpriced. You pay for the name (and the waiters' red jackets) as well as for the food. Main courses include grilled lobster, shrimp flaming in rum, turtle steaks and other exotica. Why not opt just for a daiquiri at the bar instead. Open noon–1am. $$$$

Café el Mercurio
Plaza San Francisco.
High-ceilinged, light, café-restaurant in sophisticated surroundings on the ground floor of the Lonja del Comercio. It is popular with foreign businessmen and women. Good international menu. $$

Restaurante Monseigneur
Corner of O and 21, Vedado.
Midway between the Hotel Nacional and the Capri, the Monseigneur cellar restaurant is famous as a former meeting spot for 1950s Mafia bosses. The Cuban singer, the late Bola de Nieve, made it his home, too, and his piano is still there. The restaurant now has a long seafood menu and a moody ambience. $$

Café del Oriente
Calle Oficios, Plaza San Francisco.
Tea, coffee and cocktails in elegant surroundings at reasonable prices. There is an excellent restaurant with a full international menu upstairs. $$

Papa's
5ta Avenida and Calle 248, Marina Hemingway, Santa Fé.
Tel: 22-5592, 22-8346.
Fish and shellfish are the specialties and the decor is coolly marine. Open noon–midnight. $$$

El Patio
Plaza de la Catedral, Old Havana.
Go for the fabulous location, in an old colonial palace, rather than the food. You can eat either on the ground floor, surrounded by palms and serenaded from the grand piano, or upstairs. International menu. $$$

El Tocororo
Calle 18 and 3ra Avenida, Miramar.
Tel: 33-2209, 33-4530.
An ideal place to come for a really special meal, the Tocororo is housed in an attractive Miramar

Cuba's *Paladares*: The Background

The Legalization of Paladares

For years, family restaurants were illegal, like virtually every kind of private enterprise. They operated clandestinely, yet everyone knew where they were; even policemen and party members could be seen dining there. Then, in 1994, the law was changed and "*paladares*" (the name comes from a chain of restaurants in a Brazillian soap opera) could start doing business more openly.

Cuba was suddenly full of *paladares*, offering cheap home cooking. The golden year of the *paladar* was 1995, when every other house in Havana seemd to be a restaurant – usually serving a menu of pork, beans and rice.

The Government Crackdown

In 1996, the government realized that it had created a highly successful, profitable sector of the economy that was not making money for the state – indeed, that was competing, perhaps a little too successfully, with the state restaurants that continued to serve tastless, overpriced food. So the *paladares* had to register with the state, pay a license fee, meet strict public health standards and pay devastating taxes – as much as $1,000 a month in Havana (regardless of the number of meals served), which is a hundred times a Cuban's average monthly salary. Many *paladares* were driven out of business.

A series of crackdowns closed down many more. There were commando raids (often shown on the evening news) to root out supplies of illicit lobster, shrimp, turtle and beef (all state monopolies which *paladares* cannot sell). Tax evasion, dirty kitchens, black market cheese used on pizzas – all were used as an excuse to close more *paladares* which – bitter owners believed – had become too successful for the anti–capitalist government to bear.

Survival

Government policy drastically reduced the numbers of *paladares*, and also pushed up prices. The survivors had to compete, and draw in more customers. They began to make more of an effort, erecting neon signs, placing tables in gardens, making sure there were clean tablecloths, and providing flowers and candles, even printing menus. Standards of cooking rose and menus became more imaginative – some places began to specialize in unusual cuisines – Chinese, Arabic, Spanish or Italian. These have moved beyond being traditional *paladares* – they are professional restaurants. You must book to get a table at some of the most popular establishments.

Authentic Paladares

The days of the cheap meal eaten in the family sitting room are not entirely over. These *paladares* have simply moved back underground. Refusing to register and paying no taxes, they come and go, but, as in the old days, everyone in the neighborhood knows where they are. To find a *paladar*, just ask around. Anyone will be able to tell you addresses of two or three.

Menus

Menus are often limited to fried pork, chicken or fish with rice and beans (*moros y cristianos*), salad and a starchy vegetable (*vianda*) such as yucca, plantains, malanga or boniato (*see page 120*). This is what Cubans eat at home – conservative eaters, the majority of Cubans do not seem to want anything else, and scorn even the slightest attempts to alter traditional dishes. They reject spices in favour of oil and garlic and all vegetables in favour of large quantities of meat.

villa, with a striking array of colorful art nouveau lampshades. There's no menu for the *criollo* and international dishes, but your waiter will run down everything except prices. They're high but the food is really good. Book ahead. $$$

La Torre
Focsa Building, Calle 17 and M, Vedado.
Tel: 32-4630, 32-4650.
At the top of Havana's highest building, La Torre offers a great panoramic view, but the food is rather disappointing. Steaks and fish dominate the menu. $$$

Cuban Food

El Aljibe
7a between 24 and 26, Miramar.
Tel: 24-1583.
A fine restaurant. in thatched buildings amid tropical gardens. Truly excellent Cuban cooking. Open noon–midnight. $$

La Bodeguita del Medio
Calle Empedrado 207, off Plaza de la Catedral.
Tel: 61-8442, 62-4498
Bohemian atmosphere with creole cooking in this old Hemingway haunt, but the quality of the food and service suffers due to the constant flow of tourists.
The walls downstairs are decorated with the autographs of celebrities and lesser-knowns who have eaten here over the years, but the roof terrace is actually a more congenial place to sit. Reservations advisable. Open 11.30am–6pm and 7–11pm. $$$

Casona del 17
Calle 17, between M and N, Vedado.
Tel: 33-4529.
Formerly the Don Agamemnon. Serves reasonably priced Cuban dishes and pizzas in the elegant surroundings of an old villa, opposite the Focsa Building. $$–$$$

Los Doce Apóstoles
Morro Fortress.
Tel: 63-8295.
Next to the Morro Castle and named for its battery, this restaurant serves pork dishes with all the trimmings, though the setting is arguably better than the food. Open noon– 10pm. $$

Price Guide

The following categories are for a meal for one without drinks:

$$$$	Over $40
$$$	$20–40
$$	$10–20
$	Under $10

Bar La Taska
Cabaña Fortress (next door to La Divina Pastora).
Delicious Cuban cooking, seafood a specialty. Great views from the cool balcony. Open: noon–11pm. $

Italian

D' Giovanni
Calle Tacón, behind Plaza de la Catedral.
The quality of the Italian food varies tremendously: it is sometimes excellent, sometimes poor. But the large colonial house near the harbor is magnificent. There is a café/bar downstairs, in the cool colonnaded patio, while the restaurant is upstairs. Try to get a table by a window. Often busy with tour groups in the daytime, but generally quiet at night. $

Pizza Nova
Marina Hemingway.
Tel: 246969.
The only place in Cuba that serves pizzas as good as an average high-street chain in the West. Pasta dishes and sandwiches are also available. Pleasant outdoor patio, but rather slow service. Home delivery for a few extra dollars. $$

Terraza Florentino
Hotel Capri, 21 and M, Vedado.
This rooftop bar-restaurant serves possibly the best Italian food in Cuba – thanks largely to its Italian chef. The pizzas are particularly good value. $$

Spanish

La Paella
Hostal Valencia, Calle Oficios 53, Old Havana.
Authentic, filling, tasty Spanish food in a breezy, delightfully old-fashioned room. Spanish wines. Paella is a specialty. $$

La Zaragozana
Avenida de Bélgica and Obispo, Old Havana.
Tel: 63-1062.
Filling creole and Spanish dishes, including thick bean soups, fish and paella, but quality is rather inconsistent. The restaurant tends to be livelier at lunchtime than in the evening. $$

Asian

Most of the Asian food available in Cuba is Chinese. Finding the ingredients to produce authentic Chinese meals is by no means easy, but some of Havana's Chinese inhabitants have a jolly good stab at it nevertheless.

Fonda China
Los Gardenias shopping complex, Avenida 7ma and 26, Miramar.
Excellent Chinese specialties. $$

La Torre de Marfil
Mercaderes 121, between Obispo and Obrapía, Old Havana.
Tel: 623466.
Good Chinese food in pleasant surroundings. $

Restaurante Pacífico
Calle San Nicolás, Centro Habana.
Tel: 634243.
Fairly authentic Cantonese cooking (with a little Cuban influence) in Havana's most famous Chinese restaurant, situated in the heart of Chinatown. $$

Pavo Real
7ma Avenida 205, between Calles 2 and 4, Miramar.
Tel: 296461, 242315.
Delicious Cuban-Chinese dishes served in a modern pagoda. Open noon–midnight. $$$

Sechuán
Ground floor of the Carlos III mall, Salvador Allende (Carlos III), between Retiro and Arbol Seco.
Authentic Chinese food (chef and staff are mostly of Chinese origin). Open noon–midnight. Reservations not generally needed. $$

See Man Asian Restaurant
Shanghai Theater, Zanja 306, between Lealtad and Escobar.
The See Man Asian Restaurant offers a mixture of Japanese, Chinese and Korean cuisine. Open noon– midnight. $$

Middle Eastern

Al Medina
Casa de Los Arabes, Oficios 12. Tel: 63-0862.
Serves tasty Arabic dishes, based on lamb and couscous, in a lovely old colonial mansion. The menu is padded out by Cuban dishes. $$

Oasis
Arab Cultural Centre, Prado between Trocadero and Refugio.
Good Arabic specialties, accompanied by heavily sweetened mint tea. Open 9am–midnight. $

Paladares

There are a few private restaurants on or near Calle Obispo in Old Havana, but the widest selection is in Vedado – particularly in the area bound by Línea, the Rampa and Calles O and J, where there are dozens. Below are just a few examples of the pick of Vedado's *paladares*. Prices are usually in the $10–20 range, but will rise if you drink a lot of beer or opt for wine.

El Aladino
On Calle 21 between K and L.
Open daily for lunch and dinner. Serves mostly Cuban dishes, but also occasionally couscous, lovely salads of mint and cucumber and marvelous houmous.

El Amor
Calle 23 between B and C, Vedado.
Grand surroundings in a crumbling mansion full of dusty antiques. Wonderful air of faded grandeur. Specializes in fish dishes.

De Cameron
Línea, between Paseo and 2, a block from Hotel Riviera.
Specializes in pizzas, with a good range of toppings and generous amounts of cheese. Also pasta meat and fish dishes. Meals are served in an airy room full of plants and a talkative parrot. Be warned that service is terribly slow. Also does takeaways. Open Wed–Sun, noon till late.

El Bistro
Calle K and Malecón.
Claims to serve French cuisine, but dishes are mostly Cuban – though a delicious blue cheese sauce (could it be Roquefort?) occasionally crops up on the menu. They really make an effort with service. It's popular with staff and diplomats from the nearby US Interests Section.

Jardín de los Siete Esferas
Calle 19 near the corner of B.
Here, you eat in a vine-draped garden. Mostly Cuban dishes with good pastries and an excellent chocolate coconut pie.

Marpoly
Calle K #154, corner of Línea.
Open daily from lunchtime and makes an effort to serve slightly more unusual dishes – a platter of pineapple and toasted cheese is particularly delicious.

Nerei
Calles 21 and K.
Good Cuban dishes and fast, friendly service. Fried yucca with garlic is a specialty. Open most evenings.

AROUND HAVANA

La Giraldilla
Calle 272 between 37 and 51, La Lisa, western suburb of Havana beyond Marianao.
Tel 33-6062.
La Giraldilla serves a toned-down version of Mexican food. Cubans

Cafés and Bars in Old Havana

Old Havana has an enormous number of small cafés and bars, which are good for drinks and snacks at any time of day. Most of these are found on Calles Obispo, Empedrado and Mercaderes, and also on the harborfront.
Particularly good ones are:

Bar Lluvia de Oro
Obispo 316.
A nice old bar, excellent live band. Indifferent sandwiches, pizzas and fried chicken.

Cafe La Marina
Oficios 202.
A pleasant open-air café full of palms, parrots and blue tiles. Try the delicious freshly squeezed *guarapo* (sugar cane juice), either on its own or with rum. Sandwiches, and burgers served with fresh, home-made crisps are good value. If you start hitting the *guarapo* and rum, however, the bill gets stiffer.

Cafe O'Reilly
O'Reilly 205.
An atmospheric little bar with a spiral staircase leading to a small upper room where you can sit on the tiny balcony and drink one of the best cups of coffee in Havana. The opposite balconies are so close you feel you can almost touch them. Tapas and other snacks are available.

Cafe Paris
Obispo and San Ignacio.
Live music, reasonable street-style pizza, but fried chicken and chips seems to be the most popular dish. Opposite is a good ice-cream parlor selling delicous sundaes made with rich, fruit-based ice creams for $1 to $5.

Dos Hermanos
Alameda de Paula, south of Plaza de San Francisco.
For many years, this was a rough sailors' and dockworkers' bar serving cheap shots of *aguardiente* and coffee for pesos. Now refurbished as part of the dollar machine, it now serves drinks for dollars, and reasonable tapas-style bar snacks. It is said to be an old Hemingway haunt.

La Mina
Calle Obispo, on Plaza de Armas.
This, and the adjoining Al Cappuccino, both serve excellent coffee, including cappuccino, and pastries.

Prado 264
This is the name and address of a dark and moody popular bar where Cubans and visitors mix freely. Cubans can buy rum for pesos. All other drinks are in dollars, however, and a tourist will always be charged dollars. Be warned that this is a popular haunt for *jineteros* and any foreigner is likely to be pestered to buy drinks, fake cigars and/or women.

don't believe in chillies, but you can ask for bottled Mexican sauces to pepper up the dishes. Serves a reasonable *mole* sauce. Open lunchtime till 9pm. $

La Rueda
Calles 194th and 2nd, El Chico, Wajay.
Located on a goose farm just west of José Martí airport, you can dine on that succulent bird to the accompaniment of country music. Make reservations through your hotel tourism bureau. Open noon–8pm. $$$

La Terraza
Real and Candelaria, Cojímar.
Tel: 65-3471.
This old Hemingway haunt serves some of the best seafood within striking distance of Havana: lunch here makes for an excellent day trip. The setting, with views over the Caribbean at one end of Cojímar's tree-lined promenade, is lovely. Photos of Hemingway adorn the walls. Reservations are a good idea in high season, since La Terraza is firmly on the tourist trail. Open from 10am. $$$

VARADERO

Resort hotels and villas specialize in buffets with lots of fresh fruit and outdoor grills, where you can get lunch without really leaving the beach. The specialty restaurants in the big hotels serve excellent food and are open to anyone who wants to try them.

Albacoro
Calle 59 between Avenida 1era and the beach.
Tel: 66-7320.
Excellent seafood served on a pleasant terrace overlooking the sea. Open Tuesday–Sunday, noon–10.45pm. $$

Las Américas
Hotel Internacional.
Tel: 66-7750
A stylish place for lunch or dinner, with a continental menu. Also check out the cool basement bar. Open noon–11pm. $$$

Barracuda Grill
Villa Cuba.
Excellent seafood. $$

El Bodegón Criollo
Avenida de la Playa and Calle 40.
Tel: 66-2180.
This restaurant attempts to recreate the ambience of Havana's Bodeguita del Medio, and serves similar food. Reasonable food, but it's best not to compare with the original. Open noon–10pm. $$

Capri Pizza
Ave de la Playa and Calle 42.
Pizzas and other Italian specialties. So-called Italian restaurant popular with Cubans – serves overcooked pasta and mediocre pizza. Open 11am–11pm. $$

La Casa de las Antiguedades
Retiro Josone.
Tel: 66-7898.
Located in a park with a tranquil lagoon and luxuriant trees, this restaurant specializes in carefully prepared continental cuisine. Open noon–11pm. $$$

Mi Casita
Camino del Mar between Calles 11 and 12.
Tel: 66-3787.
Intimate, capriciously furnished and specializing in tasty Caribbean dishes. Opens at 7.30pm. $$$

Halong
Camino del Mar and Calle 12.
Tel: 66-3787.
Vietnamese decor sets the tone for delicate soups and subtly flavored entrées. Open 3–11pm. $$$

El Mesón
Retiro Josone.
Tel: 66-7898.
Cuban cooking at its best. Open noon–11pm. $$$

Restaurante Venecia
Villa Tortuga, Avenida Kawama between Calles 6 and 7.
Tel: 66-4115.
Canadian-run Italian restaurant with excellent pizza. $$

Food on the Hoof

There are many street stalls selling home-made coconut and peanut sweets, roast pork rolls, pizzas, *churros* (deep-fried sugared donut sticks), coffee and soft drinks all over Cuba. Prices are just a few pesos.

Price Guide

The following categories are for a meal for one without drinks:

$$$$	Over $40
$$$	$20–40
$$	$10–20
$	Under $10

CIENFUEGOS

Cienfuegos has a good number and variety of restaurants, yet they tend to be crowded and sometimes run out of food. Make dinner reservations for no later than 7pm and get there early. The nice thing about eating out in Cienfuegos is that you will almost always have Cubans for company rather than just foreign tourists.

Casa Garibena
Calle 35 between 20 and 24.
Tel: 3893.
Excellent creole cooking in an old wooden colonial house by the sea. $

Covadonga
Calle 37 between 0 and 1, Punta Gorda.
Tel: 432-8238.
Conveniently located across from the Jagua Hotel, the restaurant serves tasty paella. $$

Palacio de Valle
Next to the Jagua Hotel, Punta Gorda.
Tel: 3021/5.
The best food in town is served in this extravagant, early 20th-century Spanish-Moorish palace. Seafood is the specialty. $$–$$$

El Polinesio
Avenida 54, overlooking Parque Martí.
Tel: 5723.
Cuban-Chinese with a Polynesian touch. Renown for its great desserts. $$

La Verja
3306 Avenida 54.
Tel: 6311.
The best place to eat in the center of town, for its shabby elegance as much as the food. Reservations claimed to be vital.
Extensive, varied and good international menu. $$

TRINIDAD

El Jigüe
Martínez Villena and Guinart.
Located in the tiny, picturesque Plaza El Jigüe, a block west of the Plaza Mayor.

This restaurant is airy with a pleasant atmosphere and good food at reasonable prices. $$

El Mesón del Regidor
Simón Bolívar 418.
Tel: 419-93756.
This restaurant's setting and decor is rather better than the food. The menu includes the usual fare, including grilled steaks and fish. Closes at 6pm. $$

Trinidad Colonial
Maceo and Colón.
Tel: 419-9 3873.
Although the food doesn't live up to the charm of this lovely colonial mansion, it is acceptable. International cuisine, slow service. $$

SANTIAGO DE CUBA

Don Antonio
Plaza Dolores.
Tel: 226-52205.
Wonderful blue and stone colonial building. Creole food. $

Casa Granda
In the Hotel Casa Granda.
Tel: 226-8 6036.
Elegant restaurant with live string quartet. Good international cooking. The complimentary house cocktail is a refreshing blend of rum, lime and tamarind. $$

El Cayo
Cayo Granma in Santiago Bay.
Tel: 226-4 1769.
Excellent seafood served in a marine setting. Open noon–9pm. $$

La Cecilia
Near El Morro castle.
Tel: 226-9 1889.
Intimate garden restaurant with limited choices. Fried chicken and shellfish brochettes are especially good. $$

Three Cuban Recipes

For anyone wishing to try their own hand at traditional, Cuban-style cooking, here are a few recipes.

Note that you can substitute the juice of the sour orange (a very popular ingredient in Cuba) with an equal mixture of sweet orange juice and lime or lemon juice.

Arroz con Pollo (serves eight)

2 chickens
3 garlic cloves
1 sour orange
one-third of a cup cooking oil
1 large green pepper
1 large onion
1 can of tomato sauce
2 cans of pimentos
1 can of small peas (petit pois)
1 can of asparagus tips
2 tsp salt
½ tsp pepper
1 laurel leaf
3½ cups of dry wine
2 cups of chicken broth
2 lbs of rice; saffron to color rice
1 egg (for garnishing)

First of all, make a broth with the chicken giblets. Cut the chicken into quarters and then roll the pieces in crushed garlic and sour orange juice. Heat the oil in a pan or flameproof casserole and brown the chicken. Add finely cut onion, the chopped pimentos (including the liquid from the can), the liquid from the peas and asparagus, salt, pepper, laurel leaf, saffron, dry wine, broth and water.

Wash and soak the rice. When the chicken is half-cooked, add the drained rice. Cook over low heat until the rice is tender. Add the peas and garnish the dish with pimentos, asparagus, peas and hard boiled egg.

Lechón Asado

Perhaps the most important traditional feast day for Cubans is *Noche Buena*, or Christmas Eve. Religious festivities are banned, but the Noche Buena feast is a timeless ritual that features the most traditional of Cuban dishes. The centerpiece is the *lechón asado*, slow-roasted pork.

6-lb leg of pork
And, for the marinade:
3 tbs chopped garlic
Pinch ground bay leaves, oregano, cumin
1 tbs olive oil
½ cup sour orange juice
½ cup dry sherry
Freshly ground black pepper
2 large onions, sliced

Trim any extra fat from the leg of pork and pierce the skin all over with the tip of a knife. Mash the garlic into a paste, then mash in the ground bay leaf, oregano, cumin and olive oil. Rub this all over the roast. Place the roast in big pan, sprinkle with pepper and sour orange juice. Scatter the onions over the roast, then wrap the whole thing in plastic and marinade overnight, turning the roast a few times.

Heat the oven to 350°F (180°C). Remove the meat from the marinade and pat it dry. Save the marinade. Put the meat in a non-aluminum roasting pan and cook for an hour, turning it to brown each side.

After an hour, reduce the temperature to 325°F (165°C) and pour the marinade over the roast. Cover loosely with aluminum foil.. Baste the meat frequently with the pan juices. Remove the foil during the last 45 minutes. Serve with *mojo criollo*.

Mojo Criollo

The classic sauce for pork.

8 garlic cloves, chopped
1 tsp salt
1 tsp ground oregano (optional)
½ tsp ground cumin (optional)
½ cup sour orange juice
½ cup olive oil

Mash the garlic with the salt to form a paste. Mash in the spices. Add the sour orange juice and stand for 30 minutes. Stir in the olive oil.

El Morro
Near entrance to Morro Castle.
Tel: 226-4 1769.
Arguably the best *criollo* cooking in Santiago. Open 9am–9pm. $$

Santiago 1900
San Basilio between Pio Rosado and Hartman, downtown.
Tel: 226-2 3507.
Set in a beautiful mansion that was the Bacardí family home. Great courtyard, grand crystal chandeliers and live music by a trio or quartet. Unfortunately, the food is rather indifferent. $$

Tocororo
Avenida Manduley 159, Vista Alegre.
Tel: 226-4 1410, 4 1369.
Like its Havana counterpart, the restaurant is expensive but elegant and atmospheric. Beef, chicken, pork and shellfish are all prepared with savor and panache. Open noon–midnight. $$$

Drinking Notes

Alcoholic Drinks

Beer and rum are the two most common alcoholic drinks in Cuba. You will find these, and a usually limited range of imported wines and spirits, in tourist shops and restaurants.

Beer You will find a whole range of imported beers in Cuba, even though the island makes its own, perfectly tasty beers. Cristal, which comes in an unmistakable green can, is the most common. Unfortunately, some of Cuba's best beers – such as Tropical and Polar – have all but disappeared while factories undergo seemingly interminable repairs. Hatuey and Mayabe, both considered good beers, are still available in many places.

Beer

Beer made in Cuba is either strong (over 6 percent) – such as Bucanero and Mayabe in black cans – or light (4–5 percent) – such as Bucanero in a white can, Mayabe in a blue can, or Cristal.

Rum Cuban rum is available as raw, home-made *aguardiente*, but you'll do well to stick to the proper stuff. The most popular brand is Havana Club. This and other brands come in three categories (according to when they were bottled):

- **Carta Blanca** (white): *tres años* (three years).
- **Oro** (gold): *cinco años* (five years).
- **Añejo** (dark): *siete años* (seven years).

The three-year-old light, dry Carta Blanca is the alcoholic ingredient in a *daiquirí*, a *mojito* (flavored with crushed mint), a *cubanito* (a Cuban-style Bloody Mary, with tomato juice), *saoco* (with coconut milk), *cuba libre* (with coke), and other mixed drinks. Rum mixed with honey, lime juice and ice, is known as a *Canchánchara*, best sampled at the bar of the same name in Trinidad.

Non-alcoholic Drinks

Juices are listed on every hotel and restaurant menu, but you may not have a choice. Fresh orange juice is served almost everywhere, as well as Cuba's own excellent packaged tropical fruit juices.

Guarapo Freshly squeezed cane juice, refreshing and creamy – is served in surprisingly few tourist establishments. It is sold in many farmers' markets, and often by the roadside, so keep your eye out. You may have to supply your own cup or bottle.

Batidos This is a delicious concoction of condensed milk and fruit or ice cream whipped up in a blender. These are increasingly served in hotels, but are often more easily bought in the street or at farmers' markets (for pesos): more often than not, these will be made with fruit, sugar and powdered milk, or even just with water.

Water Cuba produces good mineral water (fizzy and still). Local and imported mineral water can be bought in dollar stores and restaurants. Restaurants and hotels serve cold drinking water automatically. Ask if it's boiled (*hervido*) and don't drink it unless it is.

Tea Large hotels will serve tea at breakfast, but it is often rather watery. Look out for herbal and strong black tea, which is available in some cafés and bars.

Coffee The Cuban drink of hospitality and sociability. Strong and very sweet, it should be served hot in small cups: tourist establishments let you add your own sugar and almost never bring it hot enough. Breakfast buffets usually have a choice between strong Cuban and watery American coffee. *Cafe con leche* – coffee served with hot milk – is available at most cafés catering to tourists. There are even a few bars in Havana that sell cappuccino.

Milk You would do well to get used to drinking tea or coffee without milk if you are not staying only in large tourist hotels. Most hotels supply milk for breakfast, but you cannot bank on restaurants having it.

Culture

MUSEUMS

The ancient mansions and public buildings clustered around the colonial center of Cuba's older cities are now often museums. Their exhibits generally relate to local and national history, or a specific aspect of it, such as the music, decorative arts or festivals.

Entrance fees The main museums in tourist centers charge an admission fee of $1–3, but the cost is higher in some of Havana's top attractions.

Language Exhibits are generally labeled in Spanish only, though sometimes shortened notes are given in English. The most popular museums usually have at least one guide who speaks one or more European language, including English.

Opening hours are notoriously erratic, and be prepared for disappointment. Popular days for closure are Monday or Tuesday, and many museums open only for the afternoon on Sunday.

ART

Every town and city has at least one state art gallery that holds temporary exhibits and may sell works by local artists, and in recent years many others have opened.

In terms of art treasures, Havana has the lion's share – in particular at the **Museo Nacional de Bellas Artes**, which has the most representative collection of 20th-century Cuban art. The **Casa de las Américas**, also in Havana, has an interesting collection of Latin-American art.

For information on buying contemporary art and taking it out of the country, see *Export Procedures* on page 357.

MUSIC

Cubans are crazy about music. It blares from every window and accompanies every activity. Rumba, *son* and its derivative salsa, *trova* ballads and *nueva trova* political songs, jazz, country and classical can be heard and seen on TV. There is always some group performing live, but sadly many are obliged to play for tourists in their hotels rather than in local nightspots.

A visit to a traditional music hall – known as a **Casa de la Trova** – one of which is found in every Cuban town, will provide a good introduction to both Cubans and their music. A couple of nights a week, local musicians show up for an informal jam session. You may hear anything from ballads to tango, but traditional *son* is the most common. Often there's dancing and sometimes a bar.

Jazz has deep roots and Cuban musicians are creative interpreters. The genre is at its most exciting when the best Cuban and international jazz musicians gather in Havana for the annual Jazz Festival in February. At other times, it's not so easy to hear them live because of engagements abroad.

The national **opera** company is based at the Gran Teatro in Havana, off the Parque Central. Performances are posted on notices on the columns outside, or call the theatre, tel: 61 3078/9.

Opera, choral groups and the National Symphony Orchestra play with visiting ensembles at the Varadero International Music Festival in November and perform separately at other times.

DANCE

Cubans dance from the moment they can walk and, to westerners, it seems they all have the innate rhythm, impeccable footwork and the endless energy expected of a pro. Perhaps that's why the professional dance groups are so good.

Afro-Cuban dance

The **National Folklore Group** was founded to keep Afro-Cuban dance and music alive, concentrating mainly on rumba, *son* and *danzón*. Every Saturday, the group has a **Sabado de la Rumba**, when it performs outdoors at its headquarters on Calle 4 between Calzada and 5 in Havana (tel: 30-3060). It also offers **Folk-Cuba workshops** twice a year to teach rumba forms and percussion instruments to foreigners.

Ballet

The **National Ballet of Cuba**, currently directed by Alicia Alonso – who has been dancing *Giselle* for 50 years – is world-famous for its fluid grace. The company is often on tour, nationally and abroad, but you may be lucky enough to catch a performance at the Gran Teatro or the Teatro Nacional in Havana. The company's ballet school is based at the Gran Teatro, and during the day you can see the young students rehearsing.

The **November Ballet Festival** in Havana draws companies from Cuba and abroad. Some of the performances are held in provincial theaters once a week.

Modern Dance

Cuba's **Contemporary Dance Company** (Danza Contemporánea de Cuba) performs both avant-garde and traditional choreography. It runs courses, information about which is available from the Teatro Nacional de Cuba, Calle Paseo y 39, (tel: 79-2728).

CINEMA

Both Cuban and foreign films run in public movie houses. Most overseas films tend to be at least a couple of years old, often more. There used to be several showings a day, but nowadays films are often put on only at weekends or on selected evenings – other than in the main cinemas in Havana, such as those in Vedado, including the Yara, opposite the Habana Librel, and the Charles Chaplin, further along Calle 23. These same cinemas tend to show the pick of the films during the annual **New Latin-American Film Festival**, which is held every December and draws film stars, directors, critics and film buffs from around the world.

FESTIVALS

In addition to the festivals mentioned above, all Cuban provinces celebrate a **Culture Week** (*Semana Cultural*) once a year, with music, dance, arts and crafts and local culinary traditions.

Carnival is, of course, Cuba's most famous festival, and is well worth making a diversion to experience. Indeed, many people travel from abroad to take part in Santiago's carnival. A much less well-known festival, known as Las **Parrandas**, takes place in certain towns and villages of Villa Clara province, at the end of December every year – most famously at Remedios. For a description of this wild and colorful event, see page 236.

Carnival

Cuba's only real carnival is in **Santiago de Cuba**, held on the traditional dates of July 25–27. **Varadero** has a less spirited festival, with tourist participation, in January and February. **Havana** holds its carnival in November – it was moved from July (the traditional month) to fit in with the tourist high season. But it is hardly a carnival in the true sense – streets are roped off, seating is provided (with payment in dollars to enter the compound) and floats and dancers pass by with little interaction with the crowd.

The *comparsas* or street dances of Cuba's carnival are as colorful and symbolic as the floats. In Havana and Santiago, neighborhood *comparsa* groups have rehearsals at least once a week during the year, and you may be lucky enough to come across one in full flow.

Nightlife

Every hotel in Cuba has one or more bars and many also have programmed entertainment at night, often focused around the swimming pool; this may come in the form of anything from salsa classes to silly competitions. Most large hotels have their own disco and cabaret.

If you want to be more adventurous, ask around for the best local disco or cabaret, where you will be able to pay in pesos and drink rum and dance alongside the locals. Local discos are obviously at their liveliest at weekends, but don't normally get going unti 11pm or even later.

The beach resort of Varadero has abundant discos and night-time shows and cabarets, but you will find by far the best and most varied nightlife in Havana.

Havana Nightlife

As Havana is changing so fast, it is always worth asking around for the latest new arrival on the scene, but the venues listed below are long-established and are of enduring popularity. There are also a couple of "what's on"-style magazines, that are worth buying.

Casa de la Música
Avenida 35 and Calle 20, Miramar.
Tel: 33-0447.
This comparatively new venue, opened in 1994, hosts top salsa bands nightly. Music fans should definitely check out its program.

Caberet Parisien
Hotel Nacional, Calles 21 and O.
Tel: 30-3564.
If you can't be bothered to trek to the Tropicana, this show in the Nacional is the best alternative. The Capri show in the nearby Hotel Capri is also worth considering.

Havana Club
Hotel Comodoro, Calle 84 and 3era
Tel: 22-5893.
Not in a great location if you're based in Old Havana or Vedado, but still a very popular disco, with usually a good mix of Cuban and Western music.

Meliá Cohiba Hotel
Paseo and 1era, Vedado.
Tel: 33-3636.
In an effort to compete with the neighboring Palacio de la Salsa, the old Aché disco in this five-star hotel now hosts live bands – worth checking out if you don't fancy what's on at the Palacio.

Palacio de la Salsa
Hotel Riviera, Paseo y Malecón.
Tel 33-04501.
Come here to see Cuba's top salsa bands perform nightly. There is only a comparatively small dance floor, right in front of the stage, with the bulk of the auditorium being taken up with tables, but people dance in every available space. Admission is not cheap, but a lot of (nouveau riche) Cubans still come and put all the tourists to shame on the dance floor. Be prepared for an unforgettable night.

Patio de María
Calle 37 between Paseo and 2, near the Teatro Nacional.
A popular and more alternative venue, serving a mix of rock and salsa – mainly at weekends.

Tropicana
Calle 72 No. 4504, Marianao.
Tel: 33-7507, 33-0174.
This overblown 1950s show is the most elaborate and impressive of Cuba's cabarets (*see page 179*). Any hotel tourism bureau will book seats but the show is expensive – $50 minimum entrance (for which you get a complimentary, watery *mojito*). Other drinks are expensive. Afterwards, you can dance until morning to a mix of live and taped music in the attached **Arcos de Cristal** disco. (Santiago has its own version of the Tropicana cabaret.)

Shopping

What to Buy

Cigars and **rum** are the two best gifts to take home from a trip to Cuba. Most countries have import limits on both, which travelers should check out beforehand: the standard limit is 50 cigars and two liters of rum. Both items can be purchased in the big hotels or tourist stores.

If you fall under the spell of Cuban music, you will almost certainly want to splash out on a few **cassettes** and **CDs**. Many hotels have a reasonable selection, but keep an eye open for Artex shops, which tend to have a better-than-average choice. You can also pick up wonderful old **records** for a song from street vendors. They may not be in tip-top condition, but you can find great classics if you are prepared to look.

Handicrafts tend to be tasteless and overpriced in the state-run stores, but the legalization of private enterprise has meant that many Cubans have started making things – from paintings to jewelry, embroidery, ceramics, leather goods, and musical instruments. Foreign interest in Santería and other Afro-Cuban religions has also spawned the proliferation of souvenirs related to these cults, from the colorful necklaces associated with Santería to sculpted figures of the gods (*orishas*).

Secondhand **books** and fascinating **newspapers** and **magazines** from the pre-revolutionary era and the early years of the revolution are worth looking out for, too. All over Cuba you will find people selling books in the street or out of their front room.

While many peso bookshops are depressingly empty of new titles, books that are of obvious interest to tourists are being published for sale in dollar shops. The range of titles is improving, but the stock is often dominated by picture books about Cuba and Havana, expensive reprints of old Cuban revolutionary volumes (collected speeches of Che Guevara or the works of José Martí, etc.) and a limited number of novels by "safe" authors in Spanish (García Marquez is a favorite).

The shelves of **peso bookshops** are filled with cheap editions of books devoted to politics, agriculture, sociology, with the occasional dusty volume of Russian or Chinese origin.

Export Procedures

Visitors who wish to buy Cuban art should note that they need an export permit. State-run shops and galleries will issue this permit automatically.

You also need a permit if you buy a work of art from a street market, or an artist – no matter how inexpensive. Sometimes, the artist will issue a permit, but otherwise you must go to the National Registry of Cultural Goods in Havana (Calle 17 No. 1009, between 10 and 12, in Vedado), and allow a minimum of three or four days for processing. The permit costs $10 and is good for up to five art works. It is important to get a permit, otherwise the Cuban Customs will confiscate your purchases at the airport. This is also true for antiquarian books.

Buying Cigars

Cigars can be bought on any visit to a factory, such as the Partagás factory in Havana. Hotel cigar shops all have large humidors and usuallly well-informed staff; cigars here are often cheaper than in the factory shops. The cheapest place to buy cigars is at the airport, though the selection is smaller.

Don't be tempted to buy cigars on the street. Every hustler has a tale ("I have a friend who works in the factory, etc."), but almost all the cigars are fakes made from cheap tobacco. Changes in the law mean that without an official stamped receipt you will be unable to take them out of the country.

Shopping in Havana

AREA BY AREA

The shopping scene in Havana has been transformed in the 1990s. New stores and malls are opening up all the time, and the main commercial streets of the pre-revolutionary era are gradually coming to life.

Centro Habana

The main shopping streets of Centro Habana are **San Raphael, Neptuno** and **San Miguel**, where you will see many familiar names over the shopfronts – from Western Union to Woolworths, Hotpoint and Philips. The area has changed little since the 1950s, except that the stores have little to sell. Most shops are almost completely empty, or have windows filled with pitiful offerings. There are long lines, however, outside the **Tiendas Panamericanas** dollar stores.

Shops are returning to **Avenida Salvador Allende** (formerly Carlos III), the broad boulevard that runs along the southern edge of Centro Habana. A taste of things to come is the new **Carlos III shopping mall**, on Allende between Retiro and Árbol Seco. It is a fairly poor imitation of a Miami mall, with not a great deal on sale, but there are often long queues for clothes, shoes and cosmetics, and many Cubans come along every weekend just to gaze at things they cannot afford. Plenty of Cuba's new rich are also to be seen, spending hundreds of dollars on clothes and cosmetics. There is a pleasant coffee bar tucked away inside a cigar and liquor store on the ground floor, where you can get

Where to buy Crafts, Books and Music in Havana

Arts and Crafts

One of the best places for crafts in Cuba is the market held in the Plaza de la Catedral every day except Monday. You will find smaller and cheaper versions of this market dotted around the city – most notably on Calle Simón Bolívar, just off Parque de la Fraternidad (near the Capitolio), and on the Malecón a few blocks east of the Hotel Riviera.

Art lovers should check out the shops along Calle Obispo in Old Havana, where many artists have set up for themselves to sell their work. Many are artists of international renown who have exhibited abroad.

Books

A dozen or more stalls sell secondhand books at a market in the Plaza de Armas every day except Monday. Prices are fairly high, but there is a good choice. If you are looking for something specific, it's always worth asking around; even if a vendor does not have the book to hand, they may well be able to track down a copy for you if you can wait a day or two.

The bookstores worth checking out include the following:

• **La Moderna Poesia**, at the top of Obispo, just off the Parque Central. The most famous peso bookstore in Havana seems to be on the verge of being turned into a dollar store.

• **La Internacional**, opposite La Moderna Poesia on Calle Obispo. Part of this shop is dollars only, but attached is an excellent secondhand bookstore, selling a mixture of old university textbooks and an interesting and eclectic mixture of fiction, often in quite old editions, and sometimes in English. Most books are sold for pesos, though you must pay in dollars for some special titles.

• **Librería Bella Habana**, in the Palacio del Segundo Cabo (Instituto del Libro), Plaza de Armas. This shop has an extensive choice, all for dollars.

Music

Cassettes and CDs are available all over town. Most hotels have a good selection, as does the **Artex** shop on 23 and L (opposite the Habana Libre). The music shop in the **Palacio de la Artesanía** in Old Havana is good, too.

excellent coffee for just 50 cents. There is a good Chinese restaurant, the Sechuán, also on the ground floor.

Vedado

Calle 23, particularly **La Rampa** – the section that runs from the Hotel Habana Libre down to the Malecón – was once the hub of Havana's life; the street itself is inlaid with coloured panels by famous Cuban artists. The **Habana Libre Hotel** has a useful row of shops selling everything from potato crisps and Andrews liver salts to Cuba's finest cigars. (Be warned that the hotel is a hotspot for hustlers, black marketeers, prostitutes, and illegal cab drivers.) There is a small craft market just down the road from the hotel, but it's not as good as others in the city.

The **International Press Centre**, on the corner of La Rampa and Calle O, hosts exhibitions by Cuban artists, and has a shop where you can buy newspapers, magazines and books (particularly political titles), and a photo centre. You can get good, cheap photocopies here.

Between M and N, still on La Rampa, the **Pabellón** is an entertainment and computer center belonging to the Union of Young Communists (UJC).

Calle 23 continues west through a mainly suburban area until it meets the corner of Calle 12, where there is a busy little area of cinemas, shops and restaurants.

Miramar

Behind the embassy, rows of advertising billboards herald the former **Diplotienda** on 3ra Avenida and Calle 70. The shop is now open to anyone, Cuban or foreign, who can afford to shop there. Most shoppers these days are Cubans, not foreigners. It has the widest range of food on sale of any store in Cuba, but it is still very limited and dreadfully expensive. There is a small **Diplo Electrica** next door which sells electrical goods. Some of them – video-recorders for example – are forbidden to Cuban purchasers.

Other popular shopping centers in Miramar are the huge **5 Y 42** complex on 5ta Avenida and Calle 42, which has a bakery/patisserie, and stores selling clothes, fabrics, shoes, electrical goods, cosmetics – you name it – plus a handful of cafés and snackbars. It is a popular hangout for black-market vendors, who hang around outside frantically whispering what they are trying to sell – "*Queso!*" (cheese), "*Jamón*" (ham) and "*Caramelos*" (sweets). Those looking for computer supplies should check out **Tecun**, just around the corner on 42.

There is another popular dollar shopping complex at the former **Hotel Sierra Maestra** near the mouth of the bay at 1era Avenida, between Calles 0 and 2.

Havana's haute couture **Maison** on Calle 16 and 7ma Avenida (tel: 22-1906) has a series of smart boutiques, selling Cuban fashions and antiques. There are also regular fashion shows, which are very entertaining.

Sport

Beach resorts in Cuba have facilities – and often qualified instructors – for a whole range of sports, including waterskiing, sailing, snorkeling, diving, fishing, yachting, as well as basketball, volleyball, squash, tennis and horseback riding. A growing number of hotels also have bicycles and mopeds for rent.

Serious runners come for the marathons – such as the one held in Varadero in November – but Cuba's heat takes its toll.

Italian cyclists pedal the **Vuelta a Cuba** island tour every February in solidarity with Cuba, and sports teams from many countries regularly compete on the island.

Anyone interested in attending sports events should contact the nearest Cuban tourist office or the National Institute of Sports, Physical Education and Recreation (INDER), tel: 40 3581, 40 5826, 41 4300. For specific sports information, you can also call the following numbers:

- **Athletics** 97-2103
- **Basketball** 41-3248
- **Baseball** 78-1662, 78-4523
- **Boxing** 04618
- **Fencing** 40-8416
- **Gymnastics** 40-9263
- **Judo** 41-1702
- **Pelota** 41-3175
- **Rowing** 81-5979
- **Softball** 70-5907
- **Shooting** 70-5709
- **Soccer** 40-8284
- **Swimming** 40-5877
- **Tennis** 41-5394
- **Volleyball** 41-3557
- **Wrestling** 40-3978

Further Reading

General

Before Night Falls: A Memoir by Reinaldo Arenas, New York (1993).
A Continent of Islands: Searching for the Caribbean Destiny by Mark Kurlansky, Addison-Wesley, New York (1992).
Cuba (photographs) by Adam Kufeld, W.W. Norton, New York (1994).
Cuba: A Journey by Jacobo Timerman, Picador, London (1994).
Cuba In Focus by Emily Hatchwell and Simon Calder, Latin America Bureau, London (1995).
Cuba: The Land, The History, The People, The Culture by Stephen Williams, Michael Friedman, New York (1994).
The Cubans: Voices of Change by Lynn Geldof, Bloomsbury Press, London (1992).
Driving Through Cuba: An East-West Journey by Carlos Gebler, Hamish Hamilton, London (1988).
The Early Diary of Anaïs Nin by Anaïs Nin, Harcourt Brace & Co., US (1982).
The Exile: Cuba in the Heart of Miami by David Reef, Simon & Schuster, New York in the US or Vintage, London in the UK (1993).
Falling off the Map: Some Lonely Places of the World by Pico Iyer, Alfred A. Knopf, New York (1993).
Havana, Portrait of a City by Juliet Barclay, Cassell, London (1993).
Havana – 1933 Walker Evans, photographic collection re-published in the US by Pantheon and in the UK by Thames and Hudson (1989).
Hemingway in Cuba by Norberto Fuentes and Lyle Stuart, Secaucus, New Jersey (1984).
Into Cuba by Barry Lewis and Peter Marshall, Alfred van der Marck Editions, New York (1985).
Land of Miracles by Stephen Smith, London (1995).
Mea Cuba by Guillermo Cabrera Infante, Faber and Faber, London or Farrar, Straus & Giroux in the US (1994).
Memories of a Cuban Kitchen by Mary Urrutia Randleman and Joan Schwartz, Macmillan, New York (1992).
Passing Through Havana by Felicia Rosshandler, St Martin's Press, New York (1984).
Portrait of Cuba by Wayne Smith, Turner Publishing, Atlanta (1991).
Six Days in Havana by James A. Michener, and John Kings, University of Texas Press (1989).
A Taste of Cuba by Linette Green, Dutton, New York (1991).
To Cuba and Back by Richard Henry Dana Jr, Southern Illinois University Press (1966).
Trading with the Enemy: A Yankee Travels Through Castro's Cuba by Tom Miller, Atheneum, New York (1992).
When It's Cocktail Time in Cuba by Basil Woon, Horace Liveright, New York (1928).
With Hemingway: A Year in Key West and Cuba by Arnold Samuelson, Random House, Inc (1984)
I Wonder as I Wander: An Autobiograhical Journey by Langston Hughes, Farrar, Straus & Giroux (1956).

Fiction

Cuba and the Night by Pico Iyer, Quartet (1995).
Dreaming In Cuban by Christina Garcia, Knopf, New York (1992).
The Old Man and the Sea by Ernest Hemingway, New York (1952).
Our Man in Havana by Graham Greene, Penguin (1958).
The Mambo Kings Play Songs of Love by Oscar Hijuelos, Farrar, Straus & Giroux, New York (1989).
Patria o Muerte! The Great Zoo and Other Poems by Nicolás Guillén, Monthly Review Press, New York (1972).

Culture

Afrocuba by P.P. Sarduy and Jean Stubbs, Latin America Bureau, London (1993).
Los Negros Curros by Fernando Ortíz, Editorial de Ciencias

Sociales, Havana (1986).
Salsa – Havana Heat, Bronx Beat by Hernando Calvo Ospina, Latin America Bureau, London (1995).
Santería from Africa to the New World by G. Brandon, Indiana (1993).

Fidel Castro

Castro, the Blacks and Africa by Carlos Moore, Center for Afro-American Studies, University of California, Los Angeles (1988).
Castro's Cuba, Cuba's Fidel by Lee Lockwood, Macmillan, New York (1967).
Castro's Final Hour by Andres Oppenheimer, Simon & Schuster, New York (1992).
In Defence of Socialism by Fidel Castro, Pathfinder Press (1989).
An Encounter with Fidel by Gianni Mina, Ocean Press, Melbourne (1991).
Fidel Castro by Robert E. Quirk, W.W. Norton, New York (1993).
Fidel Castro by John Gerassi, Doubleday, New York (1973).
Fidel Castro y la Revolucion Cubana by Carlos Alberto Montaner, Plaza and Janes, Barcelona (1984).
Fidel: A Critical Portrait by Tad Szulc, Hodder & Stoughton (1986).
Fidel Castro: Rebel Liberator or Dictator? by Jules Dubois, Bobbs-Merril, Indianapolis (1959).
Guerrilla Prince: The Untold Story of Fidel Castro by Georgie Anne Geyer, Little, Brown and Company, Boston (1991).
History Will Absolve Me by Fidel Castro, Lyle Stuart, New York (1961).
Papa and Fidel by Karl Alexander, Tom Doherty Associates, New York (1989).
Revolutionary Struggle 1947–1958: Selected Works of Fidel Castro by Fidel Castro, The M.I.T. Press, Cambridge, Mass. (1972).
The Taming of Fidel Castro by Maurice Halpern, University of California Press, Berkeley (1981).

Politics and History

Baseball: The People's Game by Harold Seymore, Oxford University Press, New York (1990).
Baseball and the Cold War by Howard Senzel, Harcourt Brace Jovanovich, New York (1977).
Che: A Memoir by Fidel Castro, Ocean Press (1994).
Children of Che by Karen Wald, Ramparts Press, Calif. (1978).
Children of the Revolution by Jonathan Kozol, Delacorte Press, New York (1978).
Cuba: A Short History, edited by Leslie Bethell, Cambridge University Press (1993).
Cuba after Communism by E. Baloyra and J.A. Morris, New Mexico (1993).
Cuba After the Cold War edited by Carmelo Mesa-Lago, University of Pittsburgh Press, Pittsburgh (1993).
Cuba: Between Reform and Revolution by Louis A. Perez, Jr., Oxford University Press, New York (1988).
Cuba from Columbus to Castro by Jaime Suchlicki, Charles Scribner's Sons, New York (1974).
Cuba for Beginners by Rius, Pathfinder Press (1970).
Cuba in the 1970s by Carmelo Mesa-Lago, University of New Mexico Press, Albuquerque (1974).
Cuba on the Brink by James G. Blight, Bruce J. Allyn and David A. Welch, Pantheon, New York (1993).
Cuba, or The Pursuit of Freedom by Hugh Thomas, Eyre & Spottiswoode, London (1971).
Cuba: Order and Revolution by Jorge Dominguez, Harvard University Press, Cambridge, Mass. (1978).
The Cuban Revolution by Jaime Suchlicki, University of Miami, Coral Gables, Fla. (1968).
The Cuban Revolution – Origins, Course and Legacy by Marifeli Pérez Stable, New York (1993).
Cuba Roja: cómo viven los cubanos con Fidel Castro by Román Orozco, Madrid (1993).
Cuba vs. the CIA by Robert E. Light and Carl Marzani, Marzani and Munsell, Ince. New York (1961).
In Cuba by Ernesto Cardenal, New Directions, New York (1974).
The Cuban Story by Herbert L. Matthews, George Braziller, New York (1961).
The Death of Che Guevara by Jay Cantor and Alfred A. Knopf, New York (1983).
Diary of the Cuban Revolution by Carlos Franqui, Viking Press, New York (1980).
The Historical Dictionary of Cuba by Suchlicki Jaime, Scarecrow Press, Metuchen, N.J. (1988).
Khrushchev: A Biography by Roy Medvedev, Doubleday, New York (1984).
Lansky by Hank Messick, Putnam, New York (1971).
José Martí, Cuban Patriot by Richard Butler Gray, University of Florida Press, Gainesville (1962).
No Free Lunch: Food and Revolution in Cuba by M. Benjamin, J. Collins and M. Scott, Institute for Food and Development Policy, San Francisco (1984).
One Thousand Fearful Words for Fidel Castro by Lawrence Ferlinghetti, City Lights, San Francisco (1961).
Selected Works of Ernesto Guevara The M.I.T. Press, Cambridge, Mass. (1969).

Foreign Relations

Breaking with Moscow by Arkady Shevchenko, Alfred A. Knopf, New York (1985).
The Closest of Enemies by Wayne S. Smith, W.W. Norton, New York (1987).
Cuba in Transition: Options for US Policy by G. Gunn, New York (1993).
The History of Guantánamo Bay by Marion Emerson Murphy, US Naval Base, Guantánamo Bay, Cuba (1953).
Inside the Monster: Writings on the United States and American Imperialism by Jose Martí, Monthly Review Press, edited by Philip S. Foner, New York (1975).
The Soviet Union and Cuba Raymond W. Duncan, Praeger, New York (1985).
Thirteen Days: A Memoir of the Cuban Missile Crisis by Robert F. Kennedy, Norton, New York (1969).
Los Gusanos by John Sayles, HarperCollins, New York (1991).
The Missile Crisis by Elie Abel, Lippincott, Philadelphia (1966).

ART & PHOTO CREDITS

Danny Aeberhard 58, 96, 99R, 252T, 257T
Trygve Bølstad/Panos Pictures 75
Peter Brooker/Rex Features 102
M Chianura/Rex Features 65
Glyn Genin 5, 85, 86, 90, 145T, 146T, 148, 148T, 157T 163, 166, 167, 171, 174T, 187, 188T, 189, 189T, 193, 199, 203T, 204, 205, 205T, 213, 214, 214T, 215L, 218T, 219T, 223, 224, 227T, 234, 237, 237T, 239, 240, 240T, 249, 251, 255, 257, 260T, 262T, 266T, 272, 273, 275T, 277, 279T, 285, 288, 289T, 290, 290T, 291, 292T, 295, 296, 297T, 298, 298T, 303, 307, 308, 310, 311, 311T, 313, 315, 315T, 316, 317T
Eduardo Gil 2/3, 4/5, 6/7, 12/13, 14, 20, 56, 62, 67L, 70, 79, 84, 88L, 88R, 99L, 103, 106, 110, 121, 128/129, 130/131, 136/137, 145, 146, 147, 151, 159, 162, 172, 173, 175, 176L, 176R, 177, 184, 185, 188, 190, 192, 197, 214, 216, 219, 220, 221, 228/229, 233, 241, 242/243, 244, 245, 247T, 248, 248T, 253, 254L, 256, 259, 262, 267, 268/269, 276, 282, 284, 289L, 289R, 292, 299T, 314
Tria Giovan 98, 238, 280, 300/301, 302, 309T, 316T
Andreas M Gross 160
Emily Hatchwell 60, 153, 155, 155T, 169T, 173T, 231, 232, 235, 236, 239T, 278T
Miami Herald 10, 35, 36, 66
Thomas Ives 50/51, 52, 53, 87, 100, 109, 117, 161, 258, 287
Darrell Jones 114
Photographic 116L, 116R
Glyn Kirk/Action Plus/Barry Lewis/Network 8/9, 64, 115, 118/119, 132, 140, 225T, 230, 263, 264, 305, 318
Larry Luxner 212, 215R, 217, 226
David Marcus 297
Jenny Matthews/Network 91
Fred Mawer 46, 72, 78, 162, 168, 178, 183, 201T, 218, 227, 252, 254R, 261, 274, 274T, 275, 278, 279, 281, 283, 293, 304, 309, 319
Tony Perrottet 16/17, 22, 77, 80/81, 82/83, 89, 126/127, 149, 157, 158, 174/179, 181, 182, 182T, 191, 194/195, 196, 200, 201, 202, 203
Jonathan Pile/Impact 120
Private Archive 317L, 317R, 320
Revolución y Cultura 107
Richter Library, University of Miami 27, 28, 30, 32, 34, 37, 39, 40/41
Erich Schlegel 67R, 70/71, 101, 112/113, 294, 299, 306
Alfonso Silva 122/123, 124, 125, 208/209, 222, 225, 310T
Topham PicturePoint 38, 61, 73, 74
Mireille Vautier 1, 5, 25, 31, 55, 57, 59, 61, 97/104/105, 142, 143, 150, 169, 246
Francesco Venturi/Kea 18, 152
Marcus Wilson Smith 10/11, 94/95, 156, 170, 247, 266

Picture Spreads

Pages 68/69
Top row left to right: Fred Mawer, Mireille Vautier, Fred Mawer, John Denham. *Middle row left to right*: Glyn Genin, Tony Perrottet, Glyn Genin. *Bottom row left to right*: Fred Mawer, John Denham, Eduardo Gil, Fred Mawer
Pages 92/93
Top row left to right: Fred Mawer, Trygve Bølstad/Panos Pictures, Tria Giovan, Naomi Peck. *Middle row*: Rolando Pujol/South American Pictures. *Bottom row left to right*: Rolando Pujol/South American Pictures, Mireille Vautier, Emilio Jesús Reyer/Colección Museo de Guana bacoa.
Pages 164/165
Top row left to right: Francesco Venturi/Kea, Emily Hatchwell, J.L.D. Grande/AISA, Ismael R/Phototeca. *Middle row*: Peter Woloszynski, Glyn Genin. *Bottom row*: Mireille Vautier, Nicolas Sapieha/Kea
Pages 206/207
Top row left to right: AGK London, Jan Butchofsky Houser, Jan Butchofsky-Houser. *Middle row*: Mireille Vautier. *Bottom row left to right*: Fred Mawer, Mireille Vautier, Andreas M Gross.

Map Production Lovell Johns Ltd

Cartographic Editor **Zoë Goodwin**
Production **Stuart A. Everitt**
Design Consultants
Carlotta Junger, Graham Mitchener
Picture Research
Hilary Genin, Monica Allende

Index

Numbers in italics refer to photographs

d

e